PILGRIM PATH

Missionary Stations in the Hawaiian Islands. From *Missionary Album,* courtesy Hawaiian Mission Children's Society.

Pilgrim Path

THE FIRST COMPANY
OF WOMEN MISSIONARIES
TO HAWAII

Mary Zwiep

The University of Wisconsin Press

The University of Wisconsin Press
114 North Murray Street
Madison, Wisconsin 53715

3 Henrietta Street
London WC2E 8LU, England

5 4 3 2 1

Printed in the United States of America

Library of Congress Cataloging-in-Publication Data
Zwiep, Mary, 1950–
Pilgrim path: the first company of women missionaries to Hawaii, 1819–1841 / Mary Zwiep.
396 pp. cm.
Includes bibliographical references and index.
ISBN 0-299-12900-4 ISBN 0-299-12904-7 (pbk.)
1. Missions—Hawaii—History—19th century.
2. Women missionaries—Hawaii—History—19th century.
3. Hawaii—History—To 1893. I. Title.
BV3680.H3Z85 1991
266'.023730969'082—dc20 91-15555
CIP

We feel our feet to be in a pilgrim path, yet, as we tread one step after the other, the briars and thorns, which, in prospect, have so forbidding an appearance, are either so put aside, or rendered harmless, that we have the most abundant reason to thank GOD.

—SYBIL BINGHAM, LETTER TO ELIZABETH BISHOP, MAY 30, 1827

Contents

Illustrations

Acknowledgments

This book is the story of the first women missionaries to Hawaii. I owe the opportunity to read their letters, journals, and private papers primarily to the generosity of their descendants, who, over the years, have loaned or donated manuscripts to the Hawaiian Mission Children's Society Library in Honolulu. Almost all of the manuscript material that forms the core of this book comes from their Missionary Letters and Missionary Journals collections. The Bingham Family Papers deposited in the HMCS Library as well as microfilms of the Bingham Papers at Yale have been valuable. Twenty-seven letters of the Ruggles family are collected in the Bishop Museum Library in Honolulu. More letters and memoranda I found in the archives of the American Board of Commissioners for Foreign Missions (ABCFM) in the Houghton Library at Harvard; some hard-to-come-by books were available at the American Antiquarian Society in Worcester, Massachusetts, and others at the University of Michigan Library.

The amount of information available naturally varies from missionary to missionary. Every woman except Jerusha Chamberlain left some record of the voyage to Hawaii. (She wrote nothing at all, her portrait emerging solely from the writings of others, especially her husband.) Maria Loomis's journals begin with the voyage and continue through 1824; for subsequent years there are letters and a journal from 1852–54, written long after her return from Hawaii in 1827. For Nancy Ruggles, the record is even more sparse—the journal written on the *Thaddeus* and various letters. (She and her husband kept the journal together, but signed individual entries.) *The Journal of Lucia Ruggles Holman*, whose last entry is dated September 1820, was published in pamphlet form; the rest of her short stay in the islands is covered by letters and "The Holman Report," a typescript at the HMCS Library. Lucy Thurston during her last decade collected many of her own letters and journal entries—along with some newly written sketches—in the *Life and Times of Mrs. Lucy G. Thurston.* Although she probably destroyed the original material that went into her book, some letters and a section of her journal from 1821 remain. Mercy Whitney preserved twenty-three "Letter Books," keeping copies in her small, tidy hand of perhaps every letter she ever sent. She also left seven volumes (in addition to her journal on the *Thaddeus*) of the journals she kept all her life and sent home to family members. For her the record begins with letters from 1819 and continues to 1870, two years before her death. The story of Sybil Bingham's life is told in several journals: one from 1819 to 1823, excerpts from 1827, and a journal of 1843, kept after her return to New England in 1841. In addition, a private journal survives, mostly of religious meditations, beginning in 1811 and continuing off and on throughout her life. Perhaps most valuable are the uncounted and voluminous letters, drafts, and fragments in her cramped, barely legible hand. Some of the letters belong to the Bingham Family Papers in the HMCS Library; the others, to that library's Missionary Letters Collection.

Records for the men of the first company are more sparse. Daniel Chamberlain, Elisha Loomis, Samuel Ruggles, and Samuel Whitney kept journals. The men also kept the public record of missionary activities that was sent back to Boston, the "*Thaddeus* Journal" of 1819–1821 (probably written by Hiram Bingham, Asa Thurston, and Elisha Loomis in turn), and the "Journal of the Sandwich Islands Mission," from 1821 to 1825. There are some private letters as well as many public letters (some written jointly) to the ABCFM.

For the public facts of conventional history, I have relied upon standard references for the period, listed in the Bibliography. Unless directly quoting, I do not as a rule footnote pieces of information that have by now entered the public domain. I also include specialized books about Hawaiian culture and nineteenth-century women in the Bibliography. Most manuscripts I identify in the text, adding information as needed in the Notes. In quoting from manuscripts—many of which are copies or drafts—I have standardized spelling and punctuation on the rare occasions when doing so aids clarity and readability. To minimize confusion, I have used quotations marks in referring to Hawaiians of the period who sometimes used an English name, as in "Governor Adams" Kuakini. Though contemporary Hawaiian spelling uses diacritical marks, nineteenth-century writers did not, and I have followed their practice. I have anglicized the plural of Hawaiian words, adding an "s," as in *kapus.*

I owe special thanks to the staff of the Hawaiian Mission Children's Society Library for countless small acts of guidance and generosity as I was reading manuscripts, to Lela Goodell, to Daphne Yamamoto and to Mary Jane Knight, the head librarian, unerring in her ability to track down references. Barbara Dunn helped me with the records at the Hawaiian Historical Society. Margaret Schleif, curator, and Deborah Pope, director of the Mission Houses Museum, provided me with printed material and an informal education on nineteenth-century mission life. C. Holbrook Goodale sent me excerpts from an out-of-print book, *The Whitney Family of Connecticut* (1878). To Carol Silva, who taught me Basic Hawaiian, I owe many insights into the culture conveyed by its language.

Other persons read the manuscript in whole or in part: Lincoln Faller, Marjorie Sinclair, Robert Kamins, and James McCutcheon. My husband, Russell Fraser, has been a patient and perceptive reader, advising me on successive revisions of each chapter. To him especially, as to all, my appreciative *mahalo.*

For permission to reproduce prints and photographs, I am grateful to the Hawaiian Mission Children's Society, the Hawaiian Historical Society, the Bernice P. Bishop Museum, the Honolulu Academy of Arts, the Houghton Library, and the Yale University Art Gallery. A version of Chapter 6 appeared as an essay in the *Hawaiian Journal of History* 24, 1990.

This book necessarily opens up the most private thoughts of a group of women to the estimating eye of strangers. This I like to think they would have countenanced, as they did so many trials, with the understanding that the "general good" of the cause in which they were engaged took precedence over private desires. If there is a "general good" in which this book is engaged, it is the moving from oversimplification toward complexity. Inevitably, I have not told "the" story of the first company of women missionaries, filtered as this book is through my own sense of what matters and what does not in the writings left behind. Hoping they would understand the mere attempt to "get it right"—the kind of striving with which they lived their own lives—I write this book for them.

The First Company

The Reverend Hiram Bingham and Sybil Moseley Bingham

Daniel Chamberlain and Jerusha Burnap Chamberlain and five children – Dexter, Nathan, Mary, Daniel, and Nancy

Doctor Thomas Holman and Lucia Ruggles Holman

Elisha Loomis and Maria Sartwell Loomis

Samuel Ruggles and Nancy Wells Ruggles

The Reverend Asa Thurston and Lucy Goodale Thurston

Samuel Whitney and Mercy Partridge Whitney

Thomas Hopu

William Kanui

John Honolii

Introduction

Go ye into all the world and preach the gospel to every creature.

— Mark 16:15

In late October of 1819, the first of twelve companies of missionaries bound for Hawaii left Boston Harbor. The American Board of Commissioners for Foreign Missions (ABCFM) administered this mission. Donations from countless New Englanders paid for its work. The company included seven young married couples, five children, three Hawaiian youths, and one Hawaiian prince returning home. Over five months later, upon arriving in the islands, they began their work of converting the Hawaiians to Protestant Christianity. As they saw it, they were motivated by an ardent love for souls and by compassion for the perishing heathen, and were obeying the final command of Jesus to spread the gospel.

While on board the brig *Thaddeus*—from October 23, 1819, to April 4, 1820—the missionaries molded for themselves a sense of group identity. Calling one another "Brother" and "Sister," they belonged to a mission family and came to think of themselves as its Pioneer company. During the first three years, until May 1823, when the ship *Thames* arrived with reinforcements, the pioneers laid the crucial foundations for the workers who followed. They were responsible for the first precarious public successes of the mission: getting permission to land, then to build a frame house; gaining the trust, even the friendship, of important *alii* (Hawaiian chiefs, both male and female); setting up the first schools; introducing the new God and his commandments. The written word, the *palapala*, the most exciting of all the foreign material objects that had yet entered Hawaii, made this God accessible. The pressures on the group as a "family" were centrifugal, as its members dispersed to different islands or went back home to New England. But memories of communal accomplishment and the bonds of affection remained. Only two of the original seven couples remained in the islands until old age and death. By 1827, three couples had returned to the states; another left in 1834; and in 1840, the Binghams, the acknowledged center of leadership for the first and subsequent companies, departed. Having gone home temporarily for Sybil to recover her health, they never returned. An era was over.[1]

In its broadest outline, the missionaries' story begins in the late eighteenth century and continues through the nineteenth. Captain James Cook "discovered" the Sandwich Islands in 1778, followed during the next forty years by other explorers, and by traders and merchants. The missionaries came next: 153 were sent out by the ABCFM, the last group arriving in 1848. Another 28 persons arrived independently.[2] Later companies continued the work begun by the pioneers. In just a little over three decades, they wrote down the language for the first time, printed primers and hymnbooks, and translated the Bible. The physicians among them healed as well as they could the newly imported diseases that were decimating Hawaiians. Men, women, and young children together demonstrated Christian domestic life, with its different habits of clothing, eating, and childrearing. On every island, the missionaries built churches and established a system of common schools; they built high schools and a special school for the chiefs' children. Missionary influence set the Hawaiians on the track of constitutional government, fee-simple land ownership, and even, in a sense, the coup that toppled the monarchy in 1893. Some who planned the coup were missionary descendants.

By the time the Board declared Hawaii "Christianized" and dissolved the mission in 1853, over a fourth of Hawaiians were church members, many more attended church, and most could read and write. The mission's legacy, reaching far past the mid-century, is complicated, however. Charged by the Board with covering the land with homes and schools and churches—a fair description of today's thriving Hawaii—the missionaries seem to have fulfilled that charge. Some honor them for this. Others make them the scapegoat for all Western intruders, measuring the difference between then and now as loss, not gain.[3]

In telling their story, I have concentrated on the perspective of the women of the first company. This perspective—afforded by unpublished journals, letters, scrap copies, and fragments jotted down as a moment could be seized from other work – is by no means narrow or negligible. It leads both inward, toward the personality and preoccupations of each individual woman, and outward, toward the public activities of the mission as a whole. These women, sharing the ideas and values of the men, took an active interest in the primarily male jobs of printing, preaching, and translating; they paid attention to the various political crises of the nation; they taught school; they met with groups of Hawaiian women. Whenever possible, their stake in the mission's palpable achievements was more than vicarious. Not ordinary housewives, they had a finger on the pulse of a great religious experiment in the midst of a great culture about to collapse. But since the women's presence was demanded in or about the mission houses, they added to this record of public events a domestic record of how the missionaries fed, clothed, and sheltered themselves and how they raised their children. This story, by and large the doings of women that rarely get into history books, rounds out the conventional subject matter of "history."

Perhaps most important, the women's writings yield a third story, usually left to novelists – the sense of what it was like to be alive in Honolulu in the 1820s and 1830s. These well-educated, self-conscious, intensely pious young women left behind a record of rich interior lives. It tells of minds meeting daily experience – what they think, what they feel, what they make of what happens to them. They do not "tell all," but edit and shape their material according to the audience: their benefactors at the ABCFM in Boston, a ladies' society that has sent a box of food and clothing, a close friend, a beloved sibling or parent. Occasionally, though, they come close to a naked outpouring of self that gives insight into the most deeply held convictions and deeply felt needs of a particular woman. Similar assumptions, catch phrases, ways of coping, crop up in their writings, pointing toward more general characteristics of a nineteenth-century Protestant "missionary mind." Reading them, we can begin to answer the question often asked with varying degrees of exasperation or sympathy: what did they think they were doing?

Another way to put this is to ask how particular religious convictions affected their lives as women, as missionaries, and as human beings. I see myself as examining a mindset – the carefully articulated assumptions, metaphors, ideas, and emotions with which the women began missionary work, and which they found reinforced or frustrated as time went on. In what ways did this mental paradigm enable the women to see and understand the Hawaiian culture surrounding them, and in what ways did it keep them from seeing it? How well were they enabled to cope with human problems, like death and illness, that afflict us all; how well with problems, like raising children in a land of "moral pollution," peculiar to Hawaii? What happens when a group of women (and men) deeply committed to platonic truths, to invisible assets of character and soul, meet a situation that cries out not for devaluing the material, sensual world, but for paying attention to it?

My book, treating a group of women as "missionaries," is also their biography. In order to preserve and convey the sense of being alive in another time and place, vivid in the original diaries and letters, I have shaped the material as a story, paying attention to chronology and to character as it unfolds through time. The story is in one sense a great cautionary tale of the power of abstractions. It underlines for me, and I hope for my readers, the risk of "using" lives to prove a point, or of reducing them to an abstraction. The missionaries thought they could abstract from the disgusting "heathen" habits apparent to their eye an awareness of a pure soul underneath—which they could love, and which allowed them to believe in the equality of all human beings. But it was not so easy or, perhaps, salutary to separate the sinner from the sin or to substitute Christian habits for "heathen" ones. With great, even tragic irony, these helpers sometimes harmed. But the caution implicit in their story extends not only to missionary attitudes but also to contemporary observers who want to abstract a morality play from this tumultuous interaction between cultures. Modern cultural relativism, though perhaps more fruitful than the Christian absolutism with which the missionaries judged Hawaiian customs, sometimes inclines us to judge the missionaries "ethnocentric" to a fault. But the act of passing judgment on the basis of a "superior" truth is the same then and now, and gives pause. By attending to individual character—a parochial approach, not "schematic"—I hope to introduce the vitality and complexity of detail that makes it hard to box human beings into categories with labels like "heathen" and "bigot." Acknowledging as well the need to generalize or distinguish patterns, I have tried to step back as the occasion demands to ask what these lives add up to.

Examining the mission from the point of view of the women differs from an analysis of these women as "woman," potential in the material but not the single focus of my book. Their perspective is comprehensive enough to tell the public, domestic, and intellectual stories of the mission. Being female influenced that perspective, and I have sought to reflect upon the ways in which gender qualified the women's experience. An important context for this is the history of other nineteenth-century American women, the focus of many scholarly studies in recent years. Increasingly, historians have demonstrated separate "spheres" of work and influence for men and women, the idealizing of domesticity, the feminization of religion, and the roles of women's benevolent organizations in reform movements. Though many of these trends show up most clearly in the later part of the century, they are nascent (if not obvious) in the ideas and behavior of this group of women missionaries who left America in 1819. Like many a woman in nineteenth-century America, these female apostles sought a public role in improving the lives of fellow human beings. At the same time, they struggled with the demands of an idealized domesticity and "the cult of true womanhood." My commentary relates necessarily to the work of other historians (especially Patricia Grimshaw's, which focuses on all the missionary wives in Hawaii), and in the notes I have sought to tie my arguments to theirs. Readers seeking amplification will find the pertinent scholarship listed in the Notes and under "Related Sources" in the Bibliography.

Other contexts seem to me equally helpful in elucidating the women's perspective. Since, in a very large sense, the mission's story is one of interactions with Hawaiians, I have presented many details of Hawaiian culture and history (part of the public story of the mission) as well as details that suggest a particular sort of relationship between the women and Hawaiians. Related stories—that of the male missionaries, that of subsequent companies, that of the other *haoles* (foreigners) who were not missionaries, that of subsequent generations who look back on the story from another century—I introduce as the narrative moves on.

The most important context for the women's writings is religious.[4] More than all else, religious convictions shaped the lives of these women, often in ways that suggest differences from the experience of women on the mainland. Since these missionaries married either ministers or men with religious convictions as intense as their own, their lives suggest that the trend toward the "feminization of religion" in American culture was less pronounced in Hawaii than elsewhere. Shared piety tended to unite rather than differentiate men's and women's experience, helping to shape their identity as a mission "family"—men and women together, posed against the heathen. John Faragher (*Women and Men on the Overland Trail*, 1979) makes a similar point about shared convictions among his mid-century travelers.[5] Though piety, an important trait of the "true woman," invigorated all reform movements with a sense of moral authority, it had a more specialized meaning for the missionary woman. Her piety inspired her to spread not simply good works but the gospel itself. Missionaries to Hawaii felt their "bonds" with other women and often discussed their roles in Maternal Association meetings. But the ultimate arbiter of value, at least as they saw it, was less their gender than their relationship with God. Though domesticity often seemed to govern their lives, religion inspired them. The great goal they strove for was to contribute their mite to the cause of evangelizing the heathen. The tension they felt between public efforts to advance a cause and the women's work that kept them at home predicts the careers of millions of women today. But the commitment of these women to the missionary cause prompted them to devalue the domestic work that seemed to advance that cause only "indirectly." When they were frustrated in their "proper work" as missionaries, they found it hard to find solace in the typical nineteenth-century glorification of domesticity. In what was perhaps the single most traumatic decision of their lives—how and where to raise their children—they allowed concern for souls to dominate the debate. In the end, this cost some of them their families. If this story of the first twenty years of the mission is one of high hopes and arguably great achievements, it is also one of high costs, personal and public, exacted in different ways but exacted all the same for both Hawaiians and missionaries. Seen from the perspective of another century, its tone is unmistakably elegaic.

PILGRIM PATH

1. The Mission Family

For whosoever shall do the will of my father which is in heaven, the same is my brother, and sister, and mother.

— Matthew 12:50

If conditions on board the *Thaddeus* were not quite what she had bargained for, no missionary wife was going to admit it. They had prepared themselves for privations and sacrifices, for being crucified to the world for the sake of God's work. But they could not have foreseen how these grand abstractions would filter down into particularities. On the afternoon of October 23, 1819, seven missionary wives found themselves being rowed through Boston Harbor. With their husbands, five children, four Hawaiians, and twenty-three officers and crew, they squeezed onto the *Thaddeus.* The brig measured 24 feet by 85, less than half the length of a Boeing 747. For an 18,000-mile voyage around Cape Horn to Hawaii, for over five long months, this was to be home.

In 1819, the Pacific was open for exploring and trading, not quite yet for whaling, certainly not yet for passenger traffic. (The first two whaleships were visiting Hawaii at the time the *Thaddeus* left.) The *Thaddeus,* a commercial vessel, intended to trade on America's Northwest Coast after depositing the missionaries and their paraphernalia. The owners accepted $2,500 (not including provisions) for this novel charge and did what they could to accommodate the passengers on board.[1]

It was not much. Hinting at her dismay, Maria Loomis mused in her journal that they would be spending a long time "confined in this floating prison" (though she sent a copy home with a euphemism—"small vessel"). Lucy Thurston found herself and husband Asa beginning their married life in a room six feet square, jammed in some places to the ceiling with assorted chests, trunks, and bags until there was no place to put a foot down. "With such narrow limits, and such confined air," she admitted, "it might well be compared to a dungeon. This was with me a gloomy season, in which I felt myself a pilgrim and a stranger." More often, the journals describe crowding, disadvantages, and inconveniences with Yankee understatement. Daniel and Jerusha Chamberlain, with four of their five children, settled into a room "5½' square on the floor and scarcely that high." To reach the deck from this room, as Daniel explained, "we had to go half bent, sometimes over chests on our hands & knees; sometimes knocking our heads against things which hang in the way." For Mercy and Samuel Whitney, the journey back from deck to room was equally hazardous: "from deck we descended a staircase, then mounted upon a chest which stood before our door, drew a curtain and entered our room, but were unable to set our feet on the floor on account of bag and baggage." This included "one large box of medicine and a tub of sulphur soda belonging to the mission, six trunks three of which were the size of chests, bundles, boxes, writing desk, brooms, a large demijohn of spirits of turpentine belonging to the brig, a box of hardware &c. &c." Somewhere in this confusion were berths, though Mercy's was "just long enough for me to stretch myself in it by touching both hands and feet."[2]

The captain's cabin, which served as common room, offered no relief. It was a relatively spacious 20 by 15 feet, but four extra bunks lined two of the walls, while a third wall was piled high with sails blocking the light from its window. A semicircular table for twenty along with the usual chaos of hump-backed trunks, wooden boxes, and chests took most of the air space that was left. Maria Loomis, who crowded into this cabin along with her husband Elisha, the mission's doctor and his wife (Thomas and Lucia Holman), the brig's captain (Andrew Blanchard), and the first mate (James Hunnewell), repeated the refrain common to many journals: "It is but seldom we set our feet upon the floor." In the open air, Lucy Thurston surveyed the deck, where a boat, hogsheads, barrels, tubs, cables, a dog, cats, hens, ducks, and pigs contributed to the *Thaddeus*'s general air of din and commotion.[3]

Six hastily married couples (the weddings took place between September 22 and October 12) found themselves with plenty of time to get acquainted and with little space to get away from one another should the old prediction about repenting at leisure prove true. It is hard to imagine turning around in those cabins, harder still to imagine conjugal relations in them. However, no one moved much at all for the first month at sea. The *Thaddeus* lay becalmed on the twenty-third, but set sail on the twenty-fourth to rough winds. Within hours, all the passengers except the Hawaiians were seasick. "I think here was an exception to the saying that misery loves company," wrote Lucia Holman with a rare example of missionary wit, "for I believe the miseries of one was [*sic*] no consolation to those of another." To Daniel Chamberlain the vessel "appeared like a hospital for some days." Lucy Thurston described the sufferers: "some thrown on their mattresses, others seated in clusters, hanging one upon another, while here and there individuals leaned on the railing, or supported themselves by hanging upon a rope." Most of the journals begin on the first day, the twenty-third, then remain blank for the next two weeks. But by November 17, almost a month into the voyage, most of the group appeared to be recovering. By November 27, they reached a milestone—"public worship on deck without preparing beds for any." The unfortunate Samuel Ruggles, however, suffered almost to the end of the voyage, unable to sit up for a day until December 5.[4]

To add to the indignity of illness, the drinking water was brackish, the bathing water was salt, and the laundry piled up until they reached Honolulu. Sea legs developed slowly. "Often in attempting to go one way we are tossed the other," wrote Nancy Ruggles, "and if we have anything in our hands it is frequently thrown upon the floor or at the best partly spilt." For several days, meals came on deck in a communal pot, to be shared by anyone who felt capable of eating. "We had entered a new school" was Lucy Thurston's laconic comment. Within a few months, the fresh provisions gave out, and the group resigned themselves to a diet generous in rice, sea biscuit, beans, salt pork, and beef, enlivened by "water gruel," evidently palatable, at supper. Midway through the voyage, Samuel Ruggles was thrilled during a rainstorm to catch three pints of drinking water dripping off his umbrella. In late December and January, when the brig rounded Cape Horn to real gales and mountainous waves, Yankee endurance and ingenuity were put to harder tests. "It's enough to make anyone laugh," wrote the good-natured Daniel Chamberlain, "to see how many contrivances we have to keep from rolling out of bed: some have straps nailed up to hold on by; some tie a rope round them and tie it to something fast; some put up boards and when the vessel rolls bad, some lie on the floor."[5]

Nor were all the trials merely physical ones. No one expected ever to return to New England: they were missionaries for life. The newness of marriage, the strains of getting acquainted with husbands and shipmates (however compatible), and sheer physical exhaustion must have taken their toll. On December 9, a tired Sybil Bingham admitted, "To accomplish a little costs much labor on board a vessel. I am grieved to find it too much the case, that with my bodily strength my spirits sink. Several such sessions have arisen in my new situation. Tears will come unbidden and I may say without cause." When the *Thaddeus* met the ship *Mary* on December 15, the homesick missionaries were delighted, sending dozens of letters back to Boston.[6]

Yet the details were sent home in the spirit of elucidation, not complaint. Knowing their correspondents to be intensely curious, also anxious, about their welfare, the missionaries determinedly followed the accounts of trials with reassurances. In mid-summer of 1820, Lucia Holman closed her journal of the voyage and initial months in Hawaii: "Think not, my dear sisters, that I am complaining or repining at the allotment of providence, or, that I mention these things to pain you—far from it—but only that you should know the truth of my situation . . . that I may have your sympathy and prayers." Maria Loomis, finishing her portrayal of their accommodations on November 8, concluded, "We labor under some inconveniences yet we generally feel contented & happy." Jerusha Chamberlain was in good spirits, often remarking, Daniel wrote that Christmas, "that she wished our friends could know how well we fared." At the end of the voyage, Sybil Bingham wrote home to friends the extraordinary thought "that I do not remember five months in any period of my life in which I thought I had enjoyed an equal degree of happiness, with the five past."[7]

This contentment is not as surprising as it may at first seem. Having chosen their life's work, these women cultivated the attitudes that would see them through. Privation was understood as a relative term. Once Mercy and Samuel Whitney put most of their baggage in the ship's hold, they cleared a space about three feet square where they could sit to read and write, "happy as a king and queen." The Thurstons having also cleared their cabin of unnecessary articles, Lucy reflected, "Would that I could tell my dear friends that *Lucy is contented and happy.*" One evening in January, after taking some sugar and peppermint for her upset stomach, Sybil Bingham summed up the prevailing attitude: "I felt with some force, what I feel more or less, every day, that it was *unreasonable* ever to speak of the lack of one comfort, we have so many." Worried that a remark in an earlier letter might remind her sisters that she was "destitute" of many comforts, Sybil asked them "to forget every sentence which may have been bordering that way" and concluded, "I am indeed dealt with kindly. If I could count over the outward comforts I have, you would join me in saying so."[8]

Most attitudes rested upon conventional religious beliefs, a higher priority than gender. Both "outward comforts" and most of the trials aboard the ship belonged to the material world, the "vale of tears" they had learned to devalue. "This is not your rest," they told themselves, expecting their greatest happiness in heaven. They looked to the soul, which was to be saved, as the crucial element in anyone's makeup. Mercy Whitney made no complaints about "trials and privations," because "when compared to the infinite value of the soul [they] appear as the dust of the balance and altogether lighter than vanity." Such ideas were not niceties of theology; they were touchstones to live by. The tensions between this world and the next or between material and spiritual pleasures were not always easily resolved, but there was no question how they should be. In late January, as the *Thaddeus* passed by Cape Horn during rough, very cold weather, Sybil Bingham thought back to material comforts, reflecting that she had not seen a fire since leaving Boston. "Cannot you conceive it would be pleasant for me to change my apparel & take a seat with you in your rocking chair, upon your nice carpets, by a comfortable fire, your little table spread?" she asked her sisters. She urged them not to let such memories bring tears, but to remember: "God comforts her with the blessed hope that the day shall come when she shall be arrayed in robes, washed and made white in the blood of the lamb, seated with her beloved Christian sisters and all the redeemed of the Lord, in that glorious palace . . . and God shall wipe away all tears from the eyes."[9]

If the consolations aboard the brig were all in the mind, they were nevertheless very real. A sense of shared convictions bound the group together—their common Christian heritage and their unshakable desire to do the Lord's work among the heathen. They knew who they were and why they were there. On Christmas Day, Hiram Bingham preached a sermon from Luke 2:14 on the birth of a savior, concluding that "to propagate the gospel is the most desirable occupation this side heaven." Such convictions sustained them during hardships. As the brig left Boston, Maria Loomis declared herself "willing to forsake friends and country if I can be the means of promoting the blessed cause of Christ." After ninety-one days of sailing, Nancy Ruggles admitted that the voyage so far had been "long and unpleasant, yet,"—she went on in the same sentence—"we experienced no trials too great to be endured, for the sake of Christ, and the salvation of the poor heathen." Though the miseries of a late January storm drove Lucy Thurston to tears, she insisted, "I must not, I will not repine. Even now, though tears bedew my cheeks, I wish not for an alteration in my present situation or future prospects." Compared with the "degradations and misery" of the Hawaiians, she reminded herself, "all my petty sufferings dwindle to a point, and I exclaim, what have I to say of trials, I, who can press to my bosom the word of God." Sybil Bingham recorded "a little season" on February 7 "in which I think I *have felt* that the advancement of Christ's kingdom was an object which weighed down every personal consideration."[10]

An ability to shift perspectives, allowing them to think themselves into the right attitude toward the things that were going on, suggests one source of their strength. This worked against dogmatism and rigidity. Though quite certain what the "right attitude" was, they did not expect to achieve it automatically. Self-consciously wrenching themselves away from sadness or self-pity, they tried to point themselves toward the path of a cheerful heart and willing hands. Keenly aware that only God is perfect while human beings are prone to error, they never expected to depend entirely on their own efforts. A common reflection in the face of trials was the Lord's promise, "As thy day is, so shall thy strength be." But it was one measure of a fallen world that the Lord did not make acquiring that strength as easy as breathing. So far, in the infancy of the mission, the trials were easier than the ones ahead. But the women would call on the same reserves of faith and mental adroitness when the privation was the death of a child, not the lack of an orange.

Despite the discomforts, no one regretted having come on the voyage.[11] "I assure you I have not had a single desire to return to America," Nancy Ruggles wrote her mother shortly after leaving Boston, "but have felt perfectly contented with my condition, even in the darkest hours of affliction." Farther into the voyage, no one changed her mind. Lucy Thurston concluded in late January that "no trial or privation which I have experienced, or now anticipate, has ever caused me to cast a lingering look back to my native shores." Only Lucia Holman hedged a bit. A full year into the mission, on September 18, 1820, she wrote, "I have never regretted my undertaking; but, I have never seen the time, when I could say in truth (as some others, better than myself have said) that I had no desire ever to behold my country and the faces of my friends again should ever so good an opportunity present." She closed with some playful defiance: "My Country and friends are *dearer* to me than ever; and I would humbly *hope* that the cause of Christ is none the less for that." Subtly, Lucia was holding herself apart from the group, presenting herself humbly, while hinting at hypocrisy in "some others." It did prove harder for her than for the others to look to the next world, not this one, for her comforts. She and her husband would eventually conclude that to deal with the personalities of fellow missionaries and the work of the mission was too much to ask. But that decision waited for the next year's events, and for the present on the *Thaddeus,* the Holmans belonged to the family.[12]

The Bible gives an unambiguous rationale for missionary work. Both Matthew and Mark tell how Jesus, after his resurrection, commanded his disciples to go into all the world and preach the gospel to all people. The nineteenth-century missionaries traced their roots back through the apostles, who preached Christianity throughout the Mediterranean world, to Jesus himself, the first missionary as he went about doing good. Each individual missionary, male or female, taking the biblical injunction seriously, volunteered because of deeply felt religious convictions. They may have married almost on the eve of departure, but—at least in those cases for which records survive—the decision to become a missionary had been building for years. None of these women married the man first and then found herself dutifully following him into missionary work; each desired to go on a mission before she met her husband. Somewhere in everyone's background was a conversion experience in which she opened her heart to Jesus and committed herself to a Christian life. At some time also, each had begun to hope that God wanted her to devote her life to converting the heathen, rather than to serve him in some other way.[13]

But the hard question is how and why these individual minds absorbed the ideas behind missionary work in the first place. What was going on in the culture and its institutions that reinforced and—what is more interesting—inspired these personal convictions? Why, two hundred years after the Puritans fled the impositions of the Church of England, would their Christian descendants feel compelled to deliver their religion to places where Buddha, Allah, or Kane (the Hawaiian god of creation) had been worshipped for centuries?[14]

The missionary crusade coincides with the Second Great Awakening, the period of religious revivals during the first quarter of the nineteenth century. Early records from two of the women of the first company, Mercy Partridge Whitney and Sybil Moseley Bingham, confirm that revivals were on their minds. Mercy wrote to her cousin in 1819 that her church in Pittsfield, Massachusetts, had added ten members in the last half-year, that Belchertown had seen a "great outpouring of the spirit of God," and Northampton "something of a revival." In 1815, Sybil recorded her hopes (and eventual disappointment) concerning a revival among her students in Southampton.[15]

Neither woman was exceptional in her interest. The revivals brought many more women than men into the church and began a trend toward the "feminization" of religion.[16] This augured changes not only in church membership, but also in doctrine, which became more accommodating to women's concerns—for example, their distaste for ideas like infant damnation. In the multitude of church-related organizations—not only missionary societies, but prayer groups, charitable organizations, maternal organizations, and the like—women found a sense of sorority and a respectable outlet for public expression. With the confidence and moral authority born of their piety, they crusaded against all manner of vices—drunkenness, adultery and prostitution, slavery—as the century went on. When their efforts made them aware of the barriers in their way not simply as reformers, but as women, they urged political equality. In the long run, the values of Christianity (described by one historian as "humility, submissiveness, piety, and charity") came more and more to seem characteristic of women, in contrast to the qualities demanded of men earning a living in the competitive, individualistic, acquisitive world of the marketplace. This association of women with the church contributed to an ongoing division of activities and character traits into categories of male and female.

Many of these trends were nascent in the cultural attitudes and mores the missionaries imported to Hawaii. But in one important particular, this group was atavistic. In the early 1800s, the young women and men applying for missionary work were united, not divided, by religion. The most important immediate result of the Second Great Awakening was renewed fervor and piety. Some of this piety was channeled into support for foreign missions. It was a small step from accepting Jesus personally to offering him to everyone else. The emphasis from the pulpit and in printed matter was on compassion for the heathen, who lacked the advantages of living in a Christian country and whose souls were "perishing" until rescued. Those inspired to act pursued an ideal of "disinterested benevolence,"[17] a phrase of the nineteenth-century Calvinist writer Samuel Hopkins. Men and women together set out to share, not to hoard, their advantages.

But the uncomplicated piety and compassion of individual missionaries had a political component for the church hierarchy. The original Puritan experiment of theocracy had disintegrated into the separation of church and state, and into sectarianism as well, with Puritan Congregationalist, Presbyterian, Dutch Reformed, German Reformed, Methodist, Baptist, and Roman Catholic churches all competing for American souls. The West was opening up, and itinerant Methodist and Baptist preachers—with relaxed standards of orthodoxy—were claiming it. Though revivals swelled church rolls, they also brought to the forefront divisions of opinion among denominations and within each church. By the time of the Second Great Awakening, the Congregational Church was split between Unitarians, who dominated Harvard by 1805, and Trinitarians, who opened Andover Theological Seminary in 1808.[18] Andover soon became a training ground for missionaries, including Hiram Bingham and Asa Thurston.

One reading of the situation, then, is that the Trinitarian orthodoxy, losing its hold on the country, looked abroad to places like Hawaii, where a Christian community might establish itself by supplanting paganism. They were not exactly recreating a Puritan commonwealth. The missionaries were to be less strident and less fussy about doctrinal matters than the church at home: they were to preach the basic Christian truths. Despite its Congregationalist origins, the ABCFM's crusade was intended to remind Christians of their essential unity. Members from Presbyterian, Dutch, and German churches soon joined the Board. And the Board dictated a strict separation of church and state: missionaries were not to meddle with the Hawaiian government. Nevertheless, in this modified way, they planned to build the city on the hill all over again.[19]

The history of missionary activities in North America goes back as far as the early English settlements: the charter of the Virginia Company, which settled Jamestown in 1607, recommended the propagation of Christianity. In the more immediate past were attempts in the eighteenth century to convert the American Indians.[20] These were relatively unsuccessful, even though the life of the pioneer missionary to the New Jersey Indians, David Brainerd, inspired many missionaries in the next century. (His diary was edited and published as a book in 1749.) Efforts continued, the ABCFM sending missionaries to the Cherokees and Choctaws just before the Hawaiians, but the future direction of missionary work lay increasingly with foreign, not domestic, missions. Here the British pointed the way, going to India and Polynesia in the 1790s and forming the London Missionary Society in 1795. Letters and reports from British clergy and missionaries began to appear in journals and newspapers.

Although missionary societies were begun by Connecticut and Massachusetts clergy in the last years of the eighteenth century, credit for engendering widespread American support for foreign missions goes to Samuel J. Mills and some fellow students from Williams College. In an often-told story, they sheltered under a haystack during a thunderstorm in 1806 to make plans, and two years later formed the "Society of Brethren," a secret group devoted to missionary work. Later on at Andover, Mills and his friends organized the "Society of Inquiry on the Subject of Missions," to which Hiram Bingham and Asa Thurston belonged. These eager young men hoped to go abroad under American auspices. They petitioned the General Assembly of Massachusetts (the governing body of the Congregational Church), which in turn set up the American Board of Commissioners for Foreign Missions in 1810. The Board was incorporated in 1812, with a Prudential Committee, a treasurer, and a corresponding secretary to run it. An early and generous bequest of $30,000 put them on a solid foundation, and donations came in, slowly at first, then more quickly as missionary societies were set up in town after town to solicit funds and raise interest in the cause. Newspaper articles, pamphlets, periodicals, and printed sermons reached the reading public. The *Panoplist,* begun in 1805, eventually became the house organ for the ABCFM, the *Missionary Herald.* In 1817, the Board set up the Foreign Mission School in Cornwall, Connecticut, educating young men who would carry the gospel back to their own people. A slim booklet about some of its students, *A Narrative of Five Youths from the Sandwich Islands* (1816), permeated New England. Another popular tract of 1818, written by two early missionaries to Bombay, the Reverend Gordon Hall and the Reverend Samuel Newell, was titled portentously *The Conversion of the World: or the Claims of Six Hundred Millions and the Ability and Duty of the Churches Respecting Them.*[21]

Plenty of New Englanders, of course, remained unmoved by all the publicity. When the young Samuel Ruggles went on a "collecting mission" in 1817 on behalf of the Foreign Mission School, and many towns shut their doors to him, he admitted to feeling like a "stranger in a strange land," engaged in something "far more unpleasant that it will be, when I arrive at my long wished for Owhyhee [Hawaii]." What effect this publicity had on the deeply religious young men and women who volunteered for the Sandwich Island mission is hard to assess. Certainly they had read much of it. Yet it is probably too much to say that they were "taken in" by religious propaganda. More likely, the public preoccupation with missions nudged their religiousness toward that outlet instead of some other outlet for social reform. What did not motivate them were the distant problems of the church hierarchy, worried about religious divisions. As they articulated it to themselves, the decision to join a mission was entirely personal, encompassing only the individual, God, and the "perishing heathen."[22]

The Board succeeded in sending missions to Burma in 1812 (though the group ended up in Bombay), to Ceylon in 1816, and to India, Ceylon, and Palestine in 1819. But these groups were small, or were going to places where the British had already prepared the way.[23] The most promising field for a distinctly American mission appeared to be Hawaii. New Englanders were familiar with the islands located in the middle of the Pacific trade routes, where ships involved in the China trade or the fur trade along the Northwest Coast wintered and took on provisions. At about the same time that the missionary societies were being formed to reach out to heathens, Hawaiians themselves were reaching New England. For decades Hawaiian youths had been signing on as sailors with ships leaving the islands. In 1809, the most famous of the Hawaiian sailors—known to New Englanders as the orphan "Henry Obookiah" (in Hawaiian, Opukahaia)—made his way to New England. The story goes that he was found on the steps of Yale College, weeping because of his ignorance, and that the Reverend Timothy Dwight, the president, took him in. He proved a remarkable student and a pious convert. He spent the next several years moving about New England, often living with ministers as he gained an education and solicited support for a mission back to his countrymen, himself the perfect example of how the heathen could be regenerated.[24] Opukahaia is mentioned by many missionaries in their letters of application to the ABCFM.

Gradually joining Opukahaia at the Foreign Mission School were the other Hawaiians who eventually sailed home on the *Thaddeus.* Thomas Hopu ("Hopoo"), who had arrived in the United States with Opukahaia, had spent several adventuresome years on the high seas. But after privateering expeditions, shipwreck, and capture by the British, he rejoined his old friend and was converted to Christianity. Through Hopu, a third Hawaiian, John Honolii ("Honoree"), entered the school in Cornwall. Students at Yale urged William Kanui ("Tennooe"), another wanderer and sailor, to do the same. George Kaumualii ("Tamoree"), a prince of Kauai, came under the Board's patronage when they found him working as a purser's servant in the Charlestown navy yard. His father had sent him to America as a child of four to six years old, entrusting him to the care of a Captain Rowan of the ship *Hazard.* After a harrowing childhood in which, in George's words, he was "neglected" first by the captain, then by a "dirty scoundrel" of a schoolmaster who treated him "like a dog more than a human being," he joined the U.S. Navy during the War of 1812.[25]

An unforeseeable event did more than any other single promotion to open the public's hearts and purses. Opukahaia died of typhus in February 1818. The teachers and ministers supporting the mission crusade had always expected that he would lead a group back to his people. Now his words and his memory would have to be enough. Copies of the sermon delivered at his funeral along with letters and journal entries were collected into a small biography by the Reverend Edwin Dwight. *Memoirs of Obookiah* (1818) flooded New England, eventually selling over 50,000 copies in twelve editions. By November 1818, the Prudential Committee was searching for someone to superintend the preparations for a mission to the Sandwich Islands.[26]

They found their man in Hiram Bingham. A native Vermonter, he was a farmer and deacon's son and a graduate of Middlebury College. Now in his final year at Andover, he shared the interest of the times in missions. After visiting Cornwall during a school vacation in 1819, he volunteered his services to the Board. In the early summer of 1819, he was asked to organize the mission. Bingham urged in his acceptance letter that a second ordained minister be included. Soon the Board had accepted Asa Thurston and five assistant missionaries: Captain Daniel Chamberlain, who had fought in the War of 1812 and was now a farmer; Dr. Thomas Holman, a physician; Elisha Loomis, a printer; and Samuel Whitney and Samuel Ruggles, who were still students at the time they volunteered. Here then were seven missionaries ready to go to Hawaii in Opukahaia's place. The correspondence places Bingham in charge of the preparations, which suggests that his assumption of leadership once the group reached Honolulu (which the older Thurston evidently resented) had a basis in precedent as well as in Bingham's indomitable personality.[27]

If the mission was to leave by fall, there was no time to waste. Money and supplies for the mission began to reach Boston. The monetary donations were disappointing, only $3,200 more than the previous year. It would take $10,000 (including the $2,500 for passage) to outfit the mission. The missionaries themselves contributed what they could, but only two of them had any money to give. As if following to the letter Christ's advice to the rich man who wanted to get into heaven – sell all you have and give it to the poor – Daniel Chamberlain donated the $5,000 he received for his farm. Hiram Bingham's bride Sybil gave her "little patrimony" – $800 saved from schoolteaching – to form a permanent fund for the support of the treasurer of the ABCFM. The articles donated from everywhere in New England ranged from the trifling to the soberingly essential. The ledger of treasurer Jeremiah Evarts records among other items a box of raisins, ten pounds of tea, a gross of pencils, a rocking chair, a dozen axes, and a set of amputation instruments.[28]

One other sort of recruiting had to take place before the mission could depart. For six of the seven missionaries, wives had to be found. The application of Daniel Chamberlain, married with five children, forced the issue. The Board eventually not only accepted the Chamberlains but recommended marriage for the other six men and remained reluctant during the next two decades to send out unmarried men or women.[29] Not until after the Civil War, when separate women's missionary boards were formed, did women become the majority of missionaries in foreign lands. An essay written in 1836 by Rufus Anderson (by then corresponding secretary of the ABCFM) outlines the argument in favor of marriage. Good Protestants considered marriage the "natural state of man" and doubted that the cloister brought one closer to God. Although some single men might be sent with peripatetic duties—visiting schools or holding meetings in many places—as a rule a missionary in the field was as much in need of a wife as a minister at home. (Between the lines lies concern about sexual temptation, especially given the reputation of seductive islanders.) A wife could be expected to be "friend, counsellor, companion, the repository of her husband's thoughts and feelings, the partaker of his joys, the sharer of his cares and sorrows, and one who is to lighten his toils, and become his nurse in sickness."

As important as a wife might be to the personal happiness of the male missionary, she might also help with the great work at hand. Mostly this was by the power of "example"—presenting a "living illustration" of Christian family life for heathens whose domestic life was "dreadfully disordered." Women and children would also present a "symbol of peace" readily understood by the heathen. Although caring for her household would be a wife's primary duty, she might also teach infant schools and take over "the whole business of female education."[30]

Further insight into attitudes and expectations comes from the instructions Corresponding Secretary Samuel Worcester gave to the entire company before they left. Addressing a portion of his comments to "The Beloved Females of the Mission," Worcester nevertheless began with traditional assumptions about their inferiority and culpability. "Woman was designed . . . to be an help meet for Man," he said. This was "not in regard to things merely temporal," and there was no reason to exclude women from the mission's spiritual work of "recovering the common race" from the sins of human beings in general and heathen cultures in particular. (But he could not help reminding his audience that this recovery was necessary "in consequence of her being deceived who was first in the transgression"—that is, because Eve took the first bite of the apple.) He held up as models for the missionary wife the women who "attended" Jesus and the "Helpers of the Apostles" (Phebe, Priscilla, Tryphena, Persis, and the others). The woman's role in the mission would be to "help the Brethren."

The women, Worcester continued, were also expected to provide the heathen with an "example of the purity, and dignity, and loveliness,—the salutary and vivifying influence, the attractive and celestial excellence, which Christianity can impart to the female character."[31] That Christianity raised women to such heights of virtue, when various heathen cultures oppressed them with tabus on food, bound feet, and suttee argued, of course, for the advantages of the Christian civilization the missionaries intended to share. A potential missionary woman could expect to hear from the pulpit of her obligation to act on those advantages.[32]

Taken together, Anderson's essay and Worcester's address show the expectations that would become enshrined in the notion of "true womanhood" by mid-century. Though the phrase was so widely understood as to need no elaboration, the virtues of "piety, purity, submissiveness, and domesticity" summed up the requirements. Bolstered by compliments and by the moral authority (as well as the obligation) to undertake a public role, the missionary women eagerly volunteered. The contradictions of this "cult," which simultaneously insisted on women's presence in the home, were not felt until later.[33]

During the preparations for the mission, such idealizing of women led to well-intended but also patronizing solicitude. A prefabricated frame house was added to the mission's outfit but could not be squeezed onto the *Thaddeus.* Two Boston businessmen named Bryant and Sturgis shipped it without charge the next year, also ordering their ship-masters in the area to offer the women a free passage home. Concern for women as the weaker vessels was by and large unfounded (with the exception of Lucia Holman). The Board eventually concluded that "when well selected in respect to health, education, and piety, wives endure 'hardness' quite as well as their husbands, and sometimes with more faith and patience."[34]

Scattered throughout the small towns of New England were plenty of women ready to be "help meets" in the Sandwich Islands, willing to acquiesce in the fleeting courtships imposed by the sailing date of the *Thaddeus.* The dramatic urgency of these courtships had another source (in at least three cases) in the refusal of another woman to go. For some parents, it was one thing to support missions in theory, or even to send five dollars or a hundred dollars to the Board, quite another to send a daughter to the heathen. Hiram Bingham found to his chagrin, after a three-month wait, that the parents of "Sarah S." had persuaded her not to go. With less than a month before departure, Asa Thurston found himself in a similar predicament, when "Mrs. Clapp" wrote that she was "decidedly opposed to have her daughter engage in the mission to Owhyhee," and that her husband concurred.[35]

Hiram and Asa, though discouraged, did not give up. On September 17, the secret missionary society to which they belonged at Andover procured a horse and sent one of its members, William Goodell, on a "most delicate mission" to his cousin in Marlborough, Lucy Goodale. William had been corresponding with Lucy about missionary work and now asked her to consider joining a mission as the wife of Asa Thurston. Lucy had already shown herself ambitious and resourceful, pursuing an education unusual for a girl. (In her memoir, *Life and Times of Lucy G. Thurston,* she quotes a local minister who announced to her and her classmates that there was "no use in girls going as far [as they had] in arithmetic, other than setting themselves up as candidates for the wives of merchants.") Unexpectedly, her father encouraged her to attend Bradford Academy. When she met Asa Thurston, she had graduated and was teaching school. But it was not an easy time. She had just a few weeks earlier "lost" her sister Persis to marriage, and her mother had died the previous year. Writing to Persis on September 11, 1819, Lucy described her grief and tears ("I more than ever felt myself an orphan") and her source of comfort: "sacredly devoting all my leisure hours to the study of the Will of the Supreme." She gave her cousin permission for Asa to visit.

Lucy could not eat or sleep that night. Her family was supportive but left her during the next week to make her own judgment. She thought of her dear friends and country, "yet all this side the grave, how transient!" Realizing that "the poor heathen possess immortal natures and are perishing," she asked herself, "Who will give them the Bible, and tell them of a Saviour?" Despite the obvious sacrifices and dangers, she decided that if God was providing "an acceptable opportunity," she would give herself "to the noble enterprise of carrying light to the poor benighted countrymen of Obookiah." She was ready to meet Asa Thurston.

The following Thursday, Lucy and Asa parted as "interested friends." The next day, the town clerk of Marlborough was instructed to publish the marriage banns the three times required by Massachusetts law. Three Sundays took them to October 10, with little time to spare before sailing. The Thurstons were the last of the group to be married, on October 12. Lucy spent her twenty-fourth birthday, October 29, on board the *Thaddeus.*[36]

A pair of silhouettes snipped before they left shows the young couple: she pretty and he striking, with a long nose and chin. Remembrances from fellow missionaries run to character, not appearances. Mercy Whitney described them on the *Thaddeus* as "very pious, but rather reserved." In his youth, Asa was a fine athlete with a sturdy constitution. (He survived the typhus that killed his mother and brothers.) He first trained as a scythemaker, but later showed promise as a scholar at Yale and Andover. Lucy would be the wife of an ordained minister and one of the leaders of the mission. The "opportunity" was "acceptable," she decided, but she could not have foreseen the particular trials ahead. Fortunately she possessed, again according to Mercy Whitney, "superior talents and an amiable disposition, [and] has also had the advantage of a good education."[37] Asa could not have been sure—though maybe he sensed—that there was the right kind of iron in her. A late photograph of the couple in old age shows her large and apple-cheeked next to Asa's Rip Van Winkle beard. Whatever special qualities or special providences were theirs, they would grow old together in the islands, missionaries for life.

The Bingham courtship was just as brief. Hiram met Sybil

Moseley on the eve of the ordination ceremonies in Goshen, Connecticut. He was sitting out a Bible Society meeting because of a bad cold, when a minister and a young lady called to inquire about lodgings. As Hiram led them to the right place, he wondered to himself whether this Miss Moseley could be the same person his friend and fellow missionary Levi Parsons had mentioned as a suitable candidate for a missionary's wife. That evening, Hiram remembered, "I measured the lines of her face and the expression of her features with more than an artist's carefulness." Sybil was an orphan and had been teaching school for the previous nine years. Hiram soon learned that she was indeed Parsons's acquaintance, and after prudent inquiries to half a dozen persons who knew her, requested that Dr. Worcester (the Board's secretary) set up a private interview.[38]

Sybil Moseley did not need any persuading to dedicate her life to the heathen, but she had to be sure that Hiram was the right man. She was not a pretty woman: in a portrait done just before departure, she leans forward with an air of compliance and humility. Her large nose in an ordinary face does not match Hiram's dashing and regular features. (He was over six feet tall and, according to Daniel Chamberlain, "the best swimmer I ever saw.")[39] It is impossible to predict from this portrait whether Sybil's retiring pose hides a quiet strength, no less impressive than Hiram's. But the thoughts and labors of a lifetime would confirm that in intelligence, devotion to the mission's work, and kindness she had few equals.

Sybil's youthful journals, which start in 1811, leave the only record of young womanhood for the wives of the first company. These are private journals, meant for her eyes alone, as she self-consciously recorded her progress or lack of it as a Christian. They differ from the journals begun by her and the other wives on the *Thaddeus* and continued throughout missionary life, which were written with an audience of friends and family in mind. But while Sybil may have considered her meditations on holiness a private matter, their content is not idiosyncratic. Although intelligent and articulate, she is not an original or iconoclastic thinker. As is true of her "sisters" on the voyage, the received wisdom of the time informs and orders her life. In this sense, the record of Sybil's piety belongs to all of them.[40]

She dwells on the enduring twin tenets of Calvinism: the absolute depravity of humans and the absolute omnipotence of God.

The diaries begin at about the time Sybil found herself the eldest of five orphaned children. (Her father died in 1810, her mother in 1811.) At this point she began the pilgrim's life of a schoolteacher in several Massachusetts towns. The pain of her parents' deaths and the difficult memories of this period of her life would echo in journals and letters for the rest of her life. "Ah me, it seems my heart would break," she wrote on March 6, 1812. "Alas where will the wide world afford a home for an orphan girl? Gloomy indeed is the prospect before me." For consolation, she reminded herself that there was a "Father of the Fatherless" and asked, "May I be enabled to cast all into thy hands." The following year, March 16, 1813, during a sister's illness, she remembered Jesus' example, "who, in the midst of suffering even to death, could cry, Father, thy will not mine be done!" Sybil coped during this period of her life as she would in the future—by restating her faith in an omnipotent God who knows, orders, and understands all, even if human minds cannot perceive as He does. Hers was a powerful faith. In 1815 she wrote, "I think it is my comfort that the Lord reigneth even over my affairs, and that the events of this year and of my whole life, if I should live longer, even, the most minute, are all ordered by Him and that He will do all his pleasure."[41]

Still, a note of melancholy sounds through the early journal. Her parents' deaths were traumatic and her peripatetic life hard for her. On board the *Thaddeus,* on December 7, she reflected that this was "the eighth anniversary Thanksgiving which has found me in a situation new, and far from any calculations I could have made from one to the other." In a world where everyone was metaphorically on a pilgrimage to heaven, she was "literally . . . a stranger, a sojourner." She dated her journal from Westfield, Southampton, S. Hadley, and E. Windsor, Massachusetts, and from Canandaigua, New York. In August 1815, she felt "uncommonly low" because she had been disappointed in her hopes for a revival in her school. But sometimes the cause of sadness eluded her. From Southampton on June 8, 1814, she wrote, "My scholars seem happy to see me . . . my boarding place is quite agreeable . . . but still my heart is heavy—there seems a load I cannot account for."[42]

She found her joy in religion. "What a sermon have I heard!" she exclaimed one afternoon in 1811. "A day spent in the courts of the Lord," she wrote in 1816, "is indeed better than a thousand in the highest delights which earth could [have] offered." But such delight was temporary, overwhelmed not simply by melancholy but by self-derision. Church doctrine, teaching her that she was born with a sinful nature ("in Adam's fall we sinned all") provides an analogy for these swings of mood, this sense of universal frailty leading in turn to a joyful and salutary dependence on God.[43]

Sybil's religion did not allow her to be easy on herself. It exacted constant striving and constant uncertainty: one tried to be good, one tried to defend against a sinful heart, one merely hoped for salvation in the next world. In the entry of November 1811 in which she praised the sermon, Sybil wondered, "Am I not vainly imagining I have religion, love the Saviour . . . when in reality I do not? Oh, that I knew my own heart." Although making entries in her journals somewhat at random, she almost always addresses her soul on her birthday, September 14, and on New Year's Day, when she berates herself for past inadequacies and hopes for advances in holiness. On her twenty-first birthday in 1813, she wrote, "O, gracious Saviour, pity and help me who is weak. . . . O help me to begin this year anew—to strive for a closer walk with God."[44] On January 1, 1815, she noted, "Three years this day since I publicly entered into covenant with God—chose Him for my portion before the world and professed to commit my all unto his hands." She believed she had fallen short. "And Oh! how little fruit have I brought forth!" That she never seems to meet her standards is partly—as she would see it—a measure of her own frailty. She had to guard against excessive attachment to things of this earth; she also feared the "dullness," "stupidity," or "hardness of heart" that kept her from her God. It never occurred to her that the standards themselves might be impossibly high.

But no matter how exacting, Sybil's intense personal relationship with God never failed her. In the middle of the Pacific on March 27, 1820, she was still writing—as she would write for the rest of her life—"My soul, what hast thou to say of the dealings of GOD towards thee?" Though doubting her achievements, she knew what she was trying to achieve. In 1816, she had been to communion, where "if my heart did not greatly deceive me," she had felt "that if Jesus would bid me ask him what I would, it was that I might be holy—did feel as if I could say—take health, take friends, take *all* away, only that I live henceforth as one redeemed by the precious blood of Christ." Given a choice of a life's work, she wrote in 1818, "Oh may I be *perseveringly* engaged doing good, yea, humbly, and *devoutly*." As early as May 29, 1815, she was hoping that God would make her an "instrument in his hand" for the work of preaching to the heathen. Her "ardent desire," she repeated on January 7, 1816, was "to be employed in the now benighted regions of his vineyards." On her twenty-seventh birthday in 1819, in the last entry before the journal begins again the following January on the *Thaddeus*, she repeated her wish: "Should I dare to pen a request for the year following, if life be continued, it is that wholly unfit, unworthy as I am, God would be pleased of his mercy to fit me – draw my desires strongly forth and in his providence open a door for me among the heathen."[45]

Like Hiram, Sybil had a few secrets of her own to tell as far as suitors were concerned. In late December 1818, she had received a proposal of marriage from a man she does not name in her journal (perhaps Levi Parsons). Though she had been praying for four or five years for the opportunity to become a missionary, she hesitated for the most understandable and romantic of reasons. She wondered "whether it was a sacrifice to which GOD called me – to forego the sweetest comforts of life arising from a tender interest in the most tender of all connexions and unite myself to one to whom I could give no place in my heart other than that of Christian brother." Nine months later, when Hiram Bingham proposed, the question of sacrificing "the sweetest comforts of life" did not arise. She gave her answer to him a day after their formal interview. The marriage took place on October 11, 1819.[46]

Exactly what happened with Samuel Ruggles's "Mary" we do not know, except that in March 1819 he wrote asking his sister Lucia to "tell her I want her to go to Owhyhee [Hawaii] with me," and by September 22 he had married Nancy Wells. Orphaned from a "very early age," Samuel had been trying to educate himself for several years when he entered the Foreign Mission School at Cornwall in 1817. He became Opukahaia's friend and found his resolve to pursue missionary work strengthened by the calamity of Opukahaia's death. The "Owhyhee Mission will prosper," he told his brother Isaac in March 1818. "I have seen the heathen – I have seen them converted and I have seen how they may die. I feel more than ever the worth of their souls." The Board accepted Samuel as an "assistant," listing him on the published roster as "Catechist & Schoolmaster." The reasons why twenty-nine-year-old Nancy Wells went with him as his wife are not known. Perhaps she saw what his brother Isaac did, "the most amiable disposition in the world." The Hawaiians, during the years the Ruggleses spent in Kauai and Hawaii, called him, affectionately, *keiki* or child.[47]

Little is known about the remaining courtships. When the company's physician, Dr. Thomas Holman, offered to go along, he was practicing medicine and incurring debts in Cooperstown, New York. He spent the summer of 1819 at the Foreign Mission School, and the Board discharged his debts. Later on, he would be accused of having a greater interest in making his fortune in Hawaii than in serving the heathen. But for now, at least, his piety was convincing and his skills a necessity. He found Lucia Ruggles (Samuel's sister) willing to marry and accompany him. Letters survive from both Isaac and Samuel Ruggles counseling their sister on religious matters. Samuel urged her as early as July 2, 1817 (when he himself went to Cornwall) to consider "the poor benighted heathen" and to join him "and say in your heart, O my God when shall these things cease." On February 6, 1819, Isaac wrote that he thought her "almost persuaded" to join Samuel as a missionary. By June 30, the proposal from the doctor evidently having intervened, Lucia, a schoolteacher in Cooperstown, was about to give up her school and prepare for Hawaii. She married the doctor on September 2.[48]

In retrospect, some of Isaac's counsel seems ominous. As early as 1814, Lucia's brother worried that she had "a little of that disposition . . . to set too high a value on money, and not duly to estimate the worth of mental improvement and useful accomplishments." He wanted to make sure she had the "*views and feelings* which a *missionary should have,*" that she "go with an ardent love for souls," adding that missionaries "must in a peculiar manner be willing . . . to deny themselves." Since Lucia's letters do not survive, it is impossible to know whether in making her decision she stressed the perishing heathen or the doctor—whose portrait shows him a handsome man. The journal she kept during her first year as a missionary does show the expected pieties—the sense of a Providential Hand protecting them through storms, an eagerness for the work of evangelizing the heathen—and yet here and there the things she does not say, at least when her journal is compared with the others, become significant. She does not describe an all-consuming relationship with God more important than anything and anyone else (a theme that runs through Sybil Bingham's and Mercy Whitney's journals). She seems rather to emphasize the details of everyday life, as if predicting the trouble she will have in detaching herself from earthly comforts.

Lucia realized that it was impossible to "imagine what our feelings will be in any situation, till brought to the trial," a truth she learned the hard way. Knowing what she was supposed to think, she reminded herself: "We must not consult our own temporal ease as this is not our business, but to seek the good of others—is our grand object." Her journal is good-natured and cheerful; she would not have any descriptions construed as complaints; she had no regrets about becoming a missionary. Nevertheless, after a few months in Hawaii, she had to admit that she found herself in a place "where not only the comforts and *conveniences* of life are denied, but the necessaries also." In September 1820, sending the last section of her journal back to her sister, she proposed that for future missions, whenever possible, the men "go first onto the ground, and begin and prepare the rough way a little, before he brings her who, after all he has done, is capable of suffering *enough*."[49]

The young printer Elisha Loomis applied to the Board in the spring of 1819 and went to Cornwall in July, but was told on September 2 that he would not be needed that year. Resolving to work at his trade in the interim, he was in Brookfield, Massachusetts, when the Board reversed itself. "This I did not desire," he wrote to Samuel Worcester on September 16, "as I had not made the necessary preparations—I had no *female companion.* Disappointed in my expectations of finding one at Brookfield, Mass., I resolved to return home, make what preparations I could, and go out single." But in Utica, New York, he met twenty-three-year-old Maria Sartwell. A former schoolteacher now employed in folding and stitching books, she had "long been wishing to engage in a mission." He told Dr. Worcester, "I have now spent several days with her—could not be more pleased with a person. . . . I cannot but regard what has taken place as a particular interposition of Divine Providence." They married on September 27.[50]

Samuel Whitney was already in his mid-twenties but still had two years to go at Yale when he offered his services to the Board and was accepted. Help in finding a spouse came from a classmate, Josiah Brewer, who proposed his cousin and correspondent, Mercy Partridge. She replied cautiously on August 30, "I see not where would be the harm of a friendly visit from the person you mention, even if it should never be renewed." In early September, the minister in Pittsfield, Massachusetts — Mercy's home town — responded to inquiries from a Reverend Smith at Yale. The Reverend Heman Humphrey wrote reassuringly of Mercy's "uncommon, & I think undoubted evidence of genuine & ardent piety." He added, "Her constitution I take it is very good" — a remark that in retrospect is poignant, considering the procession of ailments that undermined Mercy's health in the islands. Humphrey thought she would go, "provided she should be pleased with the man, & sufficient time allowed for consideration." Since "*six weeks*" was hardly generous, he cautioned that he could not speak for her. After the wedding, according to a story passed down through the family, a friend who thought Samuel had gone hunting asked about his luck. "Through grace," said Samuel (whose sister Grace had helped with the matchmaking), "I have found Mercy, and caught a Partridge."[51]

Mercy Partridge Whitney kept exact copies of her letters and journals during the fifty-three years she spent as a missionary. Others remembered her as tall and slender, still beautiful even as an old woman. Two portraits survive: she and Samuel were one of the four couples whom Samuel Morse painted before the *Thaddeus* sailed. Dark ringlets frame her pale, pretty face; his long face, fair hair, and gentle expression make him look younger than his years. But for Mercy's early life, the written record consists only of a dozen or so letters from 1819, written to her sister Emily Dow, her brother Edward, her brother Williams and his wife Laura, and Josiah Brewer. These do not tell much about Mercy the young woman, only about Mercy the young Congregationalist. The headings say that she wrote from Pittsfield, but she rarely touched on matters of ordinary life. She offered congratulations on a marriage and remarked on the "union and cordiality" among the "band of brothers and sisters" at her church, but included no details of dresses, hairstyles, dances, or picnics. Instead, she meditated on church doctrine.

Preoccupied, like Sybil Bingham, with a sense of her own depravity and its analogue, God's omnipotence, Mercy wrote to her parents just before leaving, "I trust I feel more and more sensible of my insufficiency, & am enabled to rely more entirely on God for strength to enable me to discharge the various duties which are incumbent on me." She reminded herself again and again that she should not put up her treasures on earth; this material world—a "vale of tears for such it is truly though but few realize it"—was not meant for happiness. She urged a change of heart on her parents, her siblings, her friends. Seeing the day of judgment, when the sheep would be separated from the goats, as a fact, she reminded her sister-in-law, "we are all accountable creatures, stewards of the Lord; and must one day stand at the bar of God and give an account of our stewardship." Till then, it behooved one and all to keep their lamps lit and their loins girded for death, which could come as a thief in the night. In her statements, Mercy paraphrased the popular biblical passages of her day and dispensed the commonplace wisdom. Whatsoever we have to do as servants in the vineyard, she warned, we must do it with all our might. This is the set of beliefs she lived with and died with. Nothing in the long, strange life ahead of her caused her to stop referring to the same passages. When she was starting out, her religion sustained her with the greatest joy she had yet known. She wrote to her brother on January 7, 1819, that she "never knew what happiness was until I forsook the ways of sin & folly. I used to enjoy what I then styled happiness, but indeed it was undeserving the name."[52]

Like the other wives she would join on the *Thaddeus,* Mercy was no stranger to the missionary cause. She wrote to her cousin with eagerness, "It is a subject upon which I have frequently meditated. . . . For several years past, I have felt an earnest desire for the salvation of my fellow man, but more particularly for the poor heathen, who are groping in pagan darkness without the light of the gospel." In letters to her sister and parents she mentioned the same themes. When considering "the millions & millions of heathen, who are bowing down to idols, worshipping gods which their own hands have formed, ignorant of *Jesus* . . . my heart bleeds for them, & the tear of compassion frequently falls from my eye. I am constrained to say, Lord send me." She saw trials and sacrifices ahead, but also "the hope & prospect of being useful to the heathen." She wrote her parents, "It is this which enables me cheerfully to bid adieu to friends, & all that I hold dear in my native land. May this reflection ever offer comfort, that it is love to *Christ* & the souls of the

Reverend Asa Thurston and Lucy Goodale Thurston. Daguerreotype about 1864. Courtesy Hawaiian Mission Children's Society.

Reverend Hiram Bingham and Sybil Moseley Bingham. Painting by Samuel F. B. Morse, 1819. Reproduced courtesy Yale University Art Gallery. Gift of Honorable Hiram Bingham.

Nancy Wells Ruggles. Painting by Samuel F. B. Morse, 1819. Courtesy Hawaiian Mission Children's Society.

Samuel Ruggles. Painting by Samuel F. B. Morse, 1819. Courtesy Hawaiian Mission Children's Society.

Mercy Partridge Whitney. Painting by Samuel F. B. Morse, 1819. Reproduced courtesy Kauai Museum, Lihue, Kauai. Photo courtesy Hawaiian Mission Children's Society.

Samuel Whitney. Painting by Samuel F. B. Morse, 1819. Reproduced courtesy Kauai Museum, Lihue, Kauai, Photo courtesy Hawaiian Mission Children's Society.

Jerusha Chamberlain. Portrait from about 1845. Courtesy Hawaiian Mission Children's Society.

Daniel Chamberlain. Portrait from about 1845. Courtesy Hawaiian Mission Children's Society.

Dr. Thomas Holman and Lucia Ruggles Holman. Painting by Samuel F. B. Morse, 1819. Reproduced courtesy Yale University Art Gallery. Given by Harrison F. Bassett in memory of Elizabeth Ives Bassett and Arthur Nobel Brown. Photo courtesy Hawaiian Mission Children's Society.

Maria Sartwell Loomis. Daguerreotype about 1850. Courtesy Hawaiian Mission Children's Society.

poor *heathen,* for which I make these sacrifices." She considered this a "great undertaking," a work of "immense magnitude," but believed that God "who I trust has called me to the work, is able abundantly to qualify me. O that he would . . . make me a blessing to the poor heathen whither I may go."[53]

The month or so before sailing brought a flurry, almost a frenzy, of activity: courtship, packing, farewells. Lucy Thurston remembered that she and three friends "cut garments by dozens and by scores." Sixty "labored" for Sybil Bingham. From September 22 to October 12, six marriages took place. One high point in the preparations came on September 28, when Hiram Bingham and Asa Thurston were ordained in Goshen, Connecticut. The service was well attended by illustrious church members and mission supporters as well as the assistant missionaries. Rev. Heman Humphrey, Mercy Partridge's pastor from Pittsfield, Massachusetts, delivered the sermon, "The Promised Land." A grand apology for the mission, it is one of the best public statements of the ideas prompting New Englanders to support it.[54]

Humphrey's claims were hardly modest. He traced the missionaries' roots much farther than the New Testament model of Jesus and the disciples, back to the first books of the Old Testament. He compared the church now to the Israelites then. Just as God as a "divine grant" gave the land of Canaan to Abraham, Isaac, Jacob and their posterity, "so does the world belong to the church." The Israelites' work under Joshua was physical – to return from Egypt and to possess the land; the church's work now was a spiritual possession – to subdue the world for Christ. Thus the text from Joshua 13:1 was very much alive: "and there remaineth yet very much land to be possessed." Humphrey warned that they must not look to angels or miracles to do the work for them. God achieved his possessions through "human instrumentality." Just as he asked the Israelites to buckle on their armor and fight for their inheritance, so did he require martial zeal now. The true light must be made to shine wherever – as in Hawaii – the Prince of Darkness had reestablished his empire. Humphrey commended the apostles, who had not shut themselves up in Jerusalem waiting for the conversion of the heathen, but had gone out with energy and diligence to plant the standard of the cross on the battlements of Rome. The Protestant heroes of the Reformation—Wyclif, Zwingli, Luther, Calvin, Melanchthon, and Knox—belonged to the same tradition of fighting the church's battles "with the sword of the spirit."

The battle to reclaim the heathen world would have been over long ago were it not for the "lamentable and criminal apathy" of the church. Christendom had long been aware of heathens all over the world worshipping "stones and wood and reptiles and devils," but, as Humphrey put it, "the church slept." Now Hawaiians themselves had had to travel to America to rouse them. Appealing to duty, insisting that the church was "bound . . . to give the gospel to the heathen," Humphrey added, "This, my Brethren, is one of the few questions which will not bear argument." In yet another Old Testament image, he likened the Hawaiians' condition to a plague, whose remedy was the gospel. Humphrey finished this section of his argument by asking, "This remedy, God has sent to us and shall we, or shall we not manifest our gratitude and benevolence, by sending it to the perishing? My appeal is not so much to the understanding as to the conscience."

The sermon underlines the energy, the determination, and, of course, the arrogance of a people who believed their religion was the single truth and ought to apply to every piece of ground on the earth. Humphrey was giving his audience the sense of belonging to something much greater than themselves—the whole of human history as they saw it in the Bible. The sermon is an expression of a parochial people with the strengths and weaknesses that term implies. In the grand scheme of world civilization, they were just a small group espousing only one of the world's religions. But to them, the part equaled the whole. Without their unshakable self-confidence—their conviction that they knew who they were and what they were doing—they would never have risked doing battle with Satan in order to do good to the heathen. (Too many questions and the armor would never have been buckled.) Without that confidence, the missionaries might not have lasted a month in Honolulu. Humphrey addressed Bingham and Thurston as "soldiers of the cross" in a holy war. Armed with the truth of their religion, however, they were also shielded by it. Held in front of the eyes, the armor blocked what they did not want to see: that the Hawaiians were not necessarily "perishing" without them.

As individuals, however, missionaries cultivated humility. "The

Charge," delivered by the Reverend David L. Perry after Humphrey's sermon, spoke to proper attitudes and deportment. Perry counseled the young people to "preach even more by your benevolence, meekness, fortitude, and holy deportment, than by your precepts." They were to try, in other words, to be good, as well as to do good. For Calvinists raised on convictions of personal sinfulness, goodness was never assured. They were certain of the righteousness and necessity of their task, but they also feared that they would not be equal to it. Their calling was not for egotists: they could not expect "worldly distinction from the missionary office." If not doctrine, the task itself would humble them. In a prescient comment, Perry added, "You have put your hand to the plough . . . to labor and wear out in far distant and benighted lands." Nor was missionary work for materialists, since they would be "henceforth dead to the world, dead to the refinement of civilized society." The job was for idealists, who would cultivate an "ardent desire for the salvation of the heathen" and for whom the expected accolade was no more than Perry's wish at the close of his speech: "May the blessing of many ready to perish be your reward."

The mission's goals were next publicly articulated on October 15 at Boston's Park Street Church. Here the group (including Hawaiians) was formally organized into a church and received from Corresponding Secretary Worcester the "Instructions" of the Prudential Committee of the ABCFM. Worcester repeated familiar themes: the momentous work ahead, the sacrifice of worldly comforts, the need of the perishing heathen for the gospel. He also spoke to practical matters: the organization of mission goods into a common stock system and the need for brotherly love in cramped and isolated situations that were sure to test it.

Perhaps most important, he got down to the heart of the matter for individual missionaries—not some grand analogy comparing them to Israelites in another time and place, nor martial imagery preparing them for God's battles, but simple compassion for other human beings. "Your Mission is a mission of mercy," said Worcester, "and your work is to be wholly a labor of love." No matter how the mission's detractors—then and now—may reevaluate this motive, no matter how these intentions were thwarted or muddled in practice, there is no doubt that in personal terms, this concern for fellow humans was, in fact, each missionary's motive. Naive it may have been, but not hypocritical: there were no ulterior motives. And it was perhaps the only good reason for starting out.

Taken together, these three speeches clearly articulate the mission's identity. But they are equally interesting for what they do not examine. All rest on assumptions that will in the course of events prove problematic. To the missionaries, "civilization" was an absolute, not a relative, term, referring only to the culture of Christian New England. When Worcester said in summary, "You are to aim at nothing short of . . . raising up the whole people to an elevated state of Christian Civilization," he was not implicitly acknowledging the existence of a different Hawaiian civilization. Hawaiian customs were "pagan" and "heathen"—the opposite of "civilized"—unless they imitated the missionaries' own culture. The missionaries would bring civilization and add the good news of the gospel to the sum total of what the Hawaiians knew now (which was not worth much). The Hawaiians "have been perishing for lack of knowledge . . . they have been without God . . . living in the wretched state of uncultured man."

Though unable to conceive of civilization without Christianity, the missionaries seem to have stopped short of tautology. Making a distinction between the religious and secular details of the culture, they thought they understood a sequential relationship between the two. One of the lessons drawn from Daniel Chamberlain's failure to introduce American farming in the islands was that "mere civilization, coming in contact with savages, is an unhealthful influence: it must come to them through the gospel." Applauding the mission's achievements in 1864, Rupert Anderson thought they had got the sequence right: "One of the most obvious facts in this history is, that on the Hawaiian Islands *the gospel preceded civilization*."[55]

The imagery of the speeches is revealing. Hawaiian culture was benighted, associated with darkness; in bringing the Hawaiians new information, the missionaries would "present to them a Light, which shall dissipate the glooms." Satan had established his empire in the Sandwich Islands; as good soldiers of the cross, they were to fight a holy war against him. Success they viewed in simple terms: Christianity would supplant paganism. Hawaiians would get rid of, "cast off," the old ways. Humphrey held up an image (no doubt one of the missionaries' fondest dreams) of Hawaiians "hastening down to the shore in welcome, gathering around the missionaries by hundreds, and listening with silent amazement, while you talk to them of the babe of Bethlehem. . . . I see them casting away their idols and exclaiming with one voice, your God shall be our God, your Saviour shall be our Saviour."

The metaphors suggest a salutary supplanting—one thing taking the place of another as light conquers darkness. The missionaries seem to have supposed that one puts on and takes off whole religions as easily as a shirt. They had the example of Paul, the type of the convert, blinded on the road to Damascus, his life immediately and irrevocably changed (Acts 9:1–20). By lifting off a layer of pagan ideas and habits, the missionaries would free the true Hawaiian, whose soul was exactly the equal of any other human being's. Not stopping to wonder if they should free him, the missionaries also did not wonder if they could.

But Hawaiian religious practices permeated the islands' civilization as much as Christianity did New England's. How could one "cast off" a single part of Hawaiian civilization without profoundly disturbing the whole? Mightn't the good and evil in cultures be part of the one lump, so that in defeating what was "satanic" in Hawaiian life they would necessarily defeat with it much of the good? To phrase the issue in personal rather than cultural terms, was there such a person as a "true Hawaiian" separable from his "heathen" habits? If a Hawaiian took Christ as his portion—a change of heart in a moment of time—would he just as quickly put on the trappings of the missionaries' civilization? Better yet, should he? Could Christians still wear the *malo,* the male loincloth?

Their teachers in Boston were just as muddled. Every journal from these young persons mentions love of souls. Their primary task, "above all," Worcester told them, was to convert the heathen from idolatry. But they were also expected "to get into extended operation . . . the arts and institutions and usages of civilized life and society." In time, if the mission achieved complete success, they would have covered the land with "fruitful fields, and pleasant dwellings, and schools and churches." In time, "this little but precious Church," as Worcester addressed the newly congregated band, was "destined, we trust, to be a light shining in a dark place,—shining more and more, until those long benighted Isles shall all rejoice in the perfect day."

The trouble is that they were simultaneously to "withhold yourselves entirely from all interference, and intermeddling with the political affairs and party concerns of the nation or people among whom you reside." They were, like Paul, to "immoveably maintain the resolution, TO KNOW NOTHING AMONG THE PEOPLE TO WHOM YOU ARE SENT, SAVE JESUS CHRIST AND HIM CRUCIFIED" (I Corinthians 2:2). But how, one wonders, were they going to "know nothing . . . save Jesus Christ" and still introduce Christian civilization? And how could this introduction have nothing to do with the laws of the land? Just to introduce the seventh commandment—against adultery—put the missionaries on a collision course with Hawaii's time-honored and complicated sexual customs. But these were questions and problems for the future. In retrospect, it seems clear that the images in the missionaries' minds did not adequately match the situation they encountered in the islands—not surprising, and typical of many explorers and pioneers. In October 1819, theory had not met practice.

Finally, on the morning of October 23, 1819, the leave-taking ceremonies began. Asa Thurston gave a farewell sermon in Park Street Church. Then, on Boston's Long Wharf, everyone sang "Blessed Be the Tie That Binds." Dr. Worcester led the assembly in "fervent and affectionate prayer," and Thomas Hopu delivered the closing address. At the end, "with perfect composure," Hiram Bingham and Asa Thurston sang the hymn "When Shall We All Meet Again?" For missionaries who expected to spend their lives in service to God, and never to return to New England, the question was easily answered: "Where immortal spirits reign, / There may we all meet again." A fourteen-oared barge, courtesy of a sympathetic naval officer, rowed the young people to the *Thaddeus.* By all accounts, the ceremony had moved most of its listeners to tears.[56]

Not least among the achievements of this voyage was that they got there at all. (Later sold to the Hawaiians, the *Thaddeus* was so decrepit that before all the sandalwood to pay for it could be collected, it floated unusable in Honolulu harbor.)[57] Yet if any group could make order out of chaos and overcome trials, mental or physical, this one could. The shipboard journals attest to the high spirits, piety, and determination that enabled the missionaries not only to endure the voyage but to prosper. Their greatest achievements lay in relationships. The young marriages flourished. The women began to rely on and confide in one another, until they saw themselves as friends and "sisters." The mission as a whole began to sense its identity as a "family," even though that identity was already being shaken by petty quarrels with the Holmans.

Once under sail, with seasickness abated and returning only with storms, long hours and longer days stretched ahead, providing plenty of time to reconsider motives and marriages. The motives were secure: the decision to undertake missionary work had never been impulsive. The hasty marriages, though arranged by well-meaning friends, seem to have been made in heaven. This may have been due to good luck or astute character analysis on the part of the matchmakers or determination on the part of each woman to see the best in the spouse recommended to her. Or the couples may have stumbled upon the perfect foundation for enduring relationships in a shared devotion to the missionary cause. What does seem probable, from the accounts sent home—uniformly admiring and appreciative—is that even though they were reluctant to come right out and say it, they were falling in love.

The only couple on board who were not more or less honeymooners were Daniel and Jerusha Chamberlain, married thirteen years and parents of five children—Dexter, 12, Nathan, 10, Mary, 9, Daniel, 5, and Nancy, just a toddler. Despite their special cares and worries, with lively children to feed, entertain, teach, and nurse (Nancy was very ill at the start), the Chamberlains set an example of common sense and competence for the others. Jerusha wrote nothing, but an admiring and grateful Daniel described her as appearing "so calm and contented . . . as contented as she ever did on our old farm." On December 2, when the brig encountered rough seas, he thanked God for Jerusha's "fortitude and resignation while our little girl was sick, and indeed at all times since we have been on board." At the end of the voyage, he concluded that "no one of the females have endured the voyage as well as Mrs. Chamberlain."[58]

Sooner or later, tucked somewhere into a journal or letter, comes praise from the other women for their spouses.[59] Only Nancy Ruggles's journal is silent on this point, but then her husband was seasick for most of the voyage. She expressed nevertheless a generalized happiness, and he, still ill on December 27, mentioned his appreciation of her: "She is all and more than I could reasonably have asked." Maria Loomis sweetly but archly confided: "In the society of the brethren & dear Sisters of the Mission but more particularly in that of one nearer & dearer friend, my days glide sweetly and happily on." Though Lucia Holman would soon disengage herself from the role of missionary, she had no reservations about being the wife of Thomas Holman: a "kind husband, a faithful friend, and a pious and intelligent companion." Lucy Thurston reflected that when she married, she "felt assured of the care and friendship of one precious friend. But my expectations have been more than realized." On November 18, the *Thaddeus* recently under sail, Mercy and Samuel Whitney spent the evening in their cabin while he read to her from a book on missions, Claudius Buchanan's *Christian Researches in Asia* (1811). "I cannot retire," she wrote her parents, "without telling you we are happy." She went on to praise her "companion and friend," whom she called Mr. Whitney, who was "kind, affectionate, and faithful. O may I have a heart to praise God for such an unmerited blessing." Sybil Bingham also knew whom to thank. In an entry of January 29, 1820, in her private journal, she reflected that God had given her "a heart peculiarly formed to feel." She remembered her request that He would "in his own time . . . fill the void, by giving me one that was his servant, whose heart was formed with mine. He has more than answered the request."

The women write with solicitude for their husbands, partly explained by a natural tendency to have a husband's welfare at heart, partly by a sense of what a wife ought to do. When Mercy Whitney wrote on February 2 that she found Samuel "worthy of my sincere and lasting attachment," she continued with a resolution. "It shall ever be my constant study to make his life pleasant and useful."[60] On January 29, Sybil praised Hiram as "a treasure rich and undeserved." Her wish: "O, to prove to him what he would hope I was!" In a long passage in her private journal, written on January 15, evidently the day after an intimate conversation, Sybil made resolutions. Partly they show her kindness as a human being; partly her sense of subordination to her husband; partly that she was in love with him. When she could not "feel exactly with him in what may concern us," she resolved to recall his "uniform tenderness towards me, his attainments in the path of holiness beyond me." She would then "set a guard upon my lips that no unkind word, upon my actions, that no unbecoming carriage, wound his feelings and grieve his heart." If she saw something needing "amendment," she would watch "for the most favorable moment" and study "the kindest manner" for giving reproof. (She was not afraid to give reproof, only enormously sensitive about how she gave it.) Finally, she resolved "to watch carefully that no worldly spirit in me, no spirit of discontent, no backwardness to any exertions either on my own part or his, prove a 'weight' and hindrance to him in our Master's work."

Content with their marital relationships in private, the women also seem content with their public roles, even as they understood—from a myriad of personal experiences as well as official pronouncements—that it was not a woman's world. To add to the public statements (like those from Worcester and Anderson), every woman had personal anecdotes. On the roster of the mission, the men's vocations were listed as Catechist, Printer, Schoolmaster, or Agriculturalist, while a blank space sits next to the women's names. Only Jerusha Chamberlain was credited as the "Mother of 3 Sons and 2 daughters." When Sybil Bingham wrote to the treasurer of the ABCFM to donate her savings of $800, her new husband found it necessary to add a postscript stating that in the "disposition of her property" she had his "most full and cordial approbation." Lucy Thurston in 1870 looked back to the inequities of her childhood: that sons, not daughters, were trained for future employment, and that in dividing property, "it took *two daughters* to poise against *one son.*" Mercy Whitney protested at length in her journal against the unfair division of her father's property in 1833, apologetic about paying so much attention to "this world's good," but unable to let the matter pass when "the daughters portion [had] been so disproportionate with the sons." When, in later years, the women sent their children to New England for schooling, the Board adopted a policy of allowing $60 a year for boys and $50 for girls.[61]

Yet the women do not dwell on the inequities or quarrel with the expected divisions of labor. Though sometimes brought to tears by the domestic demands placed on them, they never thought they should not be doing the laundry. A woman's life, though different from a man's, was not necessarily inferior. In 1874, advising her granddaughter to "submit to, obey, and reverence" her husband, Lucy Thurston added, "I never felt it a servile lot." At the end of her life, Sybil Bingham was writing about the "proud post of wife & mother in a household, where a few loved beings daily feel the influence of the efforts she may make for their comfort."[62]

When a woman's lot seemed onerous, she often cast it in relief against more important issues. The women may have been "helpers" in the "Master's work" of saving souls in this world, but they understood that, ultimately, all souls—male, female, Hawaiian—were equal. And all answered the same questions on Judgment Day. (As one historian writes, Puritanism "validated" women by "setting salvation above gender.") For these missionary women, made special by their piety, a relationship with God—not with a husband now or with the children to come—was the single most important fact in their life. When Mercy Whitney's brother married in 1819, she had warned him "against placing your affections supremely upon the world, or upon the dear object of your choice." She was not trying to "lessen that affection, which ought to be cherished towards our kindred & friends; but only that it may be in subordination to the will & glory of God." Sybil Bingham confided to her private diary on January 29: "While I lean upon this beloved friend, as thy gift, gracious Saviour, save me from idolatrous affection, enabling me, at all times, to say who have I in heaven or earth, that is once to be compared with *Thee.*"[63]

The biggest shipboard challenge for these women did not concern identity as a woman, a wife, or even a Christian, but the group's identity as a "family." This was the nineteenth century's most important social unit and most powerful metaphor. Its roots went back to St. Matthew's gospel (12:50) and to Puritan covenant theology with its community of believers. The family was seen as the building block of a new nation, and those responsible for the nation's success—the women who nurtured its citizens and preserved its civilization—gained new status. For a group of strangers who had left their biological families behind and now formed a small group ready to do the Lord's will in a remote place, the word came naturally to mind.[64]

But a sense of "family" proved more elusive to achieve. It helped that the missionaries were a homogeneous group, with similar backgrounds in small towns, from respectable families but not wealthy ones. It helped that they shared similar convictions about religion. But common sense told them that however firm the foundation in Christian doctrine or good will, a group of acquaintances cooped up together for a long stretch of time risked at least intermittent discord. The sermon at the double ordination in Goshen had warned them that the "remains of corrupt nature" in every human, combined with the opportunities the ship offered "to become minutely acquainted with each other" and the condition of "being separated from the great world," would almost certainly create problems. They could expect "wounds of feeling, breaches of mutual confidence, disaffections, alienations, animosities, unkind debates, and embittered strifes." To avoid this would "require much vigilance, much prayer, much crucifixion of self, much sanctifying grace." Christian doctrine set high, if not impossible, standards. They were aiming for "brotherly love in its requisite purity, constancy, strength and tenderness,"—in the words of Rev. Humphrey—"that you may all be inseparably one, as Christ and the Father are one."

They came close. They tried very hard. They displayed the right Christian attitudes toward inconveniences. Private fears that they might be martyred or assaulted they successfully parried by remembering the promise of Jesus that he would never leave them or forsake them. They understood that even if they failed, God would raise up other instruments to work his will for the heathen. The church would triumph in the end, with or without them. Private fears of inadequacy they simply lived with as part of their religion, consoled with the knowledge that Jesus died for their sins.

Physical danger during some violent storms in January they faced with apparent "composure" (according to several journals). God, after all, controlled the seas. If he afflicted them it was with cause and for their benefit. By February 4, the most dangerous part of the voyage over, Sybil Bingham continued the analogy between the missionaries and the Israelites in the wilderness: "Over us too, has he, emphatically, watched, by night and by day,—in difficulties and in danger has he taken us in the hollow of his hand, and carried us safely through." A few days before reaching Hawaii, Samuel Whitney, who had been helping to paint the brig, fell overboard when a rope slipped. The missionaries—Mercy included—reacted without panic. Mercy ran on deck, James Hunnewell (the first mate) threw Samuel a bench, and the ship turned about almost instantly. "But the promise, 'as thy day is so shall thy strength be,' was verified to me," Mercy wrote later. "I was enabled to compose my feelings, and look to God in prayer. I felt willing to leave my dear friend in the hand of my Heavenly Father, knowing that he would do what was best." The result of the mishap was a further cementing of the family's bonds. "Never before did the mission family know how much they loved him," reads the mission's public journal. Mercy still had the bench—"Whitney's Lifeboat"—over forty years later, and intended to keep it as long as she lived.[65]

The missionaries disciplined their behavior as well as their minds. As pilgrims on the earth, it behooved them to pass the time with an eye on the final judgment when they would have to give account for their deeds. As voyagers on the *Thaddeus,* they felt a similar necessity, as Mercy Whitney put it, to "improve our time in such a manner, that at the end of our voyage we may have no occasion to say, it has been misspent." Hiram Bingham preached on December 19 from Isaiah 5:4: "What could have been done more to my vineyard, that I have not done in it?" A common lament in many journals was that the writer had not done enough. "Twenty-three Sabbaths we have spent on the water, but what improvement have I made in the divine life?" Maria Loomis asked on March 26. "I have reason to lament over my stupidity and coldness."[66]

The missionaries understood order and discipline as enabling, not repressing. With an eagerness amounting almost to impatience, they set about arranging the days and filling the hours. After seventeen days on board, on November 9 Sybil Bingham recorded that seasickness continued for most of them but that they hoped soon to begin the "systematic improvement of time." Her earnest wish was "O, to do my part towards composing a well regulated mission family." It took another ten days before everyone (except poor Samuel Ruggles) was ready "to make a regular division of time." "We breakfast at 8, dine at one, and sup at six," Mercy Whitney wrote approvingly. "Order and regularity are observed at our meals." They said a blessing before each meal, did not begin to eat until all had been served, and gave thanks at the end. Mercy planned every hour from 5:00 a.m., when she began her day with private devotions and sewing, to 9:30 p.m.:

7:30–9: "breakfast and exercises"
9–12: "writing & study"
12–1: "recitation and conversation"
1–2: "dinner, and private devotion"
2–5: "writing & reading"
5–6: "study of the language"
6–7:30: "tea, conversation, and exercise"
7:30–9:30: "private and family devotion"

Sybil Bingham's "regular system" was similar, taking her from 6 a.m. to 10 p.m., with the same three hours in the morning for study ("logic and theological reading") and four hours in the afternoon, for "miscellaneous reading" and learning the Hawaiian language. By the end of the voyage, she had reached "the last theorem in the last book of Euclid." During "recitation" hours, which the women held just after breakfast and again after dinner, Sybil deferred to their "repeated request" and instructed them, as she put it with characteristic self-effacement, "in some branches to which in the providence of God I had had opportunity to attend and they have not."[67]

The weeks and months passed with similar regularity: prayer meeting and public worship on Sabbaths, singing school one hour a week, a weekly meeting of the sisters, lessons for the Chamberlain children (each assigned a separate tutor), and the monthly "concert of prayer" (introduced by the church near the turn of the century to pray for the spread of the gospel). Special events such as Thanksgiving and Christmas they commemorated with services. Once-in-a-lifetime events, like safely rounding Cape Horn on January 30, called for a public lecture by Bingham from I Samuel 7:12. As much God's people as their Old Testament models, they erected an "Ebenezer," a monument of praise and gratitude. As the year closed, most sat down to evaluate their spiritual progress during the previous year, often berating themselves and hoping for improvement in the next. In early February, they set aside an evening to reflect on the "qualities of character" missionaries should emulate, and on the twenty-seventh, they celebrated communion. "We hope," they wrote in the "*Thaddeus* Journal," that the service "will promote our growth and piety, cement our union, and increase our strength and our preparation for our work." Late March brought them a day of fasting and prayer in preparation for landing.[68]

The little company had turned into a family. On December 28, Nancy Ruggles, whose journal is most articulate about this bonding, mused: "The sisters are very dear to me. A few weeks since, and we were all, except in one instance [she married Lucia Holman's brother], entire strangers, now the most tender love, and sisterly affection subsists between us." And the entire mission family—not just the women—felt united. Mercy Whitney wrote on the second of February, "We are happy in the society of each other. We feel the cords of love binding our hearts together, and uniting them as the heart of one man. Few in our native land can look around on a more interesting and happy family, than we daily behold." As the voyage neared its end on February 27, Nancy Ruggles reflected on the "peculiarly interesting" scene: "Here in the midst of the vast ocean, this little band of christian soldiers, who, a few months since, were for the most part entire strangers, but [are] now most tenderly allied to each other."[69]

But try as they would, they could not resolve every tension. Not a single journal or letter speaks of trouble with the Holmans. Not until 1821 did letters go back to the Board verifying the discord that stretched back to the days of the voyage. The details seem petty; the quarrels therefore ordinary and understandable. Lucia Holman hoarded oranges and sweets, a gift from another brother, defying the communal stock agreement. Thomas kept and controlled the mission's supply of wine, doling out most of the "medicine" for his own use. He was irascible, resented the elevation of the minister over the medical doctor, took an immediate dislike to Hiram Bingham, and resisted the attempts of the even-tempered Daniel Chamberlain to damp down the fires. Bingham appears to have kept his composure, but not without feeling offense and dismay. Dissension before they even reached Hawaii did not bode well. No one really knew what the "heathen" had in store for them, and a house divided against itself could not stand. The threats posed by Dr. Holman's independent spirit may have seemed more menacing than they were. In the end, the mission company bound up their wounds and pulled together as a family. But the wounds did not heal, and Thomas and Lucia Holman had the unenviable fate of uniting the mission family by becoming its scapegoat.[70]

Still, having begun the voyage "cheerfully," the missionaries closed it in good humor. "We often think and sometimes remark," wrote Mercy Whitney on February 24, "that perhaps we are spending the happiest part of our lives." They boarded the *Thaddeus* flattered to be among the chosen few, to be considered, of all the pious women in New England, among the most pious. It was an "honor & a privilege," in Maria Loomis's words, "to engage in the great work of evangelizing the Heathen." Though they would not describe themselves as enthusiasts—since they understood the term to refer to emotional extravagance as a sign of sanctification—they were enthusiastic in the root sense of being filled with God. Disquieted by the unknown, seasick, and homesick, they uniformly stood up to these tremors. They bade good-bye to their old lives "cheerfully," but not because the old life was bad, something they criticized and fled in order to attempt a better life elsewhere. The opposite was true. They left behind a world they loved and admired, hoping to spread its influence and offer it to others, buoyed up by the pleasure of sharing.[71]

These missionary women were conventional in their thinking but exceptional in their rigorous attempts to live in accord with—or up to—their ideas. Their minds during the course of their short lifetimes had been sponges for Christian doctrine. On board the *Thaddeus* one person or another recorded chapter and verse for every sermon and an outline of the argument for most. There is an ingenuous, almost schoolgirl quality to these notes. But the women's apparent lack of original thought is not a flaw, simply a given. The iconoclasts of a religion do not become its missionaries: its apologists do. "It has of late been my greatest fear," Mercy Whitney wrote to her sister Emily on January 9, 1819, "(far greater than the fear of eternal punishment) that I should be left to dishonor God—by an unholy life, an inconsistent walk and conversation." Ten months later, now a missionary, she reflected on the obligations of missionaries "to live near to God" and thought of her own "unfaithfulness, inconstancy and shortcomings." She observed that she might "justly" have been cut down, but that God appeared to have spared her to go to the heathen. Now she worried how well she would serve, "knowing that unless upheld by Almighty power I shall fall, dishonor the cause of Christ and prove a stumbling block to the world."[72]

Despite their doubts (typical for Calvinists), it is clear that these women served their religion well in the sense of trying to live their lives according to its tenets. But the more interesting question, when time has allowed distance, is how well their religion served them. It formed their minds and circumscribed their lives. How adequately did it guide them as strangers in a strange land? How well did it help them see the people they came to help? The answers to these questions—sometimes disturbing—reside in the details of seven lifetimes, yet to unfold.

The months on the *Thaddeus* were a time for pleasure in religion. The voyage was a five-month hiatus between the old life and the new during which time, in a sense, stood still. The abstractions by which the missionaries lived and with which they hoped to change the minds of another culture had not yet been put to the test of heathen experience. On board the ship they could simply enjoy them. The deists among the crew (who swayed the mind of George Kaumualii) gave them nothing like the opposition they would face from the ships' captains and crews in Honolulu. They had the opportunity to practice their missionary skills on the sailors. The voyage also marked a passage from young womanhood to the new roles of wife and mother (five of the women would deliver babies during the next year). On the *Thaddeus* they were like schoolgirls, reading and studying. They had not yet added to their lot the round of cooking, cleaning, sewing, childbearing, and schoolteaching—the particularities that would in some sense push aside the abstractions in their minds. They would never lose their commitment to Christian doctrine, their sense of its ubiquitous truth, or their pleasure in it. But they would not have the same kind of time for it. Thus the period of "happiness" of which Mercy Whitney wrote was in part a time when abstractions could thrive, supported by the culture that reared them, and unchallenged by heathen strangeness. The challenge was just over the horizon.

2. Pagan Shores

Thou shalt love thy neighbor as thyself.

—MATTHEW 22:39

The eager young Hawaiians saw land first. Thomas Hopu, "almost in an ecstasy of joy," woke Samuel Ruggles at one a.m. to tell him the news. "Owhyhee sight!" called John Honolii when he woke the Binghams at four. The brig sailed in from the west, and by daybreak Mauna Kea, the northernmost of the two volcanoes on the "Big Island" of Hawaii, rose clearly before everyone's delighted eyes. It was "truly sublime," wrote Mercy Whitney, "reaching even above the clouds. Streams of water were seen running from it in torrents, while its top was covered with a bed of snow which lasts the year round." The "Memorable day!"—as Sybil Bingham put it—was March 30, 1820.[1]

Fair winds throughout the morning carried the brig along Hawaii's northeast coast, about ten miles away. The "dark pagan land" the family had come to settle lay before them—but its darkness was only in the mind's eye. The five senses told a different story. "The country before us is beautiful," wrote Lucia Holman, "wearing the appearance of a cultivated place—with houses and huts, and plantations of sugar cane and Tarrow." Maria Loomis agreed: "The eye is feasted with a variety of interesting landscapes. Here we see gently rising hills, sloping dales, &c., verdant lawns, interspersed with groves of cocoa, bananas, and plantains." Lucia Holman spoke for everyone in her journal: "You may well suppose that after a voyage of 160 days, we were not a *little glad.*" But the Hawaiians were beside themselves, "all animation," Lucy Thurston observed, "scarcely seeking the refreshment of either sleep or food." They were home; the missionaries only hoped to make it theirs.[2]

First they needed permission to land. Since no native canoes came out to meet them, Captain Blanchard in the late afternoon sent a boat ashore. By now the *Thaddeus* had rounded the northern tip of Hawaii, passing Maui on the right, and had turned south along Hawaii's western coast. After three long hours, the ambassadors returned, having learned some astonishing news from native fishermen. "They leap on board," wrote Sybil Bingham, "and say, Tamaahmaah [Kamehameha] is dead! The government is settled in the hands of his son Reehoreeho [Liholiho] – Krimokoo [Kalanimoku] is principal chief [prime minister] – the taboo system is no more – men and women eat together! – *the idol gods are burned!*"

The missionaries knew just how to interpret this news, even more welcome than the sight of land. In their ordered world, God left nothing to chance. They were accustomed to acknowledging that he had a reason for everything even if humans did not immediately understand it. God's "piercing eye," as Sybil Bingham meditated on New Year's Day, "surveys things past present and to come as one eternal *Now,* assuring us that such is his condescension that the very hairs of our head are numbered, and that in his vast dominion not even a sparrow falls to the ground without his notice." The conclusion was inescapable: "Surely this is the Lord's doings," wrote Maria Loomis, "and it is marvellous in our eyes." Many journals took up the refrain: "What hath God wrought!" A favorite phrase from Isaiah 42:4 covered the events. "It seems as if the Lord had verily gone before us," wrote Mercy Whitney, "and that the Isles are even *now* waiting for his law."[3]

For the Hawaiian kingdom, the news summed up a tumultuous year. Kamehameha, the Hawaiians' greatest king and unifier of the islands, who saw his people through the early decades of Western visitations, died in May 1819. Kalanimoku, who as prime minister sometimes took the name "William Pitt," remained at his position through the reigns of the next two Kamehamehas, keeping the government stable. But when Kamehameha's twenty-two-year-old son Liholiho (Kamehameha II) succeeded his father, he faced immediate encroachments on his power. He was forced not only to divide his father's monopoly on the sandalwood trade among several chiefs (with disastrous results, including deforestation and a burgeoning foreign debt), but also to share administrative power with Kaahumanu, the dowager queen who had been Kamehameha's favorite. (Kaahumanu became *kuhina-nui,* holding a new office that gave her kingly authority in administering the kingdom, though Liholiho remained "technically and ceremonially" the highest officer.) Although Liholiho had been named his father's successor in childhood, he faced a potential challenge from his cousin Kekuaokalani, who had been entrusted by Kamehameha with guarding the war-god Kukailimoku. This was exactly the legacy Kamehameha himself had received from the previous chief of Hawaii, Kalaniopuu, in 1780. From Liholiho's point of view, the danger was that history might repeat itself. Kamehameha had gone on to defeat in battle every chiefly rival except the king of Kauai, who still capitulated and paid tribute. By 1796, he had turned his limited authority on one island into kingly authority over all the islands, which he ruled for the next twenty-three years.[4]

But Liholiho's most formidable challenge lay in deciding what to do about the *kapu* system. Kamehameha had kept it intact. Liholiho was initially reluctant to break with the old ways; Kekuaokalani adamantly supported them. At stake was an entire civilization. The *kapus* were the organizing principle of Hawaiian life, interwoven with its religion, its politics, its social system. They reinforced the authority of the chiefs and the division of society into four castes, each with mandates for behavior and status: *alii* or nobles; *kahunas* or priests; *makaainana* or commoners; and *kauwa*, the outcasts or slaves, though they were not numerous and little is known about them. The system rested on the notion that some things were "psychically dangerous" and must be set apart or prohibited, either because they were linked to divinity (as with the *alii*, who were descended from the gods) or to corruption (in which case both *alii* and commoner must avoid them). By honoring the *kapus*, one paid homage to the *alii* and also ensured that their superior *mana* or supernatural power did not become corrupted or endangered by contact with commoners of lesser *mana*.[5]

Some *kapus* regulated behavior, especially women's, prohibiting them from eating certain foods (bananas, pork, turtlemeat, and shark), and requiring separate eating houses and seclusion during menstrual periods. Other *kapus* dictated behavior at religious ceremonies: the *makahiki*, a yearly harvest festival, began with a *kapu* period when fleshy foods (*io*) were prohibited and moved into a period of feasting and amusement when the *kapus* were lifted. Early historians speak of chiefs and chiefesses as "having" *kapus* according to their ranks, and describe some infractions — touching the mat, tapa (bark cloth), or *malo* (loincloth) of a high-ranking chief – that resulted in death. So many *kapus* clustered about the highest ranks that such *alii* went out at night, when no one could cast a shadow on them (also a capital offense).

Whatever their flaws to the Christian mind, the *kapus* – as much as the U.S. Constitution – created a way of life. The nineteenth-century Hawaiians, whose ancestors had navigated the Pacific from Tahiti by wind, wave, and stars, expertly fished with bone hooks and nets and built elaborate fish ponds inland. With tools made only of hard wood or stone, they had reached an impressive state of sophistication in living with their land. They cultivated the staple taro plant in both dry and wet lands, with irrigation, terracing, and crop rotation. The men cooked outdoors, baking with hot stones in underground ovens (*imu*), pounding taro and water into poi. The women beat the bark of the mulberry tree into large pieces of tapa cloth, then stamped them with intricate designs. Fibers of the hala tree they wove into mats for floors. The Hawaiians knew nothing either of serious diseases like whooping cough, measles, smallpox, mumps, tuberculosis, and venereal disease or of irritants like the flea and mosquito. The culture sustained its tradition and identity with oral records, court historians keeping track of elaborate genealogies for royalty. Hawaiian art reached its apex in dance and poetry; long, intricate chants, *meles,* were composed for the hula.

Actually Liholiho was not so much deciding to initiate a change as making a formal acknowledgment of a decision that was in the making or had already been made years ago. History changed overnight for Hawaiians when Captain Cook sailed into Kaleakekua Bay in January 1778. This "discovery" by Cook belongs to that category of events in any life – of an individual or a people – that are beyond the scope of volition. It simply happened to the Hawaiians, and they could not stop time or turn it back. Roughly six hundred years of isolation – dating from the last "long voyages" from Tahiti – were over. For better or worse, Hawaii's fate would be intertwined with a much larger physical world and an increasingly influential Western culture.

Cook was the first of a geometric progression of visitors. One measure of the disequilibrium they caused by introducing new customs, new objects, and new diseases is the simple fact of depopulation.[6] Some of the decrease comes from the civil wars of unification, but by no means all. In Cook's time the islands supported about 300,000 people. By the time the missionaries arrived, a little over forty years later, estimates put the total population at half that level. To the earlier visitors' introduction of new ways, the missionaries added their disapprobation of the old. While the missionaries had nothing to do with the initial abolition of *kapus,* their attitude toward the Hawaiians' religion reinforced the continuing decline of traditional Hawaiian culture.

Pressure to abolish the system came from many directions. Hawaiians had been watching foreigners break *kapus* with immunity for years. Chiefs and chiefesses had eaten together on foreign vessels and had broken other *kapus* in private, out of sight of the priests. Kaahumanu reportedly ate shark meat and pork as early as 1810. High priests themselves, under the influence of the Westerners' rum, had broken *kapus.* After Kamehameha's death, there was evidently discussion among the chiefs. One story says that Kaahumanu requested *ai noa* (free eating), but was denied. A sympathetic Keopuolani (Liholiho's mother and the highest-ranking chiefess in the islands) then broke the *kapu* by eating with her younger son, Kauikeaouli. Hewahewa, the *kuhuna-nui* (highest priest), told the missionaries that he sided with the women. In the end, the time was right. It took Liholiho until November 1819—half a year after Kamehameha's death—to signal the end of the crucial *ai kapu,* which prohibited men and women from eating together, by sitting down to eat at the women's table during a feast. With that foundation gone, the entire system toppled.[7]

After the feast, Liholiho gave the order to destroy the *heiaus* (temples) and burn the wooden statues of the gods. Celebrations followed. The end of *kapus* allowed a kind of invigorating license. On one side it meant a release from the *kahunas'* restrictions, which had amounted sometimes to a reign of terror enforced by the death penalty. One historian suggests that Hawaiians viewed the rounds of whippings and beatings aboard Western ships as "whimsical" compared with the life-and-death brutality of the priests. In Honolulu (Daniel Chamberlain was told), "as soon as the canoe (which brought the news from Owhyhee of the Priests burning their gods,) had reached the shore, the people here ran to their temples, as if overjoyed, and set fire to them, saying to their gods, 'it has cost us a great deal to support you, and now we will take you to cook our tarrow.'"[8]

But the residue of the *kapu* system was pathos and loss as well. In the same journal entry, Chamberlain described a high priest "whose word a few months ago was death.—Now, as he comes along the boys mock him by getting a stick of wood, and saying some of his former prayers to it to deride him." Not everyone agreed with the changes. Rather than burn the gods, many hid them away and worshipped them secretly. Later in 1819, the king's army, led by Kalanimoku, had to fight and defeat the followers of Kekuaokalani, leader of the conservative faction. Nevertheless, the king's decree held, signaling a revolution. As with any revolution, there was reason to lament the passing of the old order for the sake of its formality and ceremony however much the various particulars had been discredited.

The old system endured in terms of political authority even though the basis for priestly authority was destroyed. But with the religious beliefs that inspired and unified the entire system discredited, the remaining authority rang hollow. Worse, the Hawaiians had destroyed the old *kapu* system without clarifying its replacement. The future was open. Although the Hawaiians knew something of Christianity from the merchants and explorers (Kalanimoku had even been baptized by the chaplain of the French ship *L'Uranie* in 1819) and knew that the Tahitians had adopted the new religion, Kamehameha had not been impressed. In one account, he said that "he would need good evidence of the power of this god: if the Christian would jump off a cliff, Kamehameha would watch to see if his god saved him." The Hawaiians thought they did not want the old system. But they had no urgent desire to replace the *kapus* with another set of proscriptions based on the Ten Commandments.[9]

As the *Thaddeus* continued south toward Kawaihae the day after sighting land, several canoes of Hawaiians approached the brig. The missionary wives were about to meet their first heathens. The Christianized Hawaiians on the *Thaddeus* did not count in this category. Mercy Whitney wrote home on February 4 about Thomas Hopu, "whose daily deportment has been such that he has won the affection and gained the confidence of us all." John Honolii, she continued, "manifests a mild and pleasant disposition. He is very kind and willing to lend us any assistance in his power." When the steward was dismissed for pilfering, Thomas and John joined Dexter Chamberlain in waiting on tables. George Kaumualii did not profess Christianity, but he was so acculturated to American ways that he had forgotten his native tongue and had had to relearn it at Cornwall. He played the bass viol to accompany hymn-singing. If the missionaries learned anything of Hawaiian life from these young men, they do not mention it. Their expectations seem to have been created mostly by what they had read and by what they had heard from the crew about Hawaiian "pollution and depravity." Lucy Thurston, after talking with Captain Blanchard and his officers, expected thievery, intoxication, and perhaps "the use of poisons." The Binghams and Whitneys read Claudius Buchanan's *Christian Researches in Asia* (1811). This English clergyman had returned from Calcutta (where he was vice-provost of the College of Fort Williams) to chronicle the degraded practices (such as the immolation of women) in the non-Christian world. Maria Loomis and Mercy Whitney read Miron Winslow's *A Sketch of Missions* (1819), a history of the sects and missionary societies that had previously tried to propagate the gospel. Reporting on the London Missionary Society's efforts in Tahiti, Winslow described the sexual corruption found by the English missionaries: "There was not probably one female over the age of twelve years, who had not been debased. Sodomy was not uncommon, of that scourge with which a holy God punishes lasciviousness, multitudes bore the marks in their diseased bodies." Women "so often changed their husbands and were so loose in their habits, that they could not bring up their infants"—one reason, thought Winslow, for infanticide.[10]

Mercy Whitney closed her journal for 1819 with a typical reflection: "With a select few [I] expect to spend my days in a Heathen land, surrounded by savages who are barbarous and uncivilized." Lucy Thurston thought they were all going "far, far away from civilized man, among barbarians, there to cope with a priesthood of blood-loving *deities,* and to place ourselves under the iron law of *kapus* requiring men and women to eat separately." Unaware, of course, that the *kapus* were overthrown, she reflected that women could die for eating certain foods, for entering the men's eating houses, or for even looking at an "idol's temple." In a commonly used phrase, the missionaries hoped to loose such "oppressive shackles."[11]

They did not expect the work to be easy. Samuel Ruggles wrote in his first journal entry, "Perhaps some of this little mission company are soon to fall as martyrs in the cause." In her journal on

February 7, Sybil Bingham wanted to bless God's name for bringing her this far "though it be to suffer, yea, I think to die." Even after learning that the *kapus* were overthrown, Mercy Whitney wrote on March 30 that they rejoiced "with trembling. . . . We do not expect that idolatry is utterly abolished. We probably still shall have to struggle with many difficulties and meet with much opposition, before the standard of the cross will be erected in this heathen land." Maria Loomis thought of the persecutions and deaths endured by missionaries in Tahiti and the other Society Islands during their first fifteen years, even though "all this time no visible fruit appeared." Realizing that such trials might be waiting for them, she hoped she had the strength to meet them. "O pray for us that we may have grace given us to endure every trial & to continue faithful unto the end." For consolation and comfort, the women looked to God. Sybil Bingham began her journal on November 8 wondering, "O what sufferings may be written for me in the volume of high decrees, who can tell!" She continued, "But thou bidst me, like Peter, as it were to walk upon the sea, and when the waves are boisterous and I begin to sink, wilt thou not to me, as thou didst to him, graciously put forth thine hand and bid me not to doubt? Trusting in thee, I go—." Lucy Thurston concluded in the same way, "Our only hope and trust was in God."[12]

As the canoes of Hawaiians approached, bringing gifts such as sweet potatoes, breadfruit, plantains, coconuts, and sugar cane, welcoming them to the islands with mellifluous alohas, Lucy was looking out a cabin window. Accepting a banana, she returned sea biscuits. "*Wahine maikai* (good woman)," she heard, and replied, "*Wahine.*" Encouraged by those "simple friendly pledges received and given" (which could hardly have suggested a greater contrast to the expected "pollution"), she wrote, "That interview gave me a strengthening touch in crossing the threshold of a nation." Sybil Bingham was not so calm. "For a moment my heart has failed me," she confessed. "I have been these five months, bringing these scenes to my view, so much that I thought I should in a measure stand unmoved. But I am obliged to seek my little room and let the tears flow." Over twenty years later (in *A Residence of Twenty-One Years in the Sandwich Islands,* 1847), Hiram Bingham suggested that Sybil's shock and tears were closer to the norm: "The appearance of destitution, degradation, and barbarism, among the chattering and almost naked savages, whose heads and feet, and much of their sunburnt swarthy skins, were bare, was appalling." Some missionaries, Hiram reported, turned away in tears; others "were ready to exclaim, 'Can these be human beings! . . . Can such beings be civilized? Can they be Christianized?'"[13]

The next day, April 1, Kalanimoku, his wives, dowager chiefesses, and their entourage of about thirty boarded the *Thaddeus* for a visit. Over the next several days, as the brig sailed down the west coast, the encounters continued, with shipboard visits from the *alii* and excursions ashore for some of the missionaries. Pulled two ways, the women struggled with their reactions. Like the land's "darkness," the heathens' "perishing" state was metaphorical, seen in the mind's eye. These were "children of nature alone," thought Lucy Thurston, not noble savages, Rousseauean innocents, but heirs to original sin and corruption in the grain, in need of the Christian civilization that would correct "nature." But to dwell on invisible truths was not so easy in practice. The definition of "perishing" had to expand to express the visible details of Hawaiian life. Nancy Ruggles wrote that though she had heard the name heathen, "half of their real wretchedness was never told me." Sybil Bingham, still feeling the emotional strain, neglected her journal from March 31 to April 3, when she explained, "I had intended giving particulars from hour to hour . . . [but] my feeble frame seeks the couch so as to interrupt the pen. GOD will give me strength in his own good time." In the meantime, she lamented, "O, the wretched state of this poor people still! Could your eyes behold them your hearts would melt!"[14]

One clear sign of "wretchedness" was the lack of clothing. "O, my sisters," wrote Sybil Bingham, "you cannot tell how the sight of these poor degraded creatures, both literally and spiritually naked, would affect you! I say naked. They have nothing but a narrow slip which they term a marrow [*malo*] tied around them." The women, bare breasted, wore the *pau*, several layers of tapa cloth about a yard long and three to four yards wide, wrapped about their waists. Both sexes sometimes added a *kihei* or cloak. Other visitors to the islands described tatooed bodies, front teeth knocked out or facial burns from mourning customs, whitened and closely cropped hair on the women. But in these first reports, the missionaries emphasized the nakedness; the literal lack of clothing was analogous to the lack of "civilization." Thomas Hopu passed the word to the *alii,* who by this time wore Western or native dress as it suited them, to "dress decently" while visiting the brig, "out of respect to the ladies." Understanding the directive, the chiefesses put on Western-style gowns of Chinese silk, striped calico, and black velvet. Kalanimoku appeared in a "short dimity coat, a silk vest, nankeen pantaloons, with a hat, cravat, stockings and shoes," meeting everyone's approval. Dressed properly, he seemed also to have put on civilization. "In dress and manner he appeared with the dignity of a man of culture," remembered Lucy Thurston.[15]

The size of the *alii* also demanded comments, though often conflicting ones. "Monstrous," wrote Nancy Ruggles, but the other women were more decorous. "They had limbs of giant mould," said Lucy Thurston; "large, fleshy women," observed Mercy Whitney. Maria Loomis simply stated, "The Queens are the largest women I ever beheld. It is supposed they will weigh 400 each." (In fact, Hiram Bingham called 266⅔ pounds an average weight.) But Maria also understood, with a crucial assay into accommodation, that "large women are esteemed the greatest beauties here."[16]

The missionaries' powerful sense of identity had met its equal in the Hawaiian *alii.* Well over six feet tall, statuesque, self-confident, the *alii* showed a grandness of character as well as body. They sent ahead of them "a present of three hogs and four bundles of sweet potatoes" and arrived on the brig in their uncomfortable dresses with greetings of aloha, shaking hands rather than rubbing noses in the Hawaiian style. "The effects of that first warm appreciating clasp, I feel even now," wrote Lucy Thurston a lifetime later. The three youngest Chamberlain children delighted the Hawaiians, who held them in their laps and "manifested great affection for them." The missionaries impressed the *alii* with their ability to "speak easy phrases in their language." Pleased with the introductory visit, Hiram Bingham reported, "We were assiduous in our efforts to impress them favorably, making them acquainted with our business, and our wish to reside in the country."[17]

At sunset on April 1, the day of their first visit, the royal visitors left in the impressive way they had come—seated atop the scaffolding between two large canoes, shielded overhead by a huge Chinese umbrella and flanked by *kahilis* (the feather standards of the *alii*). Nine or ten men on each side rowed in exact time. Even though permission to stay lay with the king, several days' sail further south, the missionaries were not discouraged. As the moon rose that night to reflect the setting sun, Hiram Bingham turned it into a symbol of "the approach of the Mission Church, designed to be the reflection of the sun-light of Christianity upon that benighted nation." Excited by the day's events, he and Asa Thurston climbed to the maintop of the *Thaddeus,* and as the mission family, captain, and crew watched from the deck, and as the brig floated on the "smooth silent sea," the men sang a hymn:

Head of the Church Triumphant,
We joyfully adore thee:
Till thou appear
Thy members here
Shall sing like those in glory.
We lift our hearts and voices
In blest anticipation
And cry aloud
And give to God
The praise of our salvation.[18]

The following day, the "honorable Group" of Hawaiians returned for the sail down the coast of Hawaii to the king's residence in Kailua, where the missionaries would need help with the negotiations for landing. Once there, on April 4, the period for first impressions lengthened day by day as the brig rested in the harbor and the king and his advisors debated whether or not to admit the missionaries. The missionaries continued to sort through their impressions. Although they wanted to see themselves as ardent lovers of souls, shunning worldly considerations, they found themselves in a situation where it was not souls but sensual details that clamored for attention. Often it helped to compare and contrast what they saw with what they had left behind. Attempts to describe poi compared it to "hasty pudding" or "the starch we use on muslin in thickness." In this way, they assuaged their own shock at the unfamiliar and conveyed information to their New England correspondents in terms they would understand. Various journals noted the differences in the consistency of poi, which might be eaten with one, two, or three fingers, depending on its thickness. In one entry, the Loomises described how to make it. But the missionaries knew they had not come as disinterested observers of worldly details. They often found it impossible not to recoil and difficult not to judge. They seemed to feel the eyes of the New England public and the ABCFM over their shoulders, reminding them of the criteria for a good Christian lifestyle. Praise they reserved for whatever matched the life they left behind. On April 7, when some of the mission family went ashore to dine with the king, Nancy Ruggles wrote, "We were happily disappointed to see the order and decency of the table. It was set in the American style, furnished with a baked pig, roasted fish, potatoes, tarrow etc. &c."[19]

But such approval was hard to come by. Aboard the ship, the missionaries watched as the Hawaiians ate, seated on a mat in a circle, using their fingers. "They ate with the simplicity of untaught barbarians, without any politeness or even decency," wrote Nancy Ruggles. "I know not how to describe their manners," confessed Lucia Holman, "for should I make use of language as indelicate and uncouth as they really appear, which I must do to give you any correct idea of their manners, you must be disgusted." The disgust held for an unexpected hula performance on the tenth: "I scarcely ever saw anything look more Satanic," wrote an astonished Daniel Chamberlain. Visits to ruined *heiaus* provoked expected comments on paganism. After one such visit by the men, Sybil Bingham wrote, "The feet of some of our brethren have stood upon the ground where so lately the priests of idolatry offered up their bloody victims upon their cruel altars—their eyes have seen the wide ruins of their gloomy reign." The missionaries discovered that the Western ships had introduced a companion vice to liquor. Every Hawaiian above the age of two seemed to have acquired the habit of smoking. What made it worse, according to Lucia Holman, was that they passed a single pipe from mouth to mouth and blew smoke out their noses. No missionary ever quite understood how clothes could be a "burden." Hawaiians seemed to have no sense of "shame or modesty," thought Mercy Whitney. "They appear to have but little more than the brutes." The deck of the *Thaddeus* as it sailed southward was crowded with natives "thick as bees," eating or sleeping at will, playing cards, noisily chattering in the "jargon of savage tongues." By April 3, with still a day to go before Kailua, Lucia had had enough. She wrote to her sisters: "Our deck is covered through the day with natives, and I have got so tired with the noise and sight of these naked creatures, that I could almost wish myself as far from them as you are."[20]

The regular division of hours, so cherished on the *Thaddeus*, had no place here. "They eat when hunger suggests, without any regard to time or place," wrote Lucia "—indeed they make no account of time—they eat and sleep, and eat again, frequently eight or ten times in the course of twenty-four hours." Sybil Bingham wondered after a week had passed in Kailua if these habits were not one reason why the negotiations were taking so long: "Among the obstacles in the way of dispatch, may be reckoned their great indolence and total disregard of time." The missionaries were hard put to see how such behavior differed from laziness. Fueling this impression were the habits of royalty, who had three or more attendants to fan them, brush off flies, carry a spit box, or light pipes for them. "They lie most of the time on their mats and sleep, or lounge about in idleness. They have waiters to attend upon them," wrote Mercy Whitney. When chairs became uncomfortable for their bulk, the queens "flung themselves down," and in Lucia Holman's phrase, "rolled about like so many hogs, requesting us to lie with them." Mercy's first impression of Liholiho was indolence: he looked like a man "of but little force or energy." It did not help when several missionaries called on the king at ten or eleven one morning to find "him on whom devolved the government of a nation, three or four of his chiefs, and five or six of his attendants, prostrate on their mats, wrapped in deep slumbers."[21]

Yet derision of what the eye saw occasionally vied with the nobler sentiments of Christian doctrine. The tension is important. Although they were as ethnocentric as other nineteenth-century women encountering Indians and Mexicans in the American West, the missionary wives' religious agenda made a difference.[22] Against the disgust they did feel, they put the compassion they were supposed to be feeling, their belief that souls were equal, and their desire to do something "for" members of another ethnic group besides condemn them. "The sight of these nearly naked heathen is disgusting," as Maria Loomis put it on March 31, "but at the same time increases our pity and desire for their salvation." Nancy Ruggles wrote a letter the same day reminding herself, "Much wisdom and prudence is requisite in order that we may exercise proper feelings, and conduct toward them. O may their wretchedness excite our compassion, and make their degraded appearance tolerable."[23]

The Hawaiians could not have made it easier for the missionaries to reconsider their prejudices. There was no equivalent here of Indian Wars, of "savages" murdering women and children. Both *alii* and commoner extended kind, friendly, and generous welcomes, with continuing gifts of fruit, fresh fish, roast pork, and vegetables. What these fresh provisions meant for the missionary women, "many of whom," as Maria Loomis reported toward the end of the voyage, were "drooping with the excessive heat, want of air, [and] exercise," can easily be imagined. When Elisha Loomis, Asa Thurston, and Samuel Ruggles walked about four miles inland on the fifth, the Hawaiians "embraced them [and] kissed their clothes exclaiming *miti kanaka* (good man)." Daniel Chamberlain and Samuel Whitney, returning on April 8 from a tour inland, reported the natives "kind & friendly, willing to give them the best hut in the village to lodge in, with a mat spread for a bed." Sybil Bingham, wondering on April 11 why the decision to let them stay was still pending, wrote, "There is not the least hostility on the part of the natives; on the contrary, all appear friendly." Within a few months, on July 1, Daniel Chamberlain acknowledged his complete trust. "Instead of being . . . insulted by outcasts from Botany Bay, and lawless savages," he reflected, God had "raised up many kind friends. . . . —I should not be afraid to send Daniel [his five-year-old] to any part of the Islands *alone,* on account of the natives hurting him."[24]

A determined good nature began to surface through the shock, exasperation, and condescension. The first Sabbath in Hawaii found a varied assemblage on the brig, sailing toward Kailua, with both missionary and native listeners for Bingham's sermon from Isaiah 42:4: "And the Isles shall wait for his law." Nancy Ruggles, who had been as quick as any to recognize heathenism, reflected, "How unlike to those peaceful Sabbaths I have enjoyed in America, have been the scenes of this day. Instead of a little retired spot in my chamber, I am thronged with these degraded natives, whose continual chattering has become wearisome to me, yet I think this has been the most interesting Sabbath of my life."[25]

Accounts of the Hawaiians suggest that they were not intimidated by the missionaries' condescension. The missionaries insofar as they were Westerners were not "new" to them in the same way that the Hawaiians were to the missionaries. Though Western women were a novelty, Hawaiians had been observing Western men and their material objects for over forty years. The *alii* had eagerly acquired guns, ships, and outfits of clothing. Maria Loomis reported their offers to trade coconuts, oranges, and papayas for knives, scissors, and beads. Many of the objects served as status symbols or temporary diversions for the Hawaiians. The result, as suggested by Maria's precise description of the king's house, which she visited April 7, was a mixture of Polynesian and Western customs. It was built of "round sticks of timber, some large and some small and thatched with straw. It is one story high, without chamber, cellar, or floor, but the ground is covered with straw carpets. There are no windows, but two doors. The furniture consists of five chairs, a handsome mahogany round table, two looking glasses and a dozen guns."[26]

Western customs, like the new objects, the Hawaiians adopted or not as it suited them. When the queens visited the *Thaddeus* for the first time, they wore dresses and sat on chairs out of politeness, but they also decided when they had been polite enough. They soon accepted mattresses and reclined on the deck. Then all took off their outer dresses, and one queen entered the cabin to remove everything but her *pau*. "While we were opening wide our eyes," Lucy Thurston remembered, "she looked as self-possessed and easy as though sitting in the shades of Eden." If the wives thought the queens enormous, the queens thought the missionaries "piccaninny (*too little*)." One of the queens, Lucia Holman remembered, "got me into her lap, and felt me from head to foot and said I must cow-cow and be nooe-nooe, i.e., I must eat and grow larger." The *alii* had the habit of authority. On April 2, Kalakua (one of Kamehameha's widows) presented the missionary wives with a bolt of white cambric for a dress to be made up—there and then. The women accepted the task, for, as Mercy Whitney explained in a typical blend of humility and condescension. "We esteem it a privilege to do anything for these poor degraded heathen." Nobody admitted that they did not dare to refuse before they had permission to land. The women did decline to work on the Sabbath, but sewed for the next two days straight. The queen, newly bedecked in white, stepped off the brig in Kailua to the cheers of hundreds of her subjects.[27]

The missionaries were as much the observed as the observers. When three of the wives—Lucia Holman, Nancy Ruggles, and Maria Loomis—went ashore for the first time on the seventh, they were thronged by hundreds of curious Hawaiians. "Such a noise of hallooing and shouting you never heard," wrote Lucia. "It was with great difficulty we passed the crowd, and had our guards too, some getting hold of hands and clothes . . . crying, 'Mah-ka – Mah-kah' (i.e., I love you)." All three women reported Hawaiians running up and peeping under their wide-brimmed bonnets. Lucia admitted, "I thought I had never before had my patience so much tried." The women's long necks surprised the Hawaiians, according to the nineteenth-century historian Samuel Kamakau, and earned the women an epithet that stuck: "Crowds gathered, and one and another exclaimed, 'How white the women are!' 'What bright-colored eyes!' 'What strange hats, not at all like the tall hats of the men!' 'What long necks! but pleasing to look at!' 'What pinched-in bodies! What tight clothing above and wide below!'" When the procession reached the king's grass home, he served them dinner on English china at a mahogany table. The queens, Nancy remembered, "amused themselves by looking at us & making their remarks."[28]

The Hawaiians were doing their own evaluating of the missionaries – and they held the trump card. "It is yet uncertain," wrote Mercy Whitney on April 3, "whether we shall be permitted to land or not." This uncertainty did not change the behavior of the missionaries, secure in the knowledge that God, not they, would control the decision. Still, they did not take its outcome for granted. Soon after anchoring in Kailua Bay, a party of brethren and chiefs, along with Captain Blanchard and Thomas Hopu, went ashore for an interview with the king and presented him with a Bible. "How important the moment," reflected Sybil Bingham. "The Great Hand of the Church give his servants wisdom, a sound understanding, and guide them in every step. The heart of this heathen king is in his holy hand and He can turn it as He will. O, I think, I do rest on this firm ground, that He will accomplish his blessed purposes and do all his pleasure."[29]

The next day, all the brethren went ashore to negotiate, but there was no decision. On the sixth, the family invited the king to dine on the *Thaddeus,* where he behaved, according to Maria Loomis, "with much decorum." After dinner George played the bass viol, and the mission family sang hymns. Lucy Thurston remembered that Liholiho "retired with the farewell *aloha* that left behind him the quiet hope that he would be gracious." Still he withheld permission. On the seventh, three of the wives joined their husbands on an excursion ashore, "hoping," as Lucy explained, "that social intercourse might give weight to the scale that was then poising." Nancy Ruggles admitted, "It will be a severe trial to us if we should be sent away without being permitted to tell them the way of salvation," but she was not discouraged altogether. "I think notwithstanding our prospects look rather dark at present, the cloud will soon disappear and we shall see our way before us. Our God is all powerful, his arm will protect."[30]

The immediate decision still belonged to the king, for whom Christianity had little appeal. He teased his favorite wife, Kamamalu, when she urged him to accept the missionaries: "If I do, they will allow me but one wife and that will not be you." Nor was he impressed with the new skills the missionaries could teach him. When he saw his name written down, he said, "It looks neither like myself nor any other man."[31]

Liholiho was no xenophobe, but wary: the verdict on the foreigners so far was mixed. First the exploring expeditions, then, after about 1785, the fur traders stopped at the islands. They loaded furs on America's Northwest Coast, wintered in Hawaii or bartered for fresh provisions, then sailed for China, returning to New England with teas, silks, and exotica of the East. When the Napoleonic wars entangled the European vessels elsewhere, this lucrative trade was left to American vessels for its first twenty-five years. Later, from about 1815 to 1830, Hawaiians traded their sandalwood for European goods—calico, furniture, tools, naval stores—in such abundance that they overflowed and rotted in warehouses. When possible, Hawaiians acquired European ships: Kamehameha bought six, and later chiefs soon owned more than they could use: reportedly ten brigs and numerous sloops and schooners in 1821. At first, Kamehameha and the chiefs he fought against competed with one another for foreign firearms, ships, and advisors. At least a dozen foreigners assisted Kamehameha in the conquest of Oahu in 1795. Two of the most famous foreigners, Isaac Davis and John Young, served Kamehameha long and well. Davis, the sole survivor of an attack on the British schooner *Fair American* by the Hawaiian chief Kameeiamoku in 1790, uncovered a plot to poison Kamehameha in 1810, whereupon the plotters killed him instead. John Young, who was left behind as a deserter from the vessel *Eleanora* in 1790, but who was actually forcibly detained by Kamehameha, lived the rest of his life in the islands. When the missionaries arrived, he was among Liholiho's advisors.[32]

Skilled and diligent workers were always welcome. Archibald Campbell, a Scotsman and sailor who lived a year in Hawaii and whose journal was published as *A Voyage Round the World from 1806 to 1812* (1816), reported "carpenters, joiners, masons, blacksmiths, and bricklayers" in Kamehameha's service. If these men behaved well, he wrote, they found rewards of land, wives, and status as chiefs. Campbell estimated a high of sixty foreign residents on Oahu during his stay. By 1817–18, various accounts put from 100 to 200 in all of Hawaii.

But some of the newcomers were merely tolerated. Many settlers from Christian countries were not much of an advertisement for them. Some deserted their ships; some were left behind by unscrupulous captains who exchanged them for stronger and healthier Hawaiian sailors. Some were drunkards, ne'er-do-wells, even convicts escaped from New South Wales. Campbell thought there were more of the "dissolute" among the foreign residents than the "industrious": "They have introduced distillation into the islands; and the evil consequences, both to the natives and whites, are incalculable. It is no uncommon sight to see a party of them broach a small cask of spirits, and sit drinking for days till they see it out."[33]

As early as April 5, the missionaries realized that the resident foreigners—"some wicked white men," as Samuel Ruggles put it—were not on their side. Such men "are endeavoring to prejudice them [the Hawaiians] against us, by telling them that our intention is to get possession of the Islands." One advisor, the Catholic Frenchman Jean Rives, more likely told Liholiho that the missionaries did not have the true religion. John Young, with the authority of a longtime advisor and a reputation for good character, also counseled Liholiho against the missionaries. Years later, in 1826, he would write that he was "fully convinced" that the missionaries had accomplished much good and that Christianity represented the Hawaiians' best defense against extinction, but in 1820 he was remembering his charge from Captain George Vancouver (who completed Cook's explorations from 1792 to 1794) to safeguard British interests. Vancouver had also advised Kamehameha to let no other white men settle in the islands. Since the War of 1812 had spread into the Pacific, with both England and America sending warships around Cape Horn and American trading ships being temporarily blockaded in Honolulu Harbor, Hawaiians were well aware of the rivalry between the two countries.[34]

Hiram Bingham, from the time of his first visit, was quick with reassurances that they had the approval of English missionaries, that there was no conflict between the two governments, that the missionaries had no intention of interfering with government or trade in the islands. "These considerations," he thought, "seemed to satisfy the chiefs." John Young was instructed to write to Great Britain "to prevent any misunderstanding." Still, when the missionaries asked on April 8 if they could split the company between Kailua (on Hawaii) and Honolulu (on Oahu), the king replied, "White men all prefer Oahu. I think the Americans would like to have that island." He gave them permission only to stay with him in Kailua. At this, Sybil Bingham—who went ashore that day—felt that God was "trying our faith & attachment to the cause"; there seemed nothing to do but "to plant ourselves on this dreary spot, made by volcanic eruptions, destitute of water & a spot of ground which can be tilled. Here are assembled the heads of this nation & here do they insist upon our stay." However, after inspecting the "hovel" that would house twenty-two people—"an extensive, barn-like, thatched structure, without floor, ceiling, partition, windows or furniture"—the missionaries hesitated. Captain Blanchard, impatient to get to the Northwest Coast for furs, wanted to unload everyone and everything the next day. That was Sunday, though, and as Hiram conveniently explained to Liholiho, "Jehovah has a tabu, once in seven days."[35]

Back on shore on the tenth, the missionaries found themselves waiting for the dowager queen Kaahumanu to return from a fishing trip. By now, all the ruling *alii* (except Boki on Oahu) had assembled in Kailua. But at four in the afternoon, having waited all day for an audience, the missionaries were once again delayed as two hula dancers appeared and a crowd of a thousand gathered to watch. Finally, at sunset, the missionaries had their audience and returned to the brig. John Young met them on the way and explained to their dismay that they could easily wait six months for an answer. The missionaries therefore settled quickly the next day for what they could get.

They agreed to a year's probation and promised not to send for reinforcements. At Liholiho's insistance, the medical doctor would remain in Kailua, along with Thomas Hopu and William Kanui as interpreters. The missionaries decided by ballot that the Thurstons, rather than the Binghams, should stay to provide an ordained minister. Breaking up the family was "painful," Lucy Thurston admitted, "but broad views of usefulness were to be taken, and private feeling sacrificed." With almost identical thoughts, Lucia Holman wrote that the separation was "trying to our feelings, but our path appeared to be made plain and it was our duty to submit." The other women were just as sorry. "If nature be allowed to speak," wrote Sybil Bingham, "we should say our dear brother and sister Thurston we must have with us. She is a lovely sister." But Sybil too pulled herself together: "The Lord's will be done. We hope we are able to say it from the heart." Despite past tensions with Dr. Holman, they left him behind reluctantly. Four of the five women going on to Honolulu were pregnant. "Do not be alarmed," Sybil Bingham reassured her sister with what for most other women would be bravado. "GOD will be our physician." The king insisted, she continued, that Dr. Holman remain "on account of his art. As much as we may need that, some of the female part of our little band especially, yet, all things considered, I believe we are all disposed to view a kind providence in the present arrangement."[36]

In all other aspects, the group going on to Oahu seemed the favored one. On Hawaii, there was fertile land in the interior—Captain Chamberlain thought it "the richest by far that I ever saw, with good springs of water"—but the coastal land was a barren lava plain. The village of Kailua, Nancy Ruggles observed, was "built on a bed of lava where nothing will grow but cocoanuts, tobacco, and a few shrubs." The king promised to supply fresh water, but it had to be carried on men's shoulders in large gourds called calabashes from springs four or five miles away. The Hawaiians appreciated the abundant fishing and easy swimming in the calm waters of Kailua Bay, but this hardly recommended the place to missionaries. Honolulu held out the promise of far more fertile land, which would more easily accommodate the family, and, perhaps more important, the pleasure of more regular mail. The discovery of the protected deep-water harbor around 1792 had led most foreign and American ships to that port.[37]

It took all day on the twelfth to unload provisions and baggage.

After tea that evening, the Thurstons and Holmans went ashore and the *Thaddeus* sailed on. Lucy Thurston remembered the moment in grandiose terms: "At evening twilight, we sundered ourselves from close family ties, from the dear old brig, and from civilization." Their new home was "an abode of the most uncouth and humble character. It was a thatched hut, with one room, having two windows made simply by cutting away the thatch leaving the bare poles. On the ground for the feet was first a layer of grass, then of mats." Lucia Holman thought it looked like a haystack. Taking order with their goods inside the hut, the young couples spread their mattresses on flat-topped trunks and gathered for devotions. Outside the king set his soldiers to guard them; inside an old man called "Honest Dick" kept watch. No one slept much, though not because of loneliness or fear. "We did not feel the least apprehension of danger from the natives," wrote Lucia. They were disturbed by a tiny symbol of Western influence, brought to the islands over the years on every ship. "There was a secret enemy whose name was legion lying in ambush," explained Lucy, "or rather we had usurped their rights and taken possession of their own citadel. It was the *flea*."[38]

The *Thaddeus* reached Honolulu, some 200 miles and 36 hours away, on the morning of the fourteenth. The brig sailed in from the southwest. Even while lamenting, "I believe were I to go on a dozen voyages, I should be sick every one of them," Maria Loomis took notice of a paradise:

> The first object that attracted our attention was a lofty craggy point called Diamond hill [Diamond Head], then the groves of cocoanut extending along and ornamenting the sea shore as far as the eye could reach. Then as we turned the Point our eyes were feasted with the verdant hills & fertile vallies, herds of cattle & extended plains. The little village of Witetee [Waikiki] & Hanaroora [Honolulu] making their appearance between the cocoanut completes the beauty of the landscape.

Winds were too high for the *Thaddeus* to enter the harbor safely, so it anchored outside. A small party, including Bingham and Ruggles, quickly rowed ashore, only to find that Governor Boki had gone to a distant part of the island. Instead, they spoke to Don Francisco de Paula Marin, a wealthy Spaniard and an exemplary citizen for so long that no one could remember when or how he had come. He was a great horticulturalist and sometime physician (he had been called to Kamehameha's deathbed), and was now the government's interpreter. His whitewashed stucco home and carefully tended grounds presented Hawaii's greatest evidence of refinement and civilization as the missionaries defined it. Marin cultivated almost every Western vegetable and fruit (including the pineapple), kept horses, goats, sheep, and cattle, and tended vineyards for winemaking. While he sent a messenger for Boki, the missionaries explored.[39]

They walked through dust and dirt, past clusters of grass huts—there were no straight streets in Honolulu until 1838—toward the mountains. Early maps of 1818 and 1819, made by draughtsmen of the Russian ship *Kamschatka* and the French ship *L'Uranie*, show most of the inhabitants living near the harbor and Nuuanu stream, which flows into the harbor from north of the fort. The fort itself, at the entrance to the harbor, was begun in 1816 by Russians and finished by Hawaiians. It had a stone base and walls of adobe and coral twenty feet thick at the base. The French map of 1819 (by Officer Duperrey) shows 135 houses—not far from Bingham's estimate of a couple hundred. An 1825 map by the British Lieutenant Malden of the *Blonde* shows several fish ponds to the north and south of the village. Toward the southeast lay Waikiki, then as now favored for its palm groves, surfing, and swimming. The surrounding area was swampland until the 1930s, when the Army Corps of Engineers drained it. To the northeast—between the swamp and the mountains—lay a barren, dusty area that the missionaries came to know simply as "The Plains." Engravings of Honolulu in the early decades of the nineteenth century emphasize the mountains above and the harbor in front of a random-seeming collection of huts, palm trees, dirt, and sand. There was no easy access to water in the village or in what would be the mission compound on its eastern edges until it was brought down from a reservoir in pipes in the 1850s. (The first artesian well did not appear until 1879.) Lush greenery—hibiscus hedges, rose gardens, plumeria, and shade trees—belongs to the Western fantasy of the tropical paradise, not to the dust and sun of Honolulu as the missionaries found it.[40]

The paradisiacal greenery began inland, where Hiram and his companions hiked that first day. About a mile from the village was

Punchbowl Hill, the crater of an extinct volcano. Hiram looked down over the land with a careful eye, for a moment becoming a naturalist, even a poet. He pointed out the beds of taro, with "its large, green leaves, beautifully embossed on the silvery water, in which it flourishes." Mountain streams descending to the harbor were caught in "numerous artificial canals" in order to water the taro. The seaboard plain in front stretched for twenty-five miles. Behind him, the mountains rose, the highest peak, Konahuanui, at 4,000 feet, "often touching or sustaining, as it were, a cloud."[41]

But, as a rule, Honolulu's significance lay not with the five senses, but in the mind. Hiram Bingham saw himself like Moses at the top of Pisgah, with the important distinction that he, unlike Moses, could descend to claim the land of milk and honey for Christ. He looked insistently at the land's religious significance, thinking Honolulu's "sable, interesting inhabitants far more worthy of our first attention than the inviting salubrity of its climate, the richness of its soil, or the luxuriance of its vegetation." Though Mercy Whitney appreciated the landscape she had seen so far, it was "the beauty and excellency of the Gospel of Christ"—a nonmaterial beauty—she wanted to show to the Hawaiians. Oahu was a "novel scene," but to Hiram's mind, despite the fish ponds and artificial canals, not yet a civilized one. "It was interesting, because, having been for ages past the battlefield of successive bands of pagan warriors, till the last victory of Kamehameha, it was now to be the scene of a bloodless conquest for Christ, where his ignorant, debased, and dying foes, were to be instructed, elevated, reconciled, and saved."[42]

When Boki returned to Honolulu on the sixteenth, he was too drunk to conduct business. "Intemperance," Hiram reflected, for what would not be the last time, "is as stubborn a foe as any species of idolatry." But on the seventeenth, Boki boarded the *Thaddeus*, where he appeared "mild and easy in his disposition," and though not exactly overjoyed to see the missionaries, "by no means unfriendly to us or our object." At least for now they had permission to land. The winds died down enough for the *Thaddeus* to pass into the harbor on the eighteenth and the next day the mission family disembarked. It was not an hour too soon. Maria Loomis, Nancy Ruggles, and Sybil Bingham had been seasick again on the short voyage. Sybil, when she finally began to keep her journal again after two months, remembered that she could "scarcely walk" when they landed. The women had been ashore in Kailua, but only for brief visits. Ahead lay the pleasure of losing an old habit. "I hardly know how it will seem," wrote Nancy, "to sleep on a bed and not be obliged to brace myself, to keep from rolling out."[43]

Within two or three days, the brig was unloaded, with some contention that the "obstinate" Captain Blanchard—as Samuel Ruggles wrote to his sister Lucia—was claiming some of the mission's household utensils and stores. On April 19, the family spent its first night on land in three houses belonging to foreigners—ships' captains and merchants—who willingly lent the missionaries temporary quarters and storehouses. One captain invited the group for a welcome tea in the evening. Boki received orders from Liholiho to build new homes for the missionaries, but he saw no urgency in the task and took months to comply. All these buildings were thatched, frighteningly vulnerable to fire, with mats to cover dirt floors, no ceilings, and only an occasional window—sometimes glass, more often a shuttered opening. The missionaries could add few amenities. The *Thaddeus* had had no room for furniture, with the result that there was scarcely more than one chair among them all. A crate of crockery sent out with the mission contained not a single unbroken piece.[44]

The all too short probationary year loomed ahead, and the missionaries felt considerable pressure to begin their formal and official work. They held church services on April 23 in the largest grass house and opened a school exactly a month later. These milestones were duly noted in journals. But the manual and domestic labor of settling in took most of everybody's time the first months. The metaphor of "family" continued to influence their living arrangements. Houses were shared, meals were cooked and eaten together, mission supplies were used communally. Both practical and flexible in adapting to a new place, men and women began a way of life that none of them had experienced in the United States. A sense of the great goal they were working for as well as the heathen strangeness they were posed against helped them to pull together. Sybil Bingham, thinking about their cramped quarters that July, reflected, "We have scarcely had room to move, yet we have all . . . lived in much harmony."[45]

But no one saw the need to extend the experimentation to the division of labor between the sexes. A frontier situation called for some flexibility, and men sometimes did women's work, initially helping with six months' worth of laundry. Some public work was shared, such as schoolteaching and making visits to *alii* or to the village. But carpentry, planting crops, and preaching were exclusively male, and domestic labors, like cooking, cleaning, and sewing, belonged to the women. This did not run against anyone's expectations, and there are no statements of veiled or explicit resentment from the women. What surprised them was not the kind but the quantity of their labors.

Sybil Bingham's, Nancy Ruggles's, and Daniel Chamberlain's journals simply stop for a couple of months until mid-June. Maria Loomis's journal was sparser than she would have liked. In what would be a common refrain, she wrote on May 10, "My friends would excuse me for taking my pen so seldom could they look in upon us." Nancy on June 15 apologized to her mother for the seeming neglect, but assured her that she "would think I had ample excuse if but one half were told here." Resuming her journal on June 20, after a lapse of two months, Sybil felt "awkwardness." There had been so many interesting occurrences, and "you know," she told her sisters, "it would have been a pleasure to me to have penned them had it been possible." She anticipated their reaction: "You will say there must have been new scenes if S—— could not find time to write. Indeed it has been the case as to manual labor. Each day has been filled up, with *hard work*, and when evening came 'tired nature' claimed her rest, tho sometimes so exhausted as scarcely to find it."

One reason for the "increase of labour," as Sybil explained to her friend Mrs. Elijah Bates (a lifelong correspondent from Westfield, Massachusetts), was "the want of conveniences with which to accomplish it":

> When we landed, we had the washing of a six months voyage to do, I might almost say without wood or water. Then provision was to be made for a large family under similar circumstances; with one square room, which on the sabbath was a meeting house, on the other days a school house, and at all times a place for our work, our meals & lodging. A little corner made by a partition of mats, called Mr. B——'s study, to which I could resort when not occupied with cares

> without.——— In the midst of this, a throng of the natives daily surrounded us, seated around the door, or upon the mats.

Though at first the family set one long table for meals, by late May the Chamberlains found it more convenient to cook separately until the new houses were built. The other four women divided up the duties at the cookstove outside, under the sun, each cooking for a week at a time. On June 28 Sybil prepared 33 meals. Two days later, the count was 39 meals, prepared in a room no less crowded than the *Thaddeus:* "20 feet square, where all eat,—where two beds are—where 13 persons stay—where, yesterday, were piled in 30 mats, 100 tapers, 100 cocoanuts, a quantity of calabashes, 6 chair frames [gifts from the king of Kauai] while numbers were crowding round to look on." By mid-July, Mercy Whitney admitted that thatched houses could be "very unpleasant": they were "such a rendezvous for the mice and fleas. Both are very troublesome. The former are frequently seen running about on the wall or mats, and it is not without some difficulty that we keep them off the table, and out of our dishes."[46]

To wash the accumulation of laundry—even with some help from the men—took the women until late June, when Nancy Ruggles finally sent back the Holmans' share to Kailua. Not willing to let standards slip, they ironed as well. The Hawaiians tried to help, but as Maria Loomis explained, they "know nothing of washing in our manner." For Lucy Thurston in Kailua, the result was that light cotton dresses sent with a native to be washed in a stream came back full of holes. The American women in turn knew nothing of washing under a tropical sun and reported blistered and sunburned arms.[47]

Sewing clothes for the *alii* took up untold hours. Kalakua's initial request for the dress of white cambric was not a passing fancy. Nancy Ruggles wrote to her sister-in-law in Kailua on May 10: "We have had garments on hand to make for the Governor [Boki] and Capt. Jack [a chief and captain of the king's brig *Neo*], and others almost constantly ever since we landed, which has occupied much of our time." Though Maria Loomis wrote that she was kept busy by walking a quarter-mile to prepare meals, and taking care of boxes of clothing, linen, and books in the storeroom, she also sewed shirts, pantaloons, coats, and gowns. Having made five ruffled shirts for "Captain Jack," the women excited Liholiho's envy. In early August,

Thomas Hopu arrived from Hawaii with cloth from the king and a demand for five such shirts, "made and sent back by the Schooner which sailed again in three days." As Sybil later described the crisis:

> This was sabbath. What was to be done? Monday morning I rose betimes. We were unwilling to stop the school a day—to disoblige the king we dare not. I went to work—kept up the school and by the Schooner sent one, promising to send two more by the Brig, the last of the week. In three weeks, with a little help from those I have learned [taught] to sew by taking my work into school, sitting up till half-past ten, eleven & twelve, rising early &c., I completed the five with ruffles and plaits. As large ones perhaps you never saw.[48]

These litanies of toil never let up over the years, and the work became a serious impediment to the women's sense of accomplishment as "missionaries." But for now, the mood of the mission was eager and upbeat. Sybil was much relieved by mid-summer that she had the physical strength to do the work demanded. Within three or four days of leaving the *Thaddeus*—after "breathing land air" and eating fresh food—she found her strength improving, and by June 20 she looked back almost with astonishment: "I found myself able to take hold of business which was pressing in a manner which I never did in my life." She summed up in her journal on July 19, 1820: "A missionary life, while yet tis sweet, is hard." But she would emphasize the sweetness, and as she assured her correspondents on July 14, "not a moment finds me wishing my feet had sought a smoother path." The yield for Sybil over the summer was mental as well as physical health. Writing to Mrs. Bates that first fall, mindful of the depression and sadness she had struggled with in the past, Sybil was grateful:

> But, my dear friend, in the midst of all this, so much the reverse of what my youthful fancy pictured to myself as pleasant, there has not been, through the great goodness of GOD, one gloomy day, nay, not one gloomy hour. They have flown rapidly & pleasantly along, not knowing any desire for an alteration of circumstances. Perhaps no year, since the death of my beloved parents, that there has been so little like darkness in my mind. I desire suitably to notice the mercy of GOD, for it is great.[49]

There was one reflection that silenced all murmurings. As Sybil asked when she closed her journal entry for July 20, "But where is rest on earth? I would seek it not. Lord, help us to finish our course with joy—fight the good fight of faith and lay hold on eternal life."

On July 16, the first mission child was welcomed into the family, the Loomises' son Levi. Their emotions intensified by the passing of a crisis, the family members recorded their gratitude and joy. "To this hour we have looked with trembling," Sybil Bingham wrote in her journal, a restrained statement of the truth. No help was expected from Dr. Holman, or from Jerusha Chamberlain. On the back of her letter of June 30 to Lucy Thurston, Sybil confided the worried state of the sisters in Honolulu: "O, the scene which is just before us! Where will be human help: no knowledge or experience save in one Mrs. C—— and she as she tells us *peculiarly* devoid of courage. To look upon us, a little female band, with no physician—no maternal aid———." For herself as well as for Lucy, who would soon be without physician or sister in Kailua, Sybil grasped the same consolation. "Oh—but faith—let that be strong. GOD *has* taken care of us, He *does*, He WILL take care of us. May the language of our hearts be, what time we are afraid we will trust in Him." When the whaleship *L'Aigle* returned unexpectedly to Honolulu, Dr. Williams was on hand to deliver the baby. Maria, recuperating on July 28, wrote that recent events confirmed God's goodness. She felt herself "under renewed obligations to dedicate myself & my all to his service." She also praised her husband, who had nursed her: "Among the signal favors from God is a kind & affectionate partner." Elisha reciprocated on their first anniversary, September 27, 1820: "The experience I have had convinces me that marriage is one of the greatest blessings of life, where there is a union of hearts," he wrote, "and I can truly say this happiness is my own."[50]

The first few months were in many respects a honeymoon period—not simply for the missionaries' own internal regulations, but for their relations with the Hawaiians and the other foreigners in Hawaii. Much good will was expended in all directions. A small matter, such as distributing portions of a cheese from Hiram Bingham's mother that would otherwise have been eaten by the mice, elicited a series of gifts in return. Within the hour, one native, "Captain Joe," sent a "large, sleek goat" as thanks. Scarcely a day went by without gifts of fresh provisions—pork, fruits, corn, beans, squash, potatoes—from both Hawaiians and foreign residents. Anthony Allen, a black American and former slave, now a prosperous farmer near Waikiki, sent generous supplies of vegetables and "as often as once in two weeks a goat or kid neatly dressed, every morning two bottles of goat's milk." Mr. Green, from Boston, came to tea on May 5 with a complete china tea set as a present. On May 31, Mercy Whitney counted forty articles received as gifts, ranging from a barrel of flour from two partners, Captains Meek and Pigot, to a jar of Mrs. Pigot's peach preserves. Since the apples packed on the *Thaddeus* arrived "so good as they were when first put up," Mercy could bake pies. The king gave the mission family a taro patch, telling them that when they had eaten all of the plants he would give them another. The Chamberlains, Daniel admitted, found poi a good substitute for bread: "Our family are very fond of it." Mercy summed up the ubiquitous generosity, mindful as ever of its first cause: "Thus the Lord supplies our daily wants almost without our care."[51]

"It may be supposed," Sybil Bingham wrote with prescience, "there are many who want neither us or our message among them," but for now the detractors were quiet. Samuel Ruggles wrote to his sister Lucia that the white people "are extremely kind and do all for us they are able." By May 5, the missionaries were settled enough to invite the ships' captains and merchants to tea (their evening meal), for which they set "an American table in humble but decent order." When the school opened, the foreign residents sent their *hapa-haole* (half-white) children, born of their Hawaiian wives, to fill its classes. The nubile daughters of old Oliver Holmes, longtime resident of Honolulu, learned quickly to read and spell. (Their moral development, exemplified by the "orphans" two of them bore to ships' captains, looked less promising.) When the missionaries called a public meeting on May 10, partly to suggest that the white residents help them build their houses—since Boki seemed uninterested—and partly to form a fund for the schooling of such "orphans," the residents were quick to make donations. Captain Starbuck, of the English whaler *L'Aigle*, contributed $35, and three officers added $24. By May 12, the fund had reached $300.[52]

On June 23, the entire mission family visited Anthony Allen's farm, located some two miles distant in Waikiki. As they walked, Mercy Whitney wrote, "We saw a large flock of goats and herd of cattle grazing at a distance. The prospect which presented itself to the eye, was truly delightful." Allen welcomed them to his extensive property, with its dozen houses, large garden, fish pond, sheepfold, and three hundred goats. Though they could speak very little Hawaiian to Allen's wife, who lay reclining on mats and playing with her children in a nearby room, the women communicated as well as they could by making her a gown and giving her a sewing lesson. The meal that evening was nothing less than a feast, served, as Mercy Whitney remembered it, at a "large table well furnished with glass and china." Maria Loomis listed the courses: "an excellent stew pye, after which [came] a baked pig, pork and fowls, mutton, beef, various kinds of vegetables, tarrow pancakes, hard poa [poi], a pudding, watermelon, wine and brandy, and water out of an excellent well and I believe the only one on the Islands." As Sybil Bingham concluded the description in her journal, "It was not missionary fare." After a dessert of fried cakes and good coffee served in china cups, the family walked home under the bright Hawaiian moon. The extraordinary day of luxury and repose behind them, they described it in great detail in their journals. But not having come to secure the world's riches, they stopped short of envy. As Mercy explained, "We returned to our lodging, well satisfied and contented with our little cot and homely fare." Rather, it is as if the day stood for everyone's good will that summer and captured the mood of the future they hoped for.[53]

For the most part, Hawaiian behavior toward the missionaries was so exemplary that it put to shame the missionaries' anxious expectations. When Sybil Bingham began her journal again on June 20, grateful that "the Lord has been good to us," she realized "how widely different is our situation from what it would have been had we found what we expected, an idolatrous priesthood to combat." These unnamed fears were probably on Maria Loomis's mind when she wrote, shortly after landing, "our conveniences are few and small but our trials in other respects are nothing to what we expected." The Hawaiians "appear to be very peaceable and friendly in their disposition," she wrote a few months later, though, she added (thinking of their reputation for thievery), "rather inclining to jealousy." But there had been only one instance of such thievery, and then "the things were returned so soon as information was given the Governor [Boki]." Sybil described an evening in late June when she and Hiram went out to enjoy the full moon. "In passing through the midst [of the village], on our way to the open plain," she remembered, "it was very pleasant to hear their friendly salutation, Alloah, some saying E-ho-ah (where going)? We answered, mor-oo, up yonder. Then as usual, they were pleased that we could numme-num-me (talk) Owhyhee." By July 3, Sybil could enumerate "some pleasant traits which mark the character of this poor people in the midst of their degradation. Their pacific disposition, their mild and friendly intercourse with us and with each other give us hopes of what they will be when the love of Jesus shall fill their souls."[54]

Sybil recorded one moment of skittishness, which she quickly saw was unfounded. While walking back from the Allens, Sybil and Hiram Bingham fell far behind the rest of the family. "While on the plain back of the village," Sybil recalled, "a large train seemed approaching us. At the first moment, womanish fears said, there is a heathen band approaching and we are solitary and alone." But it was "Captain Joe," the commander of one of the king's schooners. "He came up with eagerness to Mr. B., whom he seems to love, and shaking hands very heartily, says, How do you do Sir . . . such a good moon I was going to take a walk sir." Sybil concluded: "He is a pleasant youth, very active, speaks English pretty well, and has a most kind disposition."[55]

A letter the mission received from the Thurstons in early May contained an admiring report from Lucy Thurston: "On these heathen shores, even during the great feast days, I have felt as safe as if I had been in my native land; — the natives appear inoffensive and friendly and as far as has fallen under my observation have uniformly conducted themselves with propriety." Lucy — alone among all the mission women from every company — would have reason to alter her statement. In late September, an inebriated Hawaiian priest pursued her about her house several times before she was able to escape and run toward her husband in the village. She was unnerved but physically unharmed, and nothing resembling the incident ever occurred again.[56]

Since much of what the missionaries saw continued to bring out exasperation, bewilderment, or condescension, they still struggled with their reactions. Hawaiians ate dogs: Maria Loomis saw 100 of them "tied and strung on a pole" being carried through the village for a feast. "Indolence" still seemed "a native characteristic," Maria complained on June 21: "They spend many precious hours in sleep. Their women do no work of any consequence: they think it rather a disgrace. Their manner of living requires but little labor as the generality wear no clothing and live almost wholly upon raw fish and poa [poi]." There were sometimes a hundred Hawaiians staring at the missionary women as they cooked and following them whenever they left the house. "Whenever we walk out," Maria wrote, "we are generally escorted by a large concourse of men, women, and children. We are never in want of attendance." Lucy Thurston reported the same problem in Kailua. "For the sake of solitude," she wrote, "I one day retired from the house, and seated myself beneath a shade. In five minutes I counted seventy companions." On one Sabbath, Mercy Whitney's patience ran thin: "Wearied with the incessant noise of those around me, I would fain seek some silent retreat where I might spend this holy day in the enjoyment of God. We can hear little from morning till night, but the continual screaming and yelling of the Natives, who are loitering away their time in swimming, or running about the streets in idleness."

Even when feeling compassion for Hawaiians, the women judged their customs. It never occurred to them that Christian ideas and customs would not make for improvements, or that compassion for Hawaiians might mean leaving them alone. Indifference was a vice, not a virtue. Cultural relativism was unknown. Yet they realized that judgment alone was an inadequate response. As Mercy continued, the Hawaiians were "poor ignorant creatures" who had "never been taught to know God or regard the holy sabbath." Lucy Thurston concluded her description of her new life with homelier common sense: "We had entered a pathway that made it wisdom to take things as they came,—and to take them by the smooth handle."[57]

A test case came one evening in July, when a tipsy Liliha, Boki's wife, intruded at the mission tea table, leaning over the women's shoulders. Mercy Whitney remembered that their first response was "to get rid of her" by offering some tea. "She took it and sallied to her seat, and happily did not loose [spill] either the dish or its contents." Liliha had always been friendly, and on previous visits "generally sober," but, as Sybil Bingham observed, she showed "no restraint or decency tonight. . . . She immediately crowded in for a seat by my side, her breath strong with liquor,—her arms and bosom naked, and embracing me took off the flowers from her neck and fastened them on mine." Mercy was not impressed:

> We were fully satisfied with the length of her visit. You can have but a faint conception of the disgusting appearance (which we frequently have) of these almost naked natives. Boku's [Boki's] wife usually wears nothing but a piece of cloth round her waist, reaching about half way to her feet. Imagine how you would feel to see, much more to be kissed and squeezed, by these tawny creatures. Many of them likewise use so much tobacco in smoking, as to smell very offensive.

But in the end, she thought past the appearances of things to the spiritual point:

> But we seek not personal ease or pleasure; it is the salvation of their souls, for which we labour and pray, and for which we wish to live and die. May we but be instrumental of bringing them to the knowledge of God and Jesus Christ our Saviour, and we will (with the grace of God assisting us) cheerfully suffer toil and pain, endure losses, crosses and hardship; and even *then* we shall be but unprofitable servants, having done no more than was our duty to do.

Sybil's response was less doctrinaire, more sympathetic. When Liliha "commanded stillness with her attendants while thanks were given at table," Sybil realized, "O, what thanks from our hearts were due! I felt my privileges—I felt for a moment the wretched state of the heathen."[58]

By mid-summer the honeymoon was over. The mission "family" survived the voyage intact, but not the first summer in Hawaii. The challenge did not come from without, from "heathens" who exacted a confusing mix of derision and sympathy. By reminding the missionaries of what they were not, and of why they had come, the Hawaiians prompted feelings of unity. The threat came from within.

The first reports from Kailua had been encouraging: the thoughtful and hospitable royal family had provided the missionaries with mahogany bedsteads, a large Chinese table with six drawers, a cookstove, and plenty of fresh food. Asa Thurston wrote on April 27 that the king could read in words of two syllables, that his wives were eager to learn, that Dr. Holman was successful in treating the sick. But later reports built a distressing picture of the unhappy and disgruntled Holmans. Within three days of landing, Lucia Holman asked Lucy Thurston for a private conference, away from the natives, which therefore had to be held in a "mud-walled store house." There, in the dark, as Lucy remembered it, Lucia told her, "I do not find things here as I expected – I do not feel for the heathen in being among them as I formerly did – reading or hearing of their miseries." Lucia concluded that those who "do feel for them & possess that self-denying spirit which is necessary to live among them and do them good" ought to do the work – not she. Her motive in informing Lucy was that "others may place no dependence on my assistance." Having delivered her thesis statement, Lucia behaved over the next three months as if determined to give evidence of its truth.[59]

One squabble – perhaps predictable – centered on the scarcity of water. The king had promised a supply of water, but did not realize the quantity the missionaries would require: the Hawaiians bathed and swam all day long right in front of the missionaries' house. In order to wash a few clothes, Lucy and Asa spent "painful hours" collecting calabashes and "kanakas" to fill them. With the precious barrel of water thus accumulated, Lucia (as agreed) washed first. But instead of using half the water, Lucia used it all and left Lucy the rinse water. The next day the Hawaiians pleaded fatigue from the previous day's work and refused to collect any more water. A subsequent exchange between the two husbands degenerated into a spat, Asa suggesting there "might be a doubt as to the expediency of [Lucia's] washing hands, feet, etc. in fresh water," while the Thurstons made do with salt. This the doctor denied. Asa insisted he had seen her do it, and Thomas shot back, "It is none of *your* business if she did." Finally, the men decided that each would collect his own water, to be used as he and his wife pleased. Accordingly, Thomas solicited two casks from the king, water that he declared "was *his*," but that Asa later discovered was intended by the king for both couples. By the end of this week, Dr. Holman "coolly" informed the Thurstons that he intended to separate from the mission.

The family at Oahu was upset enough to send Samuel Whitney to Kailua twice during July, in an effort to "comfort their hearts," as Mercy Whitney put it. All the men of the mission (including Lucia's brother Samuel) signed a "united remonstrance" to the doctor on July 13, rejoicing in his success so far, but urging him not to leave the Thurstons alone. The family reserved its sympathy for the Thurstons. Hiram Bingham wrote praising them for their "kind, humble, patient & forbearing spirit," and Sybil responded on June 30 to a letter from Lucy with a long, consolatory one of her own. "And here my heart is joined," she wrote, "—my sympathies are awakened and I feel a love for my sister, under her trials, greater than ever. Yet I know not how to offer advice or consolation." She suggested that the trials were "not exclusively" Lucy's, but that "this favored mission family . . . has indeed a wound which cankers and preys upon its peace." But the doctrinal point, which would comfort the mission women again and again, was that this wound was somehow a part of God's plan. Here Sybil wrote:

> But GOD will glorify himself in it. Yet how does it become us, while we wonder at the mysterious providence which has permitted things thus to be, to 'stand in awe & sin not.' How peculiarly do you need that wisdom which is from above! But you do find there is a sufficiency for all your wants—that GOD will give without upbraiding. I do trust that as your day is your strength will be.

Later on, continuing to put the trials in a larger perspective, Sybil reminded Lucy "of the profiting of a pious heart in such a school of the practical influence given to the divine declaration 'this is not your rest.'" Since she and Lucy (unlike Lucia) did not suffer "the 'longing, lingering look' of sad regret," she counseled forbearance:

> Do we sufficiently notice it! We know it should make us bear patiently with those who seem without such support. I want a heart to pray for them more. I do think I can most freely forgive every bitter feeling against myself, personally, or him who is as dear as myself, but I want stronger faith & stronger desire that GOD would yet fit them [the Holmans] for their work and make them humble missionaries of the cross.———[60]

The Holmans, with the permission of the king if not the brethren, sailed for the Island of Maui on July 29. Thomas, justifying himself to the ABCFM that November, stressed the declining health and despondent mind of his wife. (Lucia did record a week-long fever one week after landing.) He insisted that the original decision to stay in Kailua was provisional; that he consented "for the good of the mission" and over the entreaties of his wife. He explained, "I told her at the same time (and I believed it to be perfectly understood by the Brethren) that if upon trial she should not feel contented, with the King's consent I would go with her to Aah-hoo [Oahu], or any other place as he should direct." Lucia's journal states simply "that we were called to leave Owhyhee, on July 29, on account of the scarcity of water—it being impossible to obtain enough for absolute necessity."[61]

These reasons, of course, tell only part of the story. One supposes that if salt water baths had not been a problem, Lucia would have found another excuse to depart. Later on that summer, when catechized by the brethren in Honolulu, she would insist, "I knew it to be my duty to go somewhere from Kirooah; I was determined to get away from that place, & I have effected my purpose by the blessing of God." "That place" was the scene of too much Hawaiian wretchedness and too many privations, even for a missionary. The natives' by now celebrated indolence did not escape her: "Two men in Owhyhee will accomplish as much work in 2 days as 1 good man in America will do in 2 hours." The only advantage she could see was that "it costs nothing to keep them," except, as she added, "the vexation of having them about, which is more than I can bear." Here was a people who had "sunk to the lowest depths of sin and depravity—they appear to glory in what should be their greatest shame." As she added with a touch of exasperated wit, "—indeed, there is nothing that disgraces them but work. In short, drunkenness is an honor, theft a virtue, and murder a mark of valour, if it can be done slyly." To a fed-up Lucia, even "the fruits and vegetables, and everything that these Islands produce, taste *heathenish*."[62]

Though hardly unusual in recoiling from native habits, Lucia had more trouble coping with her disgust than the others. Lacking Sybil Bingham's immediately sympathetic heart, or Nancy Ruggles's and Mercy Whitney's determination to remember church doctrine or Lucy Thurston's Yankee stubbornness, Lucia was inclined to regret and to wonder if she would even have enlisted in the enterprise had she known "*all* the trials and afflictions through which she must inevitably pass." She felt defensive enough to hurl a gratuitous insult at the other women, telling Lucy:

> Were the real feelings of the heart known, I believe that Mr. Thurston, Mr. Bingham or any other member of the family would *rejoice* to return to America & there spend their days, were it not that their characters are at stake, that they are getting a great name, & becoming famed for their love & zeal. It has become a fashionable thing for missionaries to disguise their feelings, & express what they do not in reality feel. But *sincerity* shall mark my words.

Lucy Thurston, as if bolstering the doctor's self-image as the protector of delicate females, agreed that it was "through her [Lucia's] influence that the Dr. wishes to separate from our family." But were that the case, the family reasoned, Lucia should have recovered at Oahu. Thomas argued that he was vulnerable in Hawaii, that his medical skills were misunderstood by the natives, and that he could be accused of poisoning every time a patient died. Furthermore, he was accountable to the king, not to the mission family. Back in Oahu, none of these reasons were seen to justify abandoning the station, leaving another couple alone among the heathen. (When Samuel Whitney came to offer the Thurstons the option of returning to Oahu, the Thurstons declined, but Lucy declared, "That visit was to us like the visit of an angel.")[63] Thomas had also abandoned his medical duties to the mission family and felt no obligation to deliver Maria Loomis's baby. (Maria had shyly asked Lucia to convey a request for help; Lucia said she had; the doctor denied having received any message and said he had been led to believe he was not to come.) Only the most providential (or fortuitous) circumstance brought a whaleship and its doctor into port at the appropriate time.

After the departure from Kailua, the rest of the Holmans' story was in a sense denouement. By then the damage had been done, the main grievances recorded. After only a month's stay in Maui, the Holmans were called to Honolulu to treat a seriously ill captain and his crew. After a week with the brethren, who, Thomas said, treated them with "indifference," the couple moved in with a Captain Dean, who lived "in a respectable style." Later that fall, when Mercy Whitney's baby was due, they traveled to Kauai and stayed on to the end of the year to attend Nancy Ruggles's confinement. By the end of 1821, with their own infant daughter, they were on their way back to New England via Canton. Reaching Boston, Thomas Holman argued his case before an unsympathetic Board, dying not long afterward in 1826. Lucia, who died in 1886, outlived every other woman of the first company. But the Holmans' formal relationship with the mission was already over in January 1821. Lucia, whose inadequacies were summed up in the phrase "walking disorderly," was suspended from the church, and Thomas was excommunicated.

In February 1821, Hiram Bingham and Asa Thurston sent a formal report back to the Board, compiling over a hundred pages of letters and documents to justify the punitive actions. To Samuel Worcester, the corresponding secretary whom they addressed as a "father," they wrote piously of sorrow, and also of resentment. Now they quoted Dr. Holman's insubordinate opinions dating back to the voyage: that he was not bound to be a missionary for life, that he could practice his medical art for material gain, that the medical supplies purchased by the Board nevertheless belonged to him, and that he would be bound by the Board's instructions, as he put it, *"so far & so long as I choose."* It appeared to Hiram and Asa as if Captain Blanchard's opinion, expressed on the *Thaddeus,* was right—that Thomas had come to make his fortune. They quoted Thomas Hopu, who divulged the doctor's dissatisfaction with the payments the natives could give him for medicine: "I cannot live upon their allohah [aloha]." Daniel Chamberlain closed a letter to Worcester of November 14, 1820, with the opinion that "money & ease were uppermost in their minds."[64]

Far from coming as a complete surprise, Thomas Holman's difficult personality had been apparent to fellow missionaries and to the Board members before he left Boston.[65] When it was too late to do anything about it, Hiram and Asa pointed out that during the voyage the Holmans practiced the "most sickening familiarity" on deck; the couple falsely accused young Elisha Loomis of lying and theft; they were so imperious at table that the young stewards asked to be excused from serving them; they refused to follow the schedule arranged for studying, indulging instead in reading medical books and imagining the symptoms their own. A meeting of the entire family to draw up the list of character traits required of missionaries prompted Lucia's suggestion: "a disposition to make the best of everything" was "strange," the others thought, since her first principle was "use the best first." In retrospect, the issue seems not whether the Holmans and their fellow missionaries would part ways, but when.

Jesus' statement that he who is not with me is against me gave the missionaries their text. The Holmans were in one sense a casualty of the tendency to see the world in terms of opposites: Christian or heathen, body or soul, saved or damned. Clarifying its identity, the "family" had survived two threats to its unity—from geographic division and now from rebellious members. But in insisting so fiercely upon that unity, the family betrayed its vulnerability. More important, its handling of the crisis had implications for the future. The Holmans were held to a strict standard of the true missionary spirit that was conceivably within their reach, but the Hawaiians would be similarly held to a standard of Christian civilization that was not.

The news from Kauai in mid-summer, unlike that from Kailua, was reassuring. Almost immediately after landing in Honolulu, the *Thaddeus* had sailed on to deliver George Kaumualii to his home island and his astonished father. Samuel Whitney and Samuel Ruggles accompanied him and on June 28, about eight weeks later, arrived back in Honolulu. In Kauai, the missionaries had received the welcome of their dreams. A twenty-one-gun salute from the *Thaddeus,* and another returned from the fort in Waimea, announced George's arrival. When George entered his father's house, Kaumualii arose, embraced him, and pressed noses in the Hawaiian manner. Neither son nor father could speak for half an hour. "The scene was truly affecting," wrote Samuel Ruggles. "I know not when I have wept more freely." Kaumualii then embraced the missionaries, calling them his friends. A few days later, Kaumualii explained to Samuel Ruggles that he thought his son was dead and had not believed the captains who told him George was living in America. Now, trying to find the right words in English, he said simply, "But he live—he come again—my heart very glad." Kaumualii rewarded Captain Blanchard lavishly, with provisions and with sandalwood valued at $1,000. To both missionaries he offered a chief's position. For the family in Oahu, he sent back thirty mats, over a hundred pieces of tapa cloth, a set of chairs, fans, fly-brushes, calabashes, coconuts, oranges, and hogs. He promised even more—to build a church, schools, and homes, and to keep the Sabbath—could he persuade them to come to Kauai.[66]

But his greatest gift to the missionaries was not material. He showed them with his actions and words the Hawaiian version of "disinterested benevolence"—aloha. He welcomed them from a sense of family just as strong as the missionaries'. In a meeting with Samuel Ruggles on May 4, the king wanted to know if he could believe what his son had told him, "that the good people of A[merica] who loved his son and loved him and his people, had sent several men and women to instruct his people to read and work as they do in America." Reassured, Kaumualii and his wife Kapule "broke out in one voice, '*Miti, miti, nooe loah aloha America*'; that is, 'good good very great love for America.'" When Samuel told him, "I wished to spend my life here and die here," the king embraced him again and said, "You, my son, I you father, my wife you mother."[67]

Though Kaumualii's initial affection arose from gratitude for the return of his son, he quickly understood that he could trust these young white men, so unlike the traders who had preceded them. The missionaries, though realizing that they were being offered women as "a token of respect and kindness," refused them on moral grounds. As Samuel Ruggles put it, "I have frequently told them that such conduct was not good, and that there was a great God who saw all their actions & was displeased with such things; but they will say all white men before say it is good, but you are not like other white men." The Americans had brought the *palapala* (the Hawaiian expression for reading and writing), which so enchanted the royal couple that they took their books into the water with them as they bathed, so as not to miss a moment of learning. By June 17, they could read in words of four letters. After listening to Samuel Ruggles read the first chapter of Genesis, the king admitted, "I can't understand it all," but insisted, "I want to know it. You must learn my language fast, and then tell me all. No white man before ever read to me & talk like you." When, after two months, the royal couple came to believe (mistakenly) that the two missionaries were leaving for Oahu never to return, they spent a sleepless, tearful night. Waiting for the men to return with their wives at the end of July, Kaumualii, schooled in wariness, or perhaps unable to believe his good fortune, often asked George if the missionaries "purposed to deceive him as other white people had done" and would never arrive.[68]

Mercy Whitney and Nancy Ruggles left Honolulu somewhat reluctantly, both of them reflecting on the "path of duty." But there was no hint of the obligatory welcome from the Hawaiians. When the *Levant* came in sight of Waimea and the passengers did not immediately disembark, an "anxious" Kapule "for some time looked constantly through a spy-glass." Meeting the queen, Mercy recorded that "not being satisfied with my giving her my hand, [she] wished me to join noses with her." No sooner had the missionaries disembarked than servants were sent to prepare their house with bedsteads layered with ten thicknesses of tapa. A feast of pork, fowl, fried fish and onions, sweet potatoes, and bananas awaited them with the royal family. Within a few days, Nancy reported that the natives brought them so much fruit that they had to tell them to stop. As Samuel Ruggles wrote later that summer to Jeremiah Evarts (the Board's treasurer), the king "says we shall never want for anything while he lives." Nancy Ruggles concluded her description of their welcome: "I think I never witnessed such expressions of joy on the arrival of friends, as I did here." The queen, she remembered, "embraced me, seated me by her side on the mat and told me I must call her mother." Mercy concurred, "The queen appears like a kind and motherly woman, and calls us good American children. The king says, as the people in America have been kind to his son and done much for him, so he will be a father to us."[69]

When, for the first time, something like empathy passed between missionary and Hawaiian, it was not based upon the "love of souls," an abstraction, but upon shared familial relationships. When the king saw Nancy Ruggles writing to her mother, she recalled, he "asked me if I loved her very much. I informed him that I did, and that it would do her heart *good* to hear that the K[ing] and Q[ueen] had kindly offered to be a father and mother to us." When the king saw Mercy writing, she told him, in answer to his questions, that her parents were still alive and that she was telling them of his and George's "kindness." For a moment, she put herself in Kaumualii's place as a parent. "He sat silent for a few moments apparently in deep thought," she recorded in her journal, "which forcibly struck me as bringing to his mind his feelings, in his son's absence."[70]

Wanting to express their affection and gratitude, Kaumualii and Kapule "wrote" letters to the missionaries and their parents. (They dictated to George, who wrote a copy they could imitate.) The queen wrote to the mothers of Nancy Ruggles and Mercy Whitney. Another letter, to Sybil Bingham, is preserved in Maria Loomis's journal:

> O Madam,
> I feel glad that your good women come here to help me. I want to learn to sew & read and do like them[.] I very glad they here. I take good care of them[;] they my children[.] I give them eat and drink. I love them much. I never see white wihena [woman] before. She mitie [*maikai*, good][.] I write letter home to America to their mothers now I be their mother[.] I be glad you do good to all the islands. except [Accept] this from
> Queen Charlotte Tapoole [Kapule].

With remarkable warmth and sympathy, a new acquaintance like Kapule wanted to reassure missionary parents halfway across the world. This aloha spirit had an analogue in the commandment Jesus gave his followers to love one another, which the missionaries were attempting to embody in their lives. Clearly, in some basic aspects of Christianity, the Hawaiians needed no "converting" at all.[71]

But the missionaries did not dwell on what they had in common with Hawaiians. The differences seemed more important. Hawaiians may have shared a sense of familial hospitality, but they lacked Christian doctrine. Hiram Bingham, quoting the letter Kaumualii wrote to Jeremiah Evarts, used it to justify the missionaries' roles in changing the Hawaiians. "I believe my idols are good for nothing," wrote the king. ". . . I feel glad your good people come here to help us—We know nothing."[72]

Both Mercy and Nancy interpreted their affectionate welcome as they had the end of the *kapu* system—as evidence of God's hand in human events, enabling them to achieve their goals more easily. In her journal for July 25, Nancy reflected, "Never before were our obligations of gratitude so great as they *now* are. Surely the King's heart is in the hands of the Lord, and he turneth it whithersoever he will." That same day, Mercy interpreted the Hawaiians' affection with great caution. She hoped it would continue, "but," she wrote, "we shall endeavor not to place too much evidence on the word of the heathen. The arm of the Lord can, and must be relied on. At present, there appears to be nothing in the way of our proceeding unmolested in our work."

As always, the missionaries tended to value spiritual truth over the vain shows of the material world. Mercy did not want to rely on the affectionate "word of the heathen" because it was one form of the worldliness she tried to shun. When she noted in her journal the next day (July 26) that the missionaries' "temporal wants" were abundantly satisfied by the natives' gifts, she went on to reflect that as missionaries, their souls must also be fed with "spiritual food," so that they would not grow "careless and remiss" in their duties. She continued, "We ought constantly to remember the admonition, 'in the day of prosperity beware,' and take heed that we prove not stumbling blocks over which the Heathen will fall and perish." In part, she felt the fragility of her situation in terms of her own inner resources. But she could not dismiss the dangers without. Kauai had neither an ordained minister nor a physician. The women thought of themselves, in Nancy Ruggles's words, as "a little number of defenseless objects, in a land shrouded in moral darkness." The temporal displays of affection—however welcome—did not diminish their assessment of "moral darkness" nor change their sense of what the Hawaiians needed. Right after Kapule said she was glad the missionaries had come to instruct her, Mercy wrote: "May the prospects which at present are thus flattering, be unobscured by clouds; and the Sun of Righteousness which has just risen, shine brighter and brighter until all this nation is illuminated by its benignant and cheering rays."[73]

By mid-summer, the mission family had dispersed to three different stations (four if the Holmans in Maui were still considered family members). It was arguably in the best interest of the mission to try to reach as many Hawaiians as possible, and the family separated in each instance with thoughts of duty. There was work to be done, and as Nancy Ruggles explained when she left for Kauai, "Daily experience teaches us this is not our rest; happy will it be if we are thereby led to lay up a treasure which will endure when all earthly things shall have passed away."[74] But to that unearthly end, paradoxically, the mission family started their earthly institutions—churches, schools, and households.

3. This Ransomed Land

> Let your light so shine before men, that they may see your good works, and glorify your Father which is in heaven.
>
> — MATTHEW 5:16

For several days on board the *Thaddeus,* the conversation at dinner had turned to discussing the character traits that seemed "peculiarly requisite in the foreign missionary." The long list of thirteen qualities the family drew up begins with "ardent love to Christ & the souls of men." The second and third requirements continue the religious theme: "a firm & habitual confidence in the blood & promises of Christ with respect to the heathen," and "a 'passion for missions,' implying an earnest desire to be useful among the unevangelized portions of our race." Lesser prominence goes to more secular traits—including the ability to teach well and learn a foreign language, habits of self-denial, self-control, Christian politeness, prudence, and "laborious diligence." The family hoped that these traits would help them achieve their most important goal: the conversion of Hawaiians to Protestant Christianity.[1]

The sense of priorities in this list—religious over secular traits—carried over into the life of the mission. The model for conversion began with the inner person and a change of heart. The gospel ought to "precede" civilization, not only being introduced first, but also taking precedence over civilization in status. The *palapala* might introduce a "better" civilization, but, more important, it opened up the Bible. Not surprisingly, the women tended to evaluate most of their domestic labors in terms of their effect on the great religious cause. With most of those labors secular and indirect—helping their husbands, presenting an "example" of domestic life, even schoolteaching—the women were often disappointed.

By January 1824, Sybil Bingham was still convinced that "vital piety is the foundation" for a missionary's character, both "male &

female." In an essay Mercy Whitney wrote in 1837, inquiring into "some of the peculiar qualifications important for a missionaries [sic] wife," she too put "ardent piety" first. As pioneers, the women could not have anticipated precisely what the life of a missionary wife would involve (certainly they did not expect to express their piety by composing sermons or translating the Bible), but they had intended to do their part in introducing Christianity, not merely "civilization." In their letters and journals, the women began to articulate their frustration and to find ways to accommodate it. Not least, they found domestic responsibilities threatening to overwhelm that precious piety. Mercy's lament from her journal of July 9, 1820 —written when she had "the care of a little school"—reverberated into the future: "I long to feel more deeply engaged in the Missionary work. How surprising that we can feel stupid when everything around us seems to invite to action and say, be up and doing, be active, be diligent and faithful in your Master's work."[2]

But only in theory could the gospel and civilization be kept separate; in practice, they were inextricable.[3] The contradiction in the missionaries' instructions between introducing "civilization"— New England schools and households as well as churches—and at the same time knowing "nothing else save Jesus Christ" was never resolved, simply ignored. If the Hawaiians changed religion, they would also want to dress differently, plant different crops, build different houses, rule the country by different laws. Christianity was after all a complete way of life, not a set of ideas to think about for a few hours on Sunday.

Religious subject matter freely mingled with secular in the schools. Their quarterly and yearly examinations evolved over the years to include recitations of the Ten Commandments and portions of the Psalms and the gospels as well as demonstrations of arithmetic and the names of lands and months. The subjects taught not only reinforced new knowledge but emphasized the decline of the old, as the students recited "a refusal to keep wooden gods." As the family set up households on each island, their tasks may have seemed entirely secular, but they were still performed within the context of establishing an entire Christian community. Their labors immediately expanded beyond schoolteaching, as they dug wells, planted beans and corn from New England, and began housekeeping with feather beds, silverware, and cookstoves, even (eventually) a shower bath outside. Later in 1821, the family persuaded the king to let them exchange thatched houses for a wooden one.[4]

Mercy Whitney explained her reasons succinctly when she wrote, years later, to Mary Clark (of the third company), "I feel it my duty to instruct them in everything which may promote their civilization, so far as I have strength, and they are willing to learn." When the families on Kauai had to make soap because the barrel they had purchased in Honolulu was bad, the only way to secure enough ashes was for Samuel Ruggles to go into the mountains for three days to burn wood. But they were compensated, in Samuel Whitney's words, with "the reflection that it is one step in teaching the natives the arts of civilization." These arts he and the others defined in terms familiar to New Englanders. The missionaries would change Hawaiians not simply from within, by introducing the gospel, but from without, by presenting an example. The Hawaiians could learn by imitation and by replacement—cloth for tapa, clothing for nakedness, the Bible and *palapala* for genealogical chants and the hula.[5]

If religion was intertwined with the details of what the missionaries called civilization, it was also inseparable from the persons who practiced it. The persuading was not entirely ideological, a matter of introducing new and exciting ideas, nor entirely practical, a matter of introducing the "arts of civilization," but also personal. Despite what they sometimes thought, the women did not bow out of the great task of converting Hawaiians. Mercy Whitney paused in 1823 to meditate on the "importance of adorning my profession as a Christian, of letting my light shine before men that others may see it & glorify our father who is in heaven."[6] The women's piety illuminated every detail of their daily lives. To be a Christian was to be like them.

In presenting their example of a better way to live, the missionaries borrowed as little as possible from Hawaiian culture, preferring instead to hold themselves apart from the Hawaiians. Like stereotypical British explorers dressing for dinner in the jungle, they were keeping up the side. Their schools, churches, and households made up the city on the hill that could not be hid; their personal piety the light that should not be hid under a bushel (Matthew 5:14–15). It never occurred to the missionaries that any changes to Hawaiians or their institutions that accompanied the change in religion might not be improvements, and they never stopped to think about costs. But one way to read the story that unfolds in the years ahead is to discover the ongoing costs of those changes not only for Hawaiians but for missionaries as well.

The church's unpretentious beginnings did not promise a quick victory for the Lord. As if to demonstrate their understanding that a church was defined by the disciplined worship of God, not by a particular building, the missionaries held services in makeshift settings—in thatched houses, on ships' quarterdecks, or at the royal lounging place of Waikiki. Nancy Ruggles described a "little sanctuary of cocoanut leaves" that served the worshippers in Waimea. Since neither Samuel Whitney nor Samuel Ruggles was an ordained minister, the couples improvised by reading printed sermons at their services, postponing communion until the Binghams could visit the following spring. In Honolulu, for the first service on land (April 23), Hiram Bingham preached from the thatched house he and Sybil were living in.

Hiram chose a reassuring text from Luke 2:10 for the first sermon: "Fear not for behold I bring you good tidings of great joy which shall be to all people." But he spoke mostly for the benefit of the thirty or so white residents and ships' officers who could understand him. Boki, his entourage, and the many Hawaiians who sat on mats or crowded about the doors and windows of the house heard the minister's words through an interpreter. The church was a novelty, its services attended through the summer by "a considerable number" of curious natives, who seemed to enjoy the singing and the music from George Kaumualii's bass viol. As eager as the missionaries were to unseat Satan's empire, they had to do it right. Hiram freely offered the preached word, but zealously guarded the sacraments for church members. "We do not approve of haste," explained the "*Thaddeus* Journal," "in admitting to the full communion of the church any of whom we have not the means of obtaining pretty assured hopes of a life and conversation becoming the gospel." The example he had set with the Holmans showed that he meant what he said.[7]

On July 9, Boki and several men lingered after the sermon to ask questions, an encouraging sign. Soon after, Hiram was visiting the governor for an hour every morning to read the Bible and instruct him in English. On July 13, when Sybil was invited to go along, Hawaiian reality for once matched the picture of missionary work she had previously imagined. She and Hiram took seats above the Hawaiians, who "placed themselves on the mats at our feet, apparently determined to learn if they could. It seemed like being where my thoughts had often, in past years, placed me—*on heathen ground.*" The journals note every mark of early success, small or large: when Liholiho understood that he must not get up from the mission table before grace, or when Hannah Holmes began to hold weekly prayer meetings at her house (though whether the attraction was her beauty or general piety is hard to tell). Hawaiians attending the Sabbath School learned Bible verses by rote, then taught them to others during the week. Over the summer, they listened to the story of Opukahaia, which John Honolii translated line by line. At the deathbed scene, when Honolii explained that he himself had announced, "Obookiah is gone," many of the scholars wept. Many said that they wanted to be like Opukahaia. "Thus," the "*Thaddeus* Journal" declared, "in a public manner the natives of the island begin the worship of the true god and we pray they may be assisted to worship him in spirit and in truth."[8]

But if the mission counted success not by the number of fledgling worshippers but by the number of professed Christians, it lost ground over the summer. Not only was it increasingly clear that the Holmans were disaffected, but the word soon came from Kailua that William Kanui was returning to Hawaiian ways. In mid-July, Sybil wrote, "*We fear* the grace of God is still a stranger in his breast. Yet we would not give him up." By July 23, however, when a public letter of excommunication was read in church, they had. "During his stay in Kiarooah [Kailua]," Maria Loomis explained, "he absented himself from public worship, was habitually guilty of intoxication, avoided the company of the brethren, etc." "Wretched youth!" Sybil added sympathetically, "and is it done? Yes, and we believe in obedience to the laws of Christ's house."

William's reaction to his banishment is not told. Like many other young Hawaiians who attended the school at Cornwall before returning home, he found it difficult to live up to the missionaries' expectations or to compete successfully with the memory of Opukahaia. The record of Kanui's long life is sparse but suggests that he continued the wandering that had taken him to the United States to begin with. According to his obituary notice, he probably spent the next twenty years attached to the royal court as teacher and translator, until the California Gold Rush lured him away from the islands. He lost his life's savings when a San Francisco bank closed its doors a few days after Kanui made his deposit. But he never completely rejected or forgot the early training from the missionaries. In California, he joined the Mariner's Church and counseled fellow Hawaiians who had gone "astray." As an old man, ill and poor, he returned to Honolulu to die. James Hunnewell, the former mate of the *Thaddeus,* and Samuel Damon, pastor of the Bethel Union Church Seamen's Chapel, shared the expenses for his burial. The excommunicated helper, having returned to his faith, lies behind Kawaiahao Church in the mission's burial plot.[9]

Soon after arriving in Kauai, yet another young Hawaiian, George Kaumualii, the returning prince who had left home as such a young child, began to feel the pressures of two competing cultures. Sybil, though pleased at the news of George's affecting reunion with his father, nevertheless worried about him, "with his wild passions, in the situation in which he now stands." Though he had "naturally an amiable disposition," he had never joined the church. Now Sybil tried to reassure herself: "It is the Arm of the Lord which must prevent his being an instrument in the Great Opposer's hand of hindering the holy work."

Sybil had reason to worry. George began to settle down in an approved manner, soon marrying (the daughter of the English seaman Isaac Davis) and begetting children, providing food and assistance for the Whitneys and Ruggleses, even writing to Hiram Bingham with apologies that he could not assist the mission more, asserting that it was his "heart's desire" that the mission prosper. But troubles dogged him: his house with all his books in it burned down, leaving him with just the clothes on his back; his eldest child died; and in his own mind, the attractiveness of New England's culture—which, after all, had given him a childhood of poverty and instability as he passed from one guardian to another—began to fade. In April 1822, in an act of foolhardiness, he drove the schooner *Young Thaddeus* onto a dangerous reef, wrecking the vessel and forcing the crew to swim ashore. Both Whitneys soon concurred in their estimate of the unhappy young man. Mercy summarized George's dwindling interest in the mission since landing: he "soon began to grow indifferent & has adopted one native habit after another; till one could scarcely suppose he had ever seen civilized societies, much less dwelt among them." Samuel called him a "dissipated wretch," adding that "his father has forbidden him ever again to come into his presence." When Kaumualii died in the summer of 1824, his will left the son who could have been his heir only a few clothes. Not long after, George joined an abortive insurrection, attempting to take over the fort at Kauai, then fleeing into the mountains for several weeks. Upon his capture – a figure now for "pity and compassion" – he was shown mercy and allowed to live in Honolulu, where he died in 1826.[10]

"Had he behaved himself as he might," Mercy wrote as early as 1821 "his influence would have been great, but now he is considered no more than a common native." Since even the "best" men had sinful hearts, this confirmed Mercy's sense that "a degraded & heathen people who are addicted to every kind of vice & iniquity" needed to be especially watchful that they were not led astray. But George, who had the burden of dual loyalty – to the culture of the West that schooled him and the culture of the *alii* he was born to – in a sense strayed from both of them. For whatever reasons, George rejected Christianity, but he could not then return to his Hawaiian heritage as though he had never left it. In being sent to America, he had forfeited his training as an *alii.* He was neither a good Christian nor a good *alii;* his story ends as a "poor outcast without power, influence, or reputation," ruined not so much by the imposition of one culture upon another as by their hopeless entanglement in his mind.[11]

Thomas Hopu and John Honolii, however, working hard as translators and teachers, remained loyal to their Christian training. Though Thomas Hopu was disappointed at being refused a license to preach in 1822 (since the missionaries reasoned that their own assistant missionaries, better qualified than he, were continuing as lay workers), he did achieve the distinction of marrying his wife, Delia, in the first Christian wedding ceremony conducted by the mission. By that time, August 11, 1822, a new and spacious church building (54 by 21 feet) had been erected, moving the services out of the Binghams' house. The church was built in the Hawaiian style, altered by glass windows and wooden doors, paid for by subscriptions totaling over $1,100 from foreigners and chiefs. One captain donated a bell, another mahogany and other wood to build the pulpit, yet another two lamps to adorn either side of the pulpit. Dedicated September 15, 1821, the building held congregations of one hundred to four hundred persons throughout the next year. "Precious privilege!" wrote Lucy Thurston after the first Sabbath services, "a sacred awe pervades the soul in treading these earthly courts." The first of four such thatched churches erected before the final stone church in 1842, it lasted until fire destroyed it in 1824.[12]

After the first summer's work in religious instruction, claims of success were necessarily guarded. The missionaries seem to have spent more time excluding than including church members. The martial imagery of the leave-taking speeches in New England was very much on their minds. "We know not how soon the scene may change," admitted Sybil that fall of 1820. "—We know not but the Prince of Darkness may yet struggle violently before he will relinquish his dominion in these fair Isles of the Sea." The first baptism (of the king's mother, Keopuolani) would not take place until 1823; the first admissions to church membership, not until 1825. Still, in the youth of the mission, optimism seemed justifiable. There was always the comfort that although the missionaries could not foresee God's "holy pleasure" toward themselves, "first called into the field," they did know that in the end, "assuredly," the victory was the Lord's.[13]

Though the church was considered the most important institution, the *palapala* caught on much more quickly than the doctrine of original sin. The first advances in "civilization" on each island emerged in the schoolrooms. There, the women's talents shone in a public forum. Though they sometimes taught Sabbath school, and of course actively participated in the services, they did not lead them. Their function in the church, as in the home, was to show the exemplary Christian woman. But in the schoolroom, they could engage in the kind of "active" missionary labor that seemed to benefit the Hawaiians directly. Since the post of teacher was shared by almost every person in the mission, it was not theirs exclusively. Whoever was not incapacitated by illness or childbirth or not needed for manual labor filled in in the schoolroom. In Kailua, even Dr. Holman instructed three persons (the chief "John Adams," a son of John Young, and a native boy favored by Liholiho). So far as the record shows, only Jerusha Chamberlain, who supervised domestic affairs in Honolulu, and Lucia Holman, who perhaps found other or better things to do, were never drafted for this vocation.[14]

In the beginning, the schoolrooms usually shared space with the living quarters or church. Along the entire front of the missionaries' house in Waimea ran a thatched extension of the roof, Hawaiian-style, creating a meeting house and schoolroom. This *lanai*, an outdoor porch shielded from sun and rain, was a perfect architectural detail for the climate. After taking about a month to settle in, the missionaries began a "regular school" on September 6. Kaumualii provided the teachers with a bell and with pupils—twenty-five children who had strict orders to obey. Fifteen adults, including the king and queen and several chiefs, also attended.[15]

In Kailua, Liholiho controlled admissions, reserving the privilege mainly for chiefs and for the wives and children of white men. He himself soon learned enough to "read intelligibly in the New Testament," but after "several months," as Lucy Thurston remembered, "the pleasures of the cup caused his books to be quite neglected." This in turn disrupted the schooling of his wives, who habitually followed their husband from place to place. Liholiho's solution was to deliver two young men, favorites of his, to Asa Thurston, explaining that teaching them would be the same as teaching him. The king did insist, however, that his younger brother and heir, Kauikeaouli, attend to his lessons, and backed up this insistence with threats of whipping. Thomas Hopu soon distinguished himself as interpreter and teacher. The king gave him a piece of land and a house; the missionaries dispensed praise. "He engages in the work with all that earnest simplicity and zeal, which has long actuated his pious heart," reported Samuel Whitney after his summertime visit. In August, Elisha Loomis arrived for a three-month stay and was soon teaching Kalanimoku and a group of young men in Kawaihae. With him came young Daniel Chamberlain, who had absorbed enough Hawaiian to help with interpreting and who would live with the Thurstons. Later that fall, the mission in Kailua was temporarily abandoned when the restless king decided to tour his kingdom. The Thurstons dutifully followed him to Lahaina, Maui, then went on without him to Oahu, where they arrived December 21, 1820.[16]

In Honolulu during the summer of 1820, most of the teaching—first an hour a day, then up to four or five—fell to Sybil Bingham, assisted by her husband, Maria Loomis, and Mercy Whitney (until she left for Kauai in mid-July). Watts's *Catechism,* Webster's *Spelling Book,* and the New Testament were the texts; instruction for the time being was in English. Within a week or ten days, the students had usually mastered the alphabet. Later they went on to spelling in unison and reciting combinations of letters. They learned to read by memorizing and reciting nonsense syllables, "running vowel changes on the different consonants in order, as: ha, ka, la, ma, na, pa, wa; he, ke, le, me, ne, pe, we, and so forth." By early August, some were writing their letters on slates.[17]

In the schoolroom – which was actually the front part of a 20-by-30-foot room partitioned off from the Bingham's living quarters with mats – Sybil found her element. Over the next few years, she described her pleasure again and again: "I could not help saying to Mr. B. as I came out of my schoolroom today I never was happier in the pleasantest school I ever had in America," she wrote in February 1821. Later that year, she reminisced to her sister Sophia about her "pretty bible class" of six scholars: "I have found many seasons in which I thought, I never before experienced equal satisfaction in any employment. *These youth & children I love.* That they love me I am satisfied." To a friend she declared:

> In America I reckoned some of my happiest hours of employment to be when surrounded by a beloved school – in this heathen school my comfort has not been less. I love them tenderly and when endeavoring in a simple way to explain to them the word of God, which some of them have now read for several months, have never failed to feel that the dearest spot among the dearest friends in my own beloved land was not so engaging a spot as that among the heathen.

Considering schoolteaching a privilege, the women took on a school eagerly and gave it up with reluctance. The grateful students buoyed their spirits. One Hawaiian woman, Sally Jackson, married to an American, brought her two daughters every day to learn to read. "I hope we shall be friends," Sally told Sybil, "And I try to do something for you when you do so much for me." When Lucy Thurston took over the school in Honolulu later in 1821, she, like Sybil, wrote of deep satisfaction:

> They make a pleasant school. One class of natives have their daily lessons with the Testament which is interpreted to the school. Every ear is open, & every eye seems fixed; & while the sacred page is read,

> here & there is heard to drop from the lips, A-lo-ha, a-lo-ha e-no— That is, I love it, I love it very much. Precious to me have been the hours thus spent. I can reckon them among the happiest of my life.[18]

Everything connected with schoolteaching brought out pleased comments from the missionaries. They remarked upon the "tenacious memories" of the students (typical in an oral culture that depended upon memory for its survival). "We are perfectly satisfied with their ability," Samuel Whitney and Samuel Ruggles wrote from Kauai, recalling "two or three instances when they have learned the alphabet the first day." Two captains observing the Sabbath school in Honolulu one day were surprised when the students repeated the ninth commandment in their own tongue after just five minutes' attention to it, especially since the same commandment was "so difficult" for American children.[19]

The school in Honolulu grew from about a dozen students in the beginning to about forty by the fall. The Chamberlain children and those of the foreign settlers attended first, then an assortment of Hawaiian adults and children. Other students were "orphans" or part-Hawaiian children whom the missionaries collected in the streets; some were brought to the mission by a parent or caretaker, or a member of the *alii.* Walking through the village, Daniel Chamberlain was reminded of the pressing need for education: he saw "so many bright children, who appear willing to learn, growing up in vice and ignorance because there is no one to teach them better." In his matter-of-fact way, he continued, "If they do not read or understand the terms of salvation, they never will accept, and if they do not accept they never will be saved. Well, then, the case requires immediate attention." Education often went beyond the training in the schoolroom, as the missionaries tried to absorb some children into their extended family, feeding and clothing them, and trying to instruct them in household chores. Many they rechristened with an American name honoring a friend or relative or benefactor, since one source of mission funds was money donated by ladies' societies and individuals for the purpose of "adopting" and educating a heathen child.[20]

One handsome boy named William Beals, son of a native mother and white father now dead, was adopted by the Binghams in all but law. When Sybil saw him peering through the gate one day and invited him to live with them, he knew enough English to answer "yes." A year later, Sybil remembered those first months of lessons, when she was surprised by the child's ability. Describing him to a friend, she could not stop until she had filled a page of cramped handwriting. When he was able to read in the Bible, she wrote, "This was like opening a gate which admitted his entrance in a wide field where all was new & wonderful." He was "much attached" to his hymnbook, delighted with his catechism. He could repeat Watts's first catechism lesson, had memorized several prayers and scriptural passages, studied arithmetic and geography, and was learning how to write. With his "amiable" disposition, the only punishment he needed was for Sybil to allow someone else to do a chore for her or to refuse to hear his lessons. "He is very affectionate & seems as happy in Mr. B. and myself as if indeed we were his parents." Realizing that she had rambled, Sybil closed her letter. "You will pardon the occupying of so much of my sheet with a relation of one small individual when the whole nation interests you," she admitted, "but I have great hopes of this child, and long for the day when I may add to this little account of him evidence of his new birth & adoption into Christ's family." Perhaps the mission was still hoping for another Opukahaia; in the meantime, the Binghams loved him as a son.[21]

William was one of the participants in the first quarterly examination, a staple of New England schools, held in Honolulu on September 12. The scholars publicly displayed their achievements for an audience composed of Honolulu's foreign residents, ships' officers, a ship's doctor, and the Holmans (recently returned from Maui). The less advanced classes of scholars, having just learned the alphabet, read and spelled out "words" of one or two syllables from a column in *The American Primer* or from Webster's. One student (probably Sally Jackson) read twenty lines from a Sabbath school card, and some of the older Hawaiian students — Hannah and George Holmes, Mary Marin, and William Beals — could read almost as much. The Chamberlain children demonstrated more advanced skills in arithmetic, geography, and writing. At the end, the entire school recited in unison — and in Hawaiian — six sentences from a "Sunday School card":

> I cannot see God but God can see me.
> In the beginning God created the heavens and the earth.

> Jehovah is in heaven and he is everywhere.
> Jesus Christ, the good son of God, died for our sins.
> We must pray to Jehovah, and love his word.
> God loves good men and good men love God.

This material had been taught in the Sabbath school, but its "cantileting," as Hiram Bingham called it, offered an impressive conclusion to the summer's work. The event was the mission's first public symbol of success. The entry in the "*Thaddeus* Journal" described the scholars' exit: "They retired in perfect order [having] much pleased themselves as well as the visitors and each turning around at the door as usual, with a bow or courtesy, very pleasantly bade us 'Good Afternoon.'"[22]

In later years, as schools spread over the islands, these examinations, held every four months, seized the Hawaiian imagination and became an institution. April 19, the anniversary of the *Thaddeus*'s landing, was often the highpoint of the school year, with thousands participating in an examination over several days' time. Without intending to, the missionaries had introduced a group performance with resemblances to the hula. The memory work and recitation were a kind of chanting; the scholars, forming themselves into disciplined rows, learned to write in unison on their slates as eagerly and skillfully as they had always moved their limbs in dance. "Some schools taught how to get ready, to stand, to speak out, to take up a slate, how to place the pencil on the slate, thus: 'Attention, get ready, wait, stand up, speak, give greeting.'" The historian Samuel Kamakau remembered when learning to read became extremely popular, sometime in late 1824: "Schools were established all over Oahu conducted like the schools of the hula in old days." After a few weeks, there would be all-night and all-day sessions, "and as April 19 of each year approached, when all gathered for the yearly exhibition (*ho'ike*), from Kepukaki you could see lights burning all the way from the Nu'uanu Pali [in the center of Oahu] to Kaimuki [north of Waikiki]."[23]

Unlike the pleasant intellectual labor required in the church or schoolroom, the manual labor of setting up exemplary Christian households for Hawaiian view demanded relentless physical endurance. It also took up most of everyone's time. Both sexes worked hard, though traditional assumptions about "men's" work and "women's" work continued.

The men's journals describe outdoor chores—building, digging, hauling—and long hikes of exploration. To get fresh meat, Samuel Whitney joined Hawaiians in hunting wild bullock. Lucy Thurston wrote sympathetically of "the toil to which Mr. Thurston has subjected himself, of cutting logs on the mountain, & sawing them with his own hands, to obtain boards for some of our doors." Although Hawaiians set up the first thatched houses for the families, the men of the mission dug the cellar and put up the frame house during the summer of 1821. Out of bits and pieces of very scarce wood, the new fathers added rockers to chairs and fashioned cradles. Daniel Chamberlain built a brick oven and fireplace for the families in Kauai. Cleaning out a spring in Honolulu that first summer, Daniel "throwed out about 350 pails of water, and considerable mud, &c. . . . I feel fatigued, and should like a half a mug of good cyder, although I very seldom think of cyder."[24]

The women continued to do most of the domestic labor—preparing food, washing, ironing, and sewing the clothes, and cleaning. They had some help from the Hawaiian children who lived with them, but as Sybil Bingham admitted to Lucy Thurston in June 1820, "You may judge what assistance are three little heathen boys, whose tongues you do not understand." As if to mute any criticism implied, she continued, "I love the little things." By this time there were twelve children in the family, doing simple chores like stirring the food on the stove.[25]

It comes as no surprise that the women continue to report domestic labors getting in the way of "missionary work."[26] One reason a drooping Sybil took such pleasure in teaching Sally Jackson and her daughters to read was that their enthusiasm revived her. "I earnestly desire to be more faithful in instructing her," she reflected. "Some little seasons spent with her in unfolding the first principles of Christianity, have been exceedingly interesting. It has awakened missionary zeal when exhausted labors have smothered it." The women did not make things easier by trying to keep up American standards when material supports were often nonexistent. "How difficult it is to have anything according to former habits," Sybil realized in 1823, "when yet, one has not help, no kitchen, no buttery, or indeed scarcely any territories at their own command.

It seems, sometimes, as if strength & spirits would all be exhausted, which are so much needed for the poor heathen, doing that which a few accommodations might render trifling."[27]

Yet it would be a mistake to see the women's story as one of continuing frustration with domesticity, questioning an ideology that "confined" them in the home even as it idealized their efforts. It is more a story of enduring tension between desire for public work and a genuine pleasure in family and household, in its own way as agreeable as the pleasure of the schoolroom. Like women on the mainland, they were increasingly self-conscious and serious about their roles as housewives and mothers. But like other reformers, their lives point out a contradiction inherent in nineteenth-century notions of womanhood. As keepers of morality and "civilization," women were justified in seeking to expand their influence in public ways, but they were also responsible for the home and family that nurtured those values. The result, as one historian puts it, was "guilt and confusion."[28]

During the first year of the mission, the women reflected more on their identity as "Christians" than as "women." But their commitment to "true womanhood" had not really been tested. They had not yet set up independent households and, more important, had not yet borne children. This was the great work of their mature lives. They would contend not only with the tension between public work and domesticity, but with the ambiguity of their own attitudes toward domestic work. This ambiguity goes farther than the conflicting emotions of pleasure and frustration. It comes from the relative value assigned to domestic labor—important enough in nurturing Christian citizens of a new nation, but less important than spreading the gospel.

Never was the pleasure in new houses or new families as intense as it was that first summer in Honolulu. The mission "family" was still communal, but moving toward separation into nuclear families. At first, the young couples moved about from thatched house to thatched house as various missionaries, merchants, and captains came and went. But finally, on the day after the school examinations, the long-promised houses, three months in the building, were finished. Both Sybil Bingham and Maria Loomis described them in detail, and one of the Chamberlain children drew a sketch: three houses standing in a row, built of poles and thatched with grass, the largest 20 by 28 feet. Connecting all three to the south (on the ocean side) was a long covered porch or *lanai,* like the one in Kauai, which Maria Loomis described as "a long shed." This served as a hall, dining room, and kitchen, although there was also a separate storehouse and cook house. The Chamberlains took the house with the communal table; the Loomises, along with their native charges, lived in a second; the Binghams moved into the back of the largest house, leaving the front for school and church. The location—roughly the same place where the mission's subsequent frame house stands today—commanded an extraordinary view. "It is a delightful spot about ¾ miles from H[onolulu] on the high road—or rather foot path to Witete [Waikiki]—" wrote Maria, "on an extensive plain with a view of the open sea in front & lofty mountains and fertile valley in the rear."[29]

In Kauai, Kaumualii, not nearly so dilatory as Boki, began building a large house (50 by 22 feet) for his missionary "children" as soon as the women arrived. Samuel Whitney still complained that thirty indolent and awkward men were slow to complete it (when "5 American farmers would do much of the work in 3 days"), but by mid-August the families had moved in. The Whitneys took the east end of the house, the Ruggleses the west, with mats between them. Three windows on each side—one of glass—added a touch of luxury. A ten-foot-high stone wall enclosed the yard, guarded every night by the king's men. Though a cook house stood in back, it was not necessary at first. Young George, who lived just ten or fifteen yards away, and had the benefit of a cook, a steward, and a dozen domestic servants, provided the missionaries' board. "George is very kind," Mercy thought, "& acts the part of a brother, in providing for our wants." Mostly the family ate fish, taro, and potatoes, but by November their garden produced "cucumbers, watermelons, corn, potatoes, beans, pumpkins, squashes, grapes, fennel, orange, tamarind, cotton, bananas, castor-oil and cocoanut trees." Water came from the Waimea River next to the village. On September 1, Samuel Whitney reported the present of a piece of land with the island's produce on it and the right to call on fifty men for any labor they wanted done. As in Honolulu, the families enjoyed an enviable view, the house standing "about 5 rods [27 yards] from the sea on a cool and pleasant spot."[30]

In writing "a family letter of little affairs" to Mrs. Bates, Sybil

Bingham recalled a "childish expression" that used to amuse her friend—*"Sybil's family all by herself."* This seems an ironic summary for the mission's bustling communal life so far. But with the new houses, Sybil achieved her goal in a modest yet entirely satisfactory way. Visiting the unfinished buildings in mid-August, Sybil had predicted that the little section set aside for the Binghams would be "my resting place—durable enough for earth." Once the houses were finished, the family partitioned the interiors with mats and a few boards. "From the large house a little room was thus taken off," Sybil explained to her friend, "into which—O,—could you enter, your heart & countenance would smile to see my comforts. Without describing it now, I will say, it is a sweet little spot, and much is the enjoyment I have, within its pleasant walls."[31]

Such contentment in the new surroundings called forth meticulous descriptions of them. With the piece of a room allotted to her, each woman created a home. Sybil Bingham and Maria Loomis surveyed their cherished possessions, some new and some carried from New England. Maria told of a ceiling of yellow tapa, the floors layered with coarse mats over straw, the walls covered with fine mats. A bedstead, a dining chair to which Hiram Bingham had added rockers, and a toilet table completed the furniture. On the table, Maria placed her few possessions: a row of books, a workbasket, an "elegant little mahogany chest," profiles of her sister and a friend, a small mirror, combcase, and pincushion. Sybil's furniture was similar: "a bed, high bedstead, and curtains . . . and a toilet, covered with a pretty mat and curtained with furniture calico, having on the back part a row of neatly bound Andover books, and on the front a little [writing] desk." In the evening, the mats lining the walls, which had "a colored straw woven in," gave "the appearance of neatly papered walls." One window, without glass, looked south toward the sea: its small white curtain partially obscured her tiny looking glass. A medicine chest, a small cupboard filled with recent gifts of china and glassware, and a shelf for books completed the picture.[32]

Outside, by the end of September, another grass house was built for John Honolii. Soon the family added a well dug about seven and a half feet through the coral to add a supply of brackish water to the clear water brought down from the mountains in calabashes. By December, they had enclosed an area of two and a half acres for their compound. The first garden met with mixed success; by

January, worms had destroyed their quarter-acre of young corn and their garden vegetables. But by March, a garden planted in December was "flourishing" with beans, corn, radishes, cucumbers, and more. Native plants like taro, potatoes, sugar cane, and bananas seemed impervious to insects or reptiles. Though everyone remarked on the benignity of the climate, they could have used more protection from the sun, since the closest trees were palm groves in Waikiki. In the summer of 1821, Kaahumanu donated a few stalks of the hala tree, which were planted in the yard for shade. In the meantime, they put up with the dust or the damp.[33]

Whatever their housing arrangements over the years—single room or entire house, frame house or grass, communal or individual—the women derived a lifetime of solace and pleasure from domestic order and a few objects. This makes perfect sense for the "true woman" of the nineteenth century, and for these particular women, pleased to be missionaries, excited by the first bloom of marriage and motherhood. But this pleasure seems contradictory for women who understood that they should not be laying up treasures on earth. As Mercy Whitney never tired of reminding her parents (who were evidently not professed Christians), "In the midst of worldly prosperity . . . the importance of securing an unfading crown . . . will be of more value in the hour of death than ten thousand worlds." This was one of Mercy's great themes, and events (as she interpreted them) tended to bear her out. In March 1821, when a fire destroyed eleven houses in Waimea, stopping within just nine yards of the Whitneys', Mercy reflected, "This event has led one to feel more sensibly than ever, the uncertainty of all worldly hopes and prosperity. . . . Let us not put our trust in uncertain riches." God, she believed, "will never leave or forsake those who put their trust in him." He sometimes worked in mysterious ways. The continuing supply of presents from ships' captains did not incline Mercy to defend those "whose sole object is *worldly gain.*" God was inclining their hearts. "He alone can dispose them to give of their abundance to supply our wants, & though perhaps unperceived by the gazing multitude, he is assuredly in *this way* building up his spiritual Temple."[34]

But Jesus' advice not to "lay up" or hoard treasures on earth was not the same as urging an absolute disregard for them. Jeremiah

Evarts, writing to the missionaries in 1822, spoke to the double focus on both "external conditions" and "higher objects" that was a continual source of tension in everyone's life: "Let the external conditions of the natives be as much improved as possible; but let their eyes be directed to higher objects than this world can afford." Though emphasizing that man does not live by bread alone, the missionaries also saw the danger of an unrelieved diet of abstractions. They were not turning their backs on the world, but on worldliness. Mercy Whitney, writing in 1827, understood the obligation to labor hard and to exercise the body; "prosperity," if it came, brought greater "usefulness." But, she warned, "if riches increase, set not thy heart upon them is the Divine admonition." The difficulty, she explained, was "not that riches in themselves are so dangerous but because we are so prone to put them in the place of *him* who has said my son give me thy heart." Sybil Bingham, writing to Hiram in 1843 with similar moderating comments, began with some reluctance to speak of "earth's cares & tossing," then defended these claims. "Earth's cares and the spiritual exercises of the heart are blended, in my experience, nor would I separate them until 'I safely reach my home—my GOD, my heaven, my all.'" In practice, the women simply balanced the claims of this world and the next as best they could.[35]

Their attachment to objects was minimal, and the mission's common stock system tended to reinforce this attitude. A bolt of cloth was routinely cut up into equal parts; only the gifts specifically labeled in New England for a particular individual were kept as personal. Religious doctrine was reinforced not only by mission policy but by particular traits of character. One ought to try, as Sybil Bingham put it, "to live not at random, guided by present impulse." In a letter giving prenuptial advice to her sister Sophia, Sybil counseled, "Gain some settled principles and let your plan of conduct arise out of these." The women tried to check their dependence on material things by making do with whatever they had and refusing to long for what they did not.[36]

Mercy Whitney's attitude, coping with a lack of milk on the *Thaddeus,* was typical. After landing, when she received a delicious portion of goat's milk for her tea, she reflected, "I have thought but little about milk since I left America, having previously resolved not to let my mind dwell upon any kind of food which used to please my taste, which I knew would not be in my power to obtain." Sybil, who admitted to "a kind of exhaustion" whenever she had to go for several days without food made from flour, wrote to two former students, remembering their kindness in bringing her nutcakes or "a cordial of some kind" when she was worn out from schoolteaching. But Sybil hoped it was not some material comfort she longed for: "If a tear found its way, I think it was the sweet remembrance of the beloved children, and friends, and not the loss of the comforts once kindly bestowed by them, which raised it. GOD in his providence, has graciously supplied our necessary wants."[37]

Although Sybil reflected in her private diary that the mission's new cottages "contrast" with dwellings in America, she could still "praise God . . . that He did not allow me to wish for one temporal comfort He had not given." This did not prevent her from appreciating the temporal comforts she did have. She checked her attachment to things; she did not entirely disregard them. Hiram made her a rocking chair that first summer. "You smile," Sybil wrote as she imagined her sisters reading her journal, "but with all my fondness for one, how do you think I have done without, with all my hard work? A box or trunk has been our only seat. My husband, I believe, was never a chairmaker before, but happy for me and the mission family, that he is *every thing.* I think no workman would have made a seat more firm and comfortable, while the sandalwood and young sealskin, with neat workmanship, render it elegant." For the rest of her life, Sybil rocked in that chair. A local merchant priced it at twelve dollars, but even now, when the chair was new, Sybil valued it much more. "I suspect you would not be purchasers," she told her sisters, "if I should put my price upon it."[38]

A list of the objects considered truly precious by the mission's wives at this point would be quite short. Elisha Loomis made Maria a chair and a cradle-swing. A piece of brown cloth fitted over an oblong frame and hung over the bed with cords allowed Levi to rock back and forth. The king gave the Thurstons a beautiful Chinese table with six drawers, which served their family for a lifetime. Asa Thurston put rockers on a plain kitchen chair for Lucy. Wood was so scarce that Mercy Whitney did not have a cradle until ten months after her baby was born, when a ship's captain, who was building a schooner with timber from America, offered a supply as a present. Both Mercy and Lucy wrote home praising wooden cupboards, which enabled them to keep food away from mice. A chest of drawers or a portable writing desk ranked high with everyone who already had one or who hesitantly requested one from supporters at home.[39]

As conditions improved over the years, there were occasional accusations that missionaries supported by the donations of the Christian public back home were living in the grand style. (Lucy Thurston, for example, was once criticized for the unseemly elegance of her daughters' bonnets.) But most articles singled out for attention during these early years had a defensible utility. (Lucy replied to the unnamed person who thought that silk and artificial flowers did not set a "good example" that it was "a good example to give durability to items." The hats—a gift from a missionary sister in Honolulu—had so far lasted seven years.) The women could welcome articles that comforted a child or allowed themselves a moment of rest; articles of adornment that merely assuaged personal vanity had no place in their lives. Individual articles of clothing—a particular style of bonnet or dress—were so insignificant, except as a utilitarian covering, that they were rarely mentioned at all. When letters went back to donors thanking them for clothing, no one mentioned that the articles were not stylish, and only rarely that they did not fit. Portraits painted in 1819, just before the *Thaddeus* left, show the women in Empire gowns. They were still wearing them in 1828 when the third company arrived in their dresses with long waists and leg-of-mutton sleeves. That first fall, Daniel Chamberlain wrote to the Board with a list of provisions for the next group of missionaries, including what the pioneers had learned about clothing. The newcomers should bring "plain clothing such as becometh followers of the meek & lowly Jesus—here is work enough to do without spending much time in doing up superfluous clothing, washing, etc."[40]

But the need for a cradle or a chair cannot be fully explained by utility. These were, of course, exemplary objects of the "civilization" the missionaries hoped to install. But the need for them was mostly emotional. For women living in dark, flea-ridden, thatched houses, the rocker and objects like it were a link with the New England of painted clapboards they left behind. Even more important, since nostalgia did not occupy many waking moments, these objects were important as symbols of contentment in a new life, not only as missionaries but as wives and mothers. Bridegrooms had fashioned many of the beloved objects. The *alii,* through their gifts, had extended a warm welcome. Honolulu was becoming home. Within two years of life as a missionary, Sybil Bingham wrote that she had never found her "heart sinking" at her decision to come to "these rude heathen shores—which helps me to add, here let me bear all the afflictions which GOD shall see good for me in this vale of tears—here let me labor, and here let me die, my bones resting in this ransomed land."[41]

The most priceless "possessions" of all were the children who began to appear in every household. Yet during the fall of 1820, as Sybil anticipated the birth of her first child, her avowed pleasure—in the new house with a partitioned area of her own, in her relatively good health, and in a rocking chair to take the edge off her fatigue—was not enough to overcome a feeling of dread. In letter after letter, she made oblique references to the childbirth ahead of her, which she called in her private journal the "hour of anguish." She struggled to control her agitation, to supplant it with brave emotions and a composed mind. When she visited the unfinished houses in August, she confided to her sisters, "I wept as the thoughts flew forward to untried scenes which awaited me there—there my eyes might be soon closed upon this sublunary world." Once settled in her house, she wrote to Mrs. Bates, "I have leisure to regulate my little concerns, take my pen & books—and listen to the solemn voice which bids me, in a spiritual view set my house in order for death may be near." Her recourse was to trust God: "To Him I would commit all, not knowing what he has written for me, but assured that *he will do right.*" Still she was afraid.[42]

In her private journal, she let her imagination range most freely. On October 22, delivery imminent, there was no medical help in sight. Dr. Holman was in Kauai, and Dr. Williams, who had recently been in port to care for a wounded seaman, would have to leave the next morning on the whaleship *L'Aigle.* Sybil reminded herself that God could carry her through "with or without human aid." "If it seems good to him," she thought, "I shall yet live to praise Him." If not, she was prepared: "Death looks not terrible to me. Praise to our Redeemer, it has long been divested of its sting, and now that I feel that it may be near, through the rich mercy of GOD, it is still without its dread array. *It is a solemn thing to die,* but with the rod & staff of Jesus—the dying head reposed on Him, the dark valley may be passed with songs of triumph." Yet death would mean "the tender parting from the beloved of my heart," and at this thought her courage failed. Her imagination veered toward morbidity as she imagined how Hiram would feel without her:

> The agonizing thought of his pressing to his lips this cold clay of one he loves so tenderly . . . the cold earth covering from his fond eyes the wife of his bosom . . . [his] solitary walk in the land of heathen darkness . . . to the little grassy spot, there to weep in silence, & alone. It is the return of night, when his weary head is laid upon his pillow —the dawn of day, when he wakes, and finds himself *without—his—friend!*

She stopped herself "—away my thoughts to *Jesus*"—and reminded herself that even if she did die, she and Hiram would be reunited "in glory when earth and all its scenes shall be no more!"[43]

Captain Starbuck promised to return with Dr. Williams if *L'Aigle* caught a whale within three days, but the time passed and no doctor arrived. Sybil carried on, teaching her school, trying to compose her thoughts. She wrote an effusive letter on October 31 to Lucy Thurston, not once mentioning the word "childbirth," but meditating on the possibility of death. Ending, she made a practical request: "My dear Sister, I would touch a tender subject. Without any gloomy presages that it *will be*, I feel that in this vale of tears, *it may be realized.* A motherless babe, in this dark land of pagans, far from the dear kindred of her who gave it birth!" Sybil commended the child to God's care:

> He will provide for it; yet will He do it by means—Those means He will appoint. Still, may I name a wish———that my dear Sister Thurston would place herself in a Mother's stead———that she would consider it, as in the providence of GOD, given to her, rather than to the Mother who in sickness & distress did bear it———that she would seek for those maternal feelings and that maternal care which she whose youthful, orphan heart has often thrilled at the tender sound of *Mother*, would have accounted amongst her greatest earthly comforts, to have exercised———.[44]

Sybil taught her school until the evening of November 8. The next day, Hiram delivered his first daughter, weighing 8 pounds, 12 ounces, given the same name as Sybil's mother and sister, Sophia Moseley. Daniel Chamberlain, writing to Jeremiah Evarts the next day, noted in his equable way that Sybil was "remarkably comfortable," adding, "I never saw parents appear to be more thankful—I left them while their hearts were overflowing with gratitude to him who is the author of all our mercies."[45]

By the end of 1820, the two households in Kauai had also welcomed daughters, Mercy Whitney on October 19 and Nancy Ruggles on December 22, though with the important difference that Dr. Holman was on hand for the deliveries. Unfortunately, everyone except Sybil Bingham left a very sparse account of this first experience of childbirth. The announcement from Kauai that "God in his good providence has given us a little daughter" survives in Samuel Whitney's handwriting. By the time he wrote his sisters on November 6, he assured them, Mercy had "now so far recovered as to be able, in a great measure, to attend to the concerns of the family." In almost the same words, Samuel Whitney recorded the birth of Sarah Ruggles: "God has again manifested his goodness by adding another little one to our number." On March 2, 1821, still in Kauai, Dr. Holman delivered his own daughter, Lucia. Back in Honolulu, the birth of Lucy Thurston's daughter Persis on September 28, 1821, meant that every missionary wife was also a mother. Once again Dr. Holman delivered the baby (though he and Lucia sailed for America a few days later), and her father announced the "occasion to sing of special mercies." Maria Loomis's second child, Amanda, was born December 4, 1821, and Jerusha Chamberlain's sixth, Alfred, the following summer on June 19, 1822.[46]

The birth of children occasioned sobering reflections and emotions in the new parents. But first, with death no longer looking so imminent, they relaxed and recorded their delight. "*Levi* lies on the bed," Maria Loomis wrote without punctuation, enchantment overwhelming her usual self-control, "with a pillow under his head that he may see his mother—kicking & laughing & talking in his pretty way his beautiful blue eyes sparkling with intelligence & animation his skin as white as a lily his little double chin his fine features make him appear to his fond mother as one of the most lovely objects she ever beheld." In several letters, Sybil Bingham attempted to answer her own question: "What can a fond mother tell you of such a darling child?" Writing to Hiram's sisters, she explained that

Sophia shared his features, "making allowance for the sweetness & delicacy of female infancy," and his eyes. "Should I pen what her fond parents discover of her opening infant mind," she added, aware of her infatuation, "I should, perhaps, raise a smile at a mother's partiality, but leave the conviction that the fondest parents are favored with the most remarkable children." When Mercy Whitney began her journal again five months after Maria's birth, she soon described her contented infant, who diverted herself with her "a-la-lo," or talking, in the morning and went to bed at night with a smile as though bidding Mercy good-night.[47]

In later years, Lucy Thurston reflected that the children had done their own kind of "missionary work." In one story, Kalanimoku walked away with young Daniel Chamberlain on his shoulders, having chosen him as a teacher. When Jerusha Chamberlain walked to church, she would begin with five children beside her and end with none, all of them claimed by doting *alii* along the way. The appearance of families (true to the Board's assumptions) did attest to the missionaries' pacific intentions; perhaps more important, the babies, who provided an occasion for personal visits, helped the missionaries nurture relationships with the Hawaiians. "The people are very fond of caressing the white children," the missionaries wrote in the "*Thaddeus* Journal." Within a few days of her birth, Sophia Bingham received a half-bushel of bananas, a half-bushel of potatoes, and a fat hog from a chiefess. When Maria Loomis and Sybil Bingham took their infants to pay their respects to Liholiho (who arrived in Honolulu in February 1821), the king slept through the two-hour visit, but the chiefesses were attentive. Each female *alii* insisted on having the babies in her arms. "The dear children," Sybil recalled, "took very patiently, much caressing which was at once bestowed upon them giving many a sweet smile for the rude attention they received."[48]

Later that year, Kamamalu (Liholiho's favorite wife) found that Maria Whitney would sit contentedly with her, while the other babies would not: the "much pleased" queen told the Whitneys they must name her "*Mah-mah-lo* after herself." The Holmans had named their child Lucia Kamamalu, but the queen's request came too late for the other families in Kauai. Early on, they had reciprocated the homage paid them by Kaumualii, who continued to regard them as part of his family and had built them yet another new house in the spring of 1821, because, as he told Mercy Whitney, "we were his children & must be nearer to him so that he could take care of us." When the Whitneys baptized their daughter that same spring, they called her Maria Tapoole "to please the Queen." The Ruggles child was named after her grandmother and the king, Sarah Trumble Tamoree.[49]

Still, as many anxious reflections as contented ones went along with new parenthood. The counsel against too great an attachment to treasures of "this" world applied to children as well as to things, prompting cautions against excessive fondness. The parents remembered the failing of the Israelites in the desert, worshipping the golden calf while Moses was communing with God: idolatrous affection. Maria Loomis worried about her attachment to Levi, "I sometimes fear the cord of maternal affection is binding my heart too close to this dear object & I tremble lest I care for him both in my heart & with my hands more than my divine Master will approve." In a world where everything that happened led back to God's design, children were evidence of God's "unspeakable goodness." They did not belong to their parents in any but the most mundane legal sense. She is "not ours," thought Lucy Thurston of young Persis, "she is God's. He has committed her to our care." "Dear as she is," wrote Sybil Bingham of her daughter, "we try to feel that she is not ours, only as loaned of our Father in Heaven." Such thoughts led logically enough, in a world where infant as well as maternal mortality rates were high, to the realization that the Lord who gave could also take away.[50]

Perhaps because her own "orphanage" was so traumatic, Sybil could not contemplate her "sweet & lovely" daughter, any more than she could await childbirth, without considering death. She confided to her sister her fear that "GOD in his wise & mysterious providence may early call her [Sophia] from these fond arms to the unfeeling grave, or parental arms may soon be taken from her support, and she be left in this dark land of heathen ignorance & pollution, a sorrowing fatherless & motherless child." In raising a third possibility, that she and Sophia might be left without Hiram, Sybil was "uttering a feeling which has never escaped my pen before." Comforted by her belief that in such an event "God would make the way clear," she retained "the blessed assurance that He would never leave me nor forsake me." But these were the comforts of ideology, existing in the mind. Here, as the desire to raise her child tugged her toward the earth, Sybil felt tension between such spiritual truths and the attraction of life in all its physicality. "But while I strive for that spirit which says, Father, thy will be done, I yet rejoice in the hope that this little one may grow & increase under the hand of her fond mother & affectionate father as a pleasant flower whose progress shall be lasting & salutary to a perishing nation and that we all together through many a toilspent year, may bring forth fruit to our divine Master's praise."[51]

The women were becoming acutely aware of the practical difficulty of training children in the way they should go.[52] The direction Sybil had in mind was toward her own vocation as a missionary, and she hoped that God would remember the "little lambs in this distant fold, . . . one day making them lights to enlighten this dark region." Lucy Thurston, holding Persis as she wrote, put it more directly: "On missionary ground, precious will be the privilege of training her up for missionary work." More important than eventual vocation was a parent's responsibility to the child's soul. As Mercy Whitney wrote, "O what a charge is such a tender offspring, a being possessed of an immortal soul the salvation of which depends in a great measure on our faithfulness." Even if the parents were faithful enough, there was the difficulty posed by polluted heathen surroundings and the innate depravity that the child shared with everyone else on earth. Sybil admitted that "many times in the course of a day," the toddler Sophia escaped outside. "In our open yard under a burning sun, where are always natives of some kind whose vulgar language cannot escape the ear, or underfoot of one of three domestic establishments where are five more little ones near her own age, all, with her, giving evidence of corrupt nature, tho no two dispositions are alike. And the great evil is not to know how to do wisely myself." These were problems of childrearing that would not disappear, but for the moment, Sybil found a generalized comfort: "If sought unto, God will give wisdom and upbraid not—."[53]

No one could foresee at this point how motherhood would affect her work as a missionary. With the birth of children into every household, the mission rounded out its presentation of the Christian family—a step in the right direction. By the time Persis Thurston was born in the fall of 1821, the wood-frame house was newly finished, so the visitors had the double attraction of the "white infant, neatly dressed in white" and the airy, light room with two glass windows, fresh paint, and delicate pink wallpaper. An exultant Lucy described her sense of the visitors' reactions: "A child dressed! Wonderful, most wonderful!! To witness home scenes and the manner in which we cherished our children seemed, in a child-like way, to draw forth their warmest affections." Like Lucy, the missionaries assumed that the picture they presented was an improvement, was, in fact, "civilization." This supposed difference between herself and Hawaiians accounts for Lucy's easy assumption of superiority as she exclaimed, "How eloquent the natives were in referring to their own naked neglected children, and their dark, dingy, thatched huts!"[54]

But this sense of superiority is carefully circumscribed. Referring to cultures, not to individuals, it emerges from the missionaries' assumption that they were bringing a better civilization, not that they were themselves better. The familiar metaphor of civilization as an overlayer, as a kind of "clothing," depends upon a perceived need to cover up or correct something—an essentially corrupt human nature. "But in these ends of the earth," wrote Daniel Chamberlain during his miserable voyage home in 1823 with an unregenerate captain, "mankind throws off the mask which custom and education seems to compel them to wear in our native country to appear respectable and show[s] the depravity of the human heart in all its turpitude and deformity." The missionaries often referred to themselves as coming from a "privileged" land where they had had a superior education in the form of medical or religious knowledge, or even training in how to keep house. What they saw when they got to Hawaii—windowless houses and naked children—tended to confirm their sense that they needed to pass along such teachings, that the Hawaiians were ignorant of "custom and education." The missionaries observed this lack with a mixture of practical resolve to do something about it, compassion, and, in Lucy's case, implicit self-congratulation. But they avoided callous self-righteousness by realizing that the differences between the two groups were a matter of "privilege" and opportunity, not of racial superiority. In the most fundamental way, they considered themselves no better and no worse than the Hawaiians. Everyone's shared human nature—before it was improved by education and the change of heart that made one a Christian—was the same. For missionary and Hawaiian, for adult and infant, it was corrupted and sinful.[55]

The missionaries' attitudes toward their children—who came into the world naked, with a corrupt nature and a need for proper training—were not far from their attitudes toward Hawaiians. The time-consuming and appealing demands of caring for their own children might be expected to diminish their interest in missionary work. But "vital piety" and "missionary zeal" remained as steadfast as ever. Sybil Bingham, drawing the analogy between her daughter and the little Hawaiian "immortals," realized that she wanted to do something more with her life than present an exemplary domestic scene to the heathen. "As a mother the sweetness, the intelligence, the thousand endearments of my little one," she wrote, "much increases my sympathy for a nation of such little immortals surrounding me, who, unless some other than their own parents care for their souls, *must forever die.*" Just how deeply Mercy Whitney felt the longing to be "up and doing" her Master's work (as she put it in July 1820) is evident from her poignant comments a full year later. She had been continuing the education of one of Asa Thurston's students, reading and explaining the fourteenth and fifteenth chapters of John. "He seemed to be deeply interested & anxious to know the meaning of every word. I have never felt more engaged in the missionary work than in the short time I have spent instructing this heathen youth."[56]

For now, the mothers foresaw no reason why they could not do their duty toward their own children and toward Hawaiians simultaneously. Experience made them conclude otherwise. For now, Sybil could dwell on likenesses, notions of soul and of innate human nature, but in the future the differences, those persistent, repugnant "heathen" habits, would loom larger. Hawaiians paid a price for this in diminished self-esteem. The price the women paid was different, but also high. Convinced that their children needed protection from Hawaiian corruption, they isolated the children. That narrowed their own choices to isolating themselves with the children or sending the children back to New England. Life did not seem to allow them simultaneously to serve Hawaiians and children, but to demand that they choose between them.

But the women's more immediate and obvious concern was how to cope with the increased labor that babies, however delightful, added to their lives. "I cannot easily recount the varieties of labor that have hitherto devolved on the female part of our little band," wrote Sybil Bingham in 1821. When Sophia was about a year old, Sybil sent a summary of a day's labor back to her sisters in order to reassure them that although she labored "under some bodily infirmities," God had not laid her aside from the work:

> "Rise each morning before the sun, if not disturbed in my rest as a nurse during the night. Consider the nursing of Sister M[aria Loomis] and her babe [newborn Amanda] as a primary labor of the week. Superintend the washing and the ironing of her family, with my own —lend my influence in entertaining strangers that may call to this our establishment. Make one visit to the village to call on the queen, some chiefesses, my scholars, etc. Observe how Somoo [Samu, a Tahitian] spends the day. Keep by me and seek the improvement of the new girl, the wife of S[amu]. See that William [Beals] receives some new ideas from books, each day. Have a careful eye to the wants of little Sophia who spends the days at this infant period, in stepping from one kind of mischief to another as fast as her little feet will carry her. Keep up my journal—give some time to the language.["] Which things, together with duties I owe my own soul, seem now necessary to be performed.[57]

As 1821 began, the journals and letters reported an increasing tension between public and private duties and described various arrangements for getting the work done. In Honolulu, Jerusha Chamberlain continued to instruct the Hawaiian children in domestic affairs and to oversee the household in general. Maria Loomis taught "reading and plain sewing" to the "family girls." The school, which Elisha Loomis took over from Sybil Bingham after Sophia's birth, was divided in January 1821 into smaller classes. Asa Thurston continued to teach the two young men he had begun with in Kailua. Elisha took the boys and Sybil the girls, as well as Mary and Daniel Chamberlain and "a native boy" (probably William Beals).[58]

Though Sybil found her general health after Sophia's birth no longer excellent, she was teaching school again in the new year. At first, she simply took Sophia into the classroom with her: "My dear little one hinders me but little in it [teaching school] though from the nature of my employment I indulge her too much, I fear, with a place in or near my arms." Two weeks after this journal entry she added another, explaining that a native woman, who seemed more than ordinarily diligent and sober, had joined the family. "I flatter myself she may eventually lighten some of our labors," Sybil wrote. "She is rather awkward with my child but [I] hope she will relieve my hands some from this pleasant little burden, and do plain sewing which will give me more time for my appropriate work." In Kauai, Mercy Whitney and Nancy Ruggles found it best to alternate the duties of the home and the classroom, switching every three or four months. Writing in August, when she was about to teach the school again, Mercy explained that it was "much more pleasant for one to have the care of the family & the other of the school for several months, than to change frequently."[59]

The fathers sometimes took over "women's" work, mostly when childbirth, exhaustion, or illness demanded it. Both the communal living experience, where everyone tried to share, and the frontier situation, where everyone had to make do, tended to blur the distinction between men's and women's work. But men's help was usually a concession to crisis and not routine. (In the 1830s, when one husband did take on a large share of childcare and domestic work, the mission censured him as a "cumberer.") But the help was much appreciated by the women. When Lucy Thurston became seriously ill after childbirth (in 1821), there was no physician available. "But I was tenderly nursed," she explained. "The ladies at the station were kind, but such were their circumstances that the principal care of the sick room devolved on Mr. Thurston. He was equal to it, even as a mother would have been." In the spring of 1822, when Sybil was coping on Kauai with two newborn babies, three more under eighteen months whose sores were "numerous," one mother (Mercy Whitney) recuperating from childbirth and another (Nancy Ruggles) with "milk fever," she had high praise for Samuel Ruggles's help. Had he not "a talent for being useful in various ways, quite above the ordinary stamp," she acknowledged, "I hardly know how I should do with all this family, this nursery, and these children."[60]

But the care of the children and the household was mostly women's work. The women expressed their frustration in terms of their religious vocation. Since their goal of converting Hawaiians was more important than anything else on earth, it tended to suppress complaints against men or reflections on gender.[61] Besides the personal unity implied by the marriage bond, missionary men and women were united both as apologists for their culture, wanting to share its advantages, and as "rebels" against sin and vice, holding that culture up to its own highest standards. Pitted against fellow expatriates, they held fast to each other.

In many ways, early mission life was atavistic, looking backward to the norms of the eighteenth century, not exemplary of the nineteenth.[62] The communal "family" reflected the homestead rather than the wage earner and his family. The work of women and men was not yet divided by the chasm of the marketplace. With a religious goal to unite them that was larger than any one individual, everyone's work was valued as contributing to the goal. The missionaries did not develop a sense (as reported by historians of American culture) of conflict between the "feminine" values associated with domesticity and Christianity and the "masculine" values encouraged by commercial ventures. Having married men who wanted to uphold rather than discredit religious values, the missionary wives never developed the notion that "women" as a group were the bastions of morality in a troubled and changing world. Men still retained the authority over religion that was theirs in the previous century.[63]

The most important clue to the women's lack of resentment lies in their own attitudes. In a letter written late in 1822, Sybil stated explicitly what everyone seemed to take for granted. The situation was the dividing up of household supplies so that each family could provide for itself for a while, the care of a single communal kitchen having proven too exhausting. "This labor comes principally upon female hands & minds. Sure I was that I could not have the serving of tables or the preparing a way for them to be served, come upon Mr. B. whose hands were more than filled with concerns of a very different kind and who was always satisfied with any manner of living provided it did not [ca]ll him from *his work*."[64]

As the months passed, the Hawaiians in the family responded to the women's training, helping with improved skill. When Jerusha Chamberlain lay ill with dysentery during the summer of 1821, Lucy Thurston took over. "But I have as much assistance from the [Hawaiian] children as I could ask for," she explained:

> The cook is the best *native* help that could be obtained, willing, faithful, & understanding. Still some one must oversee & prepare things to his hand. Then there is Dexter [Chamberlain] to spread the table; William [Beals] to sweep the kitchen & wash dishes; Delia to wipe

> dishes & sift flower [flour]; Isaac to milk & scour knives & table; Towler & Baily to wash taro & potatoes; & Henry to wait on the table & perform little calls during the day. These are their daily occupations besides attending school.

In Kauai that same summer, Mercy Whitney had grudging praise for her helpers: "We have learned the natives so that they assist us considerable," she wrote, as she repeated Lucy's proviso:

> But they still need someone constantly to watch over them or they are apt to neglect some part of their appropriate work. Each one knows what he has to do, & *generally* does it cheerfully. A great part of the hard labor is done by the natives, but still *much* necessarily devolves upon the one who superintends. . . . But I believe our children do as well as we could reasonably expect, considering their habits of indolence in which they have thus far been trained.[65]

So long as everyone stayed healthy, the women could just keep up with the labor. Gradually, reports of exhaustion gave way to reports of illness. Shortly after Sophia's birth in the late fall of 1820, Sybil caught a "severe cold" that gave her "some hours of great pain in every limb" from the rain that leaked steadily through the straw thatching and made the mats "almost rotten." Less than a year later, after giving birth, Lucy Thurston almost died from a "quick consumption." Fortunately, at first the mission babies seemed generally healthy: Maria Whitney at six months was a plump twenty-one pounds, and Sophia Bingham, Sybil reported, had not languished an hour since her birth. The journals of 1821 tell mostly of sick and dying Hawaiian children brought to the mission for healing. But as the months passed, the mission babies claimed their share of ailments—flea-bites, boils, sore eyes. Samuel Whitney seemed almost apologetic in explaining that he was sawing wood for a floor to protect his family from fleas. "I do not wish to amuse or draw pity from my friends by giving them a particular description of our situation in this respect. One instance may serve. . . . A few mornings since Mrs. W. counted 18 on our little babe's upper garment." "My little Levi is becoming quite worrisome," wrote Maria Loomis on June 18, 1821. "He has a pretty severe time getting his teeth." On August 9, Mercy confessed that she did not know what to do for Maria's dysentery: she gave her burnt brandy and loaf sugar, which gave "temporary relief, but it was considerable time before we could say she was much better. Even now she is quite feeble." Just a month and a half short of her first birthday, Maria weighed less than when six months old.[66]

In Honolulu, matters of health reached a temporary nadir during the summer of 1821. Maria Loomis took on the role of nurse not only for her own teething son but for an "orphan" baby whom the missionaries found in the village "covered with sores & reduced by hunger almost to a skeleton": the five-month-old child was the size of a newborn. "I felt as if I could not come away & leave it," she explained. With the mother dead and an indifferent white father off in the mountains cutting sandalwood, the baby's grandmother gave Maria permission to care for it. Over a month later, the child was improved, but Maria was not. The baby had broken her rest every night since she took it in. To make matters worse, as she wrote on June 18, both Captain Chamberlain and Thomas Hopu had severe dysentery. Lucy Thurston described the situation in mid-June, when she was teaching a school of six as well as supervising the "domestic concerns" of the mission family of thirty-six, which included four invalids—"Capt. Chamberlain sick with the dysentery, Mrs. Chamberlain unable even to wait on her husband, the little native babe & Mr. Lovell," a sailor dying of consumption. She continued:

> Our own house being situated at a little distance from the cook house & kitchen, & the almost numberless times I have been obliged to tread the way, multiplied my steps beneath a burning sun. It has indeed brought upon me days of toil & nights of weariness. Yesterday being [school] examination, my labors were increased, & my strength nearly exhausted.

With what must have been relief, she added, "There is a week's vacation. Today Sister B[ingham] takes my place in the family, & I am retired to recruit for further unknown duties." Lucy refrained from mentioning that she was almost six months pregnant at the time.[67]

After taking care of the family for a week in its "afflicted state," Sybil became "quite ill" on the twenty-first of June. In the meantime, on the nineteenth, Jerusha Chamberlain had delivered a baby boy. By the twenty-second, Maria Loomis noted in her journal that she herself had dysentery. On the twenty-third, she reported Hiram Bingham ill and Thomas Hopu dangerously so. By the following month, both Chamberlain parents were down with an illness diagnosed as "cholera morbus," and the consumptive sailor and pitiable orphan baby were dead.[68]

Were this a unique crisis, to be met with reserves of fortitude and good humor, it would be less significant. But the coalescing of illness, exhaustion, and disorder recurred often enough to be more commonplace than extraordinary. Half a year later, in March 1822, when both Mercy Whitney and Nancy Ruggles were expecting a second child, Sybil and Hiram Bingham traveled to Kauai to assist them. Sybil, characteristically understating her trials, called the situation they found there "far from distressing," but even she had to admit, "I think it may be termed perplexing":

> Besides the newborn infant [Mercy's son Samuel] we have in this shallow habitation three little ones, the eldest of whom is not one year and a half old – one mother confined – another expecting every day to be so – her babe [Sarah Ruggles] – though a patient little thing, so afflicted with boils as to require the most careful handling – the eldest babe [Maria Whitney] of the other, when crying, holds its breath so badly that its animal life appears extinct – the eyes of my own dear little daughter which when well sparkle so sweetly, are now so sore that for half an hour or more after she has waked in the morning it is total darkness for her. Besides this we are watching for her eye teeth. . . . My Otaheiton [Tahitian] on which I depend for working has been sick for several days. Withal a group of heathen children are in the midst of us needing care.

Sybil's next sentence would be a non-sequitur in another time and place, but for her and the missionary women like her, it was a logical response. "I cannot be sufficiently thankful for the measure of health I enjoy myself – it is excellent, my mind is saved from anything like gloom, and I never felt that I had more reason to exclaim what shall I render to the Lord for all his benefits."[69]

One important reason for the move from thatched houses into a frame one was the hope that wood floors and improved light and ventilation would produce better health among the family. After working through the spring and summer to build the house, the Chamberlain family moved into one room on August 23, 1821. By

Wood engraving of the mission house and thatched church in 1822. Courtesy Hawaiian Mission Children's Society.

Kawaiahae Bay, the first anchorage of the *Thaddeus,* as seen in 1822 by Daniel Tyerman and George Bennet. From *Voyages and Travels Round the World* (1821–29), London, 1840. Photo courtesy Hawaiian Mission Children's Society.

Thatched missionary houses in 1820. Drawing by Dexter Chamberlain sent to the ABCFM in Boston. From left, the Binghams' house and schoolroom, the Loomises' house, the Chamberlains' house, the storeroom. By permission of the Houghton Library. Photo courtesy Hawaiian Mission Children's Society.

Sketch of the Binghams' thatched house, 1820, showing the division into living quarters (left) and meeting room for church and school. By permission of the Houghton Library. Photo courtesy Hawaiian Mission Children's Society.

The southeastern part of Honolulu in 1826, with palace of Kamehameha III in foreground. Watercolor by an unknown artist. Courtesy Bishop Museum.

Kaahumanu and Hiram Bingham recommending Christianity at Waimea, Oahu, 1826. Engraving by B. F. Childs after a sketch by Hiram Bingham. Courtesy Hawaiian Mission Children's Society.

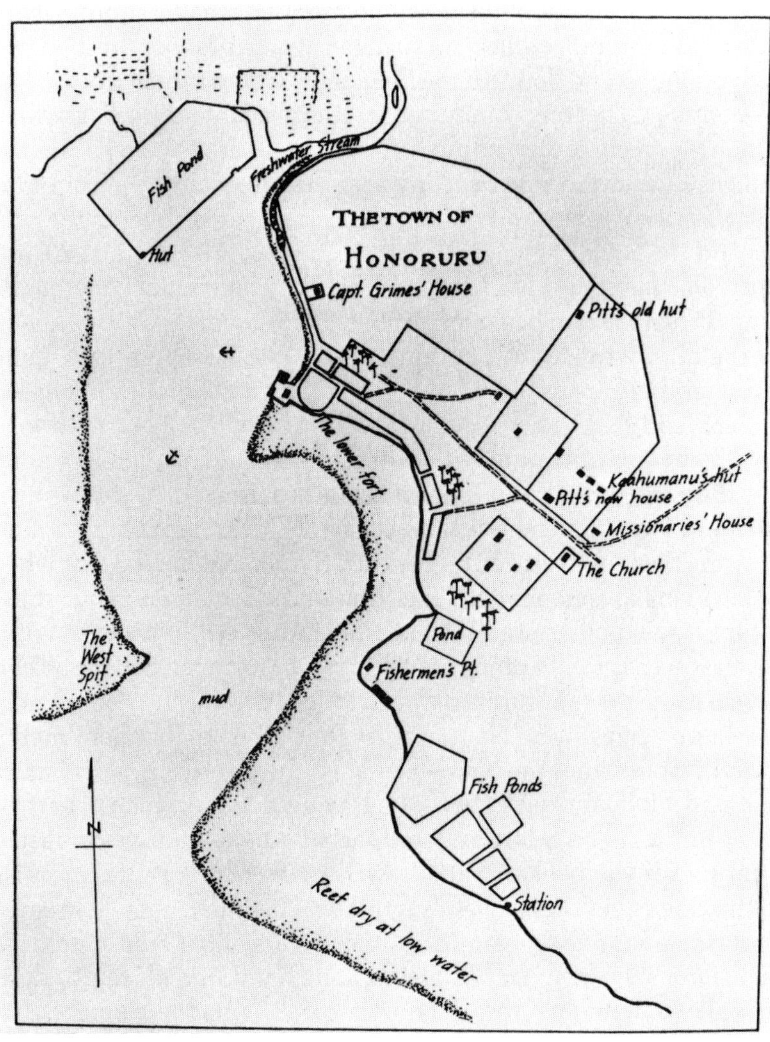

Honolulu in 1825; adapted from map by Lt. C. R. Malden of H.M.S. *Blonde*. Courtesy Hawaiian Historical Society.

mid-October, the Thurstons and Loomises each had a room, which left one room for meetings and social visits. The family finished one room on the second floor for the Binghams, who returned from Kauai in December. The long communal table moved into the cellar, which must have been cooler, though it hardly saved any steps for the women. One immediate benefit was psychological, the effect of familiar square corners and building materials. Tapa covered the ceilings and the studs of the walls, but the final covering was real wallpaper. The family found, however, that they had not conquered the damp. When the rain began in torrents that November, the roof held, but the rain, wrote Maria Loomis, "beats into every crack, & quite a number there are as the sides of our house are neither clapboarded or shingled."[70]

Their ways of coping with domestic trials were often less practical than intellectual. As they had on the *Thaddeus*, the women put mind over matter, relegating trials to their proper place and declaring them outweighed by benefits. Sybil remembered that when she lay ill in November 1820, "the rain pouring down upon our straw cottage, the name of physician nowhere near, still it was not without reason that I felt comparatively few in our wretched earth had the real comforts that surround me. I longed to have my sisters know how happy Sybil was. Never forget that all is of the mere mercy of God." Sometimes the women recalled the old truths, which may have had biblical origins but which were now so much a part of the culture as to be folk wisdom. Maria Loomis, though exhausted in caring for the orphan babe, saw herself living out the promise "as thy day is, so shall thy strength be." At other times, it seemed appropriate for one woman or another to remember admonitions—"this is not your rest" or "whatever your hand findeth to do, do it with all your might"—or to be comforted with the thought that "though affliction may endure for a night, joy cometh in the morning."

Sometimes the theology was more sophisticated. "Look at our divine Example," Sybil counseled her sisters, whose letters told her they had not been reconciled to her departure, "and hear him say, 'Wist ye not that I must be about my Father's business'—hear his gracious words, 'Verily I say unto you, ye which have followed me in the regeneration, when the Son of man shall sit in the throne of his glory, ye also shall appear with him.'—'Ye that have made sacrifices for me shall receive an hundred fold, and shall inherit eternal life.' Attend to this," she told them, "and let us be comforted. And while we look at this let us be ashamed if it has ever been in our hearts to say of any trials—it is more than I can bear."[71]

As if testing Sybil's resolve, the trials continued to pile up. When the Binghams returned from Kauai in the summer of 1822, they joined the Loomises, Chamberlains, and Thurstons (each family with children and infants), eighteen or twenty native children, Thomas Hopu, John Honolii, and Mr. Harwood, a young man from New England who was living with the mission family and repairing watches "for the public good." Three English missionaries, unexpectedly sidetracked to Honolulu on their way to Tahiti, added to the group. Feeding and caring for so many brought on the worst difficulties yet. The women described their labor in terms of how long they could "stand it." The kitchen was in the cellar, with families housed not only in various rooms on the first floor and the single room on the second, but also in the second floor area partitioned with mats. The "burning sun" of June and July beat down upon the unclapboarded frame of the mission house. Maria Loomis superintended the "long table" (to use the women's phrase) until she became seriously ill and was bedridden. Jerusha Chamberlain took over until the demands on her from her husband's severe attack of rheumatism together with one or two sick children and the washing and ironing from the recent voyage to Kauai became too much. Sybil Bingham, although exhausted herself from the difficult voyage home and from the work she had done in Kauai, realized, "There was no alternative—my duty was plain—I went below—stood at the helm and, except a few of the first days of my labor, had the care of seeing that fifty were fed with something, three times a day." That very first day, the Whitneys arrived from Kauai, a seeming godsend of fresh labor, until Mercy's own difficulties became apparent to Sybil: "Being in a new place with two children, who *both* cried *all the time,* I never looked for her out of the chamber." Sybil "stood it thirteen days and hoped to have persevered," but an alarmed Hiram intervened. Daniel Chamberlain (who needed his wife to nurse him) and Maria Loomis were both invalids. Now "Mrs. T.[hurston] took the post—stood it five days and said some other way must be devised." The unconventional solution was to "prevail upon" Mr. Harwood to take over the kitchen for a month, during which time everyone recuperated enough that, as Sybil closed her journal entry, "less difficulty was found in managing, after that."[72]

The solution was short-lived. Maria, somewhat better by the end of the summer and again taking charge of the domestic affairs, had a relapse a few months later. Trying to make soap one day and at the same time move her belongings out of her room so that the floor could be painted, she found for once her "strength unequal to the task." That morning at breakfast the women conferred about a solution. Both Sybil and Lucy had schools that they were reluctant to give up. Although Sybil's health seemed better than usual, she worried whether she would be able to care for the family when her second-floor room meant that "the cellar kitchen must unavoidably cost many a step." "It has been no uncommon thing," Sybil realized, "to give out when endeavoring to maintain that post." Lucy "plainly" declined it. Only one remedy seemed possible: deserting the long table and setting individual ones. This was still not easy, since there was only one cookstove, one small cookroom eight feet square, few cupboards or tables: they would be "as much in each other's way as we could well be in any possibly constructed house." The arduous task of dividing the communal stores into five piles made Sybil write, "Among the many times I have said, *I was tired*, I cannot tell when I was ever more so." Still, the experiment provided relief (until the summer of 1823, when the second company arrived and the long table was again put into service). The benefits of communal eating were lost, but no one seemed to mind. Sybil and Maria each remarked on the pleasure of serving her "own little family."[73]

It is hard to believe that even in their most sentimental moments, the women would have shared Hiram Bingham's view of the "good old long table" in a poem he composed in 1823:

> Convenient and needful, rough, humble and strong,
> Much thronged and admired though homely and long,
> No other can yet with thy loved form compare.
> The short, round or fall-leaf, triangled or square.

Although Sybil readily excused Hiram from domestic labor, citing his "concerns of a very different kind," and although in his book he praises the women's "spirit of self-denial" in their labors for the heathen, his poem glorifies the table as if unaware of its costs. "But rich in resources of magic and skill, / Ennui and low spirits thou canst banish at will." Maria Loomis had a different opinion. While maintaining her good humor and writing that she enjoyed herself "perfectly well," she went on, "but you know we can't be perfectly happy while the *long table* continues. By the way you would think it very broad too did you know how many faults it has to bear; for if anything goes wrong the blame is all laid to the poor table." Within a month, the family literally sawed part of it off.[74]

As the years went on, the "varieties of labor" reached into every corner of the women's lives, frustrating public pleasures like teaching, or private ones, like letter-writing, threatening their good health and their good spirits. Maria Loomis wrote during the summer of 1821 that she was neglecting "almost all" of her sewing and mending, and by 1822 the situation was more serious. Elisha's shirts had "now fallen to pieces or come to mending," she wrote. "He has now six or seven which by mending every time they are worn I hope will last as many weeks. My gowns from being most of them light colored, therefore having to be washed often & by the hands of natives too who know not how to spare them, have several of them been laid aside as past mending." She concluded, "I find when I have charge of the family I can do but little or no sewing; indeed weeks have passed when I have scarcely taken my needle into my hand tho my family were suffering for want of it." Sybil Bingham dressed the two-year-old Sophia in "one plain gong" (as the child called it) and simply ignored the need for pantaloons she had no time to make.[75]

Often the women apologized to their correspondents for writing less frequently than they would have liked. "You must not expect much from my pen," wrote Maria in April 1822, "for I am *almost* oppressed with cares as you may imagine when I tell you our family now consists of about forty." A year later, when a friendly captain was willing to take letters, Maria did not have time to write a single one. "I can hardly find time to write a word in my journal," she added, "much less copy it off." Having uncharacteristically stopped her journal from August 1820 to March 1821, Mercy Whitney began it again by explaining that the "pressure of labor together with the cares of a family sometimes force me to neglect my pen." Sybil Bingham, trying to explain her situation to Mrs. Bates in 1821, protested, "Could you know half the difficulty attendant on my writing, you would say, a little shall satisfy me. I have sent many sheets to America, but I often wonder how they were filled." To Hiram's sisters she apologized: "Could you see me now, hushing my little one to sleep, & at a late hour when the family are retiring to rest, taking up my pen to address you—my disordered eyelids kept up by the aid of one hand, (having for many months often refused to perform their office as the shades of the night drew on) methinks you would be ready to believe that there has been no *willing neglect* in times past.——"[76]

The physical consequences of the labor were obvious. "My little sister," Rev. Tyerman (one of the English visitors from the London Missionary Society) kept telling the petite Maria Loomis, "if you ever mean to be well, let well alone." Yet this advice was "impossible" to take. As a result of Maria's illness during the summer of 1822 and the pressing demands put upon her as soon as she recovered, she was the first woman of the group, though certainly not the last, to reflect, "I have reason to fear that my constitution is essentially injured."[77]

But fatigue and illness were perhaps less "perplexing" (to use Sybil's euphemism) than the effects of all this labor on the spirit. The fatigue the women could accommodate, since this life was not their "rest" to begin with. The emotional cost was higher. Maria, faced with yet another round of domestic superintending in the fall of 1822, realizing she not only had to resign her school but would miss the daily language classes the family was then arranging, finally allowed herself a moment of depression: "I feel unusually sad to day; blame me not if I write in a gloomy strain. Sisters B. & T. are both in a delicate state of health & I feeling as I do like one worn out with fatigue it sometimes affects my spirits & raises molehills into frightful mountains." The briefest touch of bitterness crept into a letter of Mercy Whitney's in 1830, when she was looking back on the toil of the early years—here the work of cutting and making clothes for the Hawaiians: "I never intend to spend month after month again at manual labour for them, as I did for several years after we arrived at the Islands, without even getting *Aloha* many times for it."[78]

The cost of this labor in terms of spiritual intensity was unexpected and perhaps hardest to bear. This was Mercy's peculiar burden in Waimea as the years passed and she and her family were often the only missionaries in the village. Since her husband was often gone all day, visiting and preaching in outlying areas, she was grateful that the king and queen continued to take the role of mother and father to their missionary children. But religious support they could not offer.

When a new church building was dedicated on March 30, 1821, in the presence of a large congregation of *alii* and their attendants, Mercy had a touch of homesickness for "sweet sabbaths" at home. "You can hardly realize the feelings of a solitary missionary, separated from all christian & civilized society, deprived of those inestimable privileges which are attached to the holy sabbath—the preaching of the word, & the blessed ordinance of the Lord's supper," she wrote. After a year in her isolated post on Kauai, Mercy felt that she had sunk into a "cold and lukewarm state. . . . O that it were with me as in days past, when I thought I enjoyed the light of God's countenance & held sweet communion with him. How changed—how lamentable is my condition!" She felt the lack of a Christian community around her and urged her correspondents to "contrast" their "situation and privileges" with hers. "It is not as I once thought, that the missionary has more spiritual enjoyment than others: no; were I to judge from my own feelings I should say it was quite the reverse."[79]

Not too long after landing, in October 1820, Sybil Bingham observed that the "labours, in some respects, have been unlike what I had conceived of missionary work." A few years later, in January 1824, she expanded on the theme:

> I have never been disappointed by finding privation & hardship greater than I had put to my account in anticipation, but I have been disappointed in finding so much apparent necessity for having so much to do with this vain world. I think I was not enthusiastic, supposing myself when saying farewell to many of the eleganc[ies] & parade of life, so taking leave of the world as not to have my hand & thoughts necessarily much engaged in worldly concerns; nor did I suppose my poor heart, so prone to cleave to earth, [would] experience any material change from lowly situation, character or name. No I think it was not so, while yet I did expect the general tenor of my employment to aid in sending my thoughts beyond these lower shores.

The laments, among thousands of words of correspondence in the first few years, are rare. No one ever retracted her commitment to the souls of the Hawaiians. Despite her spiritual trials, Mercy was convinced that her pleasure in teaching the heathen far surpassed "all temporal enjoyments; & so long as I am persuaded the Lord has any work for me to do among them," she concluded, "I think nothing would induce me to leave them to perish in their ignorance and wretchedness." Sybil typically consoled herself with something like this rhetorical question from 1824: "But if satisfied that this part, the nature of this work, and all about it is such as my Divine Master calls me to through his infinite wisdom, and such as I may hope, tho it be remotely, will act on his gracious cause, do I well to be concerned?"[80]

But it still troubled Sybil that her labors seemed to act "remotely," not directly, on the great cause. Although she loved her home, found rewards in serving her new family, and even remarked on her pleasure in bringing Hiram a cup of tea, these domestic or "worldly concerns," however exemplary, did not define the Christian life she had hoped for, where she would be actively spreading the gospel. She and her missionary sisters found themselves worrying about whether or not they would find rice or soap to replace the last in the barrel; their thoughts stayed stubbornly on "these lower shores." They remembered a time when it was easier to "feel" religious. Resentment—as against a husband who labored "directly" for the heathen or as against a woman's lot—is much too strong a word to describe these feelings that were beginning to surface. But there was a quiet undercurrent of struggle to regain something lost. It was not enough, as perhaps for ordinary housewives, simply to live out a respectable lifestyle. Though they had come to Hawaii to be "spent" in service for others, there was something they did ask for themselves. As they went about their daily lives, they wanted to be aware of a constant, reinvigorating sense of God's presence suffusing their entire being. The problem was not even remotely a matter of losing one's faith, but of meeting exceptionally high standards for religiousness, for "vital piety." The greatest discovery so far, given the life they led as missionaries, was how difficult it could be to continue to drink at what Sybil called "the Fountain of all supplies."[81]

4. The Good Fight

> Strive to enter in at the strait gate: for many, I say unto you, will seek to enter in, and shall not be able.
>
> —LUKE 13:24

Late one Sabbath evening, in early March 1821, Sybil Bingham found a moment to sit down and write, explaining, "The calm and pleasant solitude of this evening invites me to my pen." Hiram and the native children of the family had gone out, the other missionaries had retired to their own houses, and Sophia lay sleeping in her cradle. Sybil's lamp shone on the mats that covered the walls, illuminating her few possessions—books, medicines, bed and cradle, and two chairs. "All is stillness" outside this scene of contentment as well, "save the wailing note of heathen sorrow from the distant village. Death has today brought low one of high distinction." This was the *alii* woman Likelike, sedate and pleasant in manner, the wife of Kalanimoku, the prime minister. Maria Loomis mourned her as "beloved Rikarika," one of the mission's promising students, who might have been an "instrument of much good" for her nation. Likelike died from complications after childbirth. Burning with fever, she begged her attendants to carry her to a pond of cooling water, a treatment the missionaries disapproved of, though they were called in only at the end and could offer no other remedy that would save her. Her child, born alive and welcomed with incessant gunfire and explosions right outside the house, had died a few days earlier. The missionaries supposed the commotion had something to do with this.

Having recently endured her own terror of childbirth, Sybil might be expected to sympathize with Likelike as a young mother whose sufferings belonged to "this" world of flesh and blood. But while sympathy was very much on her mind, she expressed her feelings in terms of Christian doctrine: the difference between "heathen" and Christian practices of mourning and the important truth – not understood by Likelike – of judgment coming in the "next" world. "The piercing cry & wretched moans of the poor native," Sybil continued, "has sounded in our ears without cessation since twelve o'clock. O, wretched souls! I think I have never realized their unhappy situation more. How appalling must the King of Terror be to them who have never seen him divested of his sting. How awful the gloom resting upon the grave who know no victory over it!" The heathen wailing was a matter of ignorance, of not knowing how to remove the "sting." And Sybil strengthened her resolve to do something about it. "I do most earnestly desire that we may be able, ere long, to tell these people the great errand of mercy on which we come. It seems sometimes as if it must be long before we could tell them the wonderful things of the gospel in their own tongue."[1]

This small incident, which sets the heathen wail against a tiny oasis of "civilized" quiet, makes a paradigm of missionary-Hawaiian relations after the first year. The missionary compound was on the outskirts of the village. The Hawaiians overwhelmed them by sheer numbers, and Hawaiian culture, though weakened and changed by Western contact, still defined the laws and mores of the land. Defining herself, Sybil might have been speaking for every family member: "stranger as I am in this strange land." Though the missionaries felt assured they knew the "truth," they could not be complacent in it. They did not really need the intrusion of the heathen's piercing wail to remind them of where they were or of what they were up against, to remind them that their only defense was the Lord. The family's voice was like that of one crying in the wilderness, as yet merely preparing the way.[2]

Their descendants, in the last decades of the century would be able to applaud the defeat of paganism, lament the primitive conditions and sacrifices endured by their sainted forebears, and congratulate themselves on upholding a set of ideas by then clearly in the ascendancy.[3] But to the pioneers, just beginning the struggle, the Lord's victory was assured merely in the long run, not immediately. "They [Hawaiians] have indeed thrown away their false Gods," thought Maria Loomis on February 16, "but have not abandoned their vices but still continue in the depths of pollution & sin." As soon as the people realized they would have to forsake their "darling lusts," predicted Elisha, "they will oppose the progress of the gospel."[4]

In part, this distancing from Hawaiian culture was self-imposed, the missionaries recoiling from it out of a sense of superiority. But it is also true that the early missionaries were on the defensive. Their language reflects that vulnerability. Their ornate nineteenth-century prose, like their meticulously elaborated theology, has the potential for setting up a kind of decorative screen between them and the Hawaiians and, in fact, between them and all experience. It is both a way of knowing—in the sense that perceptions are filtered through a linguistic and theological framework—and a way of not knowing. It is a way of keeping unpleasant experiences, like death, at bay. When Maria Loomis referred to Likelike with a formal "thou" and lamented, "Our fond hopes are blasted and with thee mingled with the dust. Farewell! a long farewell," she meant to pay homage with formal and dignified language. But the more ornate the language and the more intricate the doctrine, the farther away Maria and the others can move from simple facts like death or fear about childbirth or physical nakedness.

The language is most ornate at moments of highest emotion—when it is expressing love, or fear, or sorrow. Then the rhetorical flourishes are a way of expressing the emotion's intensity as well as, paradoxically, a means of shying away from the emotion. (Understatement may have the same effect, though it gives the appearance of stating the bald facts. In any case, it is not the women's most characteristic idiom.) Writing about her love for Hiram to her sister and confidante Sophia, Sybil Bingham spoke more freely than most, but even she was bounded by the idiom of the nineteenth century. She imagined her sister's questions: "you would say, Sybil, has *GOD given you the heart of your husband? Has your husband yours?*" Later on, answering her own question, Sybil admitted, "I must say, the hold is stronger than I once thought any object on earth should make." As Sybil continues, her syntax, with its ongoing rush of words, may give some clue to the intensity of her emotions:

> Tho the tender acquaintance of youthful years had not made this object of my affection familiar & dear to me, yet since the memorable evening he was introduced to me, as a missionary going at his mas-

> ter's call solitary to the heathen, so much have I found of every excellence that deserved my highest approbation, that there has not been needed one of the enthusiasms of the days of youth to secure my tenderest love and warmest affection. God did, indeed, in a mysterious manner choose for me, but had he left me to have chosen as I might call it, for myself, I could not have made myself so happy, no I could not have been as happy.[5]

While the other women were less effusive when praising their husbands, they still used decorous, even ceremonial, language. The passion emerges in the flowing syntax or in between the lines. Their habit of language, which is also a habit of mind, did not allow a bald-faced confronting of facts, but preferred circumambulation (a word they might have used) in the form of ornate syntax, ceremonial diction, sentimental attitudes, or euphemism. Hence Sybil wrote of labor in childbirth as "the hour of domestic solicitude . . . a prolonged hour of distress it was." Her new baby she called "another treasure."[6]

Habits of syntax, diction, and rhythm have changed since the early nineteenth century. Sybil's effusiveness may be considered merely as a matter of style, decorative rather than plain, to be judged hesitantly, if at all, on the grounds of one century's taste versus another's. The women's reticence in discussing the most private matters with distant correspondents and their difficulty in finding a way to express deep feeling is defensible. But the conventions they fell back on kept experience at bay. Sexual passion, like the raw pain of grief or the heathen customs surrounding them, was dangerous and needed controlling. More than simply expressing or decorating experience, their language also creates it. Their need for control—whether linguistic, theological, or cultural—is evident in this overly elaborate, even obsessive, prose.

The women write in the received idiom of the time, their habits largely unselfconscious, and what their language reveals about them emerges through the hindsight of a later century. But their sense of vulnerability in relation to the surrounding world comes through as much in everyday ideas and everyday living as in linguistic habits. Here the missionaries did reflect carefully about their relationships with one another, about their sense of themselves as a "family," and about challenges to their unity. Early 1821 found them divided between Waimea on the island of Kauai and Honolulu. Things remained this way until the second company arrived in the summer of 1823. Throughout this time, the missionaries defined themselves in part defensively—by understanding how they were not like the Hawaiians, not like the Holmans, not like the nonmissionary *haoles.*

But it is in a sense their clear understanding of who they were that allowed them to resist who they were not. Their identity rested as always on shared theology and harmonious relationships among themselves (with the obvious exception of the Holmans). Affection among family members was growing, evident when Sybil Bingham entrusted her unborn child to Lucy Thurston, or when Maria Loomis assured Nancy Ruggles (apologizing that she could not attend her confinement in Kauai) that "ever since my first acquaintance with you, I have sincerely loved you." Maria had similar praise when Sybil nursed her after the birth of her daughter Amanda: "She excels in everything that is good, and is I think eminently qualified for a missionary. We have felt particularly united since we first saw each other. I could say a hundred good things, both of her and of the other good sisters." Mercy Whitney's affection for the two Rugleses was tinged with the loneliness she felt at their reassignment to Hawaii in 1823. As Samuel walked toward the beach, she remembered, "I followed him with my eyes till a high stone wall intercepted the prospect & prevented my longer viewing him." Realizing that many years might go by before the Whitneys saw him again, a man "as dear to us as our own brother," Mercy continued, "I shall feel the loss of his wife's society very much—can hardly expect to find in another so much that is amiable, lovely & worthy of imitation."[7]

Marriages seem as sturdy as friendships. The birth of a child usually reminded the couples of their claims to earthly happiness. Samuel Whitney, announcing Maria's birth to his sisters, supposed that they might well envy his state: "Indeed I would not exchange it for any on this side Heaven." When the couples had to separate briefly, as when Samuel Whitney went to comfort the Thurstons that first summer, or when Elisha Loomis left his brand-new family to teach in Hawaii, the wives acknowledged their reluctance to part. When nursed through an illness, they recorded their gratitude. Sometimes the declaration of love is understated. Mercy Whitney, reminiscing in 1832 about the years she and Nancy Ruggles spent in Waimea, recalled how they used to see their husbands at a distance, both of them the same height, wearing similar clothing, and call them the "twin Samuels."[8]

The foundation had to be firm if God, not Satan, was going to triumph. But there were times when it was easier for the family to present a united front than to be united. Their lack of rapport with the Holmans was merely the most public of such problems. By 1821, Sybil acknowledged that she did not find "perfect congeniality" with her fellow workers. "In the school of Christ," the family members all seem to have had the same "Divine Teacher," but "in the school of human affairs, a careful observer would soon discover we had had different teachers." Short tempers, resentments, or quarrelsome words do not enter into the written record (except in chronicling Dr. Holman's accusations). But it is clear that the family could not take its unity for granted.[9]

Periodically, the members gathered together to examine their goals and accomplishments. During services at the close of the year, December 31, they baptized Sophia Bingham and Levi Loomis, held communion, and reflected that in 1820 they had safely crossed two oceans and had been "allowed to take up a quiet residence." Services the next month were less pleasant. A meeting for "prayer and consultation" over the Holmans was called on January 15. The vote for censure was unanimous, but exacted a price. "This subject is too painful to dwell on," wrote Maria Loomis. "It is deeply felt by every member of the family. I believe none of us slept much last night." That Sunday, Hiram Bingham cited II Thessalonians 3:6: "Now we command you, brethren, in the name of our Lord Jesus Christ, that ye withdraw yourselves from every brother that walketh disorderly, and not after the tradition which he received of us." The repercussions reached Kauai, where the Holmans were staying while Lucia awaited childbirth. Determined to follow rules, not bend them, Samuel Whitney refused to eat with an excommunicated person: "It has laid us under new and peculiar trials but I am resolved not to violate conscience, and I think the word of God for the sake of inconvenience." The greatest suffering seems to have fallen not on the unrepentant Holmans, but on Lucia's brother, Samuel Ruggles. "The fraternal affection of my associate Ruggles is so strong," wrote Samuel Whitney, "I can hardly speak to him on the subject. It has long preyed upon his slender frame, etc. that I have sometimes feared the consequences." Samuel Ruggles acted "the part of a Christian," but by June, when the Holmans returned to Honolulu looking for a passage home, he and Nancy joined them, hoping to improve his health. Samuel Whitney predicted that when the story was printed up for the public, it would "fill New England with tears."[10]

A long and prolix letter of explanation, interwoven with copies of letters as evidence, was signed by Hiram Bingham and Asa Thurston and dated February 15, 1821. They put the emphasis not on their excommunicating Holman but on his leaving them—his "defection"—which subjected the family to the "pain & mortification of putting our unwilling hands to the work of cutting off the right hand of the mission as to Medical aid, in this land of dangers, darkness, & disease,—and then to present ourselves maimed & bleeding before our sympathising friends." They likened Holman to St. Peter, with the important difference that Peter, having denied his Master three times, repented. The next day, February 16, the family spent in fasting, humiliation, and prayer, beginning with an assembly at 10 a.m. The women did not specifically link this occasion to their recent decision about the Holmans, but they were clearly taking time off to pull themselves together. The success of the mission began with the spiritual health of each individual: "It was proposed that we inquire seriously with ourselves what ought we to confess before God—what ought we to deplore—what to abhor in ourselves—what to acknowledge with gratitude as received from God—and what ought we to pray for?" In the evening, they returned as a group to be reminded of the "great object" of the mission and "the vast importance of having our loins girded & standing in readiness should we be called to combat with the powers of darkness." Sybil and Maria reported the exhortations in almost exactly the same words—that they should live under a "habitual sense" of their dependence upon God, keeping in mind both the "greatness" of their work and the "wiles" of the Enemy.[11]

The strain began to show in the women's lives, though Sybil did no more than allude to difficulties in her private journal. She was pleased on March 18 that the events of the last weeks had "brought the hearts of this female band into closer union. I have felt & wept over the coldness that seemed creeping upon us." The problem, as she saw it, remembering Jesus' commandment to love one another (Matthew 19:19), had been "how to exercise that love in the case of each individual." It had caused her "many a groan" during the past months. On the thirty-first, encouraged, she recorded an evening spent with the sisters (Jerusha Chamberlain, Maria Loomis, and Lucy Thurston were then in Honolulu) "in free conversation & social prayer." This had been only the second such meeting since landing, and Sybil thought they had been "less happy" with one another as a result. When Lucia Holman finally left on October 2, 1821, the recipient of a great variety of presents from the mission's detractors, "in excellent spirits" and seemingly "insensible to the injury she had done and is still doing to the cause of Christ," the women were hard pressed to feel gracious. As Maria Loomis admitted, "We cannot say we are sorry to have them leave these shores."[12]

The biblical commandment to love one another contains a qualifier: as thyself. For Calvinists, raised on an assumption of personal sinfulness, in the deepest places besieged by doubts, that love came hard. The mission's enemies lay within as well as without. In her private journal that January, Sybil Bingham thought in terms of the "deceitful world," which she would defy: "But O, again, *this wicked heart*. . . . O, at last, for Jesus sake let my . . . guilty soul, rest with thee." Put more succinctly, in her words that summer, "I am a sinner." Although she continued, "but blessed be God for the hope that I am 'a sinner saved by grace,'" that hope could never be anything more. Her religion also asked her to live with uncertainty about this. Writing to her sister Sophia with the comforting thought that their earthly separation was short and that their weary feet would soon find "the inn of 'lasting rest,'" she cautioned:

> Let us remember, *if children of GOD.* O, to know we are! Is not that a concern of sufficient weight to bear down every earthly consideration, even that so near our heart—our separation? I have a comfortable hope. But I long to strive more earnestly to make my calling & election sure—I do desire in all holy conversation & godliness, to be looking for & hastening unto the coming of the day of GOD.

Given the shifting grounds of human unworthiness in the face of God's absolute power, with election never sure, Sybil's faith had constantly to be examined and renewed.[13]

In pursuing their work with such energy and zeal, the missionaries become vulnerable to the charge that they saw no difference between "preaching" the gospel (the biblical command) and imposing it. Public zeal might have been tempered by their remembering Christ's injunction that the one without sin should cast the first stone. Such restraint was rare.[14] It was not quite what they meant by "compassion for the perishing heathen," since they tended to assume a lack of knowledge to be remedied, not a set of customs to be forgiven. But since the heathen could not be expected to know any better, they still merited more respect and patience than the missionaries' fellow Westerners. Toward these recalcitrants, the missionaries' behavior looked not only as if they were forgetting the Jesus who saved the adulteress, but as if they were remembering the Jesus who threw the money-changers out of the temple. Private awareness of human frailty contrasted with the mission's public face of assured truth. This public face was responsible for heightening tensions between the missionaries and their detractors, who reacted to the face they could see.

Not caring about biblical analogues but having their own reasons, many expatriates simply wanted the missionaries gone. Like the Hawaiians who celebrated when the *kapus* were abolished, they remembered only the oppression and encumbrances of codes of behavior they thought they had left behind. Living outside the reach of church and state, they wanted to stay there. Seeing the missionaries encouraging "upright lives," wrote Kamakau, they correctly predicted that "there would be no more good times for them." Some of Liholiho's advisors, jealous and skeptical from the time of the landing negotiations, continued to make Liholiho fear a political takeover. Traders and merchants had businesses to protect and something to fear from missionaries who could tell the chiefs the fair prices for foreign merchandise or warn them against the liquor so freely offered during business discussions. In the spring of 1821, in an incident that foreshadowed greater violence to come, a seaman turned against Thomas Hopu "with unprovoked fury," attacking him with a pair of large tailor's shears and "threatening to cut his soul out." Within a year, Lucy Thurston learned to decry a "clique of foreigners whose interest and influence it was to have the reign of darkness continue, and who opposed the missionaries with all their power."[15]

The rapport of the first summer, when Lucy had written, "God bless mariners," thinking them the "links that connect us to the fatherland," was not entirely lost. Many foreigners continued to support the mission with words and acts of kindness. Throughout the early years, the women recorded presents of scarce and expensive supplies from merchants and seamen: a barrel of rice came when Sybil was down to the last quart, a barrel of soap when she was washing with the very last piece. (At $50 a barrel, the cost of soap was prohibitive, and without wood for ashes, the women could not make it.) On a single day in 1820, the mission's journal records gifts from captains and merchants of sixteen gallons of oil, six pounds of spermaceti candles, two and a half bushels of dried apples, several pounds of tea, a barrel of fish, and a cord of wood. The mission houses were always open to friendly captains, who often called when they were in port. In the spring of 1821, five whaling captains, taking tea at the mission, proposed that the women draw up a list of needed items to be circulated among the ladies of Nantucket and New Bedford.[16]

Nevertheless, even during the early days of good will, the missionaries had reason to be wary. Daniel Chamberlain predicted almost immediately after landing, on July 4, 1820, that the "greatest obstacle in the way of conversation [converting] or christianizing this people, appears to be, the bad example of the white people." The "*Thaddeus* Journal" of April 4, 1821, telling about the incident with the tailor's shears, concluded that "the practice of discharging and putting ashore turbulent seamen on these islands must have a most pernicious effect on the people in retarding the progress of the gospel." If anything, as time passed, conditions worsened. "Were it in my power to describe to you one tenth part of the iniquity and filth there is practiced you would stare with horror and amazement," wrote Maria Loomis a year later. "The village is almost overrun with runaway sailors. Almost every vessel that touches here leaves one or two." When a "wild uproar" in the village, caused by "the shameless conduct of intoxicated white men," confronted Sybil and Hiram one day, she associated the place with "the guilty streets of Sodom."[17]

One major culprit was rum, introduced as early as 1791. In 1809 Oliver Holmes showed the Hawaiians how to distill it themselves. The Hawaiians had always made an intoxicating drink from the plant *awa*, which they used in religious ceremonies or in medicinal procedures for losing weight, but its effects included nausea and vomiting, scaling of the skin (when drunk in quantity), and stupor. Rum was an improvement. Everyone—commoners as well as *alii*—

tried it. "They almost bathed in it," added the disapproving historian Samuel Kamakau.[18]

The legacy of rum went beyond personal drunkenness to political and economic difficulties. Though Liholiho "moved among his subjects with all the nobility of a king," he liked his drink and often, under the stress of governing in a difficult time, gave himself up to its pleasures. Calculating foreigners and chiefs "strove to lead Liholiho to drink more heavily," explained Kamakau, "and when he was drunk, they would run him into debt and sell him, not small lengths, but many bolts of cloth, and charge the goods to his name." The king owed money for several ships, schooners, and brigs, some of which were not seaworthy. Unneeded cloth often burned or rotted in warehouses. Chiefs turned in their debts for ships and cloth and miscellaneous other goods to Liholiho. Encouraging the sales were shrewd Yankee traders, who knew an open market when they saw one.[19]

There was hardly enough sandalwood in all of Hawaii to pay the bill. Cutting it required hard labor in the mountains, where the effects of insufficient food and cold air on men who wore only a *malo* were severe enough to cause deaths. Kamehameha I, observing this, had limited the cutting and put a *kapu* on the young trees. But Liholiho, who lost his father's monopoly, allowed the forests to be denuded. By 1826, after little more than a decade and a half of serious trading, the debts were high enough (about $150,000) for the United States to send two warships to support its commercial interests and negotiate a plan for payment. Although the trade was diminished by 1829, the various notes were not paid off until 1843.[20]

The king's drinking habits, which Lucy Thurston observed in Kailua during the fall of 1820, became a matter of common record for dismayed missionaries. Summing up the previous year in September 1821, Sybil Bingham reported that Liholiho, his wives, and attendants had spent most of the time passing from island to island, often making the decision to board one of Liholiho's recently purchased vessels "in a fit of intoxication." During the night of February 3, 1821, the family in Honolulu awoke to the noise of cannons firing at sea and being answered by the guns of the fort; as the bright flashes lit up the dark sky, the king made his "sublime" entrance into the harbor. When Hiram Bingham and Asa Thurston called to pay their respects that morning, they found Liholiho sleeping off the effects of his celebration "in a slumbering paroxysm of intoxication." They called again, but were still too early. With royal composure, Kamamalu lifted his "nerveless hand" for him, "that he might receive the missionaries' friendly 'Aloha'." Soon after, Kalanimoku, making a friendly visit to the mission houses, apologetically refused breakfast in order to get back to the king, who might take advantage of his absence to drink. Francisco Marin, recording the king's activities in his own journal, began to find it easier to mark the days the king was not drinking. Though "uniformly kind" to the family, the king clearly found that the word of God they could offer was no match for the drink of the sailors. While receiving a group from the mission one September evening, telling them they were all good, Liholiho received an invitation to drink rum with a Captain Turner. He left immediately.[21]

When Hiram Bingham, in March 1821, urged Liholiho to drink less, the king promptly replied, "By and by, by and by, not now." Part of the pathos of Liholiho's story comes from his ineffectual efforts to change himself. A month after this dismissal, a determined Liholiho remarked, "Suppose you give me glass rum in one hand $4000 other hand – suppose you tell me – suppose I drink that glass rum, you give me that $4000 I no drink it. Suppose you say, you'll kill me I no drink it – I no drink it." Sybil thought the king had a "naturally pleasant disposition, but so sunk is he in vice that no human power can raise him." The events of the next months seemed to bear her out. In March 1822, the king received his greatest scare from rum. Crowds of his subjects, thinking he was dying, set up a great wail as they passed outside the mission houses on their way to Waikiki. Hiram Bingham, quickly investigating, found the king suffering from drunken "fits" (with symptoms of reddened skin, rigid muscles, convulsion, and bleeding at the mouth). With medicine and nursing through the night and for two weeks afterward, Liholiho recovered (though in the meantime, "partially deranged," he amused himself by picking up straws and handing them about). He allowed the missionaries to give thanks to God, but his essential attitude had not changed. The following year, in a celebrated comment, Liholiho once again responded to Hiram's exhortations to repent with a plea for time: "Give me five years more, and I will become a good man!"[22]

The king's resistance was important because it set a precedent for the rest of his subjects. While the missionaries believed that the soul of a king was no different from and no better than that of a commoner, they also understood the practical truth that if the monarch and the *alii* accepted Jesus, the masses would follow them. In September 1821, after a year and a half of work, a frustrated Sybil Bingham realized that although they had "access to the heathen of every rank & age, & of both sexes," they were facing nonchalance and indifference:

> The common people appear to hear us gladly but are nevertheless content with telling us that when the king & chief, shall say, they will all attend & understand; these again hear our message & answer, '*Mite*' [*maikai;* good] but wallowing in the depths of sensual indulgence, chill our operations with the spirit of Felix's cold reply to Paul, 'go thy way for this time, when I have a convenient season I will call for thee.' [Acts 24:25]

By January 1822, it was still not a "convenient season" for most of the chiefs. On Saturdays, the missionaries found it necessary to remind the people of worship coming the next day; sometimes they tried to round up the *alii* on Sunday morning. "I am tipsy," the king said one Sunday, "and it is not right to go to church drunk; when I have got through, I will come." "Adams" Kuakini (governor of Hawaii, 1820–1845) remarked that he would attend when the king did. Kalanimoku, wanting to gamble, delivered an excuse even Hiram Bingham had to admit was courtly: "I have business and cannot go – my heart will be with you, though my body is here."[23]

Resistance from the *haoles* took various forms, not always polite. One "gentleman" attending a service in 1821, after "muttering out some restless feelings," left, saying to Sybil Bingham, "You will all go to heaven, no doubt of it." Noticing her fellow countrymen "laboring, trading, and sailing on the water" on a Sunday, Mercy Whitney was indignant: "What an example for those who come from a Christian country to act before the Heathen!" Perhaps more often than got into the record, the church services were disrupted by casual chatter or deliberate mischief. In June 1821, some of Kaahumanu's men talked loudly of the report that the newly dug cellar of the frame house would contain guns and powder for taking over the island.

Captain Davis, the often inebriated "husband" of Hannah Holmes and no friend to Hiram Bingham (whom he accused of wanting Hannah to marry Thomas Hopu), once "boldly" entered the church, where he took a seat near the king, laid his head in the king's lap, and began a conversation. On another occasion in 1822, when the missionaries barred the door to him, Mercy thought his violent beatings upon it would "burst it in." The "oaths & imprecations" of his speech, she remembered, "created such a terror in my mind, lest he should be struck dead on the spot, as I shall not soon forget." (Captain Davis died later that year.) Preaching against drunkenness, Asa Thurston provoked a Captain Porter to leave, "muttering curses . . . threatening to set fire to the house."[24]

As the charming and indignant Holmans spread their side of the story during periodic visits to Honolulu, they gathered around them a group of sympathizers. The day before the Holmans left for good, Captain Davis, John Coffin Jones (commercial agent for the United States), and a Mr. Bullard stopped Daniel Chamberlain in the village to rail against the mission's decree of excommunication: "Dr. H[olman] was a man of college education and was he to be tried by ignorant shoemakers, farmers &c.? Mr. Bingham was a scoundrel – d—n such religion as his." The doctor, they thought, could prosecute the Board and win. When pressed, the accusers declared the fuss was over Mrs. Holman's eating a few oranges and the doctor's not coming to Oahu when expected. The missionaries reported that they were reviled by ignorant men. Resentment was fueled equally by the price of sandalwood, pronouncements against adultery, and even personal dislike of Hiram Bingham. (Bingham had told one of the Hawaiian girls living in the mission family that she was wrong to go to live with Captain Suiter.) Shortly afterward, Captain Davis, predicting to Liholiho that the missionaries would multiply and take over the islands after all, proposed a kind of monument to his opposition – a second meeting house where he and Mr. Jones would take turns reading sermons. Undaunted by the possibility of an "American consul and a drunken sea captain" acting as ministers, the missionaries declared they would fear them no more than Elijah did the prophets of Baal (I Kings 18:40).[25]

Christian protest against fornication (which some captains preferred to call taking "temporary wives") provoked the most furious and lasting opposition. The wisdom of the Bible's prohibitions seemed confirmed by rampant venereal disease, but that did not matter to shiploads of men enduring hellish passages through the Pacific. The year 1819 marked not only the ominous events of Kamehameha's death and the departure of the *Thaddeus*, but the beginning of whaling in the Pacific. Soon after, every spring and fall, the ships crowded into the ports of Honolulu and Lahaina. As early as January 12, 1821, Elisha Loomis counted 10 sails in Honolulu's harbor, seven of which were American; by the latter years of the decade, over 140 whalers visited every year. These newest arrivals rarely had the scruples of young Whitney or Ruggles when offered a woman's company. When Captain Masters of the *Tamoree* visited the Whitneys in June 1821, Samuel welcomed him as "the second capt. out of 22 whom I have known since my residence on these isles who has not taken a native wife!" Everyone except the missionaries understood that you hung up your conscience as you rounded Cape Horn; the Sandwich Islands were not the United States. Here was a kind of hypocrisy shared and defended by captains and crews alike. The missionaries, lacking any such double-vision for vice, saw no shadowy areas where morality mingled with physical necessity. Their view of adultery was that "thou shalt not commit it."[26]

One afternoon during what began as a particularly convivial tea, a Captain "D" accused Captain "E" of hypocritically taking the role of a deacon in America—"on sacramental occasions, carrying around a silver platter"—while behaving no better than the rest of "us poor sinners" in Honolulu. (Captain "D" excused his own behavior, presumably just as "sinful," on the grounds that he paid no homage to God to begin with.) Captain "E," wrote Lucy Thurston knowingly, "knew where the remark fitted." Not content with watching the man's embarrassment, the missionaries followed up with a letter admonishing this "standard bearer of the church" for plunging its banner in "the slimy mire of the streets," and suggesting that his church at home ought to know this. Not long after, reported Lucy, the shamed man burst into a missionary's bedroom (presumably Bingham's), crying, "Apologize for that letter, or I'll kill you."[27]

The incident demonstrates the typical intransigence of the missionaries, not simply in defining "moral" behavior but in enforcing it. Though they fought with words against the sailors' fists, they were often at no disadvantage. Seeing themselves under the aspect of martial imagery—fighting the good fight of faith in their individual lives and fighting against Satan's kingdom in Hawaii—they by no means shrank from confrontations and won enough of them to feel encouraged. Sybil reflected in a letter of 1822 on the "multitudes of Satan's emissaries begotten from the east & the west & the north & the south as if to muster their forces to protract the long & awful revolt of this perishing people, from the King of Heaven." Encouraging herself in the face of such enemies, she continued, "Our hearts must not sink or be discouraged. . . . As Gideon's three hundred with their pitchers & their lamps we go forth against the mighty, but trusting in the same glorious Arm we shall shout like victory."[28]

This stalwart pose could not prevent defeat when the missionaries tried to make a voyage to Tahiti in the summer of 1821. The Hawaiian language proving difficult to learn and reduce to writing, they wanted to take advantage of the work and publications already accomplished in a similar culture by English missionaries. Kaumualii, who intended to send a ship in that direction, offered passage. The Binghams sailed for Tahiti (via Kauai) in early July. But the outrage of influential captains and nervous traders followed them. Commercial Agent Jones summarized their objections for Bingham: that a mission from so young a country as America would lose face by applying to the British for aid; that it was unwise to be under so great an obligation to Kaumualii; and that the two languages were so dissimilar that Tahitian publications would be of no use. The missionaries could think of other reasons. The traders (they surmised) did not want the true state of Christian success in Tahiti reported back to Honolulu, knowing as they did that as Christianity spread, it would "check [the] unrestrained indulgence of fleshly desires" and lower the price of sandalwood. The debts owed by Kaumualii to various traders put the final pressure on the chief to cancel the trip. That fall, the Binghams reluctantly returned from Kauai to Honolulu.[29]

The following spring (1822), animosity from captains and sailors again blocked the Binghams' efforts to obtain passage, this time from Honolulu to Waimea. The frustrated couple tried to appeal to the mariners' "humanity," since the errand was not directly concerned with the great cause of spreading the gospel, but with the imminent confinements of Mercy Whitney and Nancy Ruggles, each expecting a second child. Sybil's journal from February 16 to March 15 describes her discouragement as at least ten vessels—American and

English whaleships, native brigs and schooners—reached the harbor and for one reason or another declined to take the couple, even when they offered fifty dollars. "O, our poor afflicted sisters!" wrote Sybil on February 25, "the hour of danger with them both is now within a very few days. No physician, no mother, no sister or nurse with them in this strange land!" The commander of one of the native vessels confirmed what the missionaries already knew: "White men oppose the missionaries." Sybil added, "It is through their influence that this thing is. We have the fullest evidence that measures were taken to draw Capt. Lawson from the engagement which he so promptly made in his first landing." Fortunately, young Samuel Whitney waited until March 18 to be born, two days after the Binghams arrived. The birth of Huldah Ruggles followed on April 10.[30]

Jesus' words to his disciples provided some comfort for these tight situations: blessed are those who are reviled and persecuted for my sake; fear not if the world hates you, for it hated me before it hated you. Thus girded in their own minds, the missionaries could defy, though not eliminate, the criticism. But they needed to gain the Hawaiians' trust. Clearly the missionaries were different from the frequenters of beaches and grogshops, but whether they brought anything as useful as shipbuilding skills or trade goods was open to question.

That fall they were able to demonstrate their good will toward England by nursing a British sailor whose arm had to be amputated when a cannon misfired. Looking back half a year later, the event appeared as a "blessing" designed to silence the rumors of hostility between the two nations, which had almost prevented their getting permission to land. The mission's public image improved again when a Hawaiian returning from the United States with marvelous tales of wealth assured Liholiho that Americans who had everything they needed in their own country had no reason to take over his. During the spring of 1821, the Hawaiians had enough confidence in the missionaries to disbelieve the rumor that guns and ammunition would be stored in the cellar of the frame house.[31]

Perhaps the most encouraging sign of acceptance was Liholiho's permission to build the wood-frame house. The prefabricated pieces, which had arrived Christmas Day of 1820, sat in Boki's yard for almost two months (somewhat protected from pilfering), while the family waited on Liholiho. Although the mission house would not be the first frame house in the islands (Kamehameha I had built one in 1810, followed by Mr. Marin, the sandalwood trader Captain Winship, and other traders), it would be an exception to the great king's rule that foreigners could not build permanent houses. Not surprisingly, Liholiho's first response on February 5 was an emphatic no. Trying again later, the missionaries explained that the women (Sybil Bingham in particular), unaccustomed to working and sleeping on the damp floors of native houses, were becoming ill. As Lucy Thurston told the story, "One of the ladies" (herself) returned alone to the king while the other missionaries were leaving, making the argument on behalf of the women as best she could in "feeble, broken" Hawaiian. Now the king said, "Yes, build." Sixty years later, Lucy was willing to claim credit in print, but at the time she thought that she should "let the king be a king" and seem to make his own spontaneous decision. She also deferred to male ego, having "too much sympathy and reverence for the leading missionaries to drop a word to show that *her* prayer before the throne had been more availing than theirs." "A few days later," wrote Lucy, the king announced his permission for the missionaries to build the house as well as to remain in the islands past the original one year.[32]

As Lucy understood it, her success argued once again for the women's special and useful role as missionaries. Their very presence, vouching for the mission's pacific and domestic intentions, had already helped secure the original permission to land. And as Lucy retorted to one captain who thought that ladies ought not to be subjected to the trials of a heathen land, the women had secured "a footing" for their husbands, whose enemies would have driven them out were it not that they "respected the feelings of the ladies." While Lucy defended the women's importance to the mission, she also, with her secretive success, confirmed their self-image as helpmates for the men, as if the mission's success depended upon the public illusion of male authority.[33]

Samuel Kamakau, wanting to preserve the distinction between the Hawaiians and the troublemaking foreigners, wrote that "from Hawaii to Kauai, the chiefs and people received them [the missionaries] as friends. No people could have treated them more kindly. No one begrudged their coming, grumbled, spoke unkindly of them, or raised any trouble, but all dwelt with them in peace."[34] This speaks well for the Hawaiian tradition of hospitality, but Kamakau (in his eagerness to defend his teachers) overstated the case. While Hawaiian resentment certainly differed from that of the traders, it was there. The Hawaiians did not have to quarrel to resist the missionaries; they had only to be themselves. In a sense, it was easier for the missionaries to cope with their fellow Westerners, with whom the battle lines were clearly drawn and mutually understood, than with the Hawaiians, whose language they were struggling to speak and whose culture they were only beginning to observe.

The Hawaiians simply went about their lives, wearing the *malo* and *pau*, cultivating taro, dancing the hula, wailing over their dead, swimming out to the ships, and amusing themselves with dozens of sports and games like surfing, canoe racing, *holua* sledding down stone-paved courses, and boxing, often betting on the outcome. At all this, the missionaries pulled a long face.[35]

The first schools they established met serious competition from the hula, which had its own strenuous training in *halaus*, or companies. At about the time the second quarterly examinations were held (December 14, 1820), with both Hannah Holmes and William Beals earning Bibles for their achievements, Hannah and several other scholars began to be called away to practice the hula. They had to be *akamai* (expert) in time to celebrate two expected events: Liholiho's arrival and the birth of Likelike and Kalanimoku's child. Permission not to dance had to come from Boki, who gave it very reluctantly. It was as if the Hawaiians considered the *palapala* just another status symbol reserved for *alii* and *haoles*, an exotic diversion not that different from the card games the queens were so fond of. Against the mission school's enrollment of 30 or so scholars, the hula could command hundreds of dancers (270 at a December dance) and an audience of thousands. Though the scholars at the mission school were torn between their reading and their dancing, they could not easily defy the chiefs.

The missionaries had their own dilemma, a "peculiar situation" as they called it: "We have hardly thought it prudent to advise our pupils on this very delicate subject, as it is obvious that some of the enemies of our religion are seeking an occasion and would be glad to say that we were interfering with the affairs of the chiefs and opposing the orders of the government." But Hiram Bingham began an oblique offensive by preaching from Romans 13:1 ("Let every soul be subject unto the higher powers. For there is no power but of God"), explaining the importance to rulers of knowing the laws of God and keeping his moral covenant. Unable to leave heathen customs alone, Hiram led a foray to change them, not—as with the *palapala*—by adding something new to the culture, but by trying to eliminate one of its strongholds. Going on the offensive, he demonstrates how the stereotype of the pleasure-hating, impositional missionary took root.[36]

On December 20, Hiram watched a hula that had been going on for eight or ten days and would continue intermittently for several months. It looked suspiciously like a kind of idolatry. At the gate of the yard near Boki's house, where the hulas were held, stood an enclosure that held a small piece of wood draped in tapa and leaves. This was the *akua* of the hula, a goddess named Laka. As the dancers left, they piled on their decorations until it was covered with leaves and greenery. When asked why the Hawaiians had such a god, the answer was a single word, "*pone*," or "play," not something Hiram understood. Immediately he asked Governor Boki to remove the "image of abomination" and was told he could have it when the hula was over. Hiram had to content himself with trying to persuade the rulers to prohibit the hula on the Sabbath or at least to excuse the mission scholars on that day. Boki agreed to allow the scholars to attend school during the day if they danced morning and evening—not much of a concession, since those times were traditional for hula.[37]

Maria Loomis, her curiosity aroused, went along with her husband to watch in late January. It "consists principally of singing and corresponding gestures made in public," she observed:

> The dancers are arranged in several long rows; and tho there are two or three hundred of them yet each one is independent of the rest. And tho they move back and forth, to the right and left, and turn one way to the other, yet no one interferes with his neighbor or changes his place. They are composed of a mixed multitude of men, women and children both of chiefs and common people. The musicians who, besides singing, beat with a small stick upon a large one, with much force and exactness, [and] measure time by stamping upon a piece of wood placed on the ground, stand in a row behind the dancers. The whole company wear wreaths upon their shoulders and legs.

> Having satisfied our curiosity we withdrew, feeling that this place had no charms for us. We hope the time is not far distant when we shall see them engaged in more noble employment.

Maria's generalized description and her quick withdrawal from the scene give some idea of the powerful censorship operating in her mind. But at a later dance, which impressed her and Elisha as "splendid," she responded to the "regularity & order" of the event. The pageantry was impressive: the young Nahienaena (daughter of Kamehameha I and Keopuolani, and sister to Liholiho) was carried in and placed in front of the spectators—all the high chiefs and chiefesses and about two thousand commoners. One hundred soldiers in front of the crowd filed off as three young women began their dancing; a dozen men in American regimental uniforms paraded about the enclosure. But once again, after about a half an hour, the group from the mission withdrew, "feeling more than ever that we are surrounded by the heathen."[38]

The missionaries made little effort to understand this ancient art, "folly" to them. Stubbornly seeing value in nonmaterial ways, they branded the hula as one of the "transitory trifles of time" that drew attention away from "those spiritual and eternal things which belong to their [Hawaiians'] everlasting peace." The argument that the hula gave pleasure, created beauty, and combined the poetry of the *mele* (chant) and the movement of the dancers into a great artistic expression did not reach them. Hiram Bingham, describing the dancers as "often fantastically decorated with figured or colored *kapa* [tapa], green leaves, fresh flowers, braided hair, and sometimes with a gaiter on the ancle, set with hundreds of dog's teeth," ended with the crucial qualifier: "Notwithstanding their decorations, much of the person is uncovered." He concluded that the hulas "were designed to promote lasciviousness, and of course the practice of them could not flourish in modest communities."[39]

Once again the missionaries posed themselves against other foreigners, who did appreciate bright yellow tapa, the clattering of dogs' teeth at the ankles, the yellow-green of ferns or the fragrance of *maile* in leis, the extreme grace and fluidity of movement. Adelbert de Chamisso, aboard the Russian ship *Rurick* in 1816, thought that "the ungraceful contortions that we admire in our dances under the name of ballet . . . pale in comparison." In a performance of March 1794 in Waimea, about two hundred women impressed Captain George Vancouver with such "perfect unison of voice and action, that it were impossible, even to the bend of a finger, to have discerned the least variation." At one point, as the dancers fell down and covered themselves with their garments, he thought they conveyed "in some measure, the idea of a boisterous ocean becoming suddenly tranquillized by an instant calm." A botanist on the same expedition, Archibald Menzies, watched a single young girl dancing: "Every joint of her limbs, every finger of her hand, every muscle of her body, partook unitedly of the varied sympathetic impulses, while the motion of her eyes transferring their transient glances and the harmony of her features were beyond description."[40]

From these first enraptured accounts and from the later work of scholars and sympathizers, it is possible to get a sense of what the missionaries were missing. The various *halaus* where dancers were trained by a *kumu hula* (master teacher) made up part of the court society of a chief. The training was arduous, accompanied by strict standards for personal cleanliness and many restrictions—on certain foods like sugar cane, taro-tops, squid; on braiding hair, which must fall free; on sexual intercourse. The *halau* isolated itself; no one could enter without chanting a password. Students learned prayer chants (*olioli*) to Laka, the patron deity of the dance, as well as *meles* for the hula itself. Subjects for the hula's chants covered every occasion in life and every emotion, the literal meaning enriched by secret and symbolic ones. Although some hulas celebrated sexual themes (most likely many of those performed on ships for the sailors), sexuality was only one of many possible subjects. Captain Vancouver objected when he watched a hula *mai*, traditionally composed to honor the genitals and reproductive power of a chief. But he was otherwise appreciative; the missionaries condemned all the dances impartially.[41]

So seriously did they take the threat of renewed idolatry that they could not relax their pressure, as if giving way on this would open up wholesale ruin. With the *kapu* system officially gone, the Hawaiians seemed not quite sure themselves how to explain the *akua* to the missionaries. One person said that "they would never beat up for the taboos again." But others thought that keeping the "*laka*" would ensure excellence in dancing, keep them from forgetting the steps, and improve their discipline.[42]

The hula was not itself an act of worship, though its dancers, chanting prayers, paid homage to the goddess of the dance. Against "this lying vanity" the missionaries strove mightily, but their censure left the Hawaiians uncowed. Hiram Bingham, learning in February that the Hawaiians were going up into the hills to cut wood to make a new *akua*, went immediately to Boki. We must have it, Boki explained, "but it is all in play." This time (for the hula honoring Nahienaena) there was not one but three "shapeless stumps." On March 10, the indefatigable Hiram attached himself to Liholiho as the king was returning from bathing: "Taking him by the arm [Hiram] accompanied him to the house of the governor giving him here and there a message from the King of Kings . . . and endeavoring to persuade him from pursuing the intended amusement of the dance." Liholiho held his ground: "He said it was the custom of the country to dance, that it could not be hindered and besides he was going away tomorrow; he wished himself to see it." Nor would he continue to excuse the scholars from dancing on the Sabbath. Temporarily weakening, Liholiho did excuse them for the following Sabbath, but Boki now asserted himself: "Boki says no," the journal reported, "he says no, he says *we will dance*."[43]

The hula was too important and too beautiful to vanish. Not until Kaahumanu became a Christian and threw her power in with the missionaries did the interdicting have much effect. In 1830 she passed a law forbidding the dancing, but after her death two years later, the ban was generally disregarded by Kamehameha III. In the rural areas, the dancing continued through the nineteenth century. But censure was in the air, making the history of the hula after the arrival of the missionaries increasingly that of an art-in-hiding.

The deaths of Likelike and her child, which occurred at the time of the hula performances, dramatized the difference between Hawaiian and Western mourning customs. By the time the missionaries were called to Likelike's bedside on March 4, she was in agony, "beyond the reach of medical aid or religious instruction." Boki, asking Hiram Bingham if she was dead, got the answer he feared. He extended his hand and said "aloha"—"as if he wanted to retire" (or as if he wanted the missionaries to do so). He then turned his face upward and began to wail loudly in the Hawaiian manner. At this signal, about two hundred others who were gathered around began to wail and express their grief. "Some appeared to exhibit extreme anguish, crying with loud and piteous moans, wringing their hands while floods of tears ran down their sable faces, some weeping with less noise, some crying aloud without tears, and others sitting in silent sadness on the ground." The retreating missionaries were "stunned" by this "hideous din."[44]

The New Englanders had in mind a solemn funeral service followed by an orderly procession to the grave, where the body would lie straight in a coffin. Instead, during the first three years in Hawaii, they saw bodies covered with tapa, bent and tied into a fetal position, and buried in a round hole. Or they heard of bodies reduced to bones and buried in secret places, the flesh having been thrown into the sea. Instead of decorous weeping or stoical self-control, they encountered "dismal shrieking." Maria Loomis, crawling into the low doorway of a house where a friend of Boki's had recently died, reported that the gestures of six or seven women around the corpse "made them appear so frightful that I was almost afraid to stay in the house." She noticed that in order to show their regard for Likelike, "most of the people have a small lock of hair shaved off close from the sides of the head, some knock out their teeth, others burn their faces arms or neck with a piece of bark in the form of a semicircle leaving a permanent scar." The morning after Likelike's death, a man appeared at the mission house carrying two teeth in his hand, asking for alum to relieve the pain in his gums.[45]

Perhaps hardest to understand was that laughter could mix with the tears. Visiting the house of mourning, Hiram Bingham observed that while some were still wailing and some had used the bottle "too freely," others were laughing loudly as they cut their hair, and still others were "cheerfully playing cards." Mercy Whitney noticed the same practice in Kauai, after the death of a chiefess in 1823. As the mourners approached the corpse, "they commence their cries with loud & mournful wailings, proceeding very slowly & by their gestures one would suppose them to be in great agony. When they have sufficiently expressed their grief, they frequently turn from weeping to laughing, and appear as jovial as though nothing had happened." To Mercy this looked more like "affectation than real grief."[46]

Taken in their entirety, the Hawaiian customs acted out the stages of grieving necessary for a healthy recovery. Not seeing this, Hiram Bingham on the day after Likelike's death sought permission to preach a funeral sermon. He got no specific answer at first, tried again that afternoon, and heard from Keopuolani: "I will have no praying." "Something like this," the missionaries had to admit, "may be the sentiment of the nation." Hiram, persisting, finally did get to preach his sermon that Sunday in front of the house where Likelike died, to a "considerable congregation" of missionaries, ships' officers, and Hawaiians. "By the River of Babylon we sat down and wept," went the anthem. Preaching from Genesis 3:16—"in sorrow thou shalt bring forth children"—Hiram took the occasion to introduce a Christian understanding of the "creation, fall, death, and resurrection."[47]

Whenever possible during the early years—when a visiting sailor died, or when the Hawaiians permitted a mission burial for one of their own—the family demonstrated its idea of a proper funeral. The Hawaiians still had to learn to prepare themselves intellectually and spiritually for the important moment of death, to be ready because the Son of Man cometh at an hour when we think not. In their present "deplorable condition," reflected Mercy Whitney in 1821, they "believe that the spirit exists after death, but have little or no idea of a future state of rewards & punishments." Though by no means giving up their own customs, the Hawaiians were far more willing than the missionaries to acknowledge another standard. At the funeral of George Kaumualii's oldest child (February 9, 1821), Mercy remarked on "a degree of solemnity . . . visible in the countenance of the natives" as they watched a procession of mourners walking two by two to the fort for burial. Another incident, reported by Samuel Whitney, suggested the degree to which the Hawaiians were feeling the censure upon the old ways. Knowing what Samuel would say, they hesitated to show him a body whose limbs were bent in preparation for burial: "It is all bad, very bad."[48]

Any small advance in "civilized" behavior was noted in the journals. A funeral on January 11, 1821, Maria Loomis commemorated as "the first *we know* of a native buried American style." By June 2, 1823, for a chief's funeral, a "huge concourse of people" processed to the chapel for services and then to the grave. "They are very solicitous," she reported, "to have everything done in the manner of civilized people." On December 8, 1823, in Waimea, Mercy Whitney reported on a child's funeral, held at the meeting house in front of a large congregation, where Hiram Bingham (visiting at the time) preached in the native tongue, and a long procession of mourners walked to the burial ground. "This is the first time a corpse has been brought to the meeting house. They usually bury their dead in the night." (George Kaumualii's child was brought to the mission house.) The "decent black coffin" in which Thomas Hopu's father was buried impressed Lucy Thurston in 1824: "It was the first grave ever opened on the island of Hawaii to receive the remains of a fellow mortal, over whom Christian rites were performed."[49]

More than the hula kept the scholars away from school. The early enthusiasm for the *palapala* and the performances at the quarterly examinations did not immediately translate into bigger enrollments. After half a year in Kauai, in February 1822, Mercy Whitney reported that the school was reduced to twenty. When Liholiho arrived (February 13) to take a tour around the island, the children joined their parents in accompanying him. Since then, Mercy wrote, they have shown an "unwillingness to return." A few months earlier in Oahu, Sybil had noted that the number of scholars had fallen, adding enigmatically, "Various reasons have operated to produce this diminution, but none of such nature as to dampen our hopes." At least one reason, however, was clear. The scholars were running away. Many of them boarded at the mission houses, where strange behavior was demanded of them, complete with chores. On March 3, Maria Loomis reported that four more children had gone (another four had left earlier). "They be sorry by and by," William Beals told Sybil. But the *palapala* evidently was not worth the price. The women's journals add a new activity, walks to the village to look for their "lost children."[50]

Some of the girls were "decoyed away for some white man," as Maria Loomis put it, education making them more attractive as mistresses. The departures also seemed one more instance of the Hawaiian "aversion to labor." Maria added "a roving disposition & impatience of restraint" to the list of regrettable characteristics. The mission women acknowledged but did not approve the Hawaiians' division of the labor between the sexes. One difference between Hawaiian and Western practice, revealed in the first amazed glances at the mission women bending over the stove, was that Hawaiian men, not women, did the outdoor cooking. "It is generally thought disgraceful," Maria explained, "for females to work, especially the younger part of them." One father refused to return his daughter to the mission, "alleging that some of the scholars had struck her, and that we obliged her to work, which he thought disgraceful." It wasn't always the girls who balked at work. Young Isaac Lewis missed services one day because he was ashamed of his torn clothes. But since the children were responsible for mending their own clothes, and since Isaac had played instead of mending things the day before, Elisha Loomis wasted no sympathy on him. At dinner time, Elisha reported, "I told him his clothes were too bad for him to be with the other children, & asked if he were not ashamed to be seen with them. He answered 'no' but took offense . . . and at night conveyed himself away together with his books and his clothes."[51]

In another clash between Hawaiian and missionary styles of parenting, Maria tried to discipline Charlotte Holmes by tying her with a "small string" to a chest. Elisha defended his wife, explaining that Charlotte over a period of several days had shown a "disposition to be ugly, refusing to do what is told her, talking saucy, &c." When Charlotte untied herself (against orders), Maria tied her again, and there she stayed until the family was called to tea. Before the meal was over, Charlotte's Hawaiian mother, "with evident marks of anger in her countenance," came to collect her daughter. But the next day a repentant Charlotte returned. Her *haole* father, Oliver Holmes, sent word that "her education was committed to our hands and we might punish her whenever we thought she deserved it." In later years, Maria and Mercy Whitney tried having little talks with the children. Maria told two little girls who ran off with their clothes one night of the recent punishment received by a native convicted of theft (at the king's decree, he was flogged 260 times). Her point to the girls was that they might leave at any time, but not run away. "I wish her to give me notice when she is tired of living with me," Maria reported telling the instigator. In August 1823, when three boys left the family in Kauai, Mercy had a "serious talk" with them, explaining that "unless they were willing to submit to such rules as we thought expedient, they must go."[52]

The women did not part with the children easily. They report a great deal of affection for their charges. When William Beals visited Kauai in 1822 (as a tutor for Kaahumanu), Sybil Bingham began a letter to him, "My dear William, I feel as if I was writing to my little son as I take up my pen and say dear William, I hope you are a good child." She wrote solicitously, telling him that Sophia missed him so much that she talked about him night and day. Writing back, William sent a kiss to his playmate, mentioned his longing to see the Binghams, and signed himself, "I am your child." "Our little boy Eli is a pleasant child," Mercy Whitney wrote from Kauai, "we love him & should scarcely know how to part with him." When some boys did leave, she reflected that it was a "trial" to lose them, "especially the largest, who has been a great assistance to Mr. Whitney in writing the language." Maria Loomis regretted that "Sarah" had left them: she had been "a mother to my child, & he was very fond of her." She and Elisha were even sorry to see Charlotte Holmes go: "We very much regret the loss of this little girl as she generally behaved well and has been of much service in taking care of our little Levi."[53]

As the missionaries saw it, "children in this country are brought up in their own ways, the parents seldom attempting to govern them." Giving the children names like Sarah and Martha would not cancel out their earlier Hawaiian upbringing. Though the enrollment in the schools increased after the introduction of printed materials in Hawaiian in 1822, reaching two thousand pupils by 1824, the pupils were usually not children. When Laura Judd arrived with the third company in 1828, she noted that the children were "not yet tamed" or ready for instruction. Not until the end of the decade were the missionaries making special efforts to reach them.[54]

The children living in the extended mission family were being singled out as different from their contemporaries, receiving training in Western domestic skills as much as the *palapala.* Boarding at the mission must have carried, or seemed from afar to carry, status. The missionaries and their *palapala* benefited from the general attraction to all Western exotica. The mission's interactions with the king and *alii* (who of course had the first claim on any new "goods") increased its prestige even more. Foreign residents like Holmes and Marin, understanding what Western training meant, took advantage of the opportunity for their children. The Hawaiian word *luhi,* denoting temporary or foster care, describes the mission's relationship with most of the children. As Hawaiians understood the term, the parents had the option of reclaiming the child at any time. Hawaiians also allowed a child, if dissatisfied with one adult caretaker, to remove himself to another (a custom that offers perspective on all the running away). The word *hanai* (noun or verb), referring to permanent adoption, comes closer to the Binghams' relationship with William Beals.[55]

Mercy Whitney was shocked in 1821 to hear that George Kaumualii was giving away his newborn daughter to a chiefess. "I am told," she replied, that George did not want daughters. Since Mercy gave no further evidence, the exact situation was never clarified. But it is true that a complicated system of Hawaiian familial relationships escaped the missionaries' understanding. For example, Hawaiian parents might "give away" children in the sense of allowing them to be raised by someone else. A strong tradition allowed the maternal grandparents to adopt (*hanai*) the first-born female grandchild and the paternal grandparents the first-born male. This was the *hiapo,* a child in a privileged and responsible position, trained to remember and carry on the family's genealogy. But there was no such thing as an unwanted child in the *ohana* (the large, multigenerational extended family), which could easily care for one more. Words for "bastard," "illegitimacy," and "prostitution" did not even exist in the language before contact with the West. In a culture that placed much emphasis on family ties and genealogy, it was important for a child to know his parentage. A child who was *hanai*'d to another adult always knew his biological parents as well. The derisive word eventually made up for "prostitute" (*hookamakama*) literally means "ready to become a mother to any man's child."[56]

It seemed appropriate that missionary women should be taking in Hawaiian children, giving them the advantages of civilization, but the favor could not be reversed. In 1826 Kapulikoliko (a high-ranking daughter of Kamehameha I), who was moving away from Kailua, shocked Lucy Thurston with her "parting request." Lucy reported: "With great simplicity and assurance, she asked me to give her—yes, looked me full in the face, and on opening her mouth said: 'Give us your elder child' (four years old) 'and let us take her with us to our new abode.'" Lucy, who hardly needed to tell her readers that she refused, explained what was wrong with the "common customs."

> They dispose of their children without one idea of building up a family of brothers and sisters. Indeed, parents are tacked together very loosely. They come together and separate as convenience and inclination dictate. One man will have several wives, or one woman will have several husbands. Here is a mass of humanity in a chaotic state. Take half a dozen of them, and put them into some school in the United States, and something can be done with them. But it requires a great influence to lift a nation.[57]

The women saved their harshest judgments for the sexual explicitness of Hawaiian culture, which became more and more apparent as they themselves acquired the language. Mercy Whitney immediately realized the threat to her daughter, who at two and a half was "very fast getting hold of the native language." Looking back on the early years, she wrote in 1827: "Degraded as this nation was at our arrival, almost on a level with the brute creation, their conversation corresponds with their conduct, & was of the most lewd & vulgar kind." Some of the natives had since improved, she remarked, though "even now it sometimes happens that the expressions are so obscene that I cannot help reproving them."[58]

Though the women decline to give examples of obscenity, it is not hard to guess why they were shocked. Except for a desire to ensure the bloodline of the heir in the case of an *alii* woman bearing a first child, Hawaiians put no particular emphasis on virginity. After the birth, *alii* might change sexual partners without sanction, as might commoners in a particular form of marriage (*punalua*). There were sexual games (*ule* for commoners; *kilu* for *alii*) involving changes in partners. But this was not hedonism without responsibility. At least one reason for the games was to help barren women conceive. Wide-ranging promiscuity was emphatically discouraged, the language including a long list of words and sayings to express censure. Women might be offered to honor distinguished guests, like *alii* (or like young Whitney and Ruggles on their first visit to Kauai). One reason for swimming out to the Western ships was that the women attributed to the Western sailors the high *mana* (god-given power) of the *alii.* These strangers (as a modern scholar explains the misconception), "came from far away places. They had light skin. They had fire in their mouth. Some had cornered heads. They could kill—with a noise and a puff of smoke. Who wouldn't want a *moopuna* [grandchild] with some of this *mana!*"[59]

Reports of infanticide were particularly troubling. The practice has put modern apologists for Hawaiian culture on the defensive, one of them claiming that missionaries perpetuated a "myth." Others restrict the practice to narrowly defined circumstances, particularly when a child was born as a result of an alliance between *alii* and *kauwa* (the slave class). A child born so deformed as to resemble an animal or fish could be returned to this "ancestor," who properly claimed it. This is probably what Sybil Bingham had heard about when she told of being "deeply affected" by a story of "casting infants to the sharks . . . a mother throwing her little one from her breast to the devouring monster, with the belief that it would become *akua* [god]."[60]

Occasionally missionary and *alii* colluded on a punishment. In an effort to clamp down on petty theft during the fall of 1820, the missionaries reported a woman who had stolen a sheet from the clothesline. Boki promptly ordered her head shaved. Evidently the Loomises did this, though they report the punishment, as if trying to evade personal responsibility, in the passive voice: they were directed that "the head should be shaved," and Boki was satisfied except that they had missed the eyebrows. Maria reported that they hoped this would serve as a lesson. To make matters worse for the woman thief, deeply mortified anyway, she had to listen to the mission scholars chant the scripture: *"A ye na mi no hahihooa"*—thou shalt not steal. The thefts continued, however. Whenever the king, chiefs, and attendants passed through the houses, the women were on the alert. "At such time," reported Maria in 1822, "we are obliged to keep an eye constantly all over the house for they will take everything they can lay their hands on if they can do it without being discovered."[61]

Much of the time, missionaries and Hawaiians seem to have operated in different mental universes, both misinterpreting strange new details through the truths they already knew. Hawaiians might flee the sanctuary when the minister closed his eyes to pray, thinking they were being prayed to death. The missionaries, remembering the Sabbath as a day when work should cease, stopped their cooking fires on Saturday night. But the absence of work was still not play. "They spend their days in trifling, while Jesus offers them their salvation," wrote the missionaries, thinking of the constant traffic to and from the surfing beaches of Waikiki. Sybil Bingham felt hurt when Kaahumanu chose to spend Sunday surfing in Waikiki even though the services were being held in Hawaiian. As times changed and the Hawaiians improved in "modesty, industry, or religion," it seemed natural to Hiram Bingham that they should surf and swim less. "The adoption of our costume greatly diminishes their practice of swimming and sporting in the surf," he wrote, "for it is less convenient to wear it in the water than the native girdle, and less decorous and safe to lay it entirely off."[62]

The difficulties the women faced did not exclusively concern Hawaiian customs—what the Hawaiians did—but also involved who they were. The early journals talk in greatest detail about the *alii.* Here the missionaries met curiosity and friendliness, and also wariness, indifference, arrogance, and downright hostility. The *alii* had no expectations of losing political power or (at first) of turning into Christians. Like the missionaries, they knew who they were. Their authority was reinforced by their bloodlines, their childhood training, and the obedience of their subjects. To think of the missionaries only as imposing upon Hawaiians, as taking advantage of them at a vulnerable point in their history (just after the *kapus* had been overthrown), not only defies common sense but unintentionally insults Hawaiians.

In the years after Captain Cook's initial visits, the Hawaiians opened the country to Western imports—trifles like china or calico and potentially dangerous items like guns or rum. Looking with curiosity at what was new and exotic and often seemed better, they could not recognize flaws or predict dangers. They made their decisions as people do, as best they could, based on the traditions they knew and the future they could only guess at. Like the missionaries, they were victims in the sense that we all are, prone to the ironies that slip in between intention and result.

Though the missionaries had an interest in exaggerating the struggle against Satan in the Pacific, many of their early writings suggest that the balance of power was on the indigenous side. The *alii,* concerned about the changes they saw around them, were estimating the missionaries and listening to their own foreign advisors, but their behavior does not suggest that they felt threatened. Receiving a call from a missionary wife, a chiefess might or might not shift from her usual reclining position or look away from her hand of cards.

Kaahumanu characteristically raised her little finger in salutation. When the *alii* visited the mission houses, they expected an open door, immediate attention, and offers of food or tea. Early one morning (in the spring of 1821), the entire family was awakened by the loud beating of a drum outside the door. Sybil Bingham explained, "Kamamalu with her noisy throng had made us a call to request of me a button set on to a garment."[63]

A few incidents from 1822 are typical. In March, Kamamalu had delivered a piece of cloth to the women, which she wanted made up into shirts for herself (rejecting gowns as too uncomfortable). Three days later, Sybil took a tiring walk in the sun to deliver one garment. The queen's household was playing whist for cash. "Cards engrossed their attention while the nod of cold civility was all they could bestow upon us," wrote Sybil. "Seeing that little prospect but that of standing as idle spectators of a vain amusement, we, without any formality, took our leave." As Sybil thought of their "indifference to the message of eternal mercy" and their devotion to "sensual delights," she recalled, "my spirit seemed to faint within me. The falling tear was all the remonstrance I could make." Continuing on to Kaahumanu's house, she found the same card-playing going on, but received a "pleasant aloha" in greeting and an invitation to recline on a pillow. As Kaahumanu tried on the dress that had been sewn for her, "still intent at her cards, without rising, she gave me first one arm, then the other; but as the garment went on it appeared that we had not made sufficient allowance for her large shoulders and saying *pelekea-hamo* [*pilikia-hemo*] too close [she] cast [it] off." Kaahumanu returned to shuffling her cards, and Sybil retreated, "searching anew for a willingness to be servant to all if by any means we might gain some."[64]

This powerful chiefess had so far kept her distance from the mission. "Though she has never appeared our enemy," Sybil wrote in December 1821, "[she] has yet maintained such a dignified reserve as sometimes to approach a suspicious coldness." Maria Loomis thought she had "more dignity and haughtiness about her than any other woman in the Sandwich Islands." Kaahumanu (born about 1777) was now in her late forties, six feet tall, highly intelligent, and handsome. Kamakau reported what was said about her: "Of Kamehameha's two possessions, his wife and his kingdom, she was the more beautiful." She had demonstrated political shrewdness long before she nudged Liholiho into breaking the *kapus.* Alone among chiefesses she had sat in on Kamehameha I's high council, and when her father died in 1804, she, not her brothers, took his seat. To her marriage with the great king she brought her influence with the ruling chiefs and *alii* of Maui. Such was her power that she could act as a "place of refuge," saving the life of a condemned person who reached her side. In the fall of 1821, she made a "conquest" of Kauai—which had always eluded Kamehameha I—by taking its ruler Kaumualii as her second husband. Whether this marked their mutual affection is questionable, but as a political coup it was unsurpassed.[65]

By late December 1821, Kaahumanu was so ill that the Russian doctors attending her feared for her survival. The two Binghams began to call, expressing condolences. By the second visit, Sybil thought Kaahumanu's "affected airs of dignity were laid aside." Holding out a hand to each of them, the queen listened to the words of doctrine and then, silencing her attendants, commanded, "Pray to Jehovah for me." At this, Sybil wrote, "It would be impossible to speak the feeling which filled the breast." As the Binghams left, friendly alohas followed them out through the yard. "*I do feel it a privilege to be on heathen ground,*" Sybil confided to her journal. "Oh to be found faithful, humble, and devoted!" As the visits continued at Kaahumanu's request, Sybil felt that this experience was "ample recompense for a passage round Cape Horn, to point under such circumstances one dying heathen to the healing blood of Him who died on Calvary!" Within a few weeks, Kaahumanu had recovered. Hiram Bingham, paying homage, thought Sybil had "bound a silken cord around her [Kaahumanu's] heart, from which I think she never broke loose while she lived."[66]

Such visits to tell Kaahumanu of Christianity were the "direct" missionary work Sybil craved, even though she could point to no dramatic change in the queen's attitude. Kaahumanu was more interested in eradicating the old religion—burning over a hundred images in Hawaii that June—than in learning to read or attending church.[67] But the visit was still a turning point, one of a series of incidents that seemed in retrospect to have brought the *alii* to Christianity. "What" happened, however, is much easier to explain than "how" and "why." So much seemed to be working against the missionaries' efforts—the opposition from other *haoles,* the apparent resistance of Hawaiian habits, the mutual misunderstandings of one another's customs, not to mention their own bouts with illness and exhaustion—that any gains seem quite improbable.

Chiefesses like Keopuolani and Kaahumanu, having already urged the ending of the old system, had shown themselves receptive to change. The blow to the confidence and stability of the culture delivered by the loss of the *kapu* system and the ravages of Western diseases can hardly be underestimated. The missionaries benefited from the attraction to Western things that had begun forty years earlier, adding their own enticements—countless dresses sewn, a frame house for Liholiho (which they requested of the ABCFM), and most important, the printed page.

The women did their part in dispensing both the trifles and the necessities of "civilization." Sometimes they filled insensitive demands for new shirts and dresses by staying up until one in the morning. Within a three- or four-week period in late December 1822, Mercy Whitney reported cutting out over thirty garments (gowns, coats, pantaloons and so on) "principally for the Chiefs": about a third of them she had sewn herself. The Hawaiians retained their own basis for judgment. Their "favorite clothing," Maria Loomis reported in 1822, was "a man's shirt and a *pau.*" But as fashion guides, the missionary women were more reliable than anyone had been before; Hawaiians began to pay them the compliment of imitation. By the end of 1822, Sybil Bingham wrote that some "wish much to have bonnets—this is a pleasant circumstance to us." When Kaahumanu and other chiefesses once arrived for a tea party dressed in mourning clothes and caps with "the gayest and most tawdry trimmings," Sybil tried gently to explain their inappropriateness. "Some incongruity must be expected, but we would help them to avoid all we could. They take it kindly." What amused Sybil was not the attire, but the way Kaahumanu brought her handkerchief "over my shoulder as a rod of correction, because she had not been directed sooner in her dress for the occasion."[68]

To all the obstacles faced by the mission-at-large were added some that applied only to the women—the relatively inflexible division of "men's" and "women's" work, the sheer volume of domestic work, and, increasingly, the assumption that their children needed special protection. This seemed to pull them away from the heathen, back into the mission houses. It was a Christian's "privilege," as Sybil put it in March 1823, "to rise above these lower scenes, however much they may seem to perplex and distract." But it was never easy. For the rest of her life, Sybil was hoping "to labor more directly for the heathen." With her occasional dry wit, she added to her journal in February 1823, "You may wonder sometimes what in this corner of the earth I can find to be doing if it be not laboring for the heathen. I hope it is for them."[69]

Of course, the mission defined its work so broadly—including all aspects of Christianity and civilization—that the women understood that anything they could do, directly or indirectly, was valuable. Sybil reminded herself (in her journal for February 1823) that if her labor could "in some humble way, aid this holy cause, I can well call it pleasant." She fell back on her wifely duty: "I am allowed to aid one whose constant employment is in the way of direct efforts for their [the Hawaiians'] good."[70]

But the women had set their hearts on transmitting Christian doctrine. When Sybil felt such "privilege" in praying with the sick Kaahumanu, when Mercy Whitney delighted in a rare opportunity to explain the book of John to a Hawaiian, and when Maria Loomis remembered how in 1821, before she spoke the language, she explained the creation, the flood, and the stories of Abraham, Joseph, and Samson by pointing to the plates in her Bible, they were all assigning the highest value to work that concentrated on religious doctrine. They also preferred to be "up and doing" rather than setting an example. "It is now no time for inactivity" was Lucy Thurston's rallying cry in 1822. She "usually" accompanied Asa on his walks to the village every morning and afternoon, where she visited from door to door. The mission's efforts included formal activities in new institutions—church services, funeral services, Sabbath schools, singing schools, monthly prayer meetings, and schoolteaching—as well as relatively informal visits after church hours, walks through the village, social calls to deliver clothing or to answer requests for medicine. The model for personal relationships was summed up in Maria Loomis's assessment of Hiram Bingham's relationship with the king: Hiram "keeps pretty near him."[71]

But if Western paraphernalia and Christian doctrine were all the missionaries had to work with, it is doubtful that they would have had much success. Another kind of persuasion, nonmaterial, accumulated moment by moment, almost in the interstices of the active public efforts. What convinced the Hawaiians that the new religion was good were the people who practiced it. When the *alii* embraced Christianity, it was only in part because they now believed in the Christian God; they also respected the Christians themselves.

In their modesty, the women never claimed such an influence. Usually consoling themselves for contributing so little of importance, they probably underestimated the influence they did have. But gradually the image that Sybil presented in the beginning of 1821 – sitting alone at night in a grass hut, posed against the heathen wail – gave way to one of constant intermingling with Hawaiians. In being confined to the mission house by their womanly duties, the women were not isolated from the work of the mission; it was going on all around them. "One of the queens of the nation with a numerous train has just left the chair in which I have now a second time seated myself to my pen," Sybil explained early in 1821. "Familiarized to such visitants the little circumstance seems so much an everyday occurrence as hardly worth mentioning." The women's journals are filled with the incidental comings and goings of royalty and their trains, who passed through with an aloha on their way to Waikiki, bringing gifts of food, pausing to recline or, as Liholiho once did, to roll about on the feather bed. In 1822, Sybil recorded that Kamamalu "exchanges little notes" with her "almost every day." These informal interactions worked their own kind of persuasion.[72]

Hawaiians were observing the women's attempts to practice Christian virtues as much as their dislike of unironed clothes. When Maria Loomis nursed the desperately ill baby during the summer of 1821 and asked Kaahumanu to help her find a wet-nurse for the child, Maria wrote that the queen "seemed affected at my attention to a *kereka moura* [native child] and to use her own expression said 'I was very great patience.'" One day (January 1, 1822) when Sybil had just received a precious batch of letters – thirty in all – she allowed herself in a rare lapse of discipline to dismiss her school. No sooner had she counted the letters when Kamamalu and her train arrived to dine. Put to the test, Sybil admitted that she turned from the "feast" of her letters "most reluctantly to a meaner one. But the great object must be to entertain our royal guests." Reflecting upon three years of work in Kauai, Mercy remarked, "It is pleasing to see the attention of the chiefs & people to their books & their increasing attachment to our family. In cutting & making clothes for them, &c. I have so gained the confidence of many, that they think whatever I do is right, & are willing to confess themselves ignorant."[73]

In February 1823, Sybil described a few typical, hectic days at the mission house. That Sabbath, she attended the native service at nine, returned to a room filled with chiefs and attendants, went to the English service at eleven, and had to "wait upon additional company at night." Next day, as she washed and cleaned up from a recent storm, she described herself "attending to a little message on a slate from this one, a note from another; making my way all the forenoon through the house filled with chiefs and their people." Just after sunrise, the king arrived on his way to Waikiki, followed throughout the morning by one group after another, on their way to the king. Just as early the following morning, as Sybil was pouring herself a cup of tea, the king and his entourage returned from Waikiki. She distributed her plate of cakes as best she could among her guests:

> It was breakfast time in all the rooms. The queens who are always all over the house found a cup of coffee here and a cake there as it happened. The king was sober and appeared well; he seemed gratified with his morning call; observing my readiness to help him and my husband to a comfortable breakfast, he made quite a speech to honor two of the queens, desiring them to observe and imitate.

The immediate result of these visits was the familiar exhaustion and a desire for peace and quiet. "Attention to these throngs," Sybil admitted, "we always find as fatiguing as hard labor." The following evening, she confided, "I shut my door and am *still.*" The next day, she "crept away" whenever possible "into a snug little corner" to cut out some gowns for the Chamberlains. Sybil also hoped for another result from this "intercourse" between the missionaries and the nation's rulers: "O, may He bless it all for the salvation of multitudes of souls."[74]

This did not look likely by the end of 1821. At the time of Kaahumanu's illness, the best Sybil could say was, "We hope there is increasing confidence in the minds of the rulers of this land reposed in us as a body, and as individuals." The bad news followed: "Still, our hearts are pained because they seem too slow to believe the gracious message—too indifferent to exert themselves to receive the heavenly blessings proffered them." Having hoped, on finding "idolatry in ruins," that "Jesus was soon to reign," Sybil was disappointed that the Hawaiians still "lie bound in Satan's chains, the base slaves of ignorance and sin."[75]

When the missionaries' work finally received an enthusiastic response, it was not their religious ideas, or their exemplary domestic life, but a material object that made the difference. On January 7, 1822, the printing press was ready for operation. Important *alii* and foreigners in port gathered around as "Governor Cox" of Maui (Keeaumoku) pulled the lever to print the first sheet. It was a lesson from the intended Hawaiian spelling book, showing the vowels and the consonants (with examples of words in Hawaiian and English). Sixty or seventy of these first sheets went immediately to eager scholars who could not wait for the entire book. The mission's efforts now took a quantum leap forward. The spelling book, called the *Pi-a-pa,* was printed first on sixteen and then on eight pages as paper became scarce. Modeled after Webster's speller, it taught the alphabet, numbers, punctuation marks, lists of words, scripture verses, and short poems. By the end of February, Elisha Loomis had 500 copies of the first sixteen pages ready to distribute. A pleased Liholiho told Elisha he "wished there were 40 missionaries."[76]

Once Hawaiians could rapidly learn from the printed page, the number of Sybil's scholars, about 25 as of January 12, 1822, jumped to almost 500. The spelling was rationalized, with each letter standing for a single sound. With highly trained memories resulting from their oral tradition, the Hawaiians learned quickly. Some learned the alphabet through a chant, mixing the old method of learning with the new. Promising scholars who mastered the spelling book turned into teachers for others. By the end of 1824, there were 2,000 pupils, and by 1831, 52,000—about two-fifths of the population. By then, the *Pi-a-pa* had gone through nine editions of about 190,000 copies.[77]

In mid-April 1822, the missionaries were more than compensated for the previous year's disappointing attempt to get to Tahiti when a Tahitian delegation unexpectedly visited them. The Reverend William Ellis, for six years a missionary in Tahiti, two members of the London Missionary Society (the Reverend Tyerman and the Reverend Bennet), and some Tahitian Christians were on their way to the Marquesas when the captain of their ship took an unexpected detour to Honolulu. The stopover stretched out to four months of skillful help, especially with the language. Sybil called the visit "a smile upon the mission." The first Sabbath, Ellis preached a sermon in Tahitian, which the Hawaiians could just about follow. By the end of the summer, he was preaching in Hawaiian, and, more important, so was Hiram Bingham. The delegation left in late August, but Ellis, accepting the Hawaiians' invitation, intended to return with his family.[78]

Ellis's visit, following on the heels of the first printing, helped to inspire a general quickening of interest in the mission throughout the summer of 1822. By August 9, Lucy Thurston wrote, "Of late we have seen a shaking of dry bones." During the previous weeks, Sybil Bingham wrote, the missionaries had witnessed "what we have long ardently desired to see—the rulers with the people rising up to ask instruction at our hand. . . . It is so wonderful in our eyes, that it would almost seem that we dream, did not our exhausted natures, when we seek the pillow, testify that our labor, through the day has been a reality." As Maria Loomis put it, a "new era seems to have commenced."[79]

During the first week of August, "Governor Cox," after dreaming that all the islands were on fire and he was unable to escape, requested religious meetings in his home every night. Hiram Bingham, interpreting the chief's dream, linked the destructive power of a volcano to the "eternal destruction" possible for the soul. The governor now presented himself and his train as pupils and urged the other *alii* to declare their support for the new learning. Thursday, explained Sybil, "the subject was in serious agitation." On Friday, the king visited the missionaries and the next day made his decision: he sent for books and declared himself ready to learn. That Sabbath, the church was full. Monday, Kalanimoku requested books for his people. The next day, the determined Binghams took a copy of the spelling book to the still-recalcitrant Kaahumanu. To their amazement, she learned six letters on the spot. "I could scarcely believe the reality of my enrollment while leaning upon her pillow and asking her the name of this and the other letter," wrote Sybil.[80]

Roused from her indifference, Kaahumanu began to exert her enormous influence in favor of the new learning. She and Kaumualii asked Williams Beals to tutor them, calling him "our little *kumu* teacher." Sybil sent him twice a day, "cleanly dressed," to read with them for a few hours. When other scholars from the first mission school were also demanded as teachers, Sybil felt a sense of accomplishment: "I have felt a reward this week for months of labor with that little school, though sometimes it has appeared so trifling." Soon after learning to read, Kaahumanu visited Kauai with a company of eight hundred and sent back instructions for the mission: "Many are the people—few are the books. I want *elua lau* (800) Hawaiian books to be sent hither. We are much pleased to learn the *palapala.* By and by, perhaps, we shall be *akamai,* skilled or wise. Give my love to Mr. and Mrs. Bingham and the whole company of Long necks."[81]

Here was a glimmering of success as Sybil defined it. Though it was the men who first learned the language, reduced it to writing and printed the spelling book, the entire mission family took pleasure in the accomplishment. It was understood that everyone had contributed, directly or indirectly, to these achievements, and that personal ambition was subordinate to the wide-ranging goal of subduing a land for Christ; it was not a moment for egotism. Characteristically modest, yet satisfied, Sybil wrote in August 1822: "[I] have every day been permitted to contribute my mite of labor and influence in this missionary field." Sybil had another, private reason for gratitude during the recent months. Despite the "noise and bustle and seasons of fatigue and exhaustion," she had experienced "very few" moments when her "spirits have sunk and darkness rested on my mind." She continued, "God is gracious to me, my sisters, unworthy, *deeply unworthy* as I am. Help me to praise him."[82]

Still, she cautioned against exaggerating the progress. "I would not be understood as saying, by any means, now, that anything like the continuing influence of the spirit appears operating on the hearts of sinners. It is a general desire, encouraged now by the king, for the first rudiments of instruction which fills our hand and encourages our hearts." It was only the beginning. No one was yet baptized. No one had even applied to become a member of the church. But the Hawaiians, now that they had hymns and sermons in their own language, were beginning to come to services. Within half a year, the congregations were becoming multitudes. Sybil wrote eagerly, almost impatiently:

Could you see, as we have for the few past sabbaths, near a thousand heathen people gathering to the house of GOD, many of them clad in the richest, gayest dresses, while their polluted souls realized not their need of that garment of righteousness, in which alone they could stand at the last Great Day, your eye would affect your heart, and your prayer must be, "Come Holy Spirit, Heavenly Dove—With all thy quickening powers."[83]

5. *Children of Light*

For ye were sometimes darkness, but now are ye light in the Lord: walk as children of light.

— EPHESIANS 5:8

The original wood-frame mission house still stands in Honolulu, restored and open to the public as a museum. Grim in the old days, it looks better now, painted a clean white, shaded by luxuriant kukui and monkey pod trees, set off from the street by a neat fence of coral blocks and a green expanse of yard. When first built, the fence was an assortment of sticks lashed together, the "yard" no more than dirt and tufted patches of pili grass the Hawaiians used for thatch. Dust seeped through the cracks in the walls of the house, obliterating the color of the furniture and collecting in such quantities that the women sometimes emptied quarts of it from the bedclothes in the evening. To try to keep out the rain, the men filled the crevices with strips of cloth dipped in tar. The dirt walls of the cellar repeatedly caved in (even with mud and straw packed into the sides); by 1824, the house sagged in the middle and had to be propped up by beams in the cellar. The walls were not lathed or plastered until the late 1820s.

In early sketches of Honolulu, it is always possible to pick out the mission house, announcing itself with its peaked roof and straight lines, seeming to rise above the rounded thatch of native houses and define itself against its surroundings. Symbolizing "civilization," it spoke to paradox, a material object signifying a culture that put its highest value on matters not of physical fact but of spirit. Today, instead of "heathen" strangeness, the house contends with modern concrete, five lanes of city traffic, and (just visible from the Binghams' second-floor bedroom) a multi-storied parking lot. The wide-ranging views of the Pacific to the south, of the vast flat plain ahead leading to the mountains, of the palm groves to the east toward Diamond Head have been lost over the decades as the city has gradually closed in on the mission compound, placing it now in the center of downtown Honolulu, close to City Hall and the workings of modern government. Still a kind of oasis, the compound now speaks to material luxury—green lawn and foliage on ground that could be collecting rent. And, in a secular present that need not take unpeopled rooms as a serious threat, the house pays homage to "history." Since the other early buildings, whether wooden or thatched, simply wore down, or burned, or were never restored, the mission house is the oldest surviving building on the islands—all that is left of that tumultuous decade of the twenties when trading brigs and whalers crowded the harbor, and grogshops and general stores the lanes of the village. (Kawaiahao Church next door, completed in 1842, speaks more to the finished achievement of the mission than to its early struggles; the adobe schoolhouse across the street dates from 1835.) The house stands as a relic of the quixotic hope—embodied in the lives of almost two hundred men and women—that Christianity and Civilization could be transplanted and nurtured in a new place. To that hope, the house can only offer mute testimony. The active religious life of the mission, disbanded over a century ago, has long since departed.[1]

Except for the continual hum of traffic, muffled through the trees, the house is quiet now. The voices of guides lead the curious around the rooms for the kind of tour that Sybil Bingham used to give her correspondents. For the museum's purposes, most of the rooms are fixed in the 1830s, but since the interior has changed so many times, the partitions and stairways moved so often, the house seems to corroborate the women's understanding that all material creations are transitory. Outside, the various thatched houses, used for printing, or for native helpers, or as "spare bedrooms" for the overflow of missionaries, have been replaced by a stone printing house and the large stone "Chamberlain" house (finished in 1831 for the Levi Chamberlains of the second company). But while other mission families moved in and out of the frame house, the Binghams (with the exception of a short period in 1826 when they moved to the "Ellis" house across the street) always called it home. At the top of the stairs, on the Diamond Head side, stands Sybil and Hiram's bedroom. Sybil found it so pleasant that "before I am aware," she explained in her journal of October 1822, "my pen stands ready to run around it." A "charming library" of books stood on a dressing table between the two windows, hung with white curtains inside and a lattice frame on the outside to break the wind and shield from the sun. Besides the four-poster bed, its patchwork quilt, and a cradle, the room contained a new sofa, a "beautiful little mahogany work table, with trimmings" (a gift from the queen), and various "convenient and pretty things." Sybil considered "this good room . . . in accommodations and pleasantness superior to any I ever called mine."[2]

Quickly checking the seeming worldliness of her description, Sybil went on to explain that no room "ever contained anything, to me so rich, as husband and child. They are blessings loaned to me, a poor sinner, who, long ago forfeited every claim to any favor." Suddenly she added a conventional though ominous word of caution: "If this heart clings to them too closely, it may be necessary they should be recalled." About three months later, Sybil found herself in labor with her second child, at an hour "unlooked for," six or seven weeks prematurely. Even with the "anguish of body seizing hold" of her, she found time for a quick note in her private journal: "I feel that I may not see another [year] commence—it is an hour of deep trembling, but O my gracious Redeemer leave me not." Hiram's handwriting records that "a few hours after this" their son was born. "In the termination," Sybil wrote to her sisters,

> all was safe—all was well. Never was a more lovely treasure put into a mother's arms than was this tender babe. Small, but fair and comely, as of the age of several months. The little head was covered with beautiful hair, which formed little curls on its forehead as well as neck. With seeming intelligence its dark, bright eyes opened on the new scenes around. So small, and yet so perfect in every limb, its formation spoke with peculiar force a hand Divine.

The past tense was deliberate. "Such was my dear babe," she continued. The child thrived for nine days, then languished with jaundice and a bowel complaint for seven. A physician looked at him, but could not help. The evening of January 16, 1823, he died.

Anticipating the event, the parents had quickly baptized their son with the name of Levi Parsons, chosen a few hours after birth with the hope that he might take up the work of this fellow missionary to Palestine, recently dead. The king, his queens, and several of the chiefs, who had previously come to offer congratulations, came to witness the baptismal ceremony. Then, for two nights after the infant's death, as Sybil put it, "we kept the beautiful clay. New was the situation of your sister—one lovely child sweetly sleeping near her; another also near, sleeping in death." Now the *alii*, including Kaahumanu and Kaumualii, came to the room to offer condolences. Hiram asked Liholiho for a piece of ground for burial. That Sabbath, the family said prayers in Sybil's room (since she could not yet go out), then held a funeral service in the church. The *alii* joined the procession from the church to the graveyard.[3]

As Sybil spread the news to her correspondents, she repeated the standard consolations: that the Lord gives and the Lord takes away; that His name should be blessed; that although chastised by His rod, she has also been comforted. By the time she wrote, a month or so later, she was composed, devoting much of each letter to God's graciousness, compassion, and "matchless condescension," counting herself blessed to be returned to health in the company of husband, daughter, and friends near or distant. Her memory of the baby's dying gaze buoyed her up: "There fixed on me from his sweet-beaming eyes, such a happy consciousness, as thrilled my very soul. It seemed to speak of Jesus." When death came, she had been able to watch the moment with "sweet composure":

> Never did a Saviour's love appear so great, so condescending. Were we allowed to indulge the unspeakably precious hope that He, the Lord of Glory, could stoop to this little one, sprung from a sinful stock, born in sin! Did we know that he [Jesus] had died; and might we hope had made a way for such [a child] to be received to Heaven! Might my busy thought indeed leave the sad scene around, and following his little spirit, cleansed by a Saviour's blood from all pollution, exclaim, "O, the glories! O, the glories!"

Far from being dissuaded from her vocation by the baby's death, she was more than ever convinced that "it would be good to live & die making known a Saviour's precious love" to the millions who were ignorant of it.[4]

But her religious consolations did not overcome earthly sorrows. "A chastising stroke it was," she wrote Mrs. Bates, "for maternal love wept over my offspring dead." Mindful of the origin of her sorrow in "this" world, she let it breathe there, not trying to smother it with the ultimate consolation of the "next." She sought to contain and express her pain, not to deny it. This moment of suffering brought a test for the "settled principles" inspiriting her life. Her nineteenth-century diction may be euphemistic, her sentences elaborate and filled with catch-phrases, her religious doctrines the standard issue of Calvinism. But from these habits both of language and doctrine, she received the solace of form: the repetitive lull of parallel phrases ("I will sing of mercies and of judgments—The Lord hath brought low and he hath raised up—The Lord hath given & he hath taken away"); the intellectual orderliness of her religious ideas; the phrases that take their authority not only from her own deep faith but from repeated communal usage in the past. To be healed would take an effort of will over a passage of time, acknowledging both the heart that bled over the child's death and the doctrine that put that sorrow into a larger perspective. Although the consolations were powerful enough to heal in the end, they would also heal only in the end.[5]

The mission's public work was going well. In the beginning of 1823, the mission family could point to the encouraging results of almost three years of labor—a large church and the frame house, and Hawaiians themselves, eager to learn the *palapala*, increasingly willing to attend church services. But these were only external measures of achievement; it was too soon to find the changes of heart they longed for. As they waited, the missionaries continued to learn the meaning of their grand words of expectation—"to spend and be spent" in the cause of establishing a new culture and a new religion. Some costs were physical, some psychological. Some were the ordinary expenses of living in this vale of tears (whatever the geographic location), some the direct result of being on missionary ground. Some were negligible; others pierced them to the core.

In mid-February, fourteen-month-old Amanda Loomis, cutting her eyeteeth and suffering from a sore and inflamed leg, became feverish and went into convulsions. (She had "an erysipelas in her leg," an infectious disease of the skin caused by a streptococcus.) Maria immediately prepared a warm bath, but "before she could be got into it," she remembered, "I thought she was gone forever." Over the next twelve hours, Amanda had seven convulsive fits.

Throughout that "solemn & anxious" night, wrote Maria, "we kept a tub standing & water heating & whenever she was taken with a fit, to put [her] into the bath, apply ether to her nose & rub her limbs was all that we could do." Perhaps the Loomises were luckier than the Binghams, or, for this child, God had a different end in view. He "saw fit to bless these feeble means," as Maria put it, and by morning the crisis was over. "Thus," she concluded with the illogicality of deep faith, "sorrow may endure for a night but joy cometh in the morning."[6]

Since the mission houses were filling up with children, such crises as the ones confronting Sybil and Maria joined the more routine preoccupations of childrearing as a common theme in letters and journals. In this respect, life in Kauai was no different from life in Honolulu. Writing from Waimea in 1823, Mercy Whitney reported trials with her infant Samuel, who was troubled with thrush, an infection making his mouth so sore that he could not nurse. At fifteen months old, the child suffered from diarrhea, a hard cough that weakened his body, and many symptoms of worms, which left him with not much more flesh than a four- or five-month-old and a "pale *death-like countenance.*" Though Samuel recovered, his illness was alarmingly ordinary for the Whitney family over the next years. Thrush and diarrhea also afflicted Mercy's next baby: years later, she remembered sitting by his bed, watching his pulse and listening to every rattling breath while "he seemed to be on the border of the grave." Mercy and her husband repeatedly suffered excruciating pain from inflamed eyes (once she thought Samuel might lose his reason). She herself endured weeks of pain from decaying teeth until she realized that she would have to let Samuel try out the dental instruments and extract them himself.[7]

In December 1822, the Ruggleses moved about six miles to the east of Waimea, to Hanapepe, then left Kauai altogether the following summer. In Kauai, the communal part of the mission experiment was over. There would be no more sharing of household and schoolroom and, perhaps worse, no more female companionship. "You cannot tell how gratifying it would be to me, could you just stop in & spend the evening here," Mercy wrote to Nancy Ruggles about a year later. "I am all alone except my little ones who are asleep in bed." Samuel, responsible for the entire island's religious instruction, was constantly traveling and preaching in remote areas. When the second company of missionaries arrived, one couple, the Bishops, visited but did not settle in Kauai. "I believe the providence of God will order all things for the best," Mercy continued, "though I cannot but say the thought of staying alone has at times cast a gloom over my mind." Mercy's loneliness, like every other cost of a missionary life, was merely acknowledged, not resented. Answering a letter from Maria Loomis in January 1824, Mercy wrote, "I have sometimes been almost tempted to think that the dear females of the Mission, had forgotten they had a solitary sister at Tauai [Kauai], though I have never suffered my mind long, to indulge in such reflections, knowing your cares & labors."

The Whitneys had made no conversions in Kauai, but remained optimistic. As Mercy wrote, "We have very much to encourage and animate us in our work, which appears under the divine blessing to be rapidly progressing." On her twenty-eighth birthday (August 14, 1823), Mercy reflected on a year of "health, peace & prosperity." She and her husband were living in a stone house (less prone to fire than their thatched one), situated on the Waimea River not far from the ocean, shaded by kou trees in the front and a grove of coconut palms in the rear. The schools were flourishing; Samuel, now licensed to preach, was conducting services in Hawaiian; the baby Samuel was recovering from his illness; the house was "comfortable" and "very convenient." The family's garden and the "productions of the islands" fed them well, supplemented by two or three pounds of butter Mercy churned every week from goats' milk. A small detail—the fact that butter spoiled so quickly that she had to churn twice a week—was enough to point her mind toward the sort of biblical parallel that sustained her: "It reminds me of the manner with which the Israelites in the wilderness were fed from day to day—of which they [were] forbidden to lay in a store for the future, which plainly taught them to trust in God, & rely upon him for daily supplies."[8]

Back in Honolulu, there was little danger of loneliness. In early 1823, the mission compound overflowed as the family made room for the eight Chamberlains, who had returned from their visit to Kauai the previous fall. On February 3, 1823, Rev. William Ellis arrived from Tahiti as promised with his family—four children under six and a frail wife. Mary Ellis, not knowing of her husband's delay in Honolulu the previous summer, had waited five, six, then seven months and feared herself a widow before he finally arrived.

"Such long, continual and deep anxiety," wrote a sympathetic Maria Loomis, "preyed very sensibly upon her health." By the end of March, Maria reported that both Ellises had been ill since their arrival. While she insisted, "We have felt happiness in doing all that was in our power to make them comfortable," and praised the "worthy" couple for having "the true spirit of missionaries," she also admitted that their presence meant "quite an addition to our labor." Over the next year and a half, when Mary Ellis did not get better, the task of nursing her and caring for her children necessarily passed to the other women. By the fall of 1824, with Mary Ellis's health in an alarming state, the Ellises sailed for England.[9]

"Family" life in Honolulu, already weakened by the loss of the "long table," the departure of the Holmans, and geographic division, received its worst blow yet on March 20, 1823, when its "parents," Daniel and Jerusha Chamberlain, left for New England on the brig *Pearle.* The couple had been the mainstay of the mission's domestic life, supervising the stores and providing for the table until March 1822, when they resigned these duties and raised the possibility of departure. But the writing had been on the wall long before that. Daniel Chamberlain and Elisha Loomis both fell from the staging when they were putting up the frame house during the summer of 1821. They were uninjured, though it later looked as though the fall had begun the captain's decline in health, exacerbated by the usual exhaustion from hard work and several bouts of rheumatism. By the following summer (1822), Mercy Whitney reported that he was "so low it appeared as though he could not continue long with us." Jerusha too was worn out and ill. When the Chamberlains traveled to Kauai that fall to try to recuperate, they were already looking for a passage home.

Daniel Chamberlain had also discovered that his agricultural skills were relatively useless. Although Kaumualii at first was eager for instruction in American farming, the Hawaiians were the true teachers, expertly cultivating taro in both dry and wet lands. Fresh squashes, cabbages, cucumbers, and sweet potatoes were plentiful in any season; the Hawaiian melons Daniel thought superior to American ones. The image of wheat and corn fields waving in the Pacific was ludicrous. Francisco Marin and Anthony Allen produced thriving gardens, but their sites were better, watered by mountain streams. The Englishmen Tyerman and Bennet, writing a joint letter to the

ABCFM on August 9, 1822, to support the Chamberlains' decision, explained that there was "no scope for agricultural talents beyond what the natives themselves possess." Nor did the system of land ownership, concentrated in the hands of potentially capricious *alii*, seem attractive to Westerners who thought in terms of the family farm and fee-simple ownership. "Lands are so continually shifting from one to another here," wrote Daniel to the Board on November 11, 1822, "that but little calculation or dependence can be placed on it." He told of an American man on Kauai who bought land from one of the chiefs for a "good price," but from whom "a part of it has been taken away, and the produce on the rest taken away."

Still, Daniel confessed to the Board that it remained his heart's desire to labor for the heathen. According to Mercy Whitney, Jerusha had "no desire to return; & at first could scarcely reconcile her mind to such a thought." They would have stayed, explained Lucy Thurston, were it not for the children. For the first two years, Lucy remembered, the Chamberlain children "associated with the interesting native youth in our large mission family, in studies, in labors, & in amusement. . . . In native language, I think they were even before the missionaries. Who had ever conceived the idea of separating them from the natives!" Now everyone wondered how to train them up for "usefulness & for God" in a land where it was "moral death" for children to be influenced either by foreigners or by natives. The English deputation, spreading harrowing tales about missionaries' children in Tahiti, tipped the balance with their unanimous opinion—"Go home."

Unlike the Holmans, the Chamberlains received glowing testimonials. In a joint letter to the Board, Hiram Bingham, Elisha Loomis, and Asa Thurston commended the family for having "labored hard & suffered much in the cause which they left their home and country to support." In closing, they recommended them "affectionately." In Mercy Whitney's words, "They have been like parents to us and as such we love & respect them." After a miserable voyage home with an irascible captain who stole their provisions and terrorized the children (once waking up the boys by firing a gun into their berths), Daniel asked the Board to refuse payment for the passage. Eventually the legal details were resolved and the family resumed the New England life they had left only four years earlier.

In later years, an occasional report would find its way back to Honolulu from someone who had visited Massachusetts and seen one of the children. For the younger parents left behind, coping with the usual incessant labors, the Chamberlains, passing out of sight, often had to pass out of mind. But as they watched their own children growing up and reaching the age of the Chamberlains', they were reminded that the problem of "moral contamination" would not go away.[10]

By 1823, the Hawaiians had problems of a far wider scope—not a family but an entire culture disintegrating. The village of Honolulu (with about six or seven thousand inhabitants) would hardly be mistaken for Boston, but in the three years between the arrival of the first and second companies, it had begun to look less Hawaiian. Near the fort were a frame house begun in 1819 and now used for the American Consulate and two older, stone buildings (Marin's house and a storehouse for the king). Native thatched houses still clustered amid dusty lanes. But seventeen grogshops now competed with the message from the large thatched church. Kaahumanu had recently built a frame house, and the king was living in an impressive new residence. Like his earlier palaces, it was built in the Hawaiian style, with Western touches in its shuttered windows and two doors, and, inside, in its chandeliers, mahogany tables, and Chinese sofas. (At 50 by 30 feet, it was wider than the new church.) The waterfront betrayed the direction of the future. Maria Loomis remarked its "very fine appearance," the result of over fourteen vessels (mostly whalers) anchored outside the harbor and another nine within, as well as numerous native vessels. One more ship, the *Thames* that carried the new missionaries, created so little stir that until word arrived that a new group of brethren were walking toward the house, the family had scarcely noticed it.[11]

Like their town, the Hawaiians themselves presented a slightly more Western facade. The first group of men being rowed in from the *Thames* saw Kamamalu on the shore wearing a pink satin dress. But she was also wearing the yellow feather wreath of the *alii* on her head and gesturing to the men to keep them from landing in an area that was *kapu*. When Charles Stewart (of the second company) first entered the king's house, he found all the *alii* in their Sunday best. The chiefs now had the options of having clothes made by several resident tailors or of sending measurements to Canton (Liholiho had recently received four hundred garments at once from China.) Stewart, temporarily forgetting that he ought not to be swayed by appearances, described the chiefs' dress "more particularly than I should otherwise have done," but attributed his lapse to his "surprise at finding such richness of material, such variety of changes in their wardrobes, and such taste in the selection and arrangements of colours."[12]

When it was not the "tabu day" (Sunday), the *alii* would still wear the *pau* or *malo,* though they might change its material from tapa to cotton or add a shirt or a "loose slip." Kaahumanu, when Stewart first met her, wore a *pau* of twenty yards of yellow satin with a *kihei* of purple satin. But the servants and commoners still routinely wore native dress. To them Western clothing still carried the status of rare and expensive articles (one reason for continuing to visit the ships at night). Their progress was only sporadic. Even by the time the third company landed in 1828, Laura Judd remarked on the commoners "dressed and undressed": "One had a shirt *minus* pantaloons, another had a pair of pantaloons *minus* a shirt; while a large number were destitute of either. One man looked very grand with an umbrella and shoes, the only foreign articles he could command." Later on, when weddings became popular, Hawaiians would simply dress in whatever they were "privileged" enough to own—a handkerchief knotted over the head and covered with a green veil, a night-cap, a bonnet, or even a calico dress. One enterprising owner of a blue coat with gold buttons would rent it out to bridegrooms. The good-humored Laura also noticed that the appearance of the missionary women in turn afforded the Hawaiians "much amusement"—a sign that Hawaiians retained their own basis for judgment.[13]

But whatever the differences in style or material, the *alii* understood something about dress that the missionaries could not. Never losing sight of the ultimate value of the immaterial soul and the invisible asset of good character, the missionaries paid relatively little attention to the outward covering of the soul. Minimal standards of appropriateness were adequate. The first *muumuus* honored modesty and ease of construction, not fashion. Laura Judd approved of an early version (worn over the *pau*) as "a very feminine garment of unbleached cotton, drawn close around the neck." The missionary women themselves looked first to propriety, the reason why Laura

Judd had given away her "muslins, ribbons, & embroideries" upon becoming a missionary. It surprised her to discover in Honolulu that "people are estimated somewhat by the exterior."[14]

The *alii*, however, had always understood that a queen should look like a queen. One day in 1829, Kaahumanu presented the women with some expensive, heavy satin in pink, white, and blue stripes, asking that identical dresses be made for her and the missionaries to wear at the dedication of the new church. The women explained that as missionaries, "supported by the churches and the earnings of the poor," they could not make such an outward show of luxury. "*I* give it to you," said the indignant Kaahumanu, "not the church, nor the poor." The missionary women were remembering the rich man who could not enter heaven because he had laid up all his treasures on earth. Kaahumanu must have understood another truth, illustrated by the story of Jesus' accepting a woman's gift of expensive ointment for his head (Matthew 26:7–13), when the money could have been given to the poor. Though the Christian cannot serve God *and* Mammon, might she not use rich things to serve God? Why not attend the dedication of God's building in a beautiful dress? As if realizing from her aristocratic training that exterior detail might reflect interior value or (the harder truth) that it might at times even create it, Kaahumanu continued: "If it is not proper for good people to wear good things, I do not know what they are made for." The queen was "taciturn" for the rest of the afternoon, but eventually acquiesced, sending the women two rolls of black silk the next morning.[15]

The Hawaiians were negotiating their way through a minefield of American customs, many of them imperfectly imitated or partially understood. But they continued to be drawn to the new ways. For a fortnight during late April and early May of 1823, the Hawaiians held their fourth annual celebration honoring both the death of Kamehameha I and Liholiho's accession to the throne. Although the cause for festivities was distinctly Hawaiian, their manner was not. The first Sunday, April 26, Liholiho held a state dinner, inviting about a hundred guests—chiefs, ships' officers, foreign residents, and missionaries. The food, the manner of serving, the hundred-foot-long table, the music, and the style of dress (propriety dictating black) were all Western. According to Charles Stewart (not an eyewitness, but a careful second-hand reporter), "The only thing in the entertainment not designed to be in imitation of foreign custom" was a striking procession of four hundred residents of Oahu, who were paying their taxes. Wearing white tapa, the Hawaiians of each of eight districts marched in single file, carrying articles of produce neatly wrapped in leaves, each group following its headman with his torch of *kukui* nut oil.

But for the apex of the festivities, a parade held on the last day to honor Liholiho's five queens and his young brother and sister (Kauikeaouli and Nahienaena), the Hawaiians held more closely to their own traditions. To call the event "striking and interesting," as Hiram Bingham did, was understatement. Kamamalu, wearing a *pau* of scarlet silk, rode high above her subjects in a whaleboat, lined inside with broadcloth and tapa and carried by a phalanx of seventy men in the scarlet and yellow feather cloaks and helmets of the *alii.* She was shaded by an immense Chinese umbrella and flanked by thirty-foot-high *kahilis,* made with scarlet feathers and carved ivory and tortoise-shell handles. Two other queens, Kinau and Kekuaonohi, rode in similar fashion on double canoes. Pauahi, who had been rescued from fire as a child, commemorated her escape by stepping down from her elaborately decorated couch and setting it ablaze. Next she sent her expensive dress into the flames, keeping only a "handkerchief" to wrap around herself. The two royal children added to the grandeur, riding on four Chinese field bedsteads, ornamented with tapa and yellow moreen. The second company had arrived in time for this pageant, and newcomer Charles Stewart was awe-struck, calling the scene "*splendid.*" He went on to better his praise: "There was something approaching to the *sublime* in the lofty noddings of the kahilis of state . . . something conveying to the mind impressions of greater majesty than the gleamings of the most splendid banner I ever saw unfurled." Hiram Bingham admitted that the parade might be "useful" to the Hawaiians as a way of honoring the "ingenuity" and "glory" of their ancestors, but (more doctrinaire than Stewart) his sympathy was not with the display of unseemly luxury, but with "thousands" of Hawaiians who would return to their "comfortless, unfurnished, grass-thatched habitations." Man does not live by bread alone, the celebrants might have told him, but in Bingham's mind another idea was "inscribed on all"—"vanity of vanities."[16]

The king, who seemed to Stewart a noble and gentlemanly figure when sober, was not sober for this occasion. "Nearly naked" and barely managing to stay on their horses, Liholiho and his train made a "sorry exhibition." A bodyguard of more than fifty men in "shabby uniform" tried to run after the king, while "hundreds of ragged natives" hooted and shouted in their wake.

The pageant was never held again. Though the Hawaiians as they embraced the "light" of Christianity were beginning to speak of their past as the "time of dark hearts," it does not take much imagination to see that the metaphors might as easily be reversed. In terms of the survival of Hawaiian customs, it was the future that looked dark. The pageant was one of the last great formal expressions of the Hawaiians' identity and civilization as they themselves defined these things. The moment now seems bittersweet, symbolically setting off the splendid isolation of the far-distant eighteenth-century past from a costly multi-cultural future. Viewed with the knowledge of what is to come, the pageant seems less important as a "sublime" celebration of the existing culture than as a courageous act of bravado.

Every evening so far, the missionaries had watched fires being lit in the grove of trees near the *Thames;* they had listened as the Hawaiians danced and shouted in "revelry and licentiousness" until daybreak. Now, on the final night, the singing and dancing reached its peak. As Stewart described it:

> The dull and monotonous sounds of the native drum and calabash, the wild notes of their songs in the loud choruses and responses of the various parties, and the pulsation, on the ground, of the tread of thousands in the dance, reached us even at the Missionary enclosure.

Literally dancing in darkness, the Hawaiians were also dancing against it.

It was a weary group of missionary women who anticipated the arrival of reinforcements that spring. Lucy Thurston, remembering the Chamberlains, could only hope no children would be sent. Maria Loomis, who had spent much of the winter caring for a still-delicate Amanda, lamented, "I seem to have lost all the energy I ever possessed." She hoped the new missionaries "will at least revive our spirits." When they arrived (April 7, 1823), the immediate problems were practical: how to feed and house fourteen more adults, one newborn (the Stewarts' son, born on the ship), and four more Hawaiian youths from the mission school at Cornwall. To this end, one of the downstairs rooms in the house was extended into the hallway to make a large dining room (much easier on the women than running up and down the cellar stairs). The dreaded "long table" once again appeared. But there was a new stone cook house and, for the first time, some hired help for a few weeks—a cook. As soon as the new missionaries received permission from Liholiho to reside in the country—this time given readily, the king even rescinding the $80 harbor fee—everyone settled into a room of the frame house or one of the three thatched houses. Among married couples, there were three ordained ministers and their wives (Artemas and Elizabeth Bishop, William and Clarissa Richards, and Charles and Harriet Stewart), a physician (Dr. Blatchely and his wife, Jemima), and two assistant missionary couples (James and Louisa Ely and Joseph and Martha Goodrich). Levi Chamberlain, a businessman before he turned to Christianity, came to manage the supplies, and Betsey Stockton, a single black woman who had received an education while working as a domestic in the family of the president of Princeton University, came to teach and to help the Stewart family.[17]

In mid-May, Maria Loomis remarked on an "interesting" week past. "The brethren have held meetings for business almost every day," she wrote, while "the sisters have been present as much as possible and listened with much interest to the important subjects discussed." This was no improvement over the way things were handled a year earlier, when the English deputation arrived from Tahiti. Maria called that day one of the "happiest" of her life as a missionary. But she also could not avoid the analogy between herself and the biblical woman who toiled while her sister entertained Jesus: "I am like Martha," she wrote, "cumbered with much serving, and cannot enjoy their company as I would like." The division of labor at these meetings, with the men discussing the issues before the mission and the women listening or working in the background, heralded an increasingly rigid pattern.[18]

The pattern was reinforced that summer when the men wanted to explore more of the islands before deciding upon locations for new mission stations. The question of location was quickly resolved for two families when Keopuolani, returning to Maui from Oahu, asked for teachers. The Richards and Stewart families (including Betsey Stockton) sailed with the queen mother for Maui on May 28. Elisha Loomis went along to help them settle in. But further decisions were postponed until some of the other men could explore Hawaii. Asa Thurston, Joseph Goodrich, Artemas Bishop, and the young watch repairman, Mr. Harwood, left on June 24, followed by William Ellis a few days later, for a tour that would last ten weeks (until September 4). Samuel Ruggles (though not Nancy) soon left Honolulu to return to his home in Kauai, and in early August Hiram Bingham visited Maui.[19]

Back in the mission compound, the women were feeling, as Sybil put it, "the absence of our richest earthly comforts." There was plenty of companionship of a different sort from eleven children aged six and under. By this time, Mary Ellis was so ill that, in order to care for her more easily, the women moved her from a thatched house to the frame house. Lucy Thurston had given birth to her second child, a daughter, Lucy Goodale, a few days before the reinforcements arrived. Sybil's health during August, according to Maria Loomis, was "very poor." Elizabeth Bishop, one of the new missionaries, was expecting a child in September. In mid-July, high winds caused a dust storm. Several thatched houses blew down (though none of the mission's); the dust rose in such clouds that people wore handkerchiefs over their faces to protect their eyes. "The dust sifted through the thatching & every crack like snow," wrote Maria Loomis. Storm or not, the women's duties went on. Each woman took her turn at the long table for one or two days at a time. "When we get through the labors of the day," wrote Maria, "we are tired out & half-sick, & yet we have more facilities for doing work than ever before." Sybil did try to continue teaching a group of scholars in a vacant house, but gave it up after a few weeks, not wanting, she explained, "to lose my name on the list of domestic helpers." Her conclusion about the summer was sobering: "The female part of our community were, during the summer, allowed to do but little directly in the way of enlightening the heathen but we had our burdens to bear, & our various parts to perform."[20]

Although Hiram Bingham and Asa Thurston had been preaching in Hawaiian for almost a year, and Samuel Whitney began in March 1823, the women were still struggling to acquire the language. Maria admitted to Nancy Ruggles "with shame" that her progress was slow: "So many cares & interruptions to engross my time that I find but little time to devote to the language." Sybil had the same problem, explaining to her sister Lucy in January 1824 that she had laid aside her journal since the previous March from a "conviction of duty." To Mrs. Bates she explained, "I thought my pen must turn to language only for some time to come." Determined to achieve their goal, the women began in 1823 to set aside an hour or two for language lessons each afternoon, practiced writing notes to one another, and memorized sentences to recite at meals. Gradually they achieved fluency, though much more slowly than the men.[21]

After returning from Hawaii on September 4, the men began meeting twice a day "debating and discussing various points deeply interesting." Here was the first opportunity to rethink the mission's organization according to the pioneers' experience. The "hardships" the women had faced "in attempting to provide for so large and complicated a family as we then had" received some attention. The consensus was that each station would decide for itself whether to live and eat as individual families or as a group. Large boarding establishments for Hawaiian children seemed unwise, but if each woman would take three Hawaiian children into her home, then thirty-three children might be "kept perhaps in better order than if thrown together in one boarding school." These discussions were born of the men's sympathy for the women's labor. But the women's sense of acting "remotely" on the great cause was not a high priority (nor could they speak out at meetings to address the problem). More concerned about the need to reach as many Hawaiians as possible, the men debated the intended locations for various missionaries. It took until October to decide to send the Thurstons back to Kailua with the Bishops (Elizabeth being Lucy's childhood friend), the Ruggleses and Goodriches to Waiakea (close to Hilo, on the opposite side of the island of Hawaii from Kailua), and the Elys to Kauai (though this destination later changed to Kailua as well).

The new couples were not ready to leave immediately. On September 30, 1823, Elizabeth Bishop almost died during a night of "excruciating distress" as she delivered a stillborn infant. "I think it would be impossible to suffer much more & live," wrote Maria Loomis. In November, the Bishops and Thurstons left Honolulu, the Bishops visiting Kauai for several months before finally settling in Kailua in 1824, the Thurstons heading straight for Kailua. Clarissa Richards and Louisa Ely safely delivered sons on the first and nineteenth of December. Not until January 16 did the mission compound finally empty out. A chartered schooner took a group of missionaries to Hawaii—the Goodriches and Ruggleses to Waiakea, the Elys to Kailua (with the intention of ministering to Kapiolani and her people in nearby Kaawaloa), Levi Chamberlain and Rev. Ellis to the volcano, and Dr. and Mrs. Blatchely to Kailua for a few months' visit. "Thus we are left quite alone again," wrote Maria Loomis.[22]

A reduction in numbers did not necessarily imply an easier domestic life. Maria had severely bruised her knee in early January when two galloping horsemen did not give her enough warning to step safely out of the road: she fell on her face, and the horse stepped on her legs. She recovered by staying in bed for a few days; she coped mentally by filtering the incident through her religious ideas. Praising God's mercy for preserving her life, she renewed her desire to "devote that life more to his service than I have yet done." That service was still primarily domestic. Since Sybil's health continued to be poor, she could not help much. It was up to Maria to do what had to be done: care for the invalid Mary Ellis and her family, move her own household things back into the frame house, air the trunks (which were damp from standing on the ground in a thatched house), clean the frame house, and supervise the domestic chores in general. "Should I be taken down," she confessed, "I hardly know what we should all do." A few days later, on January 11, 1824, Sybil bore her third child, named after the revered Jeremiah Evarts, who had become corresponding secretary of the ABCFM in 1821. This baby (weighing eight and a half pounds) lived, but in frail health. By May, Maria reflected that the "poor afflicted child . . . has taken the whole of his mother's time and attention ever since he was 3 weeks old."[23]

In January 1824, as Sybil thought back on the previous months of crowding and labor occasioned by the arrival of the new missionaries, she realized that the situation in Honolulu was peculiarly taxing. As the central missionary station, where the supplies were located, where most of the ships landed, where the general meetings were held every spring, Honolulu was less lonely than other stations, but its steady diet of disruptions made for another kind of psychological pressure. In a letter to her sister Lucy at this time, Sybil supposed that "many of the bustling cares & labors have arisen, perhaps, from the plan of our mission [in Honolulu], and are not attendant on the situation of every missionary. This will alter," she expected, "as the calls increase for the occupying of new stations, and tho it will not make our labors less, it will cause those of the female part especially to be different, and what comforts me most in prospect of it is the hope that they will be less secular."[24]

In the long run, Sybil's assumption never proved true. The pressure on the women continued to be centripetal: the day by day demands of child care, nursing, cooking, sewing, and cleaning enforced their presence in the mission house. As the children increased in number and reached the age for formal schooling, their needs required more attention to "secular" labor, not less. Peripatetic labor routinely went to the men. The women took modest excursions – a canoe ride one morning up the Waimea River "quite refreshed" Mercy Whitney; a trip to Waikiki delighted Maria Loomis and young Levi (though the child had spent so much of his young life on the treeless plain of the mission houses that he cried from fear at seeing palm groves).[25] In 1824, Maria traveled to Lahaina on the island of Maui, the first time she had left Oahu since her arrival. But such excursions were rare compared with the constant travels of some of the men, especially in Hawaii and Kauai, as they went from village to village, preaching to as many Hawaiians as possible. When, in later years, Kaahumanu and other *alii* made tours around the islands to spread Christianity, the men of the mission often went along. What labor the men did do inside the mission houses was not domestic but intellectual – translating texts into Hawaiian, composing lyrics for hymns, and writing sermons. Though the women continued to demonstrate an example of Christian life and kept up their informal activities with ruling *alii,* the most significant work of the mission now went on in the new institutions, as schools expanded and men began conducting services for enormous congregations. The work inside the mission houses became more and more a matter of indirect influence.

This was unfortunate, since there are signs that the women were beginning to accommodate to the Hawaiians. In 1823, Maria Loomis watched the chiefs play in the Waikiki surf: "They seemed quite in their element and as much at ease as if on land." That same year, traveling back to Kailua on a native ship, Lucy Thurston found the style of eating not the most "fastidious." But she forebore: "When the faithful half-clad servant so kindly cleansed a bowl on the flap of his only garment, in which to prepare some tea, ladling in the sugar with an unsparing hand, and crumbling in the sea bread with his teeth, I could not do else than receive and drink it, saying nothing for conscience sake!" Mercy Whitney was more chagrined but equally convinced of the need for tolerance as she too reflected upon a shipboard experience:

> The interview could have been pleasant had it not been for the crowd of natives which accompanied the King & Queen, but they must necessarily have their attendants! Some to carry spit dishes, others to keep off the flies. Imagine how you would feel with thirty or perhaps forty naked Indians about you, some sitting in one place some in another & others stretched on the mats so thick that you must either step over or with difficulty get round them & then you will have some idea of my situation. But placed as we are among a heathen people we are obliged in some measure to tolerate it, if we would gain the confidence & secure the favours of the chiefs, who generally have a large train of servants about them.

Though the women remain dismayed at "heathen" habits, they remember that the true source of value lay under the skin—not with the trappings of "civilization" like proper clothing but with good character or the soul to be saved. These they hoped to secure for themselves as well as for Hawaiians. The starting point of human depravity remained the same for all. After visiting a Hawaiian home in 1823, Mercy wrote, "I thought to myself, such visits to the houses of poverty are profitable, well calculated to make me go home contented and thankful—blessing God for his distinguishing goodness"—but not because the visits made her feel superior. She herself was "one no better by nature than the vilest and most despicable heathen." When Sybil Bingham tried to introduce Hawaiians to her correspondents, she reacted similarly:

> Their yet unknown tongue, their rude unpolished manner, the vermin attached to them, with their loathsome disorder render them no very pleasant companions and would often make the sinking heart say, excuse me from farther intercourse with them, did not the *just object of this nation's accession to the kingdom of Christ,* rise paramount to every other making all else trifles.

This is not the same as modern tolerance (which has its other face, indifference), but it is something better than simpleminded recoil.[26]

But as the women struggled with their attitudes toward Hawaiians, they also continued to cope with their attitudes toward women's place. Here, little change was possible, the pressure on them (partly self-imposed) to be good mothers and "true women" very much a part of their lives. There was no easy way to relieve their labor. "We cannot, as you can," Maria Loomis reminded her family in February 1824, "go out and hire a nurse." Everyone had some help from Hawaiians, but rarely judged their labor up to mission standards. Among Mercy Whitney's "native assistants" were a cook who had been with them almost as long as they had lived in Kauai and a steward who set the table, washed dishes, helped with washing and ironing, and fetched water. Mercy called them "as faithful as we could expect, tho not to be compared with those who have been trained to habits of industry." Hawaiians, who helped care for infants, might have cared for older children as well, but the fear of "moral contamination" made that seem dangerous. The women tried to teach themselves to relax housekeeping standards a bit. "Could I let it go more as it happens," Sybil realized, "I could make it much easier." But the wisdom of relaxation, associated with laziness, was easily resisted. "Many times when I felt extremely languid," admitted Mercy, "& it seemed to require an effort to move, I have imputed it in part to sloth getting hold of me & have endeavored to shake it off." Not until 1832 did Lucy Thurston report that both men and women learned to dismiss that judgment of "indolence," realizing that "a Northern constitution can not labor here as in America."[27]

The women's correspondence, while it brought no respite from labor, still gave them pleasure and solace. The cry of "Sail O!" heralded the arrival of a whaleship with its mixed blessing—a potentially rowdy and diseased crew and precious letters. It would be hard to underestimate the emotional significance of the hundreds of letters received and sent by each woman. They wrote them when they could, often late at night after the day's chores were completed, or into the early hours of the morning when a ship's captain willing to carry them was about to leave. Writing letters enforced a period of relative calm and quiet, which for Sybil Bingham, especially, became a pleasant ritual. In the scene she painted for her correspondents, she and Hiram sit in their room in the frame house, portable desks on their laps, their pens busily covering the pages, as Sophia sleeps nearby in her cradle.[28]

But because the journals and letters had an alarming tendency to find their way back to their authors in print, they were not a perfect medium for self-expression. Mercy Whitney found herself "not a little chagrined at the sight" of her journal in print during the summer of 1822; Maria Loomis, discovering a letter of hers published in the Utica, New York, *Sentinel,* called it "extremely mortifying" and "half-resolved" not to send any more communications. Sybil was grateful to her sister in 1832 for having "acted discreetly, in making my letters in a good measure *tabu.*" Partly the women wanted the Board to control what reached the public eye so as to keep the donations coming; partly, of course, they felt their privacy betrayed. More often, simple fatigue checked the frequency of their meditations. Even the journals of prolific writers like Mercy and Sybil stop now and again for months at a time. Resuming her journal in March 1825, Mercy discovered that a year had gone by since her last entry, a year spent in a "feeble state of health." When Maria wrote in May 1824, she had been keeping up her journal for the four years since landing, but she felt discouraged about it. "I think my journal cannot be very interesting," she wrote. "I am sometimes tempted to give up writing entirely so little do I feel in a mood for saying anything that would be quite interesting. It see[m]s that such constant & fatiguing labor quite unfits my mind for writing."[29]

But there were powerful reasons for persisting, intellectual as well as emotional. As much as church services or prayer meetings, the letters helped the women nurture their religious convictions. Acknowledging letters and parcels in late April of 1824, a grateful Maria Loomis wrote, "And what return can I make for so many undeserved favors. . . . I hope I shall more entirely devote myself to my work & be more zealous to do good to the perishing souls by whom I am surrounded." As Mercy Whitney wrote, she often moved from homely detail—a bureau that allowed her to store food away from the mice and cockroaches; the leaks in her thatched roof; Samuel's efforts to secure a cow for milk—to theological meditation. One entry from July 3, 1825, moves easily from housework to the Judgment Day:

> You who are privileged with good houses & tight rooms can have but little idea of the labor which is necessary to keep thatched or mud houses clean. Destitute as we are of boards, we are obliged to dispense with a chamber floor, so that we have the dirt constantly scattering from the roof, in addition to what falls from the walls. The dust too from without, which frequently rises like a cloud, forces its way through the holes & covers everything which is in the least exposed. Houses built as ours is, cannot be expected to endure many years & considering the heavy rains we sometimes have in the wet season, it seems surprising how they stand so long. Our old house which was frequently giving way & almost ready to tumble down I have often thought a fit emblem for its occupants.

The religious perspective on these homely details is not far from her mind. The next sentence continues:

> Those who are on a journey cannot always expect the best accommodations, & it is well to have something continually to remind us, that we are strangers and pilgrims here on earth. The more homely our fare, & the fewer our accommodations, the more ardently shall we long to arrive at our journey's end, & be at home in our Father's house. But O! my dear friends—shall we ever meet in that world where the wicked cease from troubling & the weary are at rest! How important that each & all of us, should put the solemn—the momentous question to ourselves, am I prepared for death?[30]

Religious thinking filled a deep need not simply because it addressed the women's spiritual nature but because it allowed an escape from their physical one. It was a much needed solace. To have time to think at all in a life that demanded much physical labor was a kind of privilege—a respite from those labors. To think about religion was to escape from the world of the senses that was devalued in relation to the world of the mind. It was a way to put life into perspective, not as "rest" but as a journey to be endured by "strangers and pilgrims" for the sake of a final reward.

The pattern for the mission as a whole was in one sense the opposite of that for individual families. The mission spread from island to island (six stations and nine churches by mid-1824) as if responding to the centrifugal pressure implied in the command to go and preach the gospel. This pattern continued through the next decade. All the missionaries gathered only once a year, during the General Meeting, usually held in Honolulu in April. The mission family had more than doubled with the addition of new workers. The third company added sixteen more missionaries in 1828. This augured loss as well as gain. The mission could reach increasing numbers of Hawaiians, but at the cost of its own familial unity.

This dissolution had begun for the first company in the summer of 1820, when the Ruggleses and Whitneys went to Kauai. But the trend intensified as each new company of missionaries arrived and dispersed to new stations. In June 1826, Mercy reflected that she had not even met six of the missionaries who came with the second company, and that she had seen the Stewarts and Betsey Stockton for only one evening amid a large crowd of persons. "Thus you see," she wrote, "that we may be fellow labourers in the vineyard and yet as great strangers to each other, as though separated thousands of miles." Nancy Ruggles wrote from Kaawaloa in 1833 that she had not met "the last two reinforcements, besides those which have arrived this spring." Not having been to the General Meeting in three years, she saw only the missionaries who visited her station. The special bonds among the pioneers, formed during the enforced solitude of their voyage on the *Thaddeus,* could not be immediately recreated with a new company. The communal nature of the mission was not entirely lost: the stores were centrally located and parceled out in Honolulu, and roughly half the families shared stations. But, increasingly, the communal mission "family" of the first three years became a collection of nuclear families.[31]

Though the women of the first company continued to write of one another with great affection, circumstances of mission life made it impossible to maintain their earlier closeness. Distance, of course, separated them. This meant only occasional visits and letters, it being understood that correspondence with families and benefactors had higher priority. Relationships with distant shipmates receded as each woman's own family increased in size and her missionary neighbors near at hand engaged what precious time was left for friendships. Lucy Thurston welcomed her childhood friend, Elizabeth Edwards Bishop, to Kailua; after the Loomises went back to America in 1827, Sybil Bingham shared the frame house, ultimately divided in half, with Laura Judd, wife of the medical doctor who arrived with the third company in 1828. Mercy Whitney, unlike the others of the first company, was usually alone. The Ruggleses' life was more peripatetic than most, as they moved from Waimea down the coast to Hanapepe, Kauai, then lived in Honolulu, in Hilo, Hawaii, and finally in Kaawaloa (fifteen miles south of the Thurstons in Kailua).

To hold everyone together, there was always the General Meeting, as much a social event as an occasion for business. But the women did not always attend, prevented by sickness in the family or their own ill health, or simply dreading the "inconveniences" of interisland voyages. This was Mercy's euphemism (from a letter of 1831) for the real miseries of spending several days and nights scarcely able to move aboard filthy, overcrowded vessels. If the women attempted to rest below, the heat or the stench of bilge water (once it was fermented poi) drove them back on deck. Hogs squealed, Hawaiians chattered and smoked, children vomited, and the missionaries, seasick and sleepless themselves, scooped up cockroaches by the handfuls or picked off bedbugs and fleas. Mercy Whitney, who endured a lifetime of such voyages, once remarked, mildly enough, "Unless we have some important object in view, we seldom feel like undertaking it, for mere personal gratification." Lucy Thurston put it more bluntly: "After reaching Kailua, I often said with the utmost sincerity: 'Never ask me again to go upon the ocean. Let me live and die here.'"[32]

Even when the women did gather, there was not always perfect unity. There was a working assumption that everyone had the same commitment to the Lord's work. That was not always enough, perhaps one of the reasons why, as early as January 1824, the second company having very recently arrived, Sybil Bingham meditated on the "suitable qualifications" of a missionary: "Very perceptible is the difference in education, habits of life, temper of mind &c &c in our little community." Though always played down, failures of rapport among fellow missionaries, initiated so dramatically with the Holmans, continued with later arrivals. Members of later companies were inclined to resent the leadership of Hiram Bingham. The larger and more complicated the mission became, the more different personalities there were to cope with, the more there was to argue about.[33]

Even as long-range problems peculiar to the mission family were beginning to surface, what the mission had to offer was looking better to Hawaiians. In mid-September of 1823, Keopuolani, wife of Kamehameha I, mother of his next two successors (Liholiho and Kauikeaouli), the highest-ranking chiefess in the islands, lay dying in Lahaina. She was born the same year that Captain Cook reached Hawaii, 1778, so that for forty-five years her life had coincided exactly with the "new" Hawaii open to foreigners. She, along with Kaahumanu, had been responsible for persuading Liholiho to break the eating *kapus.* During the past year, she had been receiving special instruction from some of the Tahitians who had accompanied Rev. Ellis and had begun to listen attentively to what the Christians were saying. She had demonstrated her break with the past by publicly defending the missionaries against the criticisms of other chiefs, by reproving Liholiho's drunken conduct, and by casting aside her second husband in favor of a monogamous marriage to Hoapili (a high chief and later governor of Maui). Now, in her final illness, she was speaking the words the missionaries delighted to hear: "*Aroha ino iau i ke Akua*" (Great indeed is my love to God). To her children, to her husband, to the chiefs gathering around her, she delivered essentially the same message: that they should "protect" the missionaries and follow their teachings. "Walk the straight path," she charged Liholiho. "Observe the Sabbath. Serve God. Love Jesus Christ." She was especially concerned that her two youngest children (Kauikeaouli and Nahienaena) receive Christian training. She now believed, as she told Kalanimoku, that "the gods of Hawaii are false."[34]

Sixteen years earlier, during another illness, three men had been sacrificed to ensure Keopuolani's recovery. Now she refused the "death companions" who had journeyed to Lahaina to offer themselves for that purpose and forbade all Hawaiian displays of mourning except wailing. She asked for a Christian burial and, more important, for baptism—"to be washed with water in the name of God." Dr. Blatchley, summoned from Oahu by Liholiho, could not cure her, but Rev. Ellis, arriving soon after, did ease the agitation of her mind. After consulting with the other missionaries as to the propriety of giving the sacrament, and waiting in vain for the queen to rouse herself from sleep, Ellis baptized her in her dying coma on September 16, 1823. Her chosen baptismal name was Harriet, honoring a missionary wife, Mrs. Charles Stewart. So seriously did the missionaries take this sacrament that the reports home convey a sense of doubts overcome and defensiveness. The letter that reached Mercy Whitney in Kauai said, "We think she died a Christian." "I believe there was no doubt upon the mind of the brethren there," wrote Maria Loomis (thereby underlining the possibility that there might have been) "as to the propriety of administering the ordinance of baptism." But no one doubted the significance of the event. "Thus the highest tabu chiefess," wrote Kamakau, "became the first Hawaiian convert."[35]

The missionaries mourned her as a person. Maria Loomis wrote simply, "In her the brethren have lost a mother and friend." Her Hawaiian subjects paid her the tribute of mourning her as she requested—wailing in the traditional manner but (despite the easy availability of liquor) without licentious abandon and self-inflicted mutilations. Thousands assembled near the beach at Lahaina to hear the funeral sermon; four hundred joined the procession to accompany the body to its tomb. A woodcut of the funeral cortege shows the mourners in a sober and orderly line. Friends and relatives carried stones from a ruined *heiau* to build a wall enclosing the tomb, as if demonstrating that the stones of paganism were simply stones. Their actions foretold a future where Christianity would continue, literally and figuratively, to build upon the old religion's ruined foundation. But Liholiho, speaking for his people, gave the baptism a darker cast: "She was lost to them," he was reported to have said, "having some time previous given herself up to Christ."[36]

Hiram Bingham wrote of the "invigorated courage" the missionaries took from this success, reaffirming their own commitment to enlightening the nation. Many of the *alii* met them halfway, with the first of many requests for baptism coming from Kaahumanu, Opiia (Kaahumanu's sister), and Puaaiki (a blind singer in the household of a high chief, and eventually one of the earliest and most devout preachers of the new religion). Kalanimoku wanted to know if his previous baptism by the French (in 1819) was "good or not." The missionaries, finding their "duty" in these cases not "easily settled," kept the Hawaiians waiting. The following March, after the death of "Governor Cox" (the ruler of Maui and Kaahumanu's brother), the requests came "repeatedly," but were still refused. The sacrament no doubt took on greater significance for the Hawaiians for being so difficult to obtain (though that of course was not the missionaries' reason for hesitation). When Kaahumanu sent a note to William Ellis and Hiram Bingham on April 3, 1824, again requesting baptism, they again hesitated. Until they could be sure, explained the "Sandwich Islands Journal," that she understood the full "seriousness" of the sacrament, which required "holiness of heart & true & unreserved devotedness to Christ," they could not baptize her.[37]

Liholiho took no part in the importuning. The missionaries, however, still saw him as the person it was most important to convert. In August 1822 the king was receiving daily lessons at the mission house. Hiram Bingham was still tenaciously following him about Oahu, not daring to let him go north of Honolulu to Puuloa for ten days without a teacher (even though this meant, in January 1823, leaving an exhausted Sybil behind to grieve for the just-buried Levi Parsons). Kamakau had good words for Liholiho—"He was kind and gentle to the poor; he took orphans and children of the poor under his care; he treated the missionaries kindly; he saw to it that his younger brothers were educated; he could read and write"—but, the historian continued, "when it came to expressing his faith in God, he paid no attention to it." And he was still very much the king. During one visit, when Hiram Bingham placed an uncorked bottle of liquor upside-down on a mat (thereby showing his disapproval without losing the liquor), he had gone too far. The indignant king spoke in words Hiram could not translate, but in a tone that was unmistakable. The *alii* present, seeing the king's wrath (and remembering that he had recently ordered a chief beheaded), prudently urged Hiram's retreat.[38]

Liholiho was more interested in the West's secular and political side, and announced a voyage to England in November 1822.[39] Prompted in part by the increases in foreign whalers and trading vessels, with attendant disruptions in the port areas and unforeseeable implications for the future, Liholiho remembered the "special relationship" that the Hawaiians thought they had with the British. (This dated from the visits of the first explorers and found formal expression in an agreement between George Vancouver and Kamehameha I in 1794 and in subsequent correspondence from 1810 to 1812 between the monarchs of both countries; although Kamehameha I had not ceded the islands, as Vancouver believed, he had certainly wanted to protect his small country from foreign domination by allying it with the strongest naval power in the world.) The voyage was evidently a long-held ambition of Liholiho's, made possible in part by the death of his mother, who had objected to it. Now he could satisfy his curiosity about the places which had sent ships and citizens to his islands and which had already been seen by many of his countrymen. He could expect recognition and honor as a monarch as he tried to promote his country's claims. And, not least (as Kamakau believed), he could escape from the perplexing task of ruling Hawaii, which had meant contending not only with Kaahumanu but with other ambitious chiefs who had taken over his father's sandalwood monopoly and "all the larger tracts of land." This having led to various difficulties in collecting taxes and gifts, one explanation for the voyage was that Liholiho was "ashamed." During the year leading up to the voyage, Liholiho had been drinking, running up debts, gambling, and encouraging the hula.

On November 27, 1823, twelve Hawaiians, including Boki, his wife Liliha, and Liholiho's wife Kamamalu boarded the English whaler *L'Aigle.* Thousands stood on the beach wailing. Once at sea, Liholiho, evidently supposing that his departure might be prevented, soon realized that no boat was coming to take them back. "Ah," he said, "they have long despised us." (In fact, one chief who proposed detaining the king had almost had his clothes torn off his back.) Kamakau's account of the departure foreshadows its conclusion: the ship sank beneath the horizon "as if going down into the grave." In London, less than a year later, even before Liholiho could have his audience with George III, the young king at thirty-two and his queen at twenty-six were dead of measles.

Not until the following year, in March 1825, did the news reach Honolulu, followed shortly by the arrival of the HMS *Blonde* with the caskets. In the meantime, the departure of the king and Boki left the government in the hands of *alii* sympathetic to the missionaries: Kalanimoku, Hoapili, Kapiolani, Kaahumanu, and Kaumualii. With Kauikeaouli, Liholiho's nine-year-old heir, still too young to rule, Kaahumanu assumed the regency (with the other chiefs under her authority) and continued it until her death in 1832. Unlike Liholiho, torn between past and present, she had made her peace with the old religion by turning her back on it. Liquor, the equivocal gift of the newcomers and particular bane of Liholiho, she could resist. Under her tutelage, there seemed little doubt that the country was going to continue to learn about Western religion and culture.[40]

The need for some new laws, especially those that would help control the increasing numbers of sailors on shore, was obvious. In March 1822, almost as soon as the mission press began operating, two "Notices" were printed to warn that "riotous" sailors would be imprisoned in the fort until released by a thirty-dollar fine, and that foreigners "disturbing the peace" would be imprisoned and returned home. But in many of the new regulations, missionary influence is more explicit. Things began to look different after Liholiho's departure: "The chiefs were not drinking so much," wrote Kamakau, "the interest in hula, in sex-attracting games at night (*'aha 'ume o ka po*), and other defiling amusements had decreased." In December, just a month after *L'Aigle* sailed, a crier proclaimed that the Sabbath should be strictly observed, not even allowing fires to be kindled. In April 1824, in Honolulu, when the chiefs gathered for a special meeting to discuss "national reform," Kalanimoku delivered a "stirring address" recommending the new religion, the *palapala*, and missionary instruction in general: his listeners assented, "*Ae.*" Hiram Bingham and William Ellis next addressed the meeting, urging their favorite prohibitions—"waste of time by idleness & sport, the practice of gaming for money . . . the abuse of the institution of marriage as well as violations of the Sabbath." That May, in Lahaina, Kaahumanu added to the proscriptions of December: a crier announced that from now on there was to be no murder, no drunkenness, no boxing, no fighting, no theft, and no work or play on the Sabbath. The final requirement was that "all the people shall learn the *palapala*."[41]

Kaahumanu herself had demonstrated her commitment to these requirements at the quarterly examinations held in April 1824, where, amid over five hundred pupils, she was the first to be examined. On her slate she had written, "This is my word and hand—I am making myself strong. I declare in the presence of God I repent of my sin, & believe God to be our Father." Kalanimoku, who could not be present, sent a note in his own handwriting, which (as translated by the missionaries) said, "Love to Mr. B.—This is my writing which my hand has made—Just look at it. I love the words from you." The three-hour examination reached a thrilling end when the pupils as a group recited some Scripture. As Hiram Bingham described it:

> Approaching the close, the interest appeared to rise; and as the pupils who were trained to it came out in exact time upon the last line, and with elevated and united voice, shouted, "*Hoolea i Iehova,* —Praise the Lord," the queen, imagining that God was present, or was descending upon us exclaimed, "*Ua ilihia au!*" [I am struck with awe!]

Bingham, remembering the words of Eliphaz (Job 4:15), thought he knew what she meant:

> The Spirit passed before my face,
> The hair of my flesh stood up.

The next evening, Kaahumanu exhorted the scholars and the pupils to follow Christian teachings. She wondered, logically enough, why she could not now be baptized. But once again, the missionaries were not certain that she had been "born from above by the power of the Spirit of God."[42]

Taking stock in the public journal on the fourth anniversary of their landing, April 19, 1824, the missionaries applauded their accomplishments: 600 students (up from 238 in the previous quarter), 2,000 copies of the hymnbook in print, and 3,000 copies of the book of elementary lessons. (A stone printing house had been finished in December 1823.) These aids to learning and worship the missionaries could offer gladly. But they, as yet, could not bring themselves to offer the sacraments.

In the meantime, the *alii,* demonstrating their commitment to the new teachings, began to do their own missionary work. During the summer of 1824, Kaahumanu and her sister Kalakua faced down a woman who arrived in Lahaina claiming to be a prophetess of Pele, the Hawaiian goddess of the volcano. Accusing the missionaries of violating Pele's *kapus* (eating sacred berries and rolling stones into the craters), the woman was threatening retaliation if the chiefs would not dismiss the missionaries and suppress the *palapala.* "You are a woman, like one of us," Kaahumanu told her. "There is one God, who made you and us." Successful in their reproof, the chiefesses got the woman to confess her lies and go home. As visible signs of faith, churches went up at the new mission settlements. In Lahaina, a church was built and dedicated by August 27, 1823, just three months after the missionaries settled there. In Kaawaloa (fifteen miles south of the mission settlement in Kailua, on Hawaii), Kapiolani and Naihe (her husband), disappointed that teachers had not been assigned to their village immediately, built a large church, 60 by 30 feet, which was dedicated on March 29, 1824. When that did not get immediate results, they built a house for a future missionary, promising to supply the family with water. This being the kind of determination missionaries understood, they sent the Elys to the spot (instead of to Waimea, where the Whitneys consented to staying on alone). In Honolulu, in April 1824, Kaahumanu bought a two-story frame house with rooms that were papered, painted, and ceiled, and a veranda that overlooked the harbor. ("Governor Adams" had a similar house in Kailua.) The Ellises moved opposite the mission house into one made of coral rock. By mid-summer, Kalanimoku had moved next-door, into a large, two-story house built in the "modern" style with glass windows and painted walls.[43]

But, in a sense, new buildings were the least of the changes. The Hawaiians were beginning to follow the missionaries' moral ideas, especially those regulating sexual conduct. Hoapili, not long after Keopuolani's death, married one of Liholiho's wives, Kalakua, in the islands' second Christian wedding ceremony (the first for *alii*). Kaahumanu dissolved her marriage to Kaumualii's son when she was made to understand that it violated biblical teaching. By 1825, when criers proclaimed that husbands and wives must not "forsake" one another, the Christian institution of marriage was already taking root. Since in Hawaiian culture the only public ceremony relating to marriage took place among *alii,* the new ceremony, available to everyone, must have carried status. By the late 1820s, the ministers were holding mass ceremonies to meet the demand. In 1826, the old practice of living together without public ceremony was forbidden on Maui, and by 1827, in Hawaii, any new couples who were not married by a minister were punished with work on the public roads. By 1827 the first written law forbade prostitution, fornication, and adultery.[44]

But at present, in 1824, baptism continued to elude the *alii.* Only Kapiolani among the high chiefs thought herself not ready, "too wicked yet" as she put it, though she hoped "to be better by

& by." Those who coveted this nonmaterial attribute from the West continued to alter their behavior—wearing *holokus* (a long dress gathered from a yoke), saying grace at meals, observing the Sabbath. In Honolulu, Charles Stewart began a singing school at the request of Hawaiians who wanted to learn to sing as the missionaries did, succeeding with their "rude voices" much better than expected. When the meeting house burned down on May 30, 1824 (probably from arson), the pulpit, doors, seats, and windows were saved, and the entire structure (now able, at 75 by 25 feet, to hold 600 people) was rebuilt by mid-July. The few changes made for the new building speak eloquently to the desire to mold behavior during services to missionary standards of docility and silence. This time the plans included a fifteen-foot-high fence around the yard so that no one outside the church could see in. A triangular fence behind the pulpit was designed to keep the chiefs' attendants from sitting there and disrupting the services with chatter. For the *alii*, who were unused to demands not satisfied, it cannot have been easy to wait for baptism.[45]

Liholiho's absence by no means cleared the way for everyone to be interested in Christianity. Thousands of Hawaiians had yet to see a missionary; others were confused or skeptical. The practice of swimming out to the ships showed no signs of abating, though Boki was learning both to exploit such visits by charging the foreigners a dollar per head and to regulate them by firing a cannon at dusk and at dawn for arrivals and departures. Any regulation of sexual behavior that affected the dozens of libidinous sailors was ensuring future conflict. For the moment, with Kaahumanu and Kalanimoku making decisions, the trend in favor of Christian practices was strong. But the next generation of rulers would determine the future. Kauikeaouli (Kamehameha III) and his sister Nahienaena were being instructed in both the old and the new cultures. In superficial ways, this created no problems: they might arrive for a lesson in the *palapala* carried in the traditional way on the shoulders of their *kahus*. They wore elegant Western clothing or the brilliant feather cloak of their rank as occasion or mood dictated. But such ease masked profound differences between the two cultures, which came increasingly to be embodied in their lives and which could not easily be resolved by the usual route of the "pagan" custom's disappearing in the face of the Christian. For some problems there was no solution. And because the children symbolized the Hawaiian nation and culture, their suffering became that of all Hawaiians.[46]

The problem was sexual. With Kamehameha I as their father and the highest-ranking chiefess in the islands as their mother, brother and sister were under a cultural obligation—buttressed by centuries of tradition—to marry and continue their sacred bloodlines. The basis for marriage in trust and affection, even romantic love, was already in place, nurtured by the children's closeness in age (only a year and a half apart) and a shared upbringing. In another era, their union would have occasioned joy. But in June 1824, when the ruling chiefs met to discuss it (the children then being about nine and ten years old), it became an issue, dividing those chiefs who accepted the Christian prohibition against incest from those who held on to Hawaiian tradition. At Kaahumanu's request, Elisha Loomis did his best to explain the Christian disapproval of incest. But prevention, by this time, could not be part of any solution. It was "well known" in Lahaina, wrote Elisha (and according to Nahienaena's biographer was "probably true"), that sexual consummation between the two young adolescents had already occurred.

For the moment, the *alii* arguing against the marriage were successful. The missionaries in Lahaina took Nahienaena under their care, separating her from her brother in Honolulu. After Liholiho's death, Kauikeaouli (now Kamehameha III) remained in Honolulu. But these stratagems were merely a delaying action. The full burden of the clash between Hawaiian and Western morality was destined for the lives of these two children. Nahienaena's child (possibly fathered by her brother) was born and died in 1836. To Hawaiians, he represented the most sacred flower of nobility; to Christian eyes, a sin.[47]

Although, from the perspective of another century, Christianity's spread appears to have been inexorable, its progress was less like a simple forward march than an unpredictable dance—a few steps forward, a few back, a few sidesteps. Other evidence of tension between the old ways and the new—though less auspicious for lesser-ranking members of the Hawaiian population—was never far in the background. The year 1824 ushered in a series of unsettling deaths among Hawaiians connected with the mission. The missionaries noted the deaths as part of the distressing trend toward depopulation. (Mercy Whitney wrote just a year later that "the mortality of this nation is a motive which ought to excite us to steady, persevering and self-denying labors for their [Hawaiians'] good.") To some Hawaiians it looked as though disease or death was the price being exacted for their association with the missionaries. When William Richards wrote from Lahaina in June 1824 that ten out of thirty high chiefs had died within the past two years, he admitted: "Some say it is the *palapala.*" In March, when the friendly Kahekili Keeaumoku died ("Governor Cox" of Maui, and Kaahumanu's brother), the missionaries held Christian services over his body but did not know they were preaching over an empty casket. Skeptical Hawaiians had removed the bones, silently challenging the new God to tell the difference.[48]

In February, Sybil and Hiram Bingham lost their second family member, young William Beals, to a fever diagnosed as inflammation of the liver, but which was widely understood to have resulted from sexual activity. In little more than a day, he was dead. Like George Kaumualii and Nahienaena (and many other Hawaiians not so famous), William could not "put off" Hawaiian ways as easily as the missionaries expected. As a treasured *kahu,* he had been spending more and more time with the *alii.* Illogical in her grief, like the Hawaiians who blamed the *palapala,* Sybil looked to the company the boy was keeping. "Sad for him," she wrote, "was the time when royal favor first shone upon him." Mourning, she told her correspondents, "It is unnecessary for me to say to you that we loved this dear child."[49]

In Honolulu on May 26 came the most disturbing death, that of Kaumualii. Though not baptized, he appeared to remember Christian teachings as he died: "We have hope that he died in Jesus," wrote Sybil, "and that his spirit now rests with Him in glory." After a Christian burial service in Honolulu, his body was laid in Keopuolani's tomb in Lahaina. But in trusting the Christians himself, the old king of Kauai could not speak for other Hawaiians. One group who observed Charles Stewart praying and studying near an old *heiau* spread the rumor that the missionary had prayed Kaumualii to death and was beginning to do the same to Kalanimoku and the other chiefs. When the mission's men were working outside one day, some onlookers thought they should "kill the *haoles.*"[50]

Kaumualii, a skilled ruler and a decent man, was sincerely

mourned. "Some chiefs have two hearts—one good and one bad," remarked one of his stewards. "King Kaumualii, he have but one heart, and that was a good one." To describe the intensity of his emotion, he added, "I die with affection." When the news of the death reached Kauai on June 5, the king's former subjects, expressing their grief and breaking away from missionary teachings at the same time, began to spread disorder. Most of the chiefs had gone to Honolulu during Kaumualii's illness; the two or three who were left did not support the mission. Two months later, Mercy Whitney wrote, "Little or nothing has been done about the palapala—but in its stead rioting & drunkenness have been kept up." Sybil Bingham (visiting throughout the summer) remembered "the popular cry . . . 'Our king is dead, let us know no restriction,'" adding, "Every report from every part of the island was unpleasant. The house of worship was threatened with being burnt." For weeks, the church was nearly deserted on Sundays.

Sybil and Mercy had to balance their interest in this political crisis against the claims of domestic ones. Mercy's third child, Henry Martin, was born on the very day that the news arrived of the king's death. Inside the mission house during the next two months, the women lived under a kind of siege. "We were literally shut up among frantic heathen," wrote Sybil. Mercy "got up well" from childbirth after two weeks, but soon felt other ailments, badly swollen feet and ankles that made it difficult to walk, and a general frailness so pronounced by the end of the summer that she wrote to Lucy Thurston on August 5 meditating on death. Sybil had her own worries, centering on her sickly Evarts, now worsening and badly needing care from the mission's doctor, who was unable to get a passage from the windward side of Hawaii. For days and weeks, hoping for a vessel that would bring them news and return them to Oahu, she and Hiram watched for a sail.[51]

The women did not exaggerate the disquiet. Kalanimoku arrived from Honolulu on August 5 just in time for a war. The independent spirit that kept Kauai the most reluctant member of Hawaii's political union now resurfaced. Young George Kaumualii, passed over for the governorship, which Kalanimoku gave instead to his own nephew, Kahalaia, collected around him other disaffected chiefs and their men. At issue for some was the redistribution of chiefly lands upon the king's death, a custom that Kalanimoku refused to continue, telling the chiefs of Kauai that land ownership would remain unchanged. Others resented being governed by "windward chiefs" (a phrase referring to the direction of the other islands in relation to Kauai), who had dominated the political union of the islands since Kamehameha I's rule. Just before dawn on the day before the missionaries had expected to sail back to Oahu with Kalanimoku, they awoke to the sound of battle cries and gunfire. The rebels were trying to take over the fort in Waimea, which stood at the mouth of the river, not far from the mission house. Though the missionaries knew no more than this, "the whirring balls," wrote Sybil, "testified beyond a doubt that the affair was serious." The attack did not succeed, but when the firing stopped and Kalanimoku sent word for the missionary men to come to the fort, Sybil and Mercy, watching their husbands walk away, did not know this. "A few minutes passed and the firing again commenced," wrote Sybil. "Then it was my flesh & heart trembled. We looked upon one another and upon our sweet babes, but forbore to say, where are our protectors! It was a moment of heartfelt solicitude & deep suspense." The women soon learned that the men were being kept busy in caring for the wounded, burying the dead (fourteen by Sybil's count), and offering—at Kalanimoku's request—the appropriate thanks to God for the defeat of the rebels. Since this one short battle by no means signaled the end of hostilities, and since Kalanimoku was sending a vessel to Oahu to collect reinforcements, he urged the two young families to evacuate.[52]

In personal terms, the women's ordeal was not over. After hastily preparing some provisions for the voyage (while the men were conducting funeral services), the two families, with two nursing infants and three young children, set off in double canoes for the schooner. Sybil noticed the "foaming surf which . . . appeared like an enemy to resist our approach," but felt no alarm, having constantly witnessed the Hawaiian skill in paddling. But two of the waves that night were so large and fast that "we were compelled to buffet our way through them, our little ones terrified beyond reason & screaming as if the sea was about to swallow them up." Though the canoe did not capsize, all the provisions, including the drinking water and the changes of clothing for poor Evarts, were drenched. Sybil composed her thoughts to meet the crisis, remembering the "happy comfort" that "GOD our gracious preserver and protector would temper the wind to the shorn lamb." Once on board the small, uncomfortable schooner, the families were grateful for a speedy passage to Honolulu (from Sunday night to Tuesday morning), since everyone—adult or child—was seasick the entire time.[53]

The rebellion represented a serious threat to the political unity of the Hawaiian islands. The military challenge folded quickly. The rebellious Kauaians mysteriously held off from further aggression until hundreds of reinforcements for Kalanimoku's forces had arrived from Oahu and Maui. Although the rebels lost the battle fought on August 18, they then scattered into the forests, so that it took several more weeks to round them up. In early October a pitiable George Kaumualii was captured as he was quickly downing the last of his rum, hoping to make himself insensible to torture (which he never underwent). By December, the victorious chiefs (among them Hoapili of Maui) returned to Honolulu. When Kalanimoku finally returned to Honolulu in late January of 1825, having reconfirmed the political unity of the islands, he was called "the iron cable of our country," an epithet previously reserved for Kamehameha I.[54]

For the new Christian teachings as well as for the Hawaiian government, the rebellion offered a proving ground. Although this crisis seems to have been wholly a Hawaiian problem, remote from missionary concerns, it suggests the entanglement that makes the missionaries' instructions to have no "intermeddling with . . . political affairs" seem naive. Though the women were simply onlookers, the men of the mission were called in for advice. When the chiefs of Maui were gathering recruits to send to Kauai, they wondered how to square this with the Christian command to love one's enemies. The missionary there, William Richards, was uneasy, but counseled the right to defend oneself in a just war. In Lahaina and in Honolulu, the *alii* set aside days for fasting and prayer on the nation's behalf. The missionaries put their emphasis not on pacifism but on compassion for the vanquished. Hiram Bingham preached a sermon on the text "Be ye therefore merciful, as your Father also is merciful." Although one prisoner was stabbed and thrown overboard during the missionaries' voyage back to Honolulu from Kauai, that death was the exception that proved the rule. Kalanimoku, meeting the defeated George Kaumualii, said one word—"Live." To the ruling chiefs, who had met the crisis by trying to follow the teachings of the new god, it seemed that He had not failed them.

When the victorious chiefs returned to Honolulu, they requested a service of thanksgiving, with Hoapili, who had led the forces into battle, supplying the reason: "*I ke ola o kakou i ke Akua*—On account of our preservation by God."[55]

The following summer, in July 1825, over one hundred Hawaiians offered themselves as candidates for baptism, many of them explaining that they dated their love for the Christian God to the months following the insurrection. The close of the war also marked the beginning of widespread interest in learning to read. Kamakau reports that every chief's household had a teacher attached to it, forming a school. There were forty such schools in Honolulu and another forty in Waikiki. From the other islands came reports of schools established in almost every district as the missionaries and the newly trained Hawaiian teachers tried to satisfy the "multitudes" seeking the *palapala.* In May 1825, Mercy Whitney wrote from Kauai of the "unusual attention" paid to learning by the chiefs and people and of the "goodly number" meeting for prayers every Friday afternoon. Hiram Bingham recorded the words of a young supplicant asking for a book: "My desire to learn, my ear to hear, my eye to see, my hands to handle; from the sole of my foot to the crown of my head I love the *palapala.*" The distressing part of this otherwise encouraging situation was that the mission, relying on funds from the ABCFM (which was in considerable debt), simply could not afford to supply the paper and books that were needed. "Governor Adams" in Hawaii could have used 40,000 books; the missionaries there had "*not one on hand*" to give. Students crowded three, four, and five around the scarce books, some of them actually learning to read upside-down.[56]

In several dramatic incidents in which the *alii* showed their support for Christianity, they led the way for their subjects. Kapiolani, like Kaahumanu, contested with a worshipper of Pele, except that this time the refutation included more than words. In December 1824, during a hundred-mile journey from Kaleakekua to the mission in Hilo, which she undertook in order to exhort her people to Christianity and to encourage the missionaries, Kapiolani descended into the crater of the active volcano at Kilauea. Accompanied by Joseph Goodrich (one of the missionaries at Hilo) and about eighty followers, Kapiolani stood at the rim of the cauldron of molten lava and hissing gasses. "If I trust in Jehovah," she announced, "and he shall save me from the wrath of Pele when I break through her *tabus*, then you must fear and serve the Lord Jehovah." The group sang a hymn of praise and prayed, then went on, unharmed, to Waiakea the following day.[57]

Kaahumanu's demeanor during this period, according to missionary accounts, seems almost to have improved daily. Visiting Kauai during the fall of 1824, she had impressed Mercy Whitney—whose eye was so severely inflamed that even the slightest jarring of her bed put her in great pain—with her "tender feeling disposition" and concern for Mercy's comfort. At the beginning of the new year, in February 1825, when Kaahumanu returned to Honolulu from Kauai, she stood up to greet the missionaries, "and received us," the public journal notes, "with an expression of kindness, cordiality & joy which we had not before witnessed in her." Soon after, at a weekly prayer meeting for women, the most powerful woman in Hawaii rose to express her *manao* (thoughts), giving "such a relation of her past & present feelings as induced us to think very favorably of her Christian character." Kaahumanu began to take trips around Oahu to spread the first principles of Christianity, for the first time entering the houses of the poorest of the Hawaiians. She was in the process of earning a simple but distinguished epithet from her people, who began that summer to call her "Kaahumanu *hou*," the new Kaahumanu.[58]

When the bodies of the king and queen arrived from England in the spring of 1825, the Hawaiians conducted some, but not all, of their mourning in the traditional way. The HMS *Blonde* stopped first at Lahaina, where the wailing of thousands of mourners, led by Hoapili, "drowned out the roaring of the ocean." The *alii*, dressed in black, stood in a line, keeping silent until they saw the landing barge carrying their returned countrymen. The wailing began, both groups facing but not touching one another, while (as Charles Stewart wrote) "the whole air was filled with lamentation, and the ground shaken with the thunderings of the minute-guns" from the fort. Church services followed, the new customs now intermingling with the old. A changed Boki, impressed with St. Paul's and the other churches that Christendom had built, aware that the educated people in England had the governing power, had even been baptized by the chaplain of the *Blonde*. Now he stood up in a church overflowing with his people and recommended that they worship God and attend to the *palapala.*[59]

On May 11, twenty Hawaiians in black tapa, some in feather cloaks, carried gently swaying *kahilis* to lead the funeral procession. They were followed by a company of British marines, arms reversed, the ship's band, the male missionaries, the coffins—each one pulled by forty male chiefs—and the principal Hawaiian mourners, each accompanied by a British officer. The foreign residents and captains in port and the one hundred crew members of the *Blonde* in dress uniform completed the line. Inside the meeting house, the chaplain of the *Blonde* read the Episcopal Church's funeral service, and Hiram Bingham preached a sermon in Hawaiian. The bones of Liholiho's father, Kamehameha I, had been secretly buried only six years earlier; Kamehameha II and his queen rested in a stone mausoleum.[60]

During the remainder of his visit, George Anson, Lord Byron, the ship's captain, had the opportunity to meet with the chiefs to express his country's support for the missionaries. Here was more evidence for the Hawaiians that in changing to Christianity they were on the right track. By the end of May, 133 persons had asked to be considered for baptism. Still nervous, the missionaries established weekly classes for them and enforced a probationary period until the following December. Mercy Whitney, visiting Honolulu that fall, described Kaahumanu. "The change wrought in this influential Queen since I first knew her, is wonderful. Nothing short of Almighty power could have effected it. The haughty, assuming, disdainful air, which once appeared on her brow & looked so very forbidding, is now changed into a mild, tractable, childlike spirit." Mercy remembered a "gentle reproof" given to Kaahumanu at this time for sitting in church with her back to the preacher. "The thing in itself is not wrong," said Mercy, understanding that the people carrying Kaahumanu's chair had simply set her down that way. What impressed Mercy was the "docile spirit" with which Kaahumanu explained that "no one had ever told her it was wrong and she wished to know what was right." Mercy continued, "She appears to be truly sincere (as do many others) in her attachment to the cause of truth, calls the brethren of the mission *Father* because as she says, they feed her soul of the bread of life."[61]

By the end of the year, three thousand persons were coming to church in Honolulu. On December 5, 1825, Kaahumanu was one of eight *alii* in Honolulu (Hiram Bingham called them a "noble phalanx") who received the sacrament of baptism. This made her a member of the same church as the missionaries, the one that had been set up in the Park Street Church in Boston over five years earlier. (A little while later on the other islands, Kapiolani and Kalakua joined the privileged group of church members.) Each new member chose a Christian name to add to his or her Hawaiian one, Kaahumanu choosing Elizabeth, the barren woman who in her old age gave birth to John the Baptist, the harbinger of great changes in Judea. Mercy Whitney, attending the service, was much affected "to behold eight of those natives, several of whom the most influential in the nation, who a short time since were groping in all the Darkness of heathen superstition, now coming forward, & publickly dedicating themselves to the lord—taking him for their portion and their all." She thought it was "enough to draw tears of gratitude from every eye."[62]

Waimea, Kauai, 1824. Engraving by B. F. Childs after a sketch by Hiram Bingham. Courtesy Hawaiian Mission Children's Society.

Hula performed in the presence of the governor at Kailua, Hawaii. Engraving by J. McGhay after a drawing by Rev. William Ellis, about 1826. Courtesy Bishop Museum.

Drawing of Honolulu, 1840, by J. D. Dana of the U. S. Exploring Expedition. The drawing is reproduced in two sections. Kawaiahao Church, with unfinished roof, is shown on the right.

Diamond Head is shown on the right. Courtesy Hawaiian Mission Children's Society.

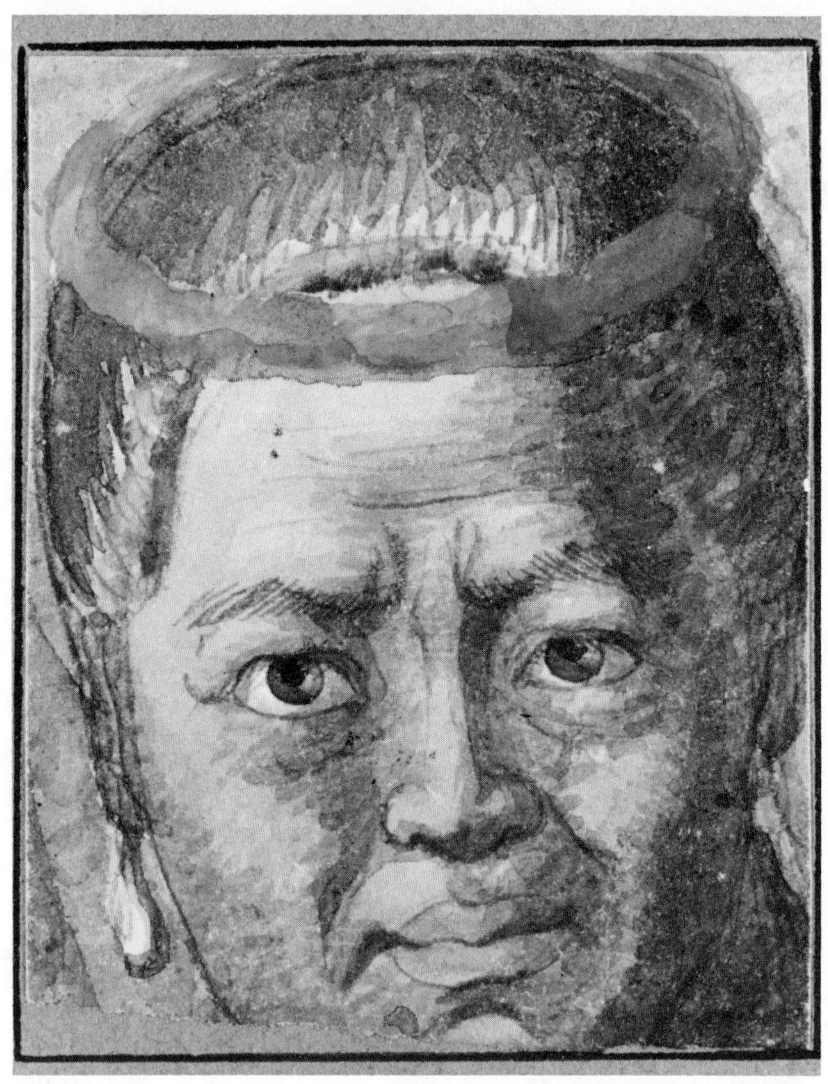

Kaahumanu. Watercolor by Louis Choris, 1816. Courtesy Honolulu Academy of Arts.

Nahienaena, about age 10. Painting by Robert Dampier, 1825. Courtesy Honolulu Academy of Arts.

Kauikeaouli (Kamehameha III), about age 11. Painting by Robert Dampier, 1825. Courtesy Honolulu Academy of Arts.

Liholiho (Kamehameha II). Engraving by unknown artist about 1819. Courtesy Honolulu Academy of Arts. Gift of Mr. and Mrs. Wallace Alexander.

Kinau leaving church in Honolulu, 1837. Lithograph. J. Masselot, artist. Courtesy Honolulu Academy of Arts. Gift of Mrs. Charles M. Cooke, 1927.

Mission house as it appears today. Second floor windows on left side belong to the Binghams' bedroom. Photo by author.

6. *The Tie That Binds*

And he that loveth son or daughter more than me is not worthy of me.

— MATTHEW 10:37

Train up a child in the way he should go: and when he is old, he will not depart from it.

— PROVERBS 22:6

At times during the late summer and fall of 1825, Sybil Bingham was not expected to live. "My feeble hand," she wrote, "could not hold a pen or attempt any thing more than to take the medicine brought me." Recuperating somewhat in September, she relapsed in October. In order to attend the December service of baptism, she had to be carried into church in her chair. Hiram attributed her symptoms to a "broken constitution," a vague diagnosis. But what set off the illness was clear enough.[1]

At the pulpit end of Kawaiahao Church, between the church and the mission house, lies the small grassed enclosure set aside for the mission's dead. Just to the left of the gate, at the end of a row of five headstones, stands a modest rectangle inscribed "In memory of two children." Here, on the twelfth of June, 1825, the Binghams laid their second son. Sixteen-month-old Evarts (as they called him) had grown strong and healthy after a delicate infancy, but could not survive croup. Within two days he was dead. Once again (as with the death of Parsons years earlier), Sybil had to repeat for herself the foundations of her faith—her own humility in the face of an omnipotent God whose reasons, though unfathomable, are always good. "O it is a bitter chastisement," she wrote her sister on the day of the funeral, "but how much less than our sins deserve. There is 'a needs be' that we are thus in heaviness. Full well we know GOD does not afflict willingly, nor grieve the children of men. Blessed be his name." Remembering what a friend from Massachusetts, Mrs. Fowler, had said through her tears after burying a daughter, Sybil repeated the words for herself: "I have known affliction from my youth, 'but tho' the LORD slay me, yet will I trust in Him.'"

Once again, Sybil wrested her ideological comforts from the pain of this world. "Strange conflicts has the sad event caused in his mother's bleeding heart," she wrote, "which sometimes says, with emphasis, the 'Lord gave the Lord hath taken away, blessed be the name of the Lord,' and yet again refused to be comforted because the lovely babe is not." "Two little lovely shoots are gone," Sybil wrote to Lucy Thurston a year later. Pursuing the biblical analogy of the vine (John 15:1–8), she compared herself to a stock that God had subjected to "digging and pruning." But she could not help mourning for her lost family. "But O, the lack of fruit! At this my soul would melt." Shock and grief took their toll on the body as well as the spirit. To one friend she explained that Evarts, the "tender vine," had "so drank of the sap . . . it had so encircled every fibre, that in sending it away, it was bringing the poor stock almost prostrate to the ground."[2]

Evarts's death did not turn Sybil into a permanent invalid—by the end of December, she was writing of comfortable health, and in future years she bore four healthy children—but it did send her into an extended physical collapse, grief pushing her past the limit of what she could bear of exhaustion and disappointment after five and a half years. The struggle against fading health—exacerbated that summer by Evarts's death—never let up in future years. The climate outside the mission houses being as healthy as anywhere in the world, the manner of living inside was the culprit. "Through much of our missionary course, thus far," Sybil wrote in 1827, "a train of circumstances have followed one the other, more especially at this central and elder station, of a nature to cause the general feature of our domestic life to be hardship, fatigue, care and withal much bustle and confusion." She saw it as her duty to bear this patiently, "not regarding what has had a slow yet sensible effect on my constitution." In 1826, during the flu epidemic (when George Kaumualii died), Sybil also became ill, describing in one letter how she attempted to finish a round of visits in the rain, then threw herself on the couch instead. She broke off her letter in tears and never finished it. Such trials were the harbingers of Sybil's chronic illness in the late 1830s, the consumption that helped persuade the Binghams to go back to New England in 1840.[3]

Sybil was hardly alone in her "feebleness"; Hiram Bingham reported several of the women suffering from "debility" during 1825. That July, Mercy Whitney looked back on a year and a half of illness when she had "been able to do but little more than oversee the concerns of my family, & sometimes not even that." She did not expect her health "will ever again be as good as formerly," adding, "My constitution seems to be considerably impaired & I am more & more convinced that my strength began to fail much sooner than I was aware." Samuel, in letters written that year, worried that she might not live. Maria Loomis had begun to remark on her "injured" constitution as early as 1822. Even Lucy Thurston, whose health improved in the islands, had to throw off a "pulmonary complaint" that had begun in New England and troubled her for ten years afterward. Nancy Ruggles enjoyed better health (according to Mercy Whitney, who had visited her in 1832), but even she had her share of common ailments—eye infections, boils—and was very ill from a miscarriage in 1833. Back in New England by 1834, Nancy had changed so much that her mother said she would not have recognized her. Reporting this in 1836, Mercy added her own conclusions:

> One reinforcement after another come on to the ground with blooming countenances, the very picture of health. For a little while, they retain their freshness, then the color begins to fade from their cheeks. As time passes on, the rosy hue that first appeared has vanished, & a pale sickly countenance or a sunburnt one is all that remain of once blooming health.[4]

Everyone suffered, not simply the women. Arguing the need for more workers in her journal entry for April 19, 1826, Mercy reflected that the few workers already there were "failing, through excess of labor, privations, & the debilitating state of the climate. Scarce any of this Mission enjoy that degree of health, which they did in America." Samuel Ruggles, she added, was "quite feeble." A half-year later (December 1826), her plea was more urgent: "With respect to most of the members of the mission, it may be truly said that we are literally sinking into the grave for want of helpers." Hiram Bingham suffered from hepatitis, which tore him away from his work in the summer of 1827 (and again in 1830), forcing a stay at a less dusty, more verdant station. By 1830, so many missionaries needed relief that the mission set up a "rest station" in the cool, high ground of Waimea, Hawaii, some 3,000 feet up and twenty miles from the snows of Mauna Kea. In 1829, Boki gave the Binghams a piece of land at Punahou, a few miles inland from the mission house, where a spring and cool mountain air allowed a comfortable retreat. In a cottage not far from one of Kaahumanu's, the Binghams could rest and work without interruptions, Sybil at her letters and journals, Hiram translating the New Testament.[5]

For some missionaries, the solution was more drastic. Elisha Loomis's health, much worse than his wife's, had so broken down that by January 1827 the family left for the United States. (Seven years later, Samuel Ruggles was too ill to stay longer, and that family reluctantly sailed back in January 1834.) Elisha Loomis continued to work for the cause, printing translations into Hawaiian of three gospels and working among the Indians of northern Michigan for two years. But he was a dying man, succumbing to consumption in 1836. Maria bore two more sons in the United States, but wrote little. A letter to her husband from 1827 complains, "I still find it hard work as ever, to put any thing on paper that suits me," no doubt unaware of the value of the detail she had recorded in her Hawaiian journal up to 1824. She followed one of her sons to Michigan, where she spent the rest of her life, tended—so a newspaper account says—in a final paralysis by her daughter Amanda. She died on September 6, 1862.[6]

Like illness, death did not respect sex or age. Elizabeth Bishop, who became in 1828 the first adult member of the mission to die, suffered horribly, unable to bear noise above a whisper, unable to eat, in excruciating pain from the slightest movement. The Binghams were the first, but not the only, missionary parents to lose a child. Fanny Ruggles died in 1827, only two years old. Nancy Ruggles's fourth child, Lucia, was born and died in 1829. The Thurstons raised their second daughter, Lucy, to the age of seventeen, only to lose her to a "lung fever" immediately upon her return to the United States for schooling. For subsequent missionary companies, both adults and children, the litany of "deaths in the field" continued. And judging from the number of Sybil's correspondents who had also buried a child (her sister Sophia, like Sybil, lost two), such bereavements were hardly limited to missionary ground.[7]

But the Lord had other ways of "chastising," "pruning," or "slay-ing" his servants. Starting in 1826, the young parents, discovering one reason after another why their school-age children should not stay in the islands, began to send them back to New England. They told themselves that it was the path of duty, that they were following God's will, that this was for the children's own good. For years, they had been worrying how to protect their children from surroundings of "moral pollution," an assessment that, strangely enough, diminished very little over the years. (In fact, as the mission began to report successful conversions, the public began to wonder why the parents could not keep their children, prompting letters in the 1830s reaffirming that Hawaii really was a land of pollution and that reports had been published—as Mercy Whitney protested in 1832—with "quite too high a colouring.") Before the missionaries could accomplish the needed changes in Hawaiian culture, it might change their children.[8]

The Society Islands, the only place where missionaries had tried the experiment of raising Christian children in the midst of Polynesian sexual habits, testified to a failed experiment. To add to the initial reports from Rev. Ellis and the other visitors in 1822, the missionaries eventually had their own eyewitness testimony. In 1832, the long-postponed journey to Tahiti finally materialized. Samuel Whitney returned with explicit tales of ruined children, which Mercy copied verbatim in a letter to her cousin Mrs. Ely, who was caring for the Whitneys' sons, in part because the shocking details helped her convince her skeptical family and reinforce her own sense that she had done the right thing in sending her children away. The account also glosses what the missionaries meant by "moral death":

> There has been only one instance, where a child of the Missionaries [in Tahiti] has been converted at the Isl—ds. Several have been ruined—one has been seduced from her Father's house, by a man in the character of a gentleman, & is now a public prostitute in the City of London. One was confined with a bastard child by a native man, not 3 months since. Three daughters of one of the Missionaries were not long since guilty of admitting 3 native men by means of a servant to their bed chamber, & secreting them under the beds till night, when the Mother hearing a noise, lit a candle & went to the room, but on seeing the men, fainted & fell & they made their escape. The daughter of a missionary, not long since while on a visit at another Missionary's house, was found in bed with a native man. Two lads, sons of

> missionaries were lately expelled [from] the [South Seas] Academy, for illicit connection with native girls. One of them on his return to his Father's house, was guilty of taking property of his Father's, & giving it to native girls as the hire of prostitution.

Mercy also mentioned in a letter of 1836 the example of "one of the pioneers," unnamed, who at first saw no harm in the children's staying in the Sandwich Islands, mingling with the natives and even marrying them. "This same brother since becoming more acquainted with the habits & character of the people, has been led to see, & I trust *feel deeply* too, the error of [his] opinion." Lucy Thurston, remarking the impurity of Hawaiian habits, referred to the reports from Tahiti as well as her own shock that children were present at childbirth.[9]

There are two kinds of documents that verify the thinking of the missionaries on this subject. The first, letters going to and from the Board, list reason after reason and attempt to make disinterested thinking triumph over parental affection. ("If this [affection] had got the better judgment," Mercy wrote just after her first child left, "we should have said, *we cannot let her go.*") The second group contains personal documents, usually letters and journal entries from a mother, showing less the finished product of rationality—the decision reached and its justification—than the costly struggle to achieve it. Here the parents, deeply shaken, write movingly, revealing not simply why they sent the children away, but what it felt like. Somewhere in the back of everyone's mind lurked the sentiment best expressed by Sybil's appeal for her daughter Lucy: *"How can we put her from us?"*[10]

The decision, difficult to begin with for emotional reasons, was made more so because the ABCFM did not approve. The members had already reviewed the situation in 1825, at the insistence of parents in Ceylon, so when the members of the Sandwich Islands mission sent back a report compiled during the General Meeting of 1826, respectfully asking for advice, but carefully listing reasons why they thought the children should be sent back to America, the Board had its reply ready.

Corresponding Secretary Jeremiah Evarts, in a long, thoughtful letter dated October 27, 1827, cautioned that there were many contaminating influences waiting for children at home, that the difference between the two places was not that of safety versus danger, but merely a difference in the degree of danger. He suggested that some difficulties with the children, which the parents might attribute to the Sandwich Islands, were to be expected as part of the normal round of childrearing anywhere. And parents were so much better suited than anyone else to raise their children that the Board urged great caution before entrusting offspring to anyone else—grandparents being notoriously indulgent and others perhaps promising more care than they could deliver. Without the children, the Board reasoned, the missionaries would not be able to demonstrate good Christian family life and would therefore lose an important aid to converting the Hawaiians.[11]

But the situation looked very different from Waimea or Honolulu. "If those who are brought up in christian lands . . . ," thought Mercy Whitney, "are so easily led astray by bad example so soon as exposed to its influence, how can we expect those who are familiar with such scenes from childhood, where everything is calculated to convey impure & vulgar ideas to the mind—to be even moral after they come to act for themselves unless the grace of God interpose & snatch them as brands from the burning." Given the assumption that the natives had a bad moral influence on the children, then what sort of life, the parents asked themselves, was going to be possible for the children and for the missionary mother trying to raise them? The perceived danger created a conviction that the children ought to be isolated to one degree or another from the natives and created worry when that proved impossible. Lucy Thurston compared the situation to a prison, where one would naturally want to separate children from inmates.[12]

In such a benign climate, where children might have spent the bulk of their time outside, exploring the hills, climbing trees, learning to swim, to surf, or to paddle canoes, they stayed inside more than was good for them, distracted by a book, by patchwork (for both boys and girls), by an hour or two of schoolwork when a busy mother could spare the time or was well enough to teach. With inadvertent poignancy, Mercy described Maria's lot: "She will sit at my bed-room window with her book or her work, & see the native children at play but a few rods distant, without manifesting the least desire to join them. She has several times reproved the[m], particularly for playing on the sabbath. I have endeavored to impress her mind with the impropriety of spending her time as these children do." The boys must have been less docile, Mercy admitting that it was "impossible to keep them wholly from the influence of the natives. We cannot confine them to the house—they must have exercise & boys especially delight to play out of doors. I sometimes endeavor to amuse them about the house, until I am fearful what effect restraints will have upon them. There is here so little variety to divert their minds that I am frequently at a loss to know what to do with them." The Binghams reconciled themselves to Sophia's departure by remembering how lonely she was in 1828, circumstances in Honolulu at the time affording her no playmates. The Loomises had left, the other mission children her age lived on other islands, and her closest sibling was six years younger.[13]

Sophia Bingham had also witnessed considerable violence before she left. Her parents could not predict whether the attacks against the mission would intensify or abate (as they did). They did realize that the child had already fled from the insurrection in Kauai in 1824; she had watched, screaming, as a mob attacked her father outside the mission house; she had listened when two men burst into the Binghams' rooms one night to protest a letter of admonition the brethren had written, ranting for two straight hours with what Sybil called "the most impious language I ever heard, too dreadful for memory to recall"; she had hidden with her family in the cellar of the mission house in Lahaina in 1827, when two cannon balls fired by the crew of the *John Palmer* narrowly missed the house. It was enough to make Sophia's safety an additional reason to remove her from the islands.[14]

The existing schools served adult Hawaiians, who were taught a limited curriculum in their native tongue, and with whom, in any case, it was not considered safe for the mission children to associate. The schooling a busy, sometimes frail mother could provide did not compare with that in a good infant school in the United States. The fathers' labors, necessarily conducted in a foreign language, were lost on the children. To build a school for the children, apart from the expense involved, seemed impractical because there were so few children scattered among the islands and, perhaps more to the point, not many teachers. (By 1828, when the third company arrived, three couples out of seven in the first company had gone home. The Ellis family had returned to England. Of the second company, the Stewarts, Betsey Stockton, the Blatchelys, and the Elys had left; Elizabeth Bishop was dying in Kailua; and Levi Chamberlain was single. That left the Binghams in Oahu, the Whitneys in Kauai, the Richardses in Maui, and three couples in Hawaii – the Thurstons in Kailua and the Goodriches and Ruggleses in Hilo. Married women coming with the third company, preoccupied with their own infants, and single women who, like everyone else, had come to serve Hawaiians, were unlikely recruits as teachers of mission children.)[15]

The more fundamental objection was to parental teaching in the first place: "What parents in America are the teachers of their own children," they wrote to the Board, "and is it to be supposed that the missionary is of all men the most free from care and labors?" Even if they did build a school, the parents worried how they would train the children for future employment in the islands. They could not prepare them for business or farming, and the best training-ground for missionaries (assuming the children even heard the call) had so far been the United States. And what if the children sank to the level of the natives or, worse, of the common sailors? Since even in the second and third generations of missionary families, marriages with Hawaiians were rare, it is not surprising that the problem of finding "suitable partners" for the children entered into the discussion. The Board counseled (with prescience) that the situation in Honolulu would improve by the time the children grew up, making their potential employment and – more important – their conversions less insecure. "You have dedicated them to God," wrote Evarts, "'have faith in God.'"[16]

But if the situation as it stood was hard on the children, it was equally trying for the women, in ways that it was perhaps hard for the men of the Board to understand. To raise children and to engage in the teaching and visiting that was "real" missionary work seemed to be mutually exclusive, not complementary, activities. The women could not simultaneously protect their children from the culture and engage with the Hawaiians as much as they wished. As Mercy Whitney expressed the dilemma, "Indeed if we would be useful to the people – we must be familiar with them. We must admit them to our houses & enter into free & cheerful conversation with them, & we must of course have our children with us." Sybil Bingham found herself in 1829 trying to teach in a newly formed school for Hawaiian children (where enrollment quickly neared three hundred) and to make systematic visits to mothers' homes. Her infant (Elizabeth, born March 8) she could "safely" carry along with her, but not the four-year-old Lucy. "Sometimes I took Lucy," Sybil remembered, "sometimes left her in her father's study, where at the translation table the sounds were altogether native—but little choice between the two situations. It was hazardous either way and often I had a conflict in my own mind."[17]

Very often, for Mercy, the demands of child care got the upper hand. In 1828, when she had three children at home with her, she wrote with frustration: "For three or four years past, they have seemed to demand what exertion I was able to make, & I have sometimes almost despaired of ever doing very much for the Heathen, except by example." Such an example of Christian domestic life, for Hawaiians to imitate, was exactly what the Board wanted to encourage. But the cost of presenting this example was the rigid division of public and private duties into male and female categories. Lucy Thurston, seeing no alternative, quoted the motto "The missionary best serves his generation who serves the public, and his wife best serves her generation who serves her family." But Mercy was sorry to see her "usefulness among the heathen . . . greatly impeded, by having to devote so much of our time to the education & care of our children." Sybil concurred, explaining, "It is quite impossible to describe the struggle sometimes existing in our breast between the mother's feelings and what appeared to be a special and almost unparalleled call from the people for all the energy of which the poor frame and burdened mind were capable." Though both parents felt the anguish of parting with the children, and shared in the decision, the argument in favor of freeing time for missionary work applied mainly to the mothers. The fathers' work went ahead with or without the children. But the women felt the dilemma in terms of their twin vocations, "laboring directly" for the "heathen" or the children.

In an imperfect world, where every wish could not be achieved, they were trying to sort through priorities. And the choices were cruel. One reading of the situation is that they did choose between their children and Hawaiians. In the end, they would either have to send their children back to be educated elsewhere, presumably saving their souls but at the cost of abandoning parental nurture, or give up missionary work—not only a great personal loss to themselves, but, more important, a betrayal of the Hawaiians "perishing" in ignorance of God's word. "Had our children remained with us," wrote Mercy in 1834, "in all probability we should ere this, have felt it our duty to leave the Islands."[19]

Though the line between reasons and rationalizations may be fine, the decision to send the children back was something more complicated than a panicky recoil from "pollution." The parents had to believe that they were acting for the children's own good—an important point because the decision then seemed less like a choice between serving their children or the Hawaiians and more like a way of serving the best interests of both. The most important question on every parent's mind, asked repeatedly in letters to the children in America, was whether or not each child had yet opened his or her heart to Christ. They were not particularly concerned that the children adopt one profession or another (though of course they hoped they might be called as missionaries), but they did emphatically hope their offspring would declare themselves Christians. The children were barraged with letters like Sybil's to Lucy about a year after her daughter left: "Dear child! and does she love the Saviour now? When I hear this—Oh! it will be beyond everything else." It would comfort her and Samuel, Mercy wrote to their ten-year-old son Henry, "to hear that all our dear children love the Saviour. This is what we most of all desire—& for this we daily carry you to God in the arms of faith & prayer, & beseech him to give you new hearts." With no illusions about childhood innocence ("Yes, even little children sin," Mercy told Henry), the parents keenly felt their responsibility to turn the children away from their natural depravity and train them up in the way they should go, as the Bible dictated. Not content with wishful thinking, the parents tried to give their children every practical advantage in attaining salvation, by removing them from bad influences and putting them in the way of salutary ones.[20]

But the missionaries wanted to act for the good of Hawaiians as well as their own children. "Their souls too," as Samuel Whitney reminded his sons, "have been purchased by the blood of Christ, and in his view are equally precious with yours." Put to the test, the needs of the Hawaiians often came first. Samuel tried to explain to his sons that if he were to leave for America, the Hawaiians would be left without a teacher, whereas there were persons other than himself in America who could give young Samuel and Henry their religious educations. On behalf of the young Hawaiians, the mission built a boarding school at Lahaina in 1831; resolved, during the General Meeting of 1836, to build one on every island; and built a school for the next generation of *alii,* the Chiefs' Children's School, in 1839—all of this preceding the opening of the school for mission children at Punahou in 1842.[21]

Just as the mission "family" as an ideal diminished under the impact of everyday experience, so too—with greater trauma—would the nuclear families give way under pressure. Despite their obvious love for their families and their high regard for the notion of "family"—which gave nineteenth-century women a respected, even sanctified, role as mothers and which gave the group their controlling metaphor—they determined that keeping their families together was not the highest priority in their lives. The insight was born of the peculiar, even unique, situation they found themselves in and of their own habits of mind. If forced into choice, what took priority was an abstraction—the soul to be saved, not the life to be lived. Here the young parents were guided once again by a tendency to devalue the material world, the here and now, in favor of "higher" objects. Though with Hawaiians it was too easy for missionaries to lose sight of souls out of disgust for "heathen" habits, with their children it was the opposite. Souls seemed more important than parental affection, the children's emotional needs, or the day to day experiences of growing up. In the end, as in so many other decisions, God's work took priority over what seemed merely personal considerations. For these women to break up their families in service of the great cause gives both a measure of their commitment to it and some measure of what that commitment cost them. "Can any sacrifice be too great," Sybil Bingham asked with ingenuous optimism, "if we may help to make the love of this compassionate Saviour known to our wretched fellow-men?"[22]

By August 4, 1826, Maria Whitney was two months shy of six years old. Her mother's journal for that date reads, "Yesterday we parted with her, little expecting to see her again on earth." Trying to describe how she and Samuel felt, Mercy wrote, "It was a most trying season to us both, but I hope we were enabled to say, 'the will of the Lord be done.'" The child was on her way to Oahu, where

Dr. and Mrs. Blatchely would take her back to America with them. Finding trustworthy adult supervision and a captain willing to take a small passenger without compensation (for the Board would not pay) helped Mercy to recognize her "duty." With just ten days to prepare Maria's belongings, Mercy needed help from Keaweamahi, the wife of Kauai's governor, who sent several of her attendants to help with sewing, and from the missionary wives in Honolulu, who finished the packing. But the physical preparations were the easy part. In early November, the ship *Connecticut,* bound for America, touched unexpectedly in Kauai for a day, and the Whitneys saw Maria once again. "Dear child," Mercy wrote, "she plead[ed] hard to stay one day longer with Ma'a." The next day, the ship out of sight and Mercy's latest journal bound up and sent back with it, she began a new one, still preoccupied with her daughter: "O the anxiety we feel on her account, & the love we bear her! None but a parent knows the anguish of a parent's heart."[23]

For the first two decades of the mission (until the school at Punahou opened), the harrowing possibility of departure had to be considered by parents as their children reached ages six to ten. The trauma was short-lived, mostly affecting families of the first two companies, and involving only 19 out of 250 mission children. The parents in the first company demonstrate the range of options available: going home with all the children (as did the Chamberlains and Loomises, though other reasons, notably failing health, affected the decision); keeping all the children to be educated by the mother (the Thurstons' choice); or sending the children home, not knowing when or if they would be reunited (the course taken by the Ruggleses, Binghams, and Whitneys). Sarah Ruggles left with the Loomises in 1827, Sophia Bingham with the Elys in 1828; Samuel and Henry Whitney went under the care of a ship's captain in 1832; and Emily Whitney and Lucy Bingham sailed home with the Ruggleses in early 1834. Lucy Thurston took her children back herself, her daughters when they were fully grown, but her son Asa when he was twelve. Over the years (by Hiram Bingham's count), three orphans and twenty-six children accompanied by their parents made the voyage.[24]

When Sybil got back to the United States in the 1840s, she went through her letters (which her sister had saved), compiling an account that would help her daughters understand what had happened to them. She had written that in the early years of the mission, whenever the subject came up for discussion, "I had to leave table or company to resume my composure." She described her tearful, sleepless night when the need to decide about Sophia pressed upon her: "I wept. I tried to pray. I sought my pillow and thought I would be composed. But it was in vain." When, in December 1833, Sybil prepared to send Lucy, the agitation began again. "I have been strengthened to the work once," she wrote, "but I cannot remember that I suffered so much in it." Not only did Lucy—this "giddy, affectionate thing"—have a different personality than her older sister, but she was being put on a ship that, despite repairs, *"still leaks."* Sybil wrote to her sister at one o'clock in the morning: "You cannot blame me that I cannot sleep. It is hard to gaze upon the sleeping features of a darling, cherished child—feel in your heart that it is the *last night* you shall be allowed to watch its slumbers, then turn quietly to your own pillow." Samuel Whitney, who traveled to Honolulu to put his two sons on the boat, admitted to them in later years that he could never forget the sound of their wails. As she readied the boys' things for the voyage, Mercy thought of "how they have entwined themselves about every fibre of my heart. . . . I am sure I feel it much more now, than when our dear daughter left." Emily, Mercy's fourth and last child, asked to sleep in her parents' room the night before sailing. "She lay awake for some time weeping," remembered Mercy, "to think the parting hour was at hand; & during this time called me several times to her bed-side, clasped her arms around my neck, & kissed me."[25]

Nor did the sadness stop with the decision to put the children on the boat. After her boys left, Mercy wrote, "I did not anticipate what a season of trial it would be, or how lonely everything would appear, after their departure," concluding, "it is well that our Heavenly Father conceals from us the future." Mail was so slow that Sybil waited a year and a half for her first letter from Sophia (though she did know from other sources that the child had arrived safely). "This poor, waiting, anxious heart," she confessed, "has been made so glad by your long, crowded pages, that it would not be easy to tell you all its joy." Sybil at least knew that her sisters, Sophia and Lucy, were both willing to take in her children; Mercy had no assurance of a family for Maria when she sent her off, merely the trust that her relatives, the Hoadly family of Worcester, Massachusetts, would find a suitable family if they could not care for her themselves. When

Samuel and Henry left a few years later, Mercy knew that the Ely family (other relations) would take them in, but did not have a mission adult, merely a trusted ship's captain — who had plenty of other duties — to see them through the voyage. In a letter written just before the boys left, Mercy appealed to them with helpless solicitude to stay with the captain and officers instead of the ordinary sailors, not to neglect their Bibles, and not to climb the ropes on the ship.[26]

As the years passed, remarks about the children crept into letters and journals as if any subject were enough to call up an association. When Sybil's third daughter, Elizabeth, reached her tenth birthday in 1839, Sybil noted with pleasure that she had never before had with her on a birthday a child who had reached that age. Mercy wrote to her absent children describing her house inside and out, trying to jog their faded memories. Worse (since daguerreotypes were not invented until 1839), she had no way of knowing what they looked like. Seeing Maria again as an adult, Mercy was surprised at her plumpness. A daguerreotype that Samuel sent her in 1848, calling it a "correct likeness," did not resemble Mercy's imagined picture of her grown-up son. Sybil did receive a large portrait of Sophia (now hanging in the mission house in Honolulu), but it arrived so spoiled by sea air after long storage aboard ship that the heartbroken parents could not make out her features. (Hiram was able to clean it later with alcohol.)[27]

Such were the day by day incidents of anxiety and loss that might have been expected. But no one had a crystal ball to determine whether or not in the long run — the course of a parent's or child's lifetime — the sadness would be worth it. The dilemma over where best to raise the children tested in fundamental ways the wisdom of the religion the missionaries were trying to spread — or, more precisely, the missionaries' particular version of that religion, with its emphasis on the Bible's platonic side, on the notion that the most important truths are the ones you cannot see. They continued to have at their fingertips the many passages that exhort believers to put worldliness aside in favor of nonmaterial things — telling us to lay up treasures not on earth but in heaven; warning that you cannot serve God and Mammon; or asking what it profits a man to gain the world and lose his soul: "Is not the life more than meat, the body than raiment?" The devaluing of material things was part of conventional piety, referred to so often that such thoughts seem to come automatically. The applications were widespread, everything from the conventionally religious ("O for the spirit—then 'let earth roll!'" as Sybil Bingham once wrote to Nancy Ruggles) to the mundane, as in Mercy Whitney's advice to her granddaughter to pay attention not to prettiness but to character. At their best, the missionaries were enabled by their platonism to look past the visible "heathenish" customs to the precious souls that made the Hawaiians anybody's equal. Now, with equally serious results, they were applying the doctrine to their children's lives. Already schooled in weaning themselves from this earth, the difficulty for the missionary women was the reverse. They were prone (even too prone) to put "higher objects" in the place of the body. And their story, in one of its largest perspectives, shows what happens as a result.[28]

Although the missionaries cited a myriad of reasons for sending their children back around Cape Horn, their subsequent letters attest to one obsessive preoccupation—that the sacrifice would enable the children to love the Savior, to get a new heart, and to save their souls. They were playing for the highest stakes with their most precious treasures on earth, their children. Judged strictly in terms of the children's conversions, the experiment was successful. Whatever combination it took—the religious atmosphere of New England, the pious family life of adopted homes, the exhortations to examine their hearts that kept coming from far-off parents—the desired effect was achieved. What the experiment cost the children in tears and confusion and loneliness is harder to assess. The Whitneys soon realized that some members of their family disapproved of Maria's arrival, and that the child had done much "wandering about" by 1830. The experience of taking care of the homesick nine-year-old daughter of fellow missionaries for two months in 1841 gave Mercy Whitney a searing insight into her own children's feelings. Often she found the child—who was older than the Whitney children were when they left—weeping for her mother. "At such moments," Mercy wrote to Henry, "your departure would rush into my mind, & I would say to myself, well, I suppose my own dear children felt very much so, after they were gone from us; & then my bosom would swell with anguish, at the thought of what you must have suffered." The children of missionaries were under a constant strain to be "good," reminded incessantly in letters of the virtues of obedience, humility, and kindness. They were to nurture a sense of gratitude to guardians who were pointing out faults for the children's own improvement (that the children might be subjected to unjust reprimands the parents never even dared to consider). Because both Sybil Bingham and Nancy Ruggles eventually returned home, they did not have to endure the separations for a lifetime, and they did not have to part from their younger children. (One thought that reconciled the Binghams to leaving in 1840 was that they would not then have to wrench themselves away from yet another child.) That left Mercy Whitney as the woman who was probably most sorely tested by her decision, for in sending her children home she risked a lifelong loss.[29]

"I long to be crucified to the world and alive to God," the young Mercy Whitney had written on board the *Thaddeus* in 1819. One reading of her story is that in one of those terrible twists of fate, she got exactly what she wished for. With her fourth child gone in 1834, she could give all her strength to the work for which she had come. A month after Emily left, Mercy wrote to Nancy Ruggles, "I feel at present quite *kaawale* [free] for missionary work—hope I shall have strength to do something more directly for the poor heathen around me, than I have ever yet done." The irony was that she did not have much strength to give. Her letter books and journals for the rest of her life tell in meticulous detail, approaching hypochondria, a story of chronic debility. Here is the source of another irony—that Mercy one by one loosened her ties to the physical world represented by her children, only to find herself intensely preoccupied with the physical details of her health.[30]

Mercy spent the remainder of her life in Waimea, living in a series of progressively more sturdy houses built of stone rather than thatch, moving farther away from the river (which flooded in the winters). The events that followed tended to keep her solitary. When Nancy Ruggles went home with her sick husband in 1834, Mercy lost her best friend among the women. Even though the Ruggleses had moved from Kauai, Mercy still remembered the close rapport of the first years and thought of Nancy as her sister. "Our acquaintance was formed," Mercy reminisced after a visit in 1832, "at a time when we felt that most of our earthly attachments were about to be sundered, which made the precious few with whom we sailed, appear more dear. And then our being separated from the rest of the mission, & living so long together at one station, & in the same family, have contributed to unite our hearts very closely, in the bonds of sisterly love, & Christian affection." In 1845, Mercy faced a much worse separation when her husband unexpectedly did not recover from an illness, but died at the youthful age of fifty-two, leaving Mercy almost three decades of widowed life on Kauai. It hurt her, Mercy wrote in one of the few critical comments that passed among the women, that Sybil Bingham, after she returned to America, never wrote to her with condolences, even though Sybil had written to some of the other missionaries.[31]

From Waimea in the 1830s, the nearest missionaries were fifteen miles away, with a second couple thirty or forty miles distant. That left Mercy few opportunities for ordinary social interactions. The General Meeting in Honolulu came only once a year (and she could not always nerve herself for the voyage). She had to mother her children as she could, by the distancing media of letter and memory. Looking at the Pride of Barbados (mimosa) and kou trees in the front yard, the tamarind and castor oil at the back, she got pleasure from thinking that her children had planted them. The cotton wool tree, she told Samuel, partly blocked the path, but the Whitneys refused to cut it down: "We let it remain there to remind us of you." Mercy kept track with relief as one by one her children professed Christianity. But the distance took its toll. She was essentially helpless when problems arose. Her parental reprimands when a child was disobedient or lax in schoolwork must have arrived over a year after the fact. Much worse was Samuel's disappearance from Amherst College in 1842, apparently because he felt pressure from his guardians to become a missionary but did not himself desire it. No one knew where he was. Three years later—when he had evidently returned—Mercy wrote to her "Dearly beloved *tho erring* Son," reassuring him that she "sincerely and heartily" forgave him, reminding him that though his crimes were great, God's mercy was greater. It distressed her that her children should not feel "*free*" to choose their professions. As the years went on, Samuel seems to have become the son that Mercy "lost"; he wrote rarely, communicating information—including his engagement—through his siblings. As Emily got older, Mercy began sending her journal home to her and not to her Pittsfield, Massachusetts, family. When Emily married a minister who contemplated missionary work, Mercy's hopes were raised for a reunion, but the couple stayed in the United States. Only once, from 1860 to 1862, did Mercy return to the mainland to visit her children.[32]

Although Maria did return to the islands in 1844 as a grown woman of twenty-three and a missionary, the long years of separation had put an irremediable strain on rapport. Maria stayed in Waimea with her mother, teaching school, until she married a fellow missionary, the Reverend John Pogue, and moved to Lahaina. The difficulties were never made explicit, but Mercy's phrasing as she informed her son Samuel of the marriage gives the suggestion of desertion: "Maria has left me, and under circumstances exceedingly trying to my feelings." Another clue to Mercy's attitude comes from her repeated advice to Emily—evidently considering missionary work—not to come as an unmarried woman if she wanted to be happy. Levi Chamberlain, present at the wedding in 1848, remarked simply that "Mrs. Whitney is not fully reconciled to her daughter's marriage." The reconciliation never came; meeting John Pogue in later years, Mercy found him "cold & distant" as an "iceberg." Mercy's prediction at the time of the wedding came true: "We shall probably not see each other very often in future." Henry too returned to Honolulu in 1849, settling down with his family, successful in his profession as printer and editor of the *Pacific Commercial Advertiser.* Mercy was pleased with Henry's wife, Kate, and the grandchildren who were born to them. (Kate evidently suffered Mercy's advice on childrearing, which included demonstrating that a six-month-old child could be made to sit still during services.) But since Mercy declined to move from Kauai, she saw her family rarely, perhaps once a year, if she went to General Meeting.[33]

"I am literally *alone* in the strictest sense of the word, my Saviour's presence excepted. You cannot imagine how *lonely* & *sad* I sometimes feel," Mercy told Emily in 1848, shortly after Maria's marriage. The challenge of Mercy's later years was to live without her family nearby. She asked Emily to "unbosom" herself in letters, continuing, "Nothing would be a greater comfort to me, than to have my dear children frank & confiding." When the Reverend George Rowell, his wife Malvina, and their family (eventually reaching seven children) moved to Waimea after Samuel Whitney's death, Mercy found that "they make up in a measure for the loss, or *absence* of my children." She did not think she could love her own grandchildren more. But most of the time she relied on spiritual comfort. Trying to express the grief of widowhood, she wrote to her brother John: "I think I may truly say, that were all the other trials which have crossed my path in life (and they are not a few) summed up into one, they would hardly compare with what I felt at the loss of my dear husband." She would have "sunk" had she not believed the Savior's promise, "Lo I am with you always." She did not rail at being singled out for affliction, relying on the same comfort Sybil Bingham found on the death of her sons. "The Lord has for wise reasons," Mercy wrote to Maria Chamberlain, "seen fit to afflict us, and though he wounds, he can also heal."[34]

The particular sorrow of widowhood came but once in her life; poor health plagued her constantly. In a comment from 1840, surprising from someone who generally spoke of the "debilitating" effect of the climate, Mercy acknowledged the cool and pleasant air caused by the trade winds: "I suppose a healthier climate is not known." But by then, her health long since shattered, it was too late to enjoy it. She spoke in 1837 of the wisdom of "exercise & simple diet in a warm climate," which she had not understood in earlier years. In 1837, she began taking a horseback ride every morning before dawn. She began to look around her at subject that had previously escaped her pen: the magnificent colors of sunrise and ocean that remarked the beauty of God's creation. In 1856, for the first time since arriving at the islands, she ventured into the ocean for a "sea bath," wading in up to her neck, holding tight to the Rowells on either side.[35]

But none of these activities reversed the image she held of herself as "feeble." In early years she complained of "ophthalmy" (inflamed eyes), an attack every year, which caused her to stay in darkened rooms, wearing green glasses if she could get them. She wrote of severe headaches (probably migraine), "dropsy" (swelling), lameness that made it difficult to walk, and a "liver complaint," cured by having a "seton" or wick surgically inserted in her side for fourteen months (1827–29) and by limiting her diet to bread and milk. In later years, she referred often to "my old complaint," chronic diarrhea that in 1841 had seemed life-threatening. In only one of four births had she the benefit of a doctor's presence. Years later she confided to her mother and sisters that complications during Henry's birth resulted in a broken "cartilage" or "ligament" near the pelvic bone. This never healed, causing her lameness and having something to do, she presumed, with a hemorrhage from a miscarriage in 1835 that brought her very close to death. In 1848, helping Malvina Rowell, who was lying down after the birth of a child now three weeks and three days old, Mercy could not help remarking the different life she had known over a quarter-century earlier, when Maria was two days younger than this current baby:

> I took care of *her*, entertained company, & did a fortnight's wash besides,—was on my feet almost all day. That is a species of the manner in which we used to get along, in former years, before the natives had learned to work. And when I think what I have gone thro' since I have been on heathen ground, instead of being surprised that my health is so feeble, I rather wonder that I am still alive.[36]

Mercy taught the station school of over 150 students in the 1830s after her sons left; in 1834, she wrote that she had been teaching over one hundred children daily for five or six weeks in reading, spelling, geography, and arithmetic. But her efforts were necessarily sporadic. In 1838, she had not taught the station school for three years, she told Samuel, taking instead a small school of twenty or thirty when she was well enough, and a Sabbath school every week. Mercy's comment to her sister in 1841 was her constant refrain: "At present, my labors *directly* for the good of the heathen, are greatly limited by feeble health."[37]

Isolated from fellow Americans and from family, Mercy lived out her life surrounded by Hawaiians. Fluent in the language by now, she visited homes and improved her knowledge of Hawaiian customs, but she shrank from intimacy or friendship. She sympathized with "Deborah" Kapule when her husband Kaumualii was taken from her by Kaahumanu (in 1821), and grieved when "Deborah"'s conduct ("living in concubinage with the husband of another woman") led to her excommunication in the late 1830s. But she seems not to have established a closeness with her resembling that between Sybil Bingham and Kaahumanu. When Maria wrote asking if her middle name should be spelled with a "T" or a "K," Mercy explained that the letters were interchangeable, adding that the name was given to her as a "mere form," and she could drop it if she wished.[38]

Mercy continued to see her own habits and attitudes as cast in relief against "heathenism," which, to her increasing frustration over the years, did not change thoroughly or quickly enough. In 1851, she thought of Hawaiians as "only children in *knowledge.*" Their dress might improve—by 1836, it was "rare" to see a woman who had not covered her breasts—but not their "moral condition." Mercy thought that very few Hawaiians were happily married: "They seem not to have acquired the art of cultivating conjugal affection." Taking walks, she noticed groups of women, "sitting or stretched out full length on the ground by the side of the road, doing nothing but talking." This was no improvement on the sloth that had affronted the missionaries in 1820. "O how much precious time is wasted by these poor natives," she lamented. Her household help still did not meet her standards in 1841; they did things "at the halves," making Mercy spend "1, 2, or 3 hours" redoing the work. At "Maternal Association" meetings, begun in the 1830s and held once a month, Mercy attempted to change Hawaiian habits of childrearing that continued to produce undisciplined and disrespectful children. ("Many seem to feel a sort of pride," she reported in 1836, "as if it were meritorious, to tell how they beat, scold, abuse & drive their children from them, calling them all manner of names, telling them they are very disobedient, ungovernable &c. &c. & the children thus treated were formerly taught by one parent to pick up stones & pelt the other, till the latter was obliged to flee for their own safety, & thus the child conquered.") In calling the Hawaiian mothers "degraded" in 1842, she was thinking of a visit to a newborn of "one of the most enlightened families in the neighborhood," where she had cleaned out the baby's navel with a syringe and found "several large maggots." In 1844, after twenty-five years, she concluded to Henry that the Hawaiians were "as yet, scarcely raised one grade above the beasts" and that it would be a "long time" before they could "justly be ranked among the civilized nations of the earth."[39]

Yet there are anecdotes of rapport with Hawaiians as well as recoil from them. Some of Mercy's criticisms were born of indignation on behalf of the poor. "If the chiefs get cheated of one bargain," she explained in 1834, "they lay heavy taxes on their subjects, to enable them to make another." Thinking the people "greatly oppressed by their rulers," she added a sympathetic perspective on their so-called sloth. "Few of them have any resolution or encouragement to be industrious & get any thing to make themselves comfortable; for they say if they do, it will all go to the Chiefs, which is frequently the fact."[40]

Mercy's comments to Hawaiians cannot have been unrelievedly critical, or they would not have shown her the respect and affection that numerous anecdotes attest. When the king and queen and windward chiefs invited her to accompany them to Niihau in 1848, Dr. Judd advised her to go: "the chiefs still have a strong attachment to the *old missionaries.*" Her scholars once presented her with a native-style dress of fine tapa cloth, matching the ones they had made for themselves; she in turn put it on "to gratify them" and wore it to the school examination. When Henry returned to Kauai in 1849, looking much like his father, the Hawaiians greeted him with a deafening wail of joy, thinking (as Mercy agreed) that it was as if Samuel had risen from the dead. Hawaiians slept inside the house, and several families camped outside in the yard, when Samuel Whitney traveled to distant villages. Mercy was grateful for the guards, even though Samuel joked that they slept so soundly you would have to throw them into the sea to wake them up. When Mercy lay in bed for months in the summer heat, recuperating from her miscarriage and hemorrhage in 1835, Hawaiians came daily to sit with her, fan her, and brush away the flies. "They were very kind indeed," she wrote to her sons, "& did everything that they could, to assist us." When she had rheumatism in her shoulder, the Hawaiians gave her *lomi-lomi,* a soothing massage.[41]

In later years, when Mercy was alone and could not afford to hire help for strenuous labor, like thatching a roof or outdoor yard work, she relied on Hawaiians. They saw it, she thought, as a "kind of play day," helping her much as they were accustomed to work for chiefs, who put on a feast when they needed a taro patch prepared or some other large job done. She was reminded of the husking, sewing, and apple-paring bees of her youth. In 1850, having made a "trial" of the Hawaiians' affection for her by asking for help with outdoor work, Mercy surprised the group of twenty-eight women with a large plate of cake. The next week, she had eighty laborers, whom she fed with a stew of corned beef, vegetables, and taro tops, and a large calabash of poi, followed by the remains of the cake and sea biscuits—a popular treat. Mercy, who mistrusted "play," still wrote in her journal of pleasure:

> You would no doubt have been interested & gratified, could you have looked down upon us, & seen the cheerful, smiling faces in every direction, the orderly, quiet behavior at their meals, the satisfaction which beamed in their countenances, the warm grasp of the hand & the hearty aloha, as they took leave & dispersed to their several houses. I have enjoyed the day much, & trust I feel truly thankful for their kindness in aiding me. May the Lord reward them.[42]

But though Mercy lived out her life in the midst of Hawaiians, she never assumed she was "of" them. She never forgot or reconsidered the instructions given the first company in 1819. In the broadest sense the mission's purpose was exemplary. As she explained in 1852:

> We were not sent out to sink down on a level with *them,* but were instructed to *raise them* to a level with the civilized nations of the earth. It is true we are like a city set on a hill, and so long as we feel that this is our position and that the world are gazing at us, it will only have a tendency if we possess the spirit & the temper of Christ, to make us *humble, holy, watchful, heavenly minded,* and *circumspect.*

In pursuit of that "spirit & temper of Christ," she never let up the pressure on herself, or on Hawaiians, to meet her exacting standards in thought or behavior. Surrounded by the "demoralizing influence" of Hawaiian culture and removed from the supportive presence of fellow Christians, she continued to struggle harder than she had expected in her youthful imaginings to nurture her own spirituality. "One is liable almost insensibly," she wrote in 1831, "unless constantly on his guard, to sink into a state of lukewarmness & spiritual languor." Orderly to the point of perfectionism, she took care with everything she did—from her neat handwriting, as she made copies of every letter and journal entry, to her routines of modest exercise and frugal diet (no coffee or tea, little meat, poi when there was no flour for bread, mostly vegetables, fruit, and milk). Resisting her children's requests that she live with them, Mercy remained in Kauai for the rest of her life. She defended her decision:

> Here I meet weekly with sisters of the church for reading and expounding the Scripture, & prayer. Here my advice & opinion is sought by those around me, & even our native preachers come occasionally to

> ask the meaning of certain texts of scripture not perfectly clear to them, & as I have commentaries, I am able to give them the views & opinions of great & learned men on these points; whereas should I leave here & go to any other place to reside & simply take care of myself, I should feel like a cumberer of the ground, a mere blank in Creation.[43]

The material conditions of life had changed much over a half-century, but Mercy had not. Occasionally she thought back to the first years of hardship. "Those who have entered the field of late years," she wrote in 1854, "know nothing of, & therefore cannot *realize* what the Pioneers were called to endure." She lived long enough to witness many improvements in material comforts—steamers that began in the 1850s to take passengers from island to island with greater speed and comfort, the arrival of mail from the United States in weeks instead of months (a journal from Emily arrived in six weeks in 1856), sewing machines and telegraphs. When Mercy returned from the United States in 1862, the journey took six weeks and one day from New York—"so short, it seemed like a dream."[44]

Yet old frugal habits died hard. She drew one of the smallest salaries from the mission ($100 in 1855), and denied herself the steamer, relying instead on native vessels, which were cheaper, even though she confessed to nausea at the mere thought of a voyage on them. Those who attended the auction of goods at her home after her death were surprised that she had saved countless relics from half a century of life in Waimea: "bolts and bolts of calico cloth, Hingham buckets filled with spools of thread, old chairs and tables, beautiful Niihau mats of makaloa reed, Hawaiian tapas, large and small, and of many colors, feather capes, and even Hawaiian idols such as modern eyes had never beheld." The need to practice economies—so as not to impose on the charitable supporters of missions—seems to have turned into hoarding (even of twigs for firewood). More interesting is the evidence of the irresistible—and very human—inclination to lay up treasures in this world. The point, as Mercy understood, was to struggle, to direct one's thoughts "from an earthly to a heavenly inheritance." Her life testifies to the struggles and contradictions that kept her religiousness in a state of living tension, not moribund abstraction.[45]

Thinking about her physical sufferings one day in 1827, Mercy had written, conventionally enough, that afflictions could turn out to be blessings. "O what a tendency do they have, to wean the heart from earth & direct it to look forward to that state where trials, conflicts & sorrows have an end." Mercy spent a lifetime trying to keep her eyes raised up from the earth. A sense of her failing health in 1848 prompted a lengthy reflection on this point: "I almost long to drop this earthly tabernacle, which is such a clog & hindrance to my spiritual enjoyment, & soar aloft to the mansions of the blest." More often than the other women, Mercy meditated on the need to be prepared for the death that might come as a thief in the night. She continued in the same journal entry:

> O to live so as to be prepared for that rest which remains for the people of God! This is the *great*—the *all important* point—the *one* thing needful. Lord, help me to live near to thee, to mortify the flesh with the affections & lusts, to overcome the world, to be crucified to it, & to rise above it in my affections, desires & aims while I live in it: that when Thou dost call me hence, I may be prepared to go, rejoicing in thy love.[46]

She persevered, "a lonely pilgrim" as she styled herself in 1854, keeping the faith, setting her example for the Hawaiians. She died in Waimea in 1872 and shares a grave marker with her husband, behind the Waimea Foreign Church. In English on the front and Hawaiian on the back, the words honor the Whitneys with an achievement Mercy hoped for: "*Pomaikai ka poe mako, ke make lakou iloko o ka Haku*—Blessed are the dead that die in the Lord." Word of mouth was unkind, passing along into the next century a view of her as the woman who became *pupule* (crazy) because she gave up her children. As for Mercy, it never occurred to her that she might have weaned her heart from earth not wisely, but too well.[47]

Lucy and Asa Thurston, like everyone else, believed that Hawaiian culture might contaminate their children. But uniquely among the pioneers, they kept their five children in Kailua, teaching them at home until their teen years, when Lucy herself accompanied the children on the ship home. (She made one voyage in 1840 leaving the three eldest, another in 1850 with one more daughter.) The Thurstons may have been prompted (as Mercy Whitney reported) by the absence of friends to whom they could entrust their children, since Lucy's parents and favorite sister Persis were dead by the time the children were old enough to return. It did make a difference, as Lucy herself admitted, that the first two children were girls. (Presumably safer from sexual temptations, the girls stayed in Kailua until they were sixteen and eighteen; Lucy's third child, a son, went home at twelve.) But Lucy also wrote that every feeling of her heart revolted against sending children away so young. And she seems not to have been as concerned as Mercy was about skirting moral dangers. "I have not felt like some of our mothers," she explained, "that children *must* be sent away or be ruined. I harp upon another string, and say, make better provision for them, or that will likely be the result." Methodical, practical, demanding, and much of the time in good health, she set about making those provisions. She was helped by living in a quiet place like Kailua, something of a backwater now that the government had moved to Honolulu, and not troubled, like Lahaina and Honolulu, by periodic disgorgements of whaling crews. (The Binghams stressed the "pollution, noise, and strife" of Honolulu more than the difficulty of Sophia's achieving a "change of heart" there. Sybil quoted a sympathetic letter from a wife in one of the "retired" stations (Delia Bishop in Kailua), who, like Lucy, could find the time for instructing her children each day. "Were I in your situation, I think I should be willing to spare my children at an early age. . . . *Your busy hurried life is not an enviable one.*")[48]

No matter what the location, the prospect of raising children was daunting. When Lucy, now the mother of two young daughters, returned from Honolulu to Kailua in 1823 to settle there permanently, she herself was ill from her old "pulmonary complaint," and temporarily overwhelmed with the difficulty of caring for two children when most of her time was spent protecting them from "dangerous" Hawaiian influences. Cooped up in a dark thatched house without windows, whose two doors were usually thronged with curious Hawaiians, Lucy felt she had to keep her elder daughter from talking with the Hawaiians, which meant that she herself was prevented from mingling and learning more of the language and culture. "In feelings," she admitted, the cottage became "the dungeon, and home the heathen world."[49]

Her solution was to make the cottage area not less of a prison, but a more inhabitable one. After a good deal of distress and sleepless nights in which she felt like a person gazing up from the bottom of a well, she put her trust in order and regularity. She divided her domestic world into three groups of persons—children, household natives, and native visitors—and designed a house (actually a group of thatched buildings and fenced yards) that would allow separate spheres of activity in daily life. Lucy had no intention of having her children mingle with the Hawaiians; she simply effected their isolation without sending them back home. She reasoned that if Jewish parents had always been able to raise their children as Jews in a Gentile culture, she ought to be able to do the same with Christian children among heathens. Since the "impurities" of Hawaiian culture were communicated through the language, she focused upon making sure her children did not learn it. "The first rule to be attended to with regard to children," she wrote, "is that they *must not speak the native language*. . . . No intercourse whatever should exist between children and heathen. On this point I am very particular." The children had their own room for instruction and a *kapu* yard—accessible only from the schoolroom—where they would retreat when their parents were speaking with Hawaiians.[50]

One crisis of childhood occurred when Persis, the oldest, rebelled against attending church services every Sunday when she understood nothing that her father was saying. Lucy sympathized, excused all the children, and began to hold Sabbath school at home. Lucy had her reward during the summer of 1836, when her daughters, declaring themselves Christians, were accepted as members of the mission church in Honolulu. At this point they were allowed to learn the language, to read any of the books available in Hawaiian, and to imitate their parents by teaching a small class of Hawaiian girls. But Lucy was taking no chances: "The restriction of non-intercourse among the natives is not removed." Another crisis arose when the Thurstons, shaken like their fellow missionaries by the news brought back by the mission delegation to Tahiti in 1832, reconsidered their decision. Asa thought the children should leave; Lucy fixed upon a twenty-year limit for missionary labor, which would bring their eldest child to the age of eighteen, an appropriate time for the entire family to leave. Thus she was able to continue her labor with an end in sight.[51]

Since Lucy's first duty lay with her family, the hours that she had available for interacting with Hawaiians were limited. The bell for classes rang at nine in the morning and continued to mark off the day in half-hour intervals as the focus of study shifted from one subject to another. In the morning, the mission area was *kapu* to Hawaiian visitors. But by afternoon, Lucy was ready to attend to Hawaiians, mostly as the master teacher of the best Hawaiian students, who were then responsible for their own classes. At various times she taught Sabbath school, a Bible class, and an "arithmetical school," while her husband cared for their children. She began a "Friday Female Meeting" in 1827, which exacted from its participants a standard of dress ("full covering") and behavior—that they "forsake all their former vile practices, and pay an external regard to the Word and Worship of God." In two years it grew from 70 to 1,500 members, then by 1830 to 2,600. But as Lucy's many letters to the depository in Honolulu attest, with her pleas for advanced textbooks in geometry, geography, and Latin, most of her energies went toward preparing her children for entrance into school in the United States. (In fact, one series of letters suggests that Lucy found herself in trouble with fellow missionaries for encouraging her daughters to sell their extra butter to earn money for books. Lucy thought this was commendable Yankee ingenuity—"God helps those who help themselves" was one of her slogans—but the practice went against the mission regulation forbidding buying and selling for profit.) Lucy's main contribution to the mission during these years lay, as the Board had expected, in holding up for the Hawaiians the standard of exemplary family life—though in such isolation that it is hard to believe many Hawaiians got an accurate picture of what went on behind the walls (even if they could have understood the English being spoken). While Lucy may also be seen as successfully combining her duties as a mother, a teacher, and a missionary, she did so with a very clear sense that her duty to her family came first. Asa's most important work was public, she wrote, hers private.[52]

There is very little evidence to clarify whether or not the other women resented or disagreed with Lucy's solution or whether or not she thought the others ought to have followed her lead. Lucy Thurston did hold up Samuel Whitney's example (in running away from college) to her own son, Asa, in 1846. Believing that young Samuel had been prematurely pressured into becoming a missionary, and wanting her own son to "be a boy, until he becomes a man," she hoped that he would take his time in choosing a profession. (The pressure in fact came from the Elys, Samuel's guardians, not from Mercy, who wrote to Samuel that there were many ways to serve the Lord.) In the only other hint of discord between Lucy and Mercy—understandable in two women who had made vastly different decisions about their children's upbringing—Mercy wrote in 1857 of Asa as a "poor reckless lad, causing his Parent and sister much trouble." She continued, "I do not see that Mrs. T[hurston]'s children with all her care & anxiety for them, prove in the end to be better than those of her neighbors, who never felt it their duty to leave their Miss*ry* work, to accompany them to the States. If she has erred in this matter, the Lord forgive her." Sybil wrote to encourage her son Hiram when he was at school in Connecticut, evidently struggling to keep up and comparing himself unfavorably with young Asa Thurston. The "*business*" of Asa's childhood, Sybil explained, had been to prepare for school, not possible in the Bingham household. But if Hiram continued to work hard, she assured him, he would advance one step at a time. Except for these brief references, the record is tactful, circumspect, and silent.[53]

Although showing her independence of mind in refusing to follow the crowd and send her children home, Lucy was no different from her fellow missionaries in her inability to question the premise that she possessed a culture and religion superior to the Hawaiians'. In her book, she unselfconsciously applauds her successes in maintaining an island of pure discourse in the sea of Hawaiian pollution. Unable to "defy" impurity of speech "in its native element," she did what she could and drove it out of her home. When Hawaiians forgot themselves and uttered something of which Lucy disapproved, she wrote it down and read it at Friday meetings. She naturally assumed that as Hawaiians "awakened into life," they would join her in criticizing their former activities and understand why she isolated her children, noting with approval in 1832, "*Now,* natives themselves are our monitors. No one is more particular than Kapiolani; and if in her intercourse among the families of the Mission, she observes native language on the lips of the children, or even if their eyes speak looks of interest and familiarity with the natives, she notes it with feelings of the deepest pity." Lucy expected Hawaiians to admire her childrearing practices, which produced docile and obedient children (in contrast to their own rambunctious ones). She quotes them as saying, "Yes, it is right. You take care of your children, but we do not take care of ours."[54]

The charge of intolerance or condescension in her attitude Lucy would not have understood. Her metaphor, like everyone else's, was of vertical movement. She had come halfway around the world to "elevate" Hawaiians, who had to "rise up" as from a pit. "We tried to give them a standard of what was right," she explained. She wrote of her daughters as "public examples." One reading of her determination to keep up a standard is that she paid Hawaiians the compliment of holding them to the same standard as herself—not a standard "half-way up" or good enough for Hawaiians. This may be one reason why a person like Kapiolani, accustomed, as an *alii,* to excellence in her own culture, would so perfectly imitate the New Englanders in dress and demeanor, becoming known as the "white (*haole*) chiefess." But like so many missionary attitudes, Lucy's have complications and contradictions. As a further reason why children should be isolated, Lucy does argue for a double standard. "Native converts to Christianity," she wrote,

> fail of being suitable models for a child's imitation. They may be clothed, they may be Christianized, yet from want of early culture from being children of nature, there is an utter destitution of those feelings of delicacy which in refined society seem inseparable from virtuous tastes and principles. Now, in estimating the character of Sandwich Islanders, we pass over what can not be corrected; it is a tarnish which reminds us of the pit from whence they were digged. Not so with the children of American extract.

These children were expected to "rise up and reflect honor upon an *enlightened origin.*"[55]

In the same contradictory way, Lucy's anecdotes include both those which unthinkingly belittle Hawaiians (as in "tarnish" above) and those which show sensitivity to their feelings. When Lucy first thought of their plan for living arrangements, she admitted, "I had a severe struggle with my own feelings in establishing these things, and passed painful, sleepless hours, lest I had offended." She took great pains to explain to the women of the Friday meetings why she was removing her children from Sunday church services. And she evidently learned over the years to accept many Hawaiian habits that she at first would have recoiled from. When another missionary wife, a newcomer, was dismayed at seeing a Hawaiian cook peeling potatoes "*with his fingers,*" an amused Lucy came to his defense. Like David, throwing down his armor in favor of a slingshot against Goliath, the cook, as soon as the missionary turned away, would discard the "awkward irons" of knife and fork and skillfully use "those facilities which nature furnishes."[56]

Lucy Thurston, alone of the women in the first company, sorted through her journals and letters to collect them into a book (which she wrote not for her own fame but to secure an income for her widowed daughter Mary and her children). Since she therefore had the opportunity to purge her record of embarrassing or excessively private details, it is difficult to read her autobiography without wondering what she left out. (Was she, like Sybil Bingham and Mercy Whitney, periodically worried about spiritual dullness; did she succumb to moments of depression or, in solitude, to words of self-depreciation?) The few letters that do survive are copied into the book more or less verbatim; it seems unlikely that Lucy purged much. Lucy does leave a trail of embarrassing admissions, mostly in dismissing Hawaiian culture, but these are unselfconscious. Because Lucy's tone is self-assured and her anecdotes often pragmatic—a record of trials resolved and problems overcome—she seems less vulnerable than either Sybil or Mercy, the only other pioneer women who left a comparable amount of writing. One speaker at her funeral mentioned a "commanding" presence. She gives the impression that she could solve any problems that came her way. But she could only solve them by relying on the Lord. When she learned that her daughter Lucy would die, after having been pronounced out of danger, Lucy remembered, "It was a very great shock to me, both in body and mind. I felt like Belshazzar when his knees smote together." Her recovery at this moment did not depend upon the niceties of theology—though she did later express the ideas of her faith. Now she discovered the strength of her character. "I retired and was alone with God. A simple thought passed through my mind. 'I will try to bear whatever is laid upon me.'" This is *the* Lucy Thurston, meeting her challenges without flinching. She is at her best in shrugging off self-pity. Never murmur that your lot is a hard one, she advised her daughter Persis. It comes as no surprise that a young Lucy could hang on in Kailua for half the year in 1820, when Lucia Holman could not.[57]

She coped with her share of medical problems (which tended to take the form of emergencies, not, as for Mercy Whitney, lingering ailments). In 1831, en route to the General Meeting, she bore her fourth child in the cramped hold of a storm-tossed native ship, which stank of bilge water and resembled, in Lucy's mind, the Black Hole of Calcutta. In 1838, she suffered a "paralysis" on one side, possibly a stroke; in 1850, she nearly killed herself by mistakenly dosing herself with strychnine instead of quinine.[58]

In 1855, she faced her most difficult physical trial, an operation to remove a cancerous breast, which—because of concern about Lucy's previous paralysis—had to be done without chloroform. The operation lasted an hour and a half. As the surgeon cut, Lucy found herself beginning to talk. She was sorry that her husband had not been able to arrive in time to be there, she said:

> But it is not necessary. So many friends, and Jesus Christ besides. His left hand is underneath my head. His right hand sustains and embraces me. I am willing to suffer. I am willing to die. I am not afraid of death. I am not afraid of hell. I anticipate a blessed immortality. Tell Mr. Thurston my peace flows like a river.

Lucy's son Asa and daughter Persis were present. The cutting over, Lucy asked Persis to tell her when each stitch began, so that she could bear it. The doctor spoke at the end: "There is not one in a thousand who would have borne it as you have done." In this crisis, as in all the others, Lucy practiced the attitude she had recommended to Persis in 1842, the kind of toughness that transcends cultures and centuries: "I will not disguise it,—life is replete with anxieties, perplexities, cares, toils, sufferings, and sorrows. Well, let them come."[59]

There were future trials, deaths of her grandchildren, her son Asa, and her husband. "Mr. Thurston," as she called him, lapsed into senility (his mind "deranged") during the last nine weeks of his life before he died in 1868. Lucy spent her last years in Honolulu, applauded and sentimentalized by those much younger than herself. She was given the honor (unprecedented for a woman) of addressing a public meeting with her reminiscences. Honolulu had not exactly been won for the Congregationalists, but it had been won for the *haoles.* A different sort of person was being bred for this new era. Lucy—despite the isolation she enforced for her children —had spent a lifetime in Kailua among Hawaiians, speaking their language. It was "compassion," she thought, that motivated her desire to "raise" Hawaiians to her own position, to teach them to think like her. But the belittling judgments nascent in her attitudes blossomed into results she would not have approved. Her efforts and those of her fellow missionaries were directed, however imperfectly, toward preserving the nation: they looked with horror at the depopulation; they maintained the Hawaiian language in the schools; they were urged by Rufus Anderson (secretary of the ABCFM) in 1846 *"to get a NATIVE MINISTRY,"* because without self-government, "the Sandwich Islands people are marked for speedy extinction." Thinking Hawaiians lived in "darkness," Lucy's generation wanted to give them the "light" they themselves had. Later generations, thinking Hawaiians lived in darkness, had no time for them. By the late nineteenth century—by now two generations removed from the disinterested idealists of the *Thaddeus* who tried to know nothing but "Jesus Christ and him crucified"—a group of *haole* businessmen, led by Lucy Thurston's grandson, overthrew the Hawaiian monarchy and set the stage for U.S. annexation and statehood.[60]

Lucy Thurston had a heart attack in 1876, but lived through six months of "spasms of pain" and difficulty in breathing before she died. She is buried in Oahu Cemetery in Honolulu, as she directed, above her husband.[61]

7. *Pilgrim Path*

Come unto me, all ye that labor and are heavy-laden, and I will give you rest.

— MATTHEW 11:28

From 1827 (when the Loomises went home) on through the 1830s, the record for the women of the first company concentrates on three women — Mercy Whitney, Lucy Thurston, and Sybil Bingham — and three islands — Kauai, Hawaii, and Oahu. There are so few papers from Nancy Ruggles that her story in Hawaii falls away. With great reluctance, the Ruggleses returned to the United States in 1834, citing Samuel's poor health (consumption) and their children's welfare. Like Mercy, Sybil was affected by the news of departure. She felt a chill run over her, then wept. "We came together — have lived much together — " she wrote to Nancy, "have borne the heat & burden of the day together; and much more I might add, that makes me feel." On the way home, during a stopover in Tahiti, Samuel wrote that if they could now set their course for the Sandwich Islands (not the United States), they would be "happy." For a time Samuel toured New England churches, telling about Hawaii, but his health did not immediately improve with the change of climate, and the family never returned. They were living in Wisconsin when Nancy Ruggles died eighteen months after her husband, on February 28, 1873.[1]

Unlike Mercy and Lucy, who spent their lives in relatively quiet places, it was Sybil Bingham's lot always to live in "tumultuous" Honolulu. Sitting down in 1833 to reflect (as she had so often) on why it was difficult for her to engage in "direct instruction" of the heathen, Sybil described her surroundings:

> There are those on mission grounds, who are better able to realise the anticipation of sitting down systematically, to the direct work of

> instruction. But a female member of a mission—a mother of a rising family, placed at a post like this, where reinforcements land—where the disabled reembark—where invalids come for medical aid—where general meetings are often held—where the king and principal rulers dwell—where other chiefs from other islands often assemble—whom the thousands of the inhabitants of the land who claim to be known & remembered, go & come—where foreign visitors of various ranks & languages and minds & manners [go & come], some honestly desiring attention, that they may correctly gain information, others *not less needing* it, to counteract their prejudices or to correct my statements, as their report may be borne abroad on the four winds of heaven—I say, a feeble woman, placed in such circumstances must be content to realize but little of the picture her youthful mind had formed of sitting down, quietly day by day, surrounded by heathen women & children, to lead their minds to the sources of knowledge, both human and divine.[2]

In estimating what was wrong with that "youthful picture" in the 1820s, one of the key words was "quietly." Not surprisingly, the mission's success in December 1825—when the most important *alii* in the kingdom became church members—coincided with the first acts of violence against the mission by other foreigners. While on probation, from July to December, the chiefs put their first *kapu* on the women's visits to the ships. "The Enemy is busy—truly on the alert," Sybil predicted that September. "It seems sometimes, with reference to this little spot of the vast territory over which he had been allowed so long to reign, it might be said that 'he had come, having great wrath, knowing that he has but a short time.'" The great wrath did not take long to surface. In October, in Lahaina, whalers armed with knives threatened William and Clarissa Richards at the door of their house. In Honolulu, Hiram Bingham was the obvious target. A mob of whalers surrounded him in January 1826 as he fled from a prayer meeting at Kalanimoku's house toward the mission house. Stopping at the door (which Sybil, not seeing him, had barricaded), he warded off blows with the help of Hawaiian defenders. For one terrible moment, Sybil lost sight of Hiram in the crush and feared the worst. The following year the Binghams (visiting Lahaina on their way back from a rest cure in Hawaii) found themselves once again under attack. This time the Richards and Bingham families hid in the cellar with five small children while two cannonballs came perilously close to the house. About two weeks later, news came that some English whalers were on their way, threatening to level the town if the missionaries were not turned over to them. Sybil knew that the "final victory" had to be the Lord's. In the meantime, the families composed themselves to meet the danger, singing hymns and praying through the night as they deliberated the safest course of action—fleeing into the center of the island or sailing to Honolulu.[3]

As it looked to Sybil by December of 1827, "The wrath of man seems ready to swallow us up." And she was willing to admit (in an undated fragment from these years), "I have been more tremblingly alive with fear, than I ever remember to have been, for any length of time in my life." She found herself waking up at night, listening "for every sound." Even though in retrospect it is hard to believe the mission ever faced ruin, the immediate danger was real. Both missionary and chief took the threats from knives and cannonballs seriously. Though officers kept their men in order—even "Mad Jack" Percival, who sympathized with his crew, broke up the attack on Bingham and punished its perpetrators—many did so grudgingly. The chiefs in Oahu, Sybil reported, felt agitation and "no little awe" at the threat from the English whalers in 1827 to level Lahaina.[4]

As befitted a serious situation, the defense of the mission and in fact of the nation itself (for one issue was the chiefs' right to make laws for their own subjects) took many forms. Sybil reasoned that when faced with such "real hatred to the gospel . . . nothing short of the *Grace* of *GOD* can cure it," but she also pondered what might "disarm it." "Female influence" came to mind: as the only missionary woman in Honolulu at the moment (April 1827), the responsibility fell on her, and she resolved on a course of behavior. "I would make it my daily prayer, that in every thought, word, or step relative to those who so ungenerously oppose themselves, I may have the spirit of meekness & of wisdom." But direct action seems to have been more effective than demeanor in securing the mission's defense. The simplest solution was to meet force with force, as when the Hawaiians readied the cannon at the fort in Lahaina in 1825, signaling to the *Daniel*'s men that they intended to protect the Richardses. As another alternative, Boki temporarily "gave in" to the *Dolphin*'s crew in early 1826, defusing the violence by rescinding the *kapu* on women for a few months. Various meetings and councils attempted diplomatic solutions. A meeting of 1826, heavily attended by the foreign community, was supposed to state grievances against the mission (which had issued a "Circular" challenging its critics), but instead collapsed when no one had specific charges. In December 1827, when the chiefs met to consider the charges leveled by Captain Buckle (of the *Daniel*) against William Richards, the missionary wrote a conciliatory letter explaining that he had not expected his account of Buckle's behavior (in "purchasing" a woman) to be published. Many of the more distinguished visitors to the islands—Lord Byron of the HMS *Blonde* in 1825, Lieutenant Thomas ap Catesby Jones of the U.S. Navy sloop *Peacock* in 1826, Captain William Finch, also from the Navy, on a good-will tour in the *Vincennes* in 1829—earned respect from the chiefs for their own actions and put in a word of support for the missionaries.[5]

Still, none of this cleared up the somewhat murky relationship between church and state. Though pleased to give advice when asked, the missionaries claimed that they did not interfere in the daily governing of the country. When sailors confronted Hiram Bingham in August 1825, after the first *kapu* on prostitution, he referred them to Kaahumanu. The queen enforced the *kapu* on Oahu, lecturing women and even ordering that two offenders have their heads shaved. At a council meeting in 1826, she told a bullying Lieutenant Percival that she was responsible for the *kapu* and that God had taught her. (Percival protested that it was Hiram Bingham.) If the chiefs began to govern with new rules derived from the newly adopted religion, Bingham argued in his book, this situation was no different from that in "civilized" countries like the United States, where leaders of church and state shared moral convictions.[6]

But some defense of the mission was prompted as much by private affection as by public policy. When the Bingham and Richards families were fired on in Lahaina in 1827, they fled to Honolulu, considerably worried about the reception they might receive (the offending ship having preceded them to the port). Once there, they were reassured. Manuia, the commander of the fort in Honolulu, sent out a boat to ferry them in and saw that they were conducted inside the fort, guarded by armed men on either side. "But what affected us to tears," Sybil recalled, "was the sight of our beloved Elisabeta [Kaahumanu] who, in dignified & tender attitude, met us at the gate, gave us, in silence, her hand, kissed us, and wept." The queen then walked them over the plain to the mission house. "A considerable company attended us," Sybil continued, "of the serious part of our congregation and others, extending, one after the other, the hand, and giving the salutation *aloha.*" This was something different from the behavior of the noisy crowds of April 1820 in Kailua, gazing discourteously into the women's faces under their bonnets. As the potential for violence continued, the defense tightened. Sybil described their protection at this time: "There is almost every high chief of the nation with each a number of people, either within or about our house. It is a guard to defend us from violence, determined that if a blow is struck it shall [be] against them as well as their teachers."[7]

As much as the missionaries saw themselves as beleaguered by detractors, they stayed on the offensive, continuing to implant their own uncompromising sense of the true religion and the good life and to oppose anything—heathen or *haole*—that got in their way. The good life was defined in large part by what it excluded: fornication and drinking rum, of course, and increasingly in the 1830s all spirits and tobacco. In 1827 Kaahumanu tried to prevent Catholic missionaries from landing, and in 1831 she expelled the last two priests. (She was technically acting with independent authority, but it is clear that she did what her missionary friends hoped she would, and they did not urge her to let the priests stay.)[8]

Ever fond of quantifying, the missionaries continued to keep track of the figures that seemed to prove their success—the attendance at schools and churches, the numbers of buildings, and the thousands of books printed and distributed. Hawaiian congregations sat patiently on mats in churches in Lahaina, Kailua, and Honolulu that held three to four thousand persons. Those who could not fit inside sat in the yard, catching a word or a hymn as they could. Only a few, relatively speaking, were being admitted to church membership and allowed to take communion. (In 1833, Sybil reported six to seven hundred members; by 1837, there were fewer than twelve hundred members, though half the population attended church.) Lahaina in 1828 had 174 schools and 11,881 students (almost a third of the population in Maui); Kauai in 1829 had 74 schools, each staffed by a native teacher, meeting in new schoolhouses that were usually the largest buildings in the village. As the male missionaries toured the villages, they were much in demand for conducting *hoikes,* the school examinations that routinely had a thousand or more participants, and marriage ceremonies, often dozens at one time. (Richards once married 59 couples in one day, and 1,222 in one year.) No matter how many times the missionaries insisted that the souls of *alii* and commoner were equal, there was special joy in January 1827 when the princess Nahienaena joined the church in Lahaina. In Honolulu, Kauikeaouli had no interest in joining the church, but still earned the approbation of the mission community when he stood up unexpectedly at the end of the dedication ceremony for a new church in 1829 and "with dignity, clearness, and appropriateness of diction, voice, and manner" acknowledged his respect for Christianity.[9]

Sybil Bingham reported in her journal of 1830 a high pitch of interest in all activities to do with the church. Her part lay in gathering the women into weekly Female Prayer Meetings. These had begun back in January 1825, when Kaahumanu had given an account of her hopes as a fledgling Christian. As with Lucy Thurston's meetings in Kailua, membership required a statement of resolve—"casting off all former evil courses & seeking to walk according to the rules of the blessed gospel." Sybil wrote the names of members in a copybook. From seven hundred at the end of 1825, the members in Honolulu reached over fifteen hundred by 1830. By then the group had outgrown its meeting place, making Sybil worry about unwieldiness and disorder. She revised the organization into more manageable groups of forty to eighty women, assigning each a leader who could keep track of church attendance and who made weekly visits to members' homes, checking on families and children's instruction, ascertaining any distress or illness, whether physical or spiritual. The missionary women (Laura Judd and Mary Ward—later Mrs. Edmund Rogers—as well as Sybil) then spread their presence among the groups at their weekly meetings and visited the homes of the leaders.[10]

Toward the end of 1829 and during the new year of 1830, the women found themselves thronged with children instead of adult students. Hiram Bingham had compiled a thirty-six-page primer for children (with the alphabet, spelling and reading lessons, hymns, a catechism, even some pictures), whose first copies were being promised as a new year's present for all who applied. On January 2 it rained all day, but even with a ten-feet-wide "brook" in front of the house, the children kept coming. Just at dark, the first seventy copies were ready for them; two months later, Bingham counted 1,144 children happily turning pages. That April, when over 6,000 students performed at the annual *hoike,* Sybil counted 300 children. The past several months had given her the kind of missionary "work" she valued and craved. After one January meeting, attended by both women and children, she had written, "Seated in the midst of the group, literally surrounded and kneeling with them, I experienced some of the comfort I once thought I should feel in being with the heathen."[11]

It would be a misconception to suppose that a missionary wife's lot was mostly a matter of romantic expectations reversed and toil endured. The greatest "comfort" continued to come from "direct" labors for the Hawaiians. But there were also momentary occasions that gave pleasure. Sybil and Clarissa Richards once gave a tea party for thirty of the highest-ranking chiefs, who had gathered in Honolulu for a council in December 1827. Kaahumanu sent over sugar that morning; the two women spent the day baking cakes and biscuits. "I could not help laughing in the midst of my work," Sybil later wrote to Nancy Ruggles:

> Everything was perfectly orderly, but the cups passed back from the hands of those old veterans of Tamehameha, and the cake plates went round it unlike what they used to do in a circle of young ladies of whom you know. But I will not dwell longer here. It was a novel and pleasant scene. We do not remember that we have met so many of the high chiefs together, certainly not in such a way before.

The missionary women also knew the satisfaction not only of believing themselves engaged in a worthwhile cause, but of believing that they were appreciated. Especially during the period of intensified interest around 1830, Sybil described the pleasure and frustrations of popularity. She wrote to Sally and Jane Howell on March 17, 1830:

> At this station we meet the people or at least a portion of them, in various ways, many times a week; but such appears to be the desire to learn something more from our lips, or to expect their satisfaction in having learnt something, that if we did not set ourselves against it, we should not have an hour from morning til night without some

> of them about us. We do not know what to do. It is an uncomfortable feeling to turn away from them. But the scriptures must be translated, other books must be written—sermons prepared—schools attended—communications made home, &c., &c. Family wants must be attended to, or these feeble bodies fail and that must be done with comparatively few conveniences and little help. . . . As my dear husband went from tea to his study this evening, full twenty stood about the door, with longing looks to be invited in. We could only say, *aloha*, and pass along, telling them we were both very much engaged.[12]

These constant interactions—formal and informal, with *alii* and commoners—continued to nurture familiarity and (with some *alii*) even friendships. Many *alii* still dropped by at their pleasure, expecting the attention that the missionaries were almost always sure to give. One evening in 1827, Kaahumanu and her adopted grandchild drove up just as Sybil was preparing for bed. "But I thought again—" she wrote, "had the tea-kettle boiled, prepared tea, and went the usual round—body and mind more comfortable than to have failed in anything." During what was supposed to be a rest cure on the island of Hawaii in 1830, Sybil spent the first three weeks feeding and attending to royal visitors and their attendants who were making a tour of the windward island. Kaahumanu and young Kauikeaouli lodged and took meals with the Binghams in their thatched cottage there. But there were also signs that aristocratic prerogative was subsiding; the days of drums pounding to get a button sewn on were over.[13]

Kaahumanu and Opiia (her sister) were visiting the Binghams one evening in 1827 when word came that a ship willing to take letters was leaving the next morning. "She soon kindly took our hands," Sybil reported with gratitude, "and, with Opiia, leaving her kind salutations for the *poe hoa hanau* [kindness] in A[merica], retired to the apartment she terms hers." By 1827, Kaahumanu was often spending the night at the mission house even though she had two houses of her own nearby. Hiram Bingham, acceding to her frequent requests, in 1830 made her a rocking chair similar to one he had made for Sybil. The relationship Sybil enjoyed with the queen was not one she had ever anticipated—to "know the comfort of loving and showing kindness to her as a Christian sister." The affection was reciprocated. In the spring of 1827, Kaahumanu, who had been touring the windward islands, paid a visit to the mission house along with her sister, Lydia Namahana. "We sat a little while," Sybil remembered, "then sang a hymn & joined in prayer, after which I made a comfortable little breakfast, and by what kind attentions I could, sought to cherish the affectionate *aloha* which they manifested toward us." When Sybil's fifth child (and third daughter) was born on March 8, 1828, she was baptized Elizabeth Kaahumanu Bingham.[14]

In May 1832, Kaahumanu finished what would be her last tour around the islands as a witness for Christianity. She was ill when she returned to Honolulu, just able to welcome the fourth company of missionaries (who arrived May 17) before retreating to her small house in the cool valley of Manoa. Chiefs and missionaries attended her as she lay in her bed scented with *maile* leaves and ginger; for a square mile around, commoners set up temporary houses and waited. Hiram Bingham presented the first copy of the New Testament in Hawaiian, which had been rushed off the press and bound in red leather with Kaahumanu's name imprinted on the cover in gold. The Whitneys, the Judds, the Chapins, and the Binghams were with Kaahumanu when she died near dawn on June 5. "I am going now," she said, "where the mansions are ready." (Many writers have assumed that she was collating the words of Jesus—"In my father's house are many mansions. I go to prepare a place for you"—with the Hawaiian custom of having attendants go ahead of chiefs to prepare a lodging after a day's journey.) "Thanks be to GOD," Sybil wrote, "for the precious hope that she went in peace, and 'entered into rest.'" Mercy Whitney was deeply impressed to be "sitting by the bed-side of this dying saint. . . . O may this be the happy lot of us all, when our pilgrimage on earth shall cease. To see one who was a heathen thus die, was well worth thirteen years of toilsome labour in this land of darkness." As the word of the queen's death passed rapidly from mouth to mouth, the "doleful wail" of the crowd (as Laura Judd remembered it) "echoed from the hills and mountains' side with appalling reverberations."[15]

At the funeral, Hiram Bingham compared Kaahumanu to the apostle Paul, another Christian who came to belief late in life. Like him, she could say, "I have fought a good fight. I have finished my course. I have kept the faith." Even one of the mission's detractors, who wanted to believe that Kaahumanu adopted Christianity out of political shrewdness—and a conviction that her people as Christians would have a better chance of adapting to the changes thrust upon them by Western discovery—had to admit, "She died a *Christian*. . . . She really believed in and practiced the principles of the Christian religion." Sybil, who never doubted Kaahumanu's conversion, simply mourned her loss. "The nation feels—the mission feels it—the church feels it—my individual heart and that of my beloved husband feel it," she wrote. "There is a great blank here. It seems as if nothing could fill it." In her correspondence months after the events, Sybil called back her friend from memory—the summer day in 1822 when she and Hiram first interested Kaahumanu in the alphabet, and the many times since when they had sought "to make her happy in the bosom of our family." Kaahumanu rarely gave advance notice of a visit, and Sybil recalled being often so exhausted that it took an effort to do her duty. She remembered the queen's last call at the mission house for tea, just before the arrival of the fourth company. "But the vivid impression which is on my mind of that fixed, composed, complacent look, as she sat for the last time by my side at table, seems a reward for all. I believe she truly loved us."[16]

Everyone wondered what direction the nation would take after Kaahumanu's death, some, as Sybil clearly realized, hoping that "the whole fabrick of what is denominated moral improvement in the land would fall." The detractors were able to see the "fabrick" shake. The challenge came this time not from whalers and other foreigners but from the Hawaiians themselves, many of whom, especially on Oahu, longed for forbidden pastimes. Once again they surfed, boxed, danced the hula, listened to chants, renewed sexual games and plural marriages, and opened up the distilleries, grogshops, and billiard rooms. The king himself, Kauikeaouli, led the way, encouraged by a group of companions known as the *Hulumanu*. He resisted the efforts of Kinau (daughter of Kamehameha I and niece of Kaahumanu), the new *kuhina-nui* and a resolute Christian, to discipline him. Told in early 1833 that he could not afford to buy a brig he coveted, he plunged into two years of riotous living, as if he had the excuse he needed. Criers went through the streets, not to proclaim prohibitions but to rescind them. At one point, Kinau went to Laura Judd in despair, ready to renounce her rank and responsibilities and either emigrate to America or live at the mission.[17]

Yet in the midst of this, Kauikeaouli seemed to reserve a part of himself for soberly estimating his responsibilities. Although asserting his independence of the regency—he told an assembly in March 1833, "I alone am the one"—he did not (as rumored) try to replace Kinau as *kuhina-nui* with someone more indulgent, nor did he disband the council of chiefs. After 1835, when a new code of laws was drawn up, the king, having resolved his differences with Kinau, left most of the governing to her. Despite the rebellious beginning to his reign, he ended it in 1854 receiving tribute. "Perhaps no king born to the throne ever made a better ruler," wrote Kamakau. "He made all men free and equal." The constitution written in 1840, thought Kamakau, gave the commoners a better life, freeing them from some onerous *kapus* and taxation; the king's decree of 1839 upheld the practice of any religion (thus ending the persecution of Catholic priests and native believers). A religious revival of the later 1830s saw thousands of Hawaiians (especially on the island of Hawaii) baptized by ministers such as Titus Coan and Lorenzo Lyons, who did not demand the probationary periods of the first company. In 1841, the missionaries finally began to license Hawaiians as preachers (Puaaiki, or "Blind Bartimeus," first, then David Malo in 1843, and nine others by 1848). By 1854, the General Meetings were disbanded in favor of governance by the Hawaii Evangelical Association, one sign that the country was Christianized and its churches independent. (In 1864, the ABCFM severed all financial connections.)[18]

But in the 1830s, to see his people through these changes, Kauikeaouli had also to watch them in the throes of deracination and depopulation. The population in 1840 was down to 100,000 from at least a quarter of a million at the turn of the century. Typhoid, measles, whooping cough, syphilis, even the common cold plagued Hawaiians; Kinau died of mumps in 1839; a smallpox epidemic in 1853 killed between 2,500 (an official estimate that many considered too low) and 10,000—Kamakau's estimate was still higher. Others died of a misery that was less physical than psychological, born of confusion and despair in a changing world. One historian calls this the "*okuu* phenomenon," after the Hawaiians' saying: "*Na kanaka okuu wale aku no i kau uhane,*" or "The people dismissed freely their souls and died." Now the young king led his people in mourning.[19]

To marry and rule jointly with his sister Nahienaena would have presented Kauikeaouli with his greatest opportunity for personal happiness.[20] The event would also have symbolized the continuation of Hawaiian culture. This he sacrificed. After childhood, brother and sister grew up separately, Nahienaena in Lahaina, where she was greatly influenced first by the Stewart family and then by the Richardses. She also remembered her mother's dying command to follow the missionaries. In January 1827, she professed her Christian faith and received baptism. In Honolulu, Kauikeaouli's *kahu* (guardian) was Boki, who, despite his baptism on board the *Blonde*, was never an ardent supporter of the mission. (He was Kaahumanu's archrival in politics.)

As brother and sister matured, and now and again spent a few months together, the gossip about incest—though denied by Nahienaena and others—never subsided. The behavior of both siblings began to suggest their frustration and confusion. Nahienaena, like so many of her countrymen during the early 1830s, "slid back" into the old pleasures of cards, chants, hula, and rum. For drinking, she was suspended from the Lahaina church in 1831; in later years she went back and forth between periods of pious regret and rebellion. Her brother made a suicide attempt in 1834 (possibly after his sister refused marriage). A few months later, the two gave up their resistance and married, after the Hawaiian custom, by sleeping together in the presence of various high chiefs. The union was not to last; the ruling chiefs did not recognize the marriage. A half-year later, in January 1835, Nahienaena left the king in Honolulu, impulsively returning to Lahaina. She did not return to the church, and that May she was excommunicated. She was still allowed a Christian ceremony, however, for marrying the man the chiefs had chosen for her, Leleiohoku. Her child, born in September 1836, could have been her husband's or her brother's. The baby boy lived only a few hours. Nahienaena, ill from a lingering fever, died on December 30, 1836, not much more than twenty years old.

There were two funerals, one at Kawaiahao and another at Lahaina, where a procession wound from the mountains to the sea while the commoners wailed. Kauikeaouli mourned in his own fashion, remaining in Lahaina for eight years, building a house that preserved on its second floor the coffins of his mother (Keopuolani), his sister, and the child. For years he took himself away on the anniversary of his sister's death to mourn alone. As his behavior as a ruler began to change, it looked as if the terrible event had shocked him into responsibility and sobriety.[21]

The missionary women of the first company, none of whom lived in Lahaina, had little direct contact with Nahienaena. They mentioned her with pity, but saw her in terms of their own—not Hawaiian—standards, the terms of Christian behavior and preparation for death superseding the imperatives of "heathenism." When Nahienaena shortly before her death told Samuel Whitney that she felt an angry God was judging her for her sins, Mercy agreed with the moral lesson: "This has indeed been a fact so far as we can see, & the change has been so striking, that it appears to be the general impression of the natives, that her illness was a judgment from the Lord. Hers is an awful case of apostasy, & O may it lead us all to look well to our ways, lest we also fall & deny the faith we now possess." The Hawaiian reaction was doubtless more complicated. Certainly the non-Christians among them saw no such cause and effect in the princess's early death. Nahienaena, despite her rank, had not yet exercised political power, so Hawaiians venerated her and felt her loss not for what she had done but for who she was. Her very existence was a physical reminder of the generations of high chiefs whose blood ran in her; her death a confirmation of a glorious Hawaiian past no longer being passed along into the future.

Nahienaena uneasily put on the vestments of the new religion, having so much personal happiness to sacrifice in so doing that she could not, like Kaahumanu, unequivocally embrace it. In the end, the struggle was too much for her. Hers is not a story of triumphal mediating between new and old but of vacillation and a final succumbing. It is hard to suppose that, for her, Christianity brought the message Hiram Bingham had promised that first Sunday—good tidings of great joy. Her mother had died in the first flush of hope for what the new religion would bring her people. Nahienaena's last words (as recorded by Laura Judd) spoke to unease and confusion: "Can there be hope for one who has sinned as I have?"[22]

Though life was hard for missionary women, the wrench they felt in leaving behind the culture of their New England girlhoods never approached the anguish of Nahienaena. They were not trying to lose a past, but to recreate it in another place. They never had to reassess the value of the way of life they had grown up with, merely to determine the best way to go about persuading others to adopt it.

During the first five years, the women of the first two companies did some of their most important work by inspiring important *alii*, especially Kaahumanu, to share their piety. Without that foundation of support from *alii*, the rest of the mission's story would have been one of demise, not consolidation and expansion. In later years, the women continued to pursue forms of "direct" labor, which after 1830 increasingly meant not simply teaching the *palapala* but also conducting Female Prayer Meetings and Maternal Association meetings that imitated organizations for women in New England.[23] If Mercy Whitney, whose children were all gone from the islands by 1834, and Lucy Thurston, whose children were all with her until she took the eldest home in 1840, represent two extreme responses to the problems of rearing children, Sybil Bingham's life presents a middle ground. Though she parted with two daughters, she bore two more children, Hiram Jr. in August 1831 and Lydia on Christmas Day 1834, and so spent her second decade in Hawaii with a family to raise. Now the tension she felt between domestic labor and public work for the mission—which never entirely went away—became most acute, as she juggled as best she could the roles of mother, minister's wife, hostess, schoolteacher, correspondent, seamstress, counselor, and visitor of Hawaiians.

When Sybil began a journal again in the spring of 1827 (after a four-year hiatus and roughly two years after Evarts's death), she wanted in part to strengthen her spiritual life, to examine more often "*how, and for what purpose I live,*" but she also needed an outlet for the mundane thoughts and activities that so quickly filled her days. Without mentioning the orderly divisions of hours on the *Thaddeus*, but implicitly inviting the comparison, she confessed that June, "I once thought much of system, but I have none now—My time, from beginning of the week to the end seems to be at anyone's command rather than my own." It was the "irregularity" of her domestic life that frustrated her in 1829. Nor did the situation improve. Ten years later, in February 1839, Sybil wrote, "I have often filled up my hasty pages, leaving, I suppose, an impression of being myself, as an individual, in a bustling, unquiet state in regard to domestic order and regularity." So far as she could tell, such "sacrifices" had not been called for from every missionary wife and resulted from the "peculiar" circumstances in Honolulu, dating from the time the *alii* had first responded favorably to the mission.[24]

It did not seem to make much difference that as the years went by, various physical improvements made chores easier. Sybil was grateful for a new cookstove, varied tinware, and a cupboard (which kept out rodents and roaches) in 1827. (Without a cupboard when they first arrived, the Judds had to take a wooden trunk and put it on stilts in tar-water.) The Binghams no longer lived in one room but in half the house, with a kitchen and two bedrooms eventually added on at one side. In 1829, Sybil wrote to Maria Loomis that she would probably think herself a stranger if she returned to Honolulu and gazed at plastered walls, painted casings, a carpeted floor, crimson curtains, and a handsome clock. Comparing her situation in 1837 with earlier days, she exclaimed, "It is so different! I mean the manner of living—." She went on to list the "minor things" that came to mind:

> Such, for instance, as little or no bread, and bread in plenty—no milk & butter and milk & butter in abundance—no chair to rest the weary limbs in and chairs many, no table to put the scanty food, and nice tables adorned perhaps occasionally with rare shells and neatly modern-bound choice books—straw houses, on a dry plain, where scarcely a green leaf met the eye with out stretching to the vallie for it, and comfortable permanent houses, with neat yards attached, and here & there a pretty garden of plants & shrubs.[25]

Like the other wives, Sybil had help from Hawaiians. But she often mentions preparing and serving meals herself, and her "native family," as she called them in 1827, were "awkward & inexperienced" —a boy who looked after the cattle and milked, another who did housework, a girl who was learning to sew and who looked after the infant Lucy, a husband and wife who did the washing. The man was also making the difficult shift from cooking an entire pig in an underground oven to cooking small pieces on a stove. "But they are all improving," Sybil kindly concluded. Ten years later, even though the situation was more trying—Sybil was preparing rooms for the new company of thirty-two missionaries as well as missionaries from other stations—her comments varied little. "I have only native help —never indeed any other. But they are kind—do as well as they know how." Over the years, Sybil stopped doing laundry, one of "many things" which she no longer looked upon as "pressing duties." "We were slow to come into the practice," she wrote in 1837, "but we do it universally now—send our clothes back to the stream, to be washed in cold water. You can readily perceive that we cannot have such care of them as we would like." But she went on to ask with unassailable—and new-found—common sense, "If we should devote the good part of one day every week [to laundry], how little would it avail to this nation's good?"[26]

In the same letter, Sybil reflected on what was perhaps her greatest privation over the years: "One must be in a situation to realize how precious a thing *time* is where thousands surround one, ignorant, and needing help of every kind." The difference was measured by numbers of students—not thirty or forty but eight hundred, whom Sybil (or one of the other missionary women) met in Friday prayer meetings in 1829. Sybil taught a school of women whenever she could, remarking that students "of any age and rank" could be assembled "at any time I would say." Sybil's own family was growing larger; even in 1827, when she had only two children, she wrote, "A sense of maternal care overwhelms me." A few years later, now with three at home, she answered a correspondent who may have indulged a "misconception" that a missionary's children were "peculiarly favored" by daily closeness to their mother. If Mrs. Collins could imagine a missionary woman's life, Sybil predicted that she would see

> no small demands made upon [her] time by foreign company, to say nothing of various interruptions there must be from a close association with 56 individuals forming the mission company. See her at one time with some half doz[en] of the [na]tive population pressing at any hour they chose upon her attention within her own doors—at another going abroad, having perhaps, some concern in children's school; again read the scriptures with a class of native females—to prayer meeting or something of the kind, for there is much that invites not to say demands attention abroad. See this mother striving to obtain an hour for her pen. . . . Again look at her heart oppressed by a sympathy in the great responsibilities [that] press upon her beloved husband, sometimes a juncture of affairs which speak a nation's fate at stake. Add to these a feeble frame, often apparently ready to [s]ink under the accumulated weight, and many other things which

> might be named, and tell me what you think of this mother's children—where, and how think you are they engaged?

In 1839, Sybil gave a humorous example of the demands on her time, when she had to stop writing a letter after about fourteen lines to admit, "If I do not connect two thoughts, you will none of you blame me. You may smile, and if it were not for your partiality might think it schoolgirl like, when studying for her first composition, if I tell you I had left my seat since I dipped my pen more times than I have lines—though I have not counted." She could not walk outside without pursuit: "As well may one involved in debt step abroad, when officers are in pursuit of him as we step about our house without demands upon our time, our ears and our tongues such as you would hardly understand, at once, if I should try to tell you."[27]

There were times when Sybil felt she simply had to be alone. There were days when she rarely sat down; days when she went to bed at the same time as the children; other days when she could not allow herself the couch until a late hour. She described herself as "overwhelmed" one day in 1836—"Find myself sometimes with my hand pressing my head as if that would help to determine which of some half dozen matters, of equal claim, to dispose of first." Amid this busyness Sybil seemed to believe that she was not doing enough for the Hawaiians—"the poor people for whom I thought I left my country." She assessed her efforts in 1829 at a school of "interesting females" that she had been managing for a year: "We hope [the Hawaiians] have been benefited by what has been done for them, tho so little in comparison with what we could desire to do."[28]

Sybil coped with her "miscellany of labor" and desires by disciplining her attitudes. Again and again she admitted that she had not expected missionary life to place her so much among "the drawers of water & hewers of wood," as she mourned in 1837. This is the gist of an entry in her journal ten years earlier: "I think I did not give place to wild & visionary ideas, in contemplation of missionary life, but really; I did not realize how much of precious time would be demanded for the things of the body." Her inclination was to devalue these demands in favor of "higher objects" and the great work to be done. "I feel ready to think house, clothing, food, and almost anything, shall go as it happens," she wrote in 1829, "rather than that time & strength be consumed upon them, when other things of such importance, have much demand." Still, Sybil had learned early on, that she could not neglect "food, clothing, cleanliness, &c. or our health must suffer." She never questioned that such matters were women's responsibility, not men's. But she did lament the degree of attention and precious time these things demanded. Her regret (which she expressed as early as 1825) was that domestic chores "should so take up the life of a missionary wife. . . . O, that is a *very small* part of what a missionary wife in such a land as this at this interesting moment should do!"[29]

Always concerned that she not appear to be complaining to her correspondents, Sybil kept undervaluing her trials: "Multitudes have had more cares and labours devolving upon them than I," she wrote in 1827. Thinking that her domestic conveniences had improved enormously in 1830, she told her amused husband, "I am very rich—have nothing left to wish for, in these matters," even though she was stepping round puddles in the kitchen during a heavy rainstorm and pulverizing flour that looked "as much like lime as anything." She reminded herself that she had set no stipulations as to the kind of work she would or would not do for the Lord. Instead of feeling self-pity, she chastised herself for falling short of the divine command—"Whatsoever ye do, do it heartily as to the Lord." Much of the work she had done for fourteen years, as she realized in 1833, was "altogether uncongenial with the natural turn of my mind." But, she continued, "it has seemed to bear to my mind the stamp of divine appointment, and I have been made not only comfortable, but I believe uniformly cheerful in it." By 1839, she was able (as she realized she would not have been in youth) to call it a "privilege" to be hewing the wood. It was all the Lord's work. Looking back over twenty years of labor, she thought she could "mark the fulfillment of the gracious promise, 'As thy days, so shall thy strength be.'"[30]

At times for Sybil (as for Mercy Whitney) the labor crowded out spiritual well-being, perhaps the greatest trial. Several references in 1827 suggest an interlude when she felt particularly sluggish, dull, and languorous—her vocabulary. An entry from her journal for June 16 is typical:

> I look at myself, the favored wife, almost the sole companion of a missionary, whose labours, whose perplexities, whose responsibilities, to say the least, are many and important; and I feel sometimes

> less than nothing; and that it would not need the hundredth part of what seems pressing, to crush me in the dust. I am, as it were, compelled to fly for strength—wonder at my stupid heart, and am ready to say, woe is me, if I am not daily and habitually at the Fountain of all Supplies. But, alas! I go barren—allowing these very duties where I so absolutely want help to come in among hindrances.

It is hard to suppose from Sybil's writings that she presented a public face of arrogance or unyielding righteousness. Her modesty was not calculating (not Uriah Heep's) but flowed from its counterpart in her religion, a sense of her own imperfection and inadequacy—the reason why she needed to seek the "Fountain of all Supplies." "Dust and ashes as I am," she wrote in May 1827, "let me set the Mighty GOD before me as my strength—his glory as my object. Alas for this deceitful heart! It is an easy thing to talk of glorifying God, accustomed to the language from early lispings; but O, to have the one steady desire, in all that is done, said or thought!" Sybil's private journal, in which she still made a few entries every year, is largely preoccupied with these spiritual flagellations. Looking over ten years of entries in 1829, she thought she saw "a *readiness to wander from thee.*" Summarizing again in 1834, she could find "little in the period which speaks much for me as following the blessed Savior with alacrity & joy. Complaints of sluggishness & deadness mark the years." She wrote from the little cottage at Punahou, where she retreated when she could with the children for a quiet day of domestic order, fasting, and meditation.[31]

Since Sybil does not write of "having fun," it is easy to forget that her religion, just as it had in her youth, brought "alacrity & joy." There was the pleasure, in moments of spiritual intensity, of being "dead" to the world but alive to God. There are no references in Sybil's letters to hellfire and brimstone, to a fear of God's wrath motivating her to walk the straight and narrow. God tempers the wind to the shorn lamb. The promises he makes "chase away the darkness." One letter to a childhood friend, written in 1830, anticipates the last judgment. "And to what are we hastening? Yes, even to our *last great change!* Happy happy those who are prepared to meet it!" The "light" of Christianity was as much a truth as the "darkness" of paganism. Although Sybil continued to feel that she had not done enough to transform the "darkness" surrounding her in

Hawaii, she did not finally measure success in material ways. It comforted her that Hawaiian converts to the religion would enjoy the same rewards she herself hoped for. In late 1832, mourning for four *alii* (Kaahumanu, Naihe, Kalanimoku, and Opiia), Sybil asked: "Do the voices of these four, born in paganism and reared under its dark & cruel reign now join with angels above? We do feel as if we had good reason as to believe that even so it is."[32]

Sybil could ask for no better end for a Christian's earthly pilgrimage than to join the "angels above." But to speak of the life of a culture—rather than an individual life—keeps the focus on the "here and now." Unlike the missionaries to heavily populated countries like India and China, where the existing government and religion could absorb a small dose of Christianity without much ado, the missionaries to Hawaii found themselves in a tiny country whose institutions were much more vulnerable. Hawaii had already overthrown its former religion, was fast losing its population, and was converged upon by whalers, warships, and trading vessels from foreign powers. When the missionaries came to turn a heathen nation into a Christian one, they could not have predicted what effect all of these changes might have on nationhood itself. From one point of view, the distant perspective of two hundred years in the future, the legacy of Western contact for Hawaiians looks like religious, cultural, and political loss. The monarchy no longer rules (since 1893); the *alii* no longer own the land; the population of full-blooded Hawaiians is a tiny fraction of what it was when Captain Cook arrived; taro fields and fish ponds are comparatively rare; Hawaiian is spoken routinely mainly on the small, privately owned island of Niihau. Already in the 1860s the historian Samuel Kamakau took this decline as his subject. Writing a chapter on "Hawaii Before Foreign Innovations," he described ancient expertise in composing genealogical chants, building canoes, weaving mats, and creating tapa designs, as well as skill in line, rod, net, and torch fishing. Then he turned his refrain into a lament: "Today there are no more such." There is no cure for such loss. No doubt an intellectualized solace can be derived from an even larger perspective, suggesting that this ascending and descending of cultures makes up the history of the world. If Hawaiians in Kailua in 1823 took the stones from an old *marai,* or temple foundation, to make the foundation for a Christian church, the Roman Christians had built churches on the sites of their pagan temples: "Santa Maria sopra [over] della Minerva."[33]

But modern Romans have had two thousand years to absorb Christianity; after only two hundred years, wounds can still smart. Since the Hawaiians never expected to lose cultural sovereignty, this outcome can seem especially poignant or bitter. The *alii* gave Westerners permission to land and to build, never dreaming that their own descendants would not have this power. They eagerly embraced the *palapala,* never anticipating that their newly written language would cease to predominate. They sang the missionaries' hymns and composed beautiful ones of their own, not realizing that they had permanently laid aside many chants and dances. They accepted the sailors' rum and distilled their own *okolehao,* not foreseeing, in a time of cultural trauma, how seductive and addictive an escape drunkenness would prove for both *alii* and commoner, nor how damaging to good rule. They bartered for the firearms that enabled Kamehameha I to win the wars of unification, only to find, one hundred years later, that same firepower backing up the coup that ended the monarchy.

The irony is tragic because the Hawaiians' greatest asset, the empathic, hospitable "spirit of aloha" that accounted for the welcome given to new people, new things, and new ideas, also made the Hawaiians less suspicious and more vulnerable than they might have been. They could not resist a Pandora's box of items—nails first, then china, bolts of cloth, wooden furniture, even the *palapala*—not realizing that they opened the lid to both advantage and harm. (The *palapala* preserved the language but not Hawaiian subject matter.) Hawaiians lacked protection from diseases their bodies could not fight, from shrewd trading practices that ran them into debt, and, most damagingly, from the malaise that crept over them when changes came too fast for assimilation or protest. Buoyantly confident in the beginning, they thought that they could control the effects of foreign influence. This made their failure to do so that much more cruel.

In adopting Christianity, Hawaiians exchanged their own culture, nurtured in a climate of benignity and abundance, for one whose roots led through Europe to the desert and Semitic tribes. The missionaries tended to underestimate the difficulty and cost of making such a change, assuming that the past would be shed without regret. The archetype here is Saul, the Roman citizen blinded with light on the road to Damascus, who never looked back. Or it is the Day of Judgment, when, in the twinkling of an eye, we shall all be changed. The missionaries were well aware of what they themselves had sacrificed—the farms, schools, churches, the families and friends in New England. But they counted this world well lost if they could thereby work as God's instruments to the heathen. They were less aware of what they were asking the Hawaiians to sacrifice.

Even so, the story is more than a simple one of rejecting the past for a new future. To some extent, the success of Christianity in Hawaii comes from its similarities to Hawaiian culture.[34] Hawaiians did have to deny their "heathen" past in order to accept Christianity. But another reading of events says that they found in Christianity a way to continue their past into the present. This may seem like another cruel irony, if the restrictions of the *kapu* system were merely exchanged for those of the Ten Commandments (which were some of the missionaries' earliest teachings). Sometimes the missionaries themselves did not want to face the similarities—that the "pagan" practices they were trying to stamp out had correspondences in the Old Testament. Hiram Bingham, criticizing the "heathen rites" performed at a funeral in 1822, "using incantations, offering sacrifices of hogs, dogs, and fowls, so sickening to the missionaries, so offensive to God, and so degrading and ruinous to the people," seems to have forgotten that the entire book of Leviticus prescribes sacrificial offerings as a "sweet savour unto the Lord." The Hawaiians, however, having access to the unexpurgated Bible as it was translated, must have seen this for themselves, just as they recognized in the biblical lists of "begats" the counterpart to their own genealogical chants. Some of the similarities were cultural rather than doctrinal. The practice of having a *kahu* or special teacher responsible for the training of an individual *alii* perhaps made it easier for the minister to be accepted as an authoritative teacher. The extended mission family, bursting the seams of the frame house, living communally, calling one another "brother" and "sister," might not have seemed that different (except for the building material of the house) from the sense of community in the Hawaiian *ohana.* The enormous popularity of the *hoikes,* with their memory work, dramatic precision of movement, and pageantry, owed much to the performance of chants and hulas in the not-too-distant past.

For many Hawaiians caught up in the moment, the day by day living of the 1820s and 1830s, the new contacts with foreigners brought expectations of gain and advantage, not loss. To increasing numbers of *alii* and commoners, Christianity did seem to bring the "light" and "good tidings" the missionaries spoke of. The legacy of this point of view is the community of Christian Hawaiians that continues to this day. Every Sunday at Kawaiahao Church, worshippers speak Hawaiian as well as English, the choir joining in again and again with anthems and responses in Hawaiian. When Hawaii became the fiftieth state in 1959, the Reverend Dr. Abraham Akaka, then pastor or *kahu* of Kawaiahao Church, saw the event as merging the best of two cultures. "Since the coming of the missionaries in 1820," he said in his sermon, "the name of God to our people has been *aloha*":

> One of the first sentences I learned from my mother in my childhood was this from Holy Scriptures: "*Aloha ke akua.*" In other words, *aloha* is God. *Aloha* is the power of God seeking to unite what is separated in the world—the power that unites heart with heart, soul with soul, life with life, culture with culture, race with race, nation with nation. . . . Thus when a people or a person live in the spirit of *aloha*, they live in the spirit of God.

This point of view accepts both the good intentions of the missionaries and their message, "grateful that the discovery and development of our islands long ago was not couched in the context of an imperialistic and exploitative national power but in the context of *aloha*." This word, Akaka thought, was the "real Golden Rule." He concluded with the hope that statehood would "reaffirm" for a multicultural present the words planted 139 years earlier—the text for Hiram Bingham's first sermon: "Fear not, for I bring you good tidings of great joy, which shall be to *all* people." The italics are Akaka's.[35]

The notion that Hawaiians, coached by missionary denunciations, learned to be ashamed of their traditions suggests why the Hawaiians might have rejected old customs. But it does not explain why the Hawaiians should (illogically) have been willing to imitate and to follow those who were the source of the criticism. The answer, in part, is that neither the message nor the messengers were entirely negative. "To hear them preach and pray," wrote Jackson

Jarves, a Honolulu journalist in the 1840s, "you would suppose all mankind—excluding themselves and their friends—damnable scoundrels; to see them act, you felt sure they did not, at heart, feel that the human race was so unmitigatedly bad after all." The Hawaiians perhaps found in the missionaries the continuation of what they knew to be good in their own culture. The missionaries brought with them the desire to love your neighbor as yourself, even carrying it to the extreme belief that you could love your enemies and do good to those that hurt you. (After the spelling book, one of the earliest publications was the Sermon on the Mount.) Most important, they brought the idea that of faith, hope, and charity, the greatest was "charity," called "love" in later translations of the Bible and, by the Hawaiians, *aloha*. This ideal of Christian love, which the missionaries attempted to embody in their earthly lives, is one component of the light that shone as the mission took root.[36]

Many of the effects of Western influence were felt by Hawaiians in the long run, as their culture declined and politics changed. This was less true for the missionaries. The greatest cost of their "great experiment" they bore in private, in individual lives. For Sybil, the cost was exacted in deteriorating health in the late 1830s. In mid-1836, she became seriously ill with the "dropsical" symptoms, cough, and severe pain in the lungs that indicated consumption. She collapsed, unable to raise her head for days, while on a missionary tour of the island with Hiram, and had to be carried home. Physicians agreed that if she was ever to recover her health, she would have to go back to New England. The physician of the ship *Peacock* put this in writing as early as 1836. The subject had come up six to eight years earlier, Sybil admitted in 1839, but, as with the thought of sending Sophia home, she could not bear to confront it. "I do not readily admit that I am an invalid," she wrote in March 1837, when she felt she had recovered. But by September she admitted that she had "been an invalid through the year." By the fall of 1839, she remarked on a "strange subject" for her pen, a sense of equivocation replacing her refusal to consider departure: "It would be good to stay, it would be good to go." Evidently not bedridden, but contending with bouts of illness, Sybil continued to report busy days in her letters. She told her old friend Mrs. Johns in October 1839 that her health had generally been sustained during the last three years. But even so, she was not optimistic about recovery: "I am indeed at times, entirely prostrate—I often think of a watch 'run down,' but like that with a little attention go again. But it will not always be thus. Ere long the 'main spring' must fail. Sometimes I feel this."[37]

The Thurston family was planning to sail home in the fall of 1839. Sybil began to think of sending Elizabeth back with them. But the Thurstons were delayed for a year, and the following August it was the entire Bingham family that embarked with some of the Thurstons, Lucy and her five children. (Asa declined to leave his post.) Since Hiram Bingham was the acknowledged leader in the most important mission station, the departure of the Binghams after twenty years signals the end of an era. It makes a convenient moment to pause and take stock of accomplishments.[38]

When the Thurstons and Binghams sailed from Hawaii, there were hardly any of the pioneers left—only Asa Thurston and the Whitneys (with Samuel Whitney's death only six years away). None of the couples had shared a station for over a decade (since the Loomises had left Honolulu in 1827). The communal sharing of houses belonged to the pioneering past. In this sense the life of the "family" was over. But the group lived in one another's memory, thinking of shared accomplishments, reflecting on how much had changed. A decade after the Binghams left, on April 19, 1851, Mercy marked the thirty-first anniversary of the pioneers' leaving the *Thaddeus* by noting that only she and Asa Thurston were at their posts (Lucy was making her second trip to the United States for the sake of her children), and that four of the company were dead. But then, as in 1840, there was much to look back on. Having gained the trust of important *alii,* the first company had had the privilege of beginning the work of the mission.[39]

The Binghams had been synonymous with the mission in Honolulu, like the Thurstons in Kailua and the Whitneys in Waimea. Hiram Bingham in his book cites a half-page of statistics to document the changes that validate the most important two decades of their lives. He points to the constitution (of 1840), two editions of the Bible of 10,000 copies each, "six boarding schools, 12 station schools and 357 common-schools, embracing 18,000 scholars," and eighteen churches with 20,000 new members admitted in the last four years. Although the missionaries left plenty of unfinished business—like the construction at Kawaiahao of a stone church that Hiram Bingham had designed—they understood their work as part of a continuum that could be carried on by the missionaries who remained. In one sense, they carried out the charge they had received in 1819, laying the foundation for the land covered with homes, schools, and churches that is Hawaii today. Other efforts ended in failure, at least in terms of the missionaries' hopes. The 1839 decree of religious tolerance opened the islands to Catholics, Mormons (who arrived in 1850), and Episcopalians (in the 1860s). By then, one historian sees the "unfashionable" values of the mission as "in retreat." When Mark Twain labeled the islands "Christian" in the 1860s, he meant that they were Christian in the same sense as other nations, with sin no longer flourishing in name, only in reality.[40]

This great story of missionary activity, played out under the aspect of Western influence in Hawaii, is more than a simple story of imposition and acquiescences. It doubles back on itself, overlaid with irony, a story of newness welcomed and only later seen as dangerous, of the desire to do good and the result sometimes working harm. The missionaries, among them some of the best their civilization could offer, were not simply "what was good enough for Hawaiians." They came with their minds on "higher objects," brandishing in their service the "sword" of the spirit against Satan's kingdom. Announcing their love for souls, they put their highest priority on salvation. They got themselves into a quagmire of material and spiritual values. Their instructions were contradictory, telling them to pay attention only to spiritual truths ("Jesus Christ and Him crucified") and yet somehow to effect a visible transformation of the indigenous Hawaiian culture. In teaching Hawaiians about the "spirit," they succeeded best by offering one more exotic, irresistible, and, above all, material Western object, the *palapala.* The women came with their minds on "ardent piety" and discovered how much of their work would involve physical needs. Reversing the order of philanthropists today, who offer economic aid to relieve human wretchedness, the missionaries offered a change of heart. They thought they could separate Hawaiians from their culture, and have them change to Christianity as simply as they might take off one suit of clothes and put on a new one. They thought they scorned the culture only—its hula, infanticide, idolatry, human sacrifice—not the Hawaiians and their souls, for whom they had compassion. But when the Hawaiians changed their hearts, they often "somehow" had not changed enough. The bad habits of heathenism did not entirely go away. Fearful that their children might pick up those habits, they put them back on the boats to America. The story of "paradise lost" offers a tempting analogy for both Hawaiians and missionaries, not, though, with the missionaries resembling the serpent. Innocence was lost, but on both sides.

They came to do good, one might say, adding in exasperation and sympathy that they were not good enough. With complete unselfconsciousness, Mercy Whitney wrote of Hawaiians in terms that might have described herself: "[I] cannot but look with pity, when I see how tenacious they are of habits & customs, to which they have been accustomed from infancy."[41] Not understanding that cultures can solve similar problems in different ways, they made the Hawaiians ashamed of their culture. They did not know that "wasting time" could be a pleasure; they could not enjoy games or sexuality as the Hawaiians did. They could not save the Hawaiians from new and mortal diseases. They could not save them from the annexationists at the end of the nineteenth century. They remind us how easy it is to condemn differences. Condemning the missionaries on the basis of a "superior" understanding of cultural relativism, some in the twentieth century differ little from the missionaries condemning the Hawaiians on the basis of a "superior" truth.

The famous joke about the missionaries is that they came to do good and did well. But this first company lived for subsistence, not profit. Their own perspective was not ironic; they understood life as a straightforward pilgrimage, responsive to cause and effect, effort and achievement. When they failed, they thought they had not tried hard enough or in the right way. They aimed high: "Be ye therefore perfect, even as your father which is in heaven is perfect" (Matthew 5:48). They understood this charge as impossible, since humans are imperfect by nature. But inspired by the magnitude of their goal—"the great work of doing good to souls"—they tried to improve on nature. In one sense, all the quarrels with fellow *haoles* signify the missionaries' attempt to make Hawaii a more perfect place than the one they had left behind in New England. But their legacy is not measured in generalities—souls saved, or nations "raised." They left something more personal and particularized—a legacy of effort against their own fallen natures in a fallen world. Like the Hawaiians, who made the best of a new and difficult situation, the missionaries tried to do good and to be good: down the road lay the not always predictable, not always explicable results. Sybil believed she had not tried hard enough or that God had a plan she could not expect to understand perfectly. "But my fleeting days pass on," she berated herself in 1826, "and the good that I would I do not." But a different reading of the lines from Paul's letter to the Romans (7:19) suggests paradox. ("The good that I would, that I do not; the evil that I would not, that I do.") Why things do not turn out as planned is a mystery at the heart of volition. This is glossed by the Christian notion of original sin, or the knot in the grain, or, as Shakespeare puts it, "the imposition . . . hereditary ours." This imposition is a burden, and also a mystery not to be solved.[42]

After the first decade, the women increasingly identified their "direct" and "active" labors not simply with teaching the *palapala* and the gospel, but with helping Hawaiian women and children through a system of home visits and meetings. The women continued to feel that they could not do enough and in the end (as one historian has demonstrated) felt that their efforts to transform Hawaiian women to the model of "true womanhood" had failed. They had kept up a standard of Christian civilization for themselves—by the 1850s life in Honolulu was little different from that on the mainland—but not for the majority of Hawaiians. But the women also realized that their distinctly female efforts to "civilize" Hawaiian women were only one part of a cause of "magnitude and grandeur" focused on Christianizing Hawaiians. In this larger effort, the women continued to identify with the seeming success of the mission, measuring it as the men did, with visible signs like churches built, laws changed, books translated and printed, and the conviction that many Hawaiians had been reborn from within.[43]

In 1840, none of those who were leaving assumed that the great work of saving souls was finished, but no one thought it had been in vain. In 1837, Sybil had written, "We receive encouragement by looking back. The contrast of present-things with things, with which we began, has a happy effect upon the mind." She did not, of course, measure their achievement in material terms. After eighteen years, she reflected, she and Hiram had nearly the same furniture they had begun with—a writing desk and her rocking chair. But she thought there was enough evidence to be able to say, "A great work has been accomplished." For those who would carry on that work, she did not emphasize the "vital piety," which had seemed so important on the *Thaddeus*, but a "*persevering spirit.* Faith and patience will be often tried." Schooled in patience, Sybil realized that "to raise a nation from the dust and place them where our idea of comfort, virtue & happiness would have them is not the work of a day."[44]

A younger generation of missionaries would carry on, working with a younger generation of chiefs, most of them now being trained by the mission at the Chiefs' Children's School. With Kinau's death in 1839, the generation of high chiefs reared under the *kapu* system, the special friends of the Binghams and Thurstons and Whitneys, was gone. In a pensive moment, after the General Meeting of 1839, Sybil wrote:

> I looked upon the nation. That phalanx of Christian chiefs—pillars on which the nation was rising—stood not in their place. . . . I would pause on these things, then turning my eyes to my dear husband would say within myself, no Karaimoku—no Kaahumanu, Opiia, Naihi, Kaikioewa—no Kinau now turns the trusting eye to him saying, Help us in our perplexities by something from the blessed book you bring. They need you not. Your peculiar work there is finished.

Keopuolani, Liholiho, Kaumualii, were long in their graves. Boki had sailed off looking for sandalwood in 1829, never to return. Before the Binghams left, Liliha (Boki's wife) and Hoapili (governor of Maui and husband of Keopuolani) would die. Kapiolani would submit to an operation for breast cancer (like Lucy Thurston fourteen years later, without an anesthetic), but would die of infection afterward. The changes in the mission, with its burgeoning numbers—the largest company yet came in 1837—and younger faces, foreboded contentious times ahead. Some simply resented Hiram Bingham's prominence; some, fueled by a temperance movement in the United States, disapproved of his moderating comments about smoking and drinking wine. Some thought he had been too strident in discouraging Roman Catholicism. The "Great Awakening" of the late 1830s—adding more church members in a day than the pioneers had in seventeen years—implicitly criticized the earlier caution. Such tensions came home to Sybil during the General Meeting of 1839. With sympathy and sadness, she watched Hiram as he argued for the minority on many issues. "There is yet comfort," Sybil held on to the thought, "in the hope that there is union—oneness of purpose in the mission, numbering so many of different callings,—of minds cast in different molds—of education and habits different—so different as to give great force to the remark, 'your mission is a great experiment.'" Sybil would never say the experiment had failed, but at the end of that General Meeting, even as she insisted that "the bond of union is unbroken," she continued, "but a sadness which has been gathering through the years, now began to settle on my spirits. Every retrospective thought seems to mingle with the heavy one, 'The glory is departed.'"[45]

When they heard that the Binghams and Thurstons were leaving, Mercy and Samuel Whitney endured the voyage to Oahu, "feeling," as Mercy explained, "that we must see them once more before they sailed." She found everyone in "good spirits" except Hiram Bingham. Although Lucy Thurston was going without her husband, Sybil, as Hiram realized, could not manage without his help. But the Binghams had received an eighteen-month leave of absence, not a dismission, and expected to return. Perhaps they had their suspicions. When at ten o'clock on the morning of August 3, 1840, the group of missionaries gathered for communion, Mercy called it a "trying season" because they knew they were "about to separate, perhaps for life." Mercy continued, "Bro[ther] B[ingham] was completely overcome. He could say little more than bid us farewell, ask our forgiveness if he had in any way wronged us, & entreat us to be more faithful in the service of our Lord, than he had been." At noon, the party "were hurried away" to the bark *Flora.* Stephen Reynolds, merchant and diarist, watched the departure, glad to see the end of the "blood-sucking, cash-sucking—lazy—lying wretches," gossiping that Hiram Bingham collected donations from the crowd. The Hawaiians, however, seemed to share Bingham's woe. They stood packed on the shore, wailing for "Binamu."[46]

Now it was Mercy's turn for sadness. Within a few hours, the sails had vanished from sight:

> I sat pensive musing on the past, & thought of the time when I embarked on board the Brig *Thaddeus* with 6 Missionary sisters for these Islands, & now I have given the parting hand to the last of them,

> perhaps to see them no more on earth. I felt alone in the midst of my friends, & a feeling of indescribable sadness came over me, similar to what I have repeatedly felt, when parting with beloved children. There was an aching void within, which nought on earth could fill. And it was a consoling thought to reflect, that tho earthly friends must part, there is a friend whose *presence* can *always* cheer the sinking hearts, & revive the drooping spirits of his people. O that my soul may ever be filled with *his* fulness.[47]

About a month after arriving in the United States (February 4, 1841), Sybil wrote of the pleasures of homecoming. On the train to her sister's home in Connecticut, she looked with "sensations . . . altogether indescribable" at winter scenery she had had to imagine for over twenty years. Patches of woods, orchards, enclosed fields, barns and barnyards of domestic animals, "plain comfortable houses" —all "charmed" her and brought back such recollections of an earlier life that (had she not been on a train) she could have wept. She did weep after being reunited with her daughters. Sophia was already married and a mother; Lucy, almost fifteen, had grown to womanhood. "But where were my two little girls," Sybil wondered, "who each in their turn had received their mother's farewell kiss, as one after the other was embarked on the wide waters?"[48]

The stage was being set for reversals of expectations, large and small. The Binghams began what they expected to be a visit to New England, settling the three younger children in schools, renewing friendships, visiting relatives. Hiram began to write a memoir of Kaahumanu, which eventually exploded into a 300,000-word history of the mission, *A Residence of Twenty-One Years in the Sandwich Islands* (1847). Every fall for five years, they thought of the ships departing for the islands, but Sybil's unimproved health or Hiram's unfinished book held them back. Having begun her adult life as a "pilgrim," an orphaned and peripatetic schoolteacher, Sybil found the word applying once again in a literal sense to the life she was leading. "Comforts in our daily path, are many," she wrote in October 1842, as ever not wanting to complain or take a narrow view of things, "but 'pilgrim & sojourner' are for us fitting terms." A partial list of the return addresses of Sybil's letters tells the story —her sister's home in Connecticut; Bingham relatives in Bennington, Vermont; the Pomeroys (Sybil's mother's family) in Brooklyn;

friends in Westfield, Massachusetts; Manlius and Canandaigua, New York (where Elizabeth and Lucy were in school); even Ann Arbor, Michigan, where Sophia and her husband had moved. Putting young Hiram on the stage to go to school in New Haven one day in 1843, Sybil realized that her family was "indeed a scattered flock." So many letters to her husband Hiram were addressed to "Missionary Rooms, Boston," that it comes as no surprise to find Sybil commenting in 1843 that they have spent their last three wedding anniversaries apart. "I feel some loneliness —," she wrote to her daughter Sophia in June 1844:

> no little spot on the wide earth to call home. — Of all my young, rising family, not one to be my daily charge, while the maternal heart flutters over them as if by its fluttering the little scattered brood could be brought again under the wing. Not unfrequently your dear father is away for a few days, and then it is, that with a certain indefinable feeling I look around and find nothing to call mine.[49]

The longer the Binghams stayed in America, the more "embarrassments" accompanied their unsettled state. The Board gave grants to returning missionaries, but no salary; the Binghams wanted to call upon the treasury as little as possible. They were depending on others for necessities like clothing, lodging, and their children's tuitions. Even postage was a source of worry. Sybil apologized to her son for not writing more often: "My purse will not easily meet all that my feelings would ask." She told her husband that she had delayed sending one of her letters until she had heard from him, "and thus save postage — seeing the post office charges in one way and another, make such demands upon a light purse, kept from being empty, only by gifts."[50]

Sybil's cough did not improve; sometimes she was too weak to write much to her children; in November 1845 she admitted that her cough was becoming "a serious matter. . . . This morning, waked by it, a little before dawn, and for two hours, buckled down to it. Am not free now, ten minutes at a time." The following December she wrote that the nights were "generally comfortable," but she spent the mornings in "hard coughing."[51]

As bad as the situation was in America, it was news from Honolulu that brought the worst trials. In 1843, Hiram Bingham was surprised to learn that the temporary substitution of the Reverend Richard Armstrong for himself at Kawaiahao Church had been made permanent. Sybil, feeling that she could confide in Levi Chamberlain, wrote, "A shade is thrown over our whole missionary course." She thought she must be dreaming to find "any other man" taking Hiram's place. With perhaps more indignation than she had ever expressed in her life, Sybil defended her husband:

> Why should such a step be taken without his consent, without a trial, and without giving him opportunity to speak on the subject at all? Was that solemn act, in the vestry of Park St. Church, twenty four years ago, when a charge was given him by that holy man of God, Dr. Worcester, all a farce?

In another development, she felt hurt and indignation on her own behalf. The lands at Punahou on which the Binghams had their cottage had been used by the mission to build a school for its own offspring. Reading a letter at the Missionary Rooms in Boston, Sybil objected to a description she found of the land as "given by Government to the *Mission.*" The land had been in Boki's power, and he had given it to the Binghams before he left on his final voyage in 1829. But that was not the problem: Sybil had never thought of the land as going to her heirs. In letters to Levi Chamberlain and Laura Judd, Sybil explains that she and Hiram had always seen the land as connected with the Hawaiians' church, Kawaiahao, and as "the inheritance of the congregation" to support a pastor when the mission was eventually disbanded. "I saw in it, as I supposed, the permanent support of the preaching of the gospel, in the 1st church at Honolulu, independent of funds appropriated expressly to extending the Redeemer's kingdom among the unevangelized"—that is, independent of the ABCFM. She recalled the "*hoomanawanui*" (patience) with which she and her fellow laborers, mostly Hawaiian women, day after day had reclaimed the area from "commons," building a wall and a road, filling in the land, smoothing it over, planting a border of bananas, and stocking nine or ten acres nearby with cane. No mission funds had been used for the improvements. "There is one object for which I have labored—that Church—," she concluded to her old friend Laura Judd. "My thoughts turn there and I am disquieted."[52]

Time was running out for both Sybil and Hiram after five years in America. Though she did not yet mention it, she was dying. Hiram's book, nearing completion, lost its promised publisher. Instead, he had to sell advance subscriptions for 4,000 copies for a printer in Hartford. He had thought the book would provide for his family's future; it now looked doubtful that the book would earn anything. Together, with great sorrow, Sybil and Hiram faced the inevitable. They asked to be dismissed as missionaries from the ABCFM. The Board accepted the request, having in the intervening years heard from those remaining in Honolulu that the "domineering" Bingham was not missed, an opinion corroborated by complaints over the last two decades from returning merchants and ships' captains. Members tried to word a bequest of $800 in such a way that the oversensitive Binghams would not take it as a return of Sybil's original donation but as a grant for educating their children. The offended Sybil (needy but proud) still viewed it as a "quit claim."[53]

Throughout these hard, lean years, Sybil had been relying primarily on a single idea for comfort, what she called, in one letter, "this precious doctrine of *GOD's particular providence.*" Thinking, for example, of Hiram's loss of Kawaiahao Church, she wrote, "Our Heavenly Father saw a reason why such a cloud should envelop us in our setting day, and he is good: yes, *he is good.*" Sybil was no sentimental optimist. She never lost sight of herself as "dust," or of depravity as the natural human state. But the consolation was there. It came from her sense of a God who keeps his eye on the sparrow. Hers was no frivolous hope that "things will work out in the end." It was rather a sense that however things work out, they are part of God's plan. "They [events] are good as they are," she had written to Nancy Ruggles back in 1825. "Their being the reverse of what we would have planned, by no means proves them not good." Sybil's ideas had never been put to such a trial. Seeing herself in a "labyrinthe," she began in some letters in 1846 to think the unthinkable, "whether they had been wise to leave Honolulu—whether we have not mistaken duty—are doing penance never required of us by our gracious Heavenly Father." They had not acted "rashly," she explained to the Hunnewells (James Hunnewell, the first mate of the *Thaddeus* and now a merchant, had aided the Binghams). "But," she added,

> could we then have seen how, by following in such a path we came suddenly to a point in our missionary course where we found ourselves stopped in the midst of the race—set aside, before our strength had departed, while nothing else was given us to do, we must have exclaimed 'this cannot be the way!' But here we are.

Her comfort arose from the same idea that sustained her through the deaths of her infant sons so many years ago—her "full persuasion that through all this 'mist,' part of a *perfect plan*, extending into Eternity, is being wrought out."[54]

Sybil was not getting any better. A letter written in December 1846 to her daughter Sophia suggests the low point for her living conditions, when she was boarding in North Haven, Connecticut, and Hiram was often traveling, looking for places to live or overseeing the printing of his book. She was cold as she wrote to Sophia, "fire all out in my stove—chamber cold—fingers numb. I have a foot stove with chestnut embers in it, or I could not stand it." She was also hungry. "We catch as we can get," she continued, "with four hungry children, the fifth in arms, around a small kitchen table." The family could only afford a half-pint of milk each day, a pound of cheese each month. Still, she could not end the letter with complaint: "You know we count none of these things sorrows. . . . He [God] is teaching us that we are but pilgrims & strangers here—having no abiding place."[55]

At about this time, the Bingham family was rescued by a distant relative on Sybil's side, Samuel Williston, a wealthy manufacturer of buttons in Easthampton, Massachusetts. He provided places for Elizabeth, Hiram, and Lydia in the seminary that bore his name and helped the family find a house to rent. By that summer, Sybil had her three children with her again. In June, Hiram finished correcting the proofs of his book. "How will it seem to begin life anew as a family!" he exclaimed. "How will it seem to consider our missionary work *done!*—and our *book* done! and ourselves allowed a little time to sit down and think, and talk with our children, without saying 'don't interrupt us now—wait till the book is finished!'"[56]

But Sybil was coughing blood. She wrote one of her last letters in December 1847, trying to comfort her recently widowed sister Sophia even as she herself, "trembling and afraid," faced her death.

Toward the end of February, she was not moving much from her rocking chair. ("She had before requested," Hiram explained to his daughter Sophia, "that if God should send the summons, she might be in her rocking chair.") The night of February 26, the family gathered round, supporting her emaciated limbs and her cold, swollen feet, and recording her last words. These were disconnected, spoken at intervals. "'The Lord comes for me'—'Stop—stop—I *live*'—'Almost overcome'—'Break the bands [bonds].'" She was in her dying coma and did not answer when Hiram called her name an hour later. The family sang a hymn Hiram had composed for the *Sandwich Islands Hymnbook,* "The Dying Pilgrim." Near one o'clock on the morning of February 27, 1848, Sybil Bingham died.[57]

She was buried first in Easthampton, then reburied almost a half-century later in New Haven, Connecticut, after Hiram's death, to move her bones closer to his. (Hiram's second wife separates them.) Hiram stayed in New England and reapplied for missionary work, but was never offered an acceptable position by the Board. He never returned to Honolulu.[58]

A NOTE ON SOURCES AND ANNOTATION

NOTES

BIBLIOGRAPHY

INDEX

A Note on Sources and Annotation

For many of the facts of this book, I am indebted to a few histories. Of nineteenth-century missionary accounts, Hiram Bingham's *A Residence of Twenty-One Years in the Sandwich Islands* (1847) is the most thorough and useful. For the perspective of a Hawaiian writing about Hawaiians, Samuel Kamakau's *Ruling Chiefs of Hawaii* (translated and published in 1961) is the only complete history. The standard modern history is R. S. Kuykendall's *The Hawaiian Kingdom, 1778–1854* (1938). Also useful were Harold Bradley's *The American Frontier in Hawaii* (1942) and a more recent general history by Gavan Daws, *Shoal of Time: A History of the Hawaiian Islands* (1968). Bradford Smith's *Yankees in Paradise* (1956) is the only modern, book-length history of the mission, useful for chronology though dated by a patronizing tone. Patricia Grimshaw's *Paths of Duty: American Missionary Wives in Nineteenth-Century Hawaii* (1989) takes all the missionary women as its subject and has helped me to say whether the experiences of the first company were typical or not. I have kept some references to her dissertation of the same title in my notes because it treats this subject in greater detail. Robert Benedetto's *The Hawaii Journals of the New England Missionaries: 1813–1894* (1982) describes the journal collection at the HMCS Library.

In the interest of readability, I have kept note numbers in the text to a minimum. Numbers are placed at the end of a paragraph or a section of thought and signal an endnote giving sources for the entire paragraph or section. I identify individual quotations or sentences in the text by a few key words—whenever possible the last words of the quotation.

In referring to books, I cite in the Notes only authors (with abbreviated titles for first references) and reserve full citations for the Bibliography. Where dates of journal entries are given in the text, I do not repeat them in the Notes. In referring to the letters of the women and men of the first company, I have shortened the first and last names to two capital letters (SB for Sybil Bingham).

Notes

Abbreviations

ABCFM Papers of the American Board of Commissioners for Foreign Missions. Houghton Library, Harvard University.

ABCFM-HEA General correspondence between the Sandwich Islands missionaries (Hawaiian Evangelical Association) and the ABCFM. Holograph. HMCS.

ABCFM-HAWAII Letters from the missionaries in Hawaii to the ABCFM. Collection at HMCS. Copies of originals at Houghton Library, Harvard University.

BP Bingham Family Papers. This collection includes some of Sybil Bingham's letters and her journal fragments of 1827 and 1843. HMCS.

HJH *Hawaiian Journal of History.* Periodical.

HMCS Hawaiian Mission Children's Society Library. Honolulu, Hawaii.

J Journal (from the collection at HMCS).

MLC Missionary Letters Collection. HMCS.

MLC-ts Typescript of letters of the Sandwich Islands Mission to the ABCFM. 1819–1837. 8 vols. HMCS.

RP Ruggles Family Correspondence. Manuscript Letters in Bernice Pauahi Bishop Museum. Honolulu, Hawaii.

SB-PJ Journal of Sybil M. Bingham, 1811–1839; some entries from 1847. Original at Yale University; microfilm at HMCS. This is Sybil's "private" journal and the journal for her youth.

SIJ "Journal of the Sandwich Islands Mission, 1821–1825." Typescript in HMCS of original at Houghton Library, Harvard University.

TJ "*Thaddeus* Journal": Journal of the Sandwich Islands Mission, 1819–1821; written by Hiram Bingham, Asa Thurston, and Elisha Loomis. Holograph and typescript. HMCS.

Introduction

1 Era was over: Walter Frear (a missionary apologist) called 1820–1840 "The Crucial Period" in "A Century of Achievement," in *The Centennial Book*, p. 8; see also Gavan Daws, *Shoal of Time*, p. 103.

2 Number of missionaries: my count from the *Missionary Album*; see also Rufus Anderson, *Memorial Volume*, p. 273; Robert Schmitt, "Religious Statistics of Hawaii, 1825–1972," *HJH* 7 (1973): 41–45.

3 "Christianized": Anderson, *Memorial Volume*, p. 253. Statistics: ibid., p. 254; Bradford Smith, *Yankees in Paradise*, p. 319; Ralph S. Kuykendall, *The Hawaiian Kingdom*, p. 109.

4 Religion as most important context: my argument here is along the lines of Christine Stansell's insistence on the importance of class conflicts as a variable in the "cult of true womanhood." Critical of the "home-visiting" program of middle-class members of the New York City Tract Society in 1829–1860, she describes their misapprehensions of lower-class women, and sees the entire effort as "a mission of social domination in the language of ethical mandate." Their lack of success in spreading middle-class mores is analogous to that of missionary wives with Hawaiians. See *City of Women*, pp. 64–68.

5 Shared convictions on the overland trail: for a group of midwestern farm families going west in mid-century, John Faragher found that two-thirds of the content of both men's and women's journals covered the same three themes. "First and foremost," this indicates that both men and women "were part of a common culture, that they were, indeed, more alike than different": see *Women and Men*, pp. 14–15.

Chapter 1: The Mission Family

1 *Thaddeus* information: *Missionary Album;* Maria Loomis J., Nov. 8, 1819. Whaleships: Kuykendall, p. 70. Fare: Bingham, *Residence*, p. 63.

2 "Small vessel": Maria Loomis J., Oct. 23, 1819; two copies of this journal were kept, one staying with the Loomises, the other sent to Utica, N.Y., and known as the "John C. Williams" version. "Pilgrim and a stranger": Lucy G. Thurston, *Life and Times*, p. 20. "Hang in the way":

Daniel Chamberlain J., Nov. 21, 1819. "Touching both hands and feet": MW to "My Dear, Dear Bros. & Sisters," Feb. 4, 1820, MLC.

3 The captain's cabin: Maria Loomis J., Nov. 8, 1819; also MW to "My Dear, Dear Bros. & Sisters," Feb. 4, 1820, MLC. The deck: Thurston, p. 20.

4 "Misery loves company": Lucia Ruggles Holman, *Journal,* p. 7. "Hospital": Daniel Chamberlain J., Nov. 21, 1819. "Upon a rope": Thurston, p. 20. "Beds for any": Nancy Ruggles J., Nov. 27, 1819. Samuel Ruggles's discomfort: Nancy Ruggles J., Dec. 5, 1819.

5 "Partly spilt": Nancy Ruggles J., Nov. 6, 1819. "New school": Thurston, p. 21. Fresh provisions gave out: Samuel Ruggles, J., Dec. 26, 1819. Diet: Maria Loomis J., Feb. 16, March 13, 1819; MW to "My Dear, Dear Bros. & Sisters," Feb. 4, 1820, MLC; Holman, p. 8. "Water gruel": Holman, p. 8; Daniel Chamberlain J., Dec. 27, 1819; Samuel Ruggles J., Dec. 25, 1819. Drinking water . . . umbrella: Samuel Ruggles J., Dec. 26, 1819. "Some lie on the floor": Daniel Chamberlain J., Dec. 31, 1819.

6 "Tears . . . without cause": Sybil Bingham J.

7 "Sympathy and prayers": Holman, p. 33. "Happy": Maria Loomis J. Jerusha contented: Daniel Chamberlain J., Dec. 2, Dec. 25, 1819; see also March 23, March 29, 1820. "The five past": SB to Mr. & Mrs. Bartlett, "1820, Brig *Thaddeus,*" BP, Box 3; see also Nancy Ruggles J.: not "unhappy," Nov. 6, 1819.

8 "King and queen": MW to "My Dear, Dear Bros. & Sisters," Feb. 4, 1820, MLC. "*Happy*": Thurston, p. 21. "In saying so": Sybil Bingham J., Jan. 14, 1820; Sybil's journal is addressed to her sisters.

9 "Lighter than vanity": MW to Dr. C. Goodrich & Wife, Dec. 4, 1819, MLC. "Tears from the eyes": Sybil Bingham J., Jan. 28, 1820.

10 "This side heaven": Sybil Bingham J., Dec. 26, 1820. "Cause of Christ": Maria Loomis J., Oct. 23, 1819. "Poor heathen": Nancy Ruggles J., Jan. 22, 1820. "Word of God": Thurston, p. 23. "Personal consideration": Sybil Bingham J., 1820.

11 No one regretted having come: this contrasts with the reluctance of many women pioneers to travel west, the decision having been made by husbands; see Faragher, pp. 163–68, 171–73. The comparison with missionary women is useful generally, since the westward journey was undertaken by similarly isolated groups of men and women for roughly similar lengths of time, but with greater travail and less of a sense of group unity; see also Julie Roy Jeffrey, *Frontier Women.* Sandra Myres, *Westering Women and the Frontier Experience,* reviews both books (pp. 10–11) and questions the picture of women as "solely" reluctant to leave (pp. 99–102).

12 "Affliction": Nancy Ruggles J., Nov. 6, 1819. "My native shores": Thurston, p. 22. "*Hope*": Holman, p. 37; see also p. 26.

13 Women's background: the education, motivation, and hasty courtships of the women of the first company were typical; see Patricia Grimshaw, "Christian Brides," in *Paths of Duty*, pp. 1–23; see also her "'Christian Woman, Pious Wife,'" *Feminist Studies* 9 (1983): 493–97.

14 Ideas behind missionary work: for much of this section of the chapter, I am indebted to John Andrew, *Rebuilding the Christian Commonwealth*, pp. 70–119 and generally; to Oliver Elsbree, *The Rise of the Missionary Spirit in America*; and to Stow Persons, *American Minds*. For a summary of British missions in Polynesia, see R. K. Howe, "To Recover the Remnant," in *Where the Waves Fall*, pp. 109–21. Missionaries as descendants of Puritans: see the Rev. Orramel H. Gulick and Anne Gulick, *The Pilgrims of Hawaii*, pp. 11–12, 36–38; Andrew (p. 119) calls the mission an "attempt to re-create a seventeenth-century New England Christian Commonwealth in the middle of the Pacific Ocean."

15 Great Awakening: Persons, pp. 85–89, 103, 169; Elsbree, pp. 25–46; Andrew, pp. 4, 8, 71; Sydney Ahlstrom briefly summarizes the important thinkers in *Religious History of the American People*, pp. 415–28; see Sandra Wagner's summary of Calvinistic thinkers, "Sojourners Among Strangers," pp. 47–86; she also covers the conversion experiences of the first two companies on pp. 87–113. "Revival": MW to Josiah Brewer, Feb. 4, 1819, MLC; SB-PJ, June 4, 1815.

16 "Feminization" of religion: I am summarizing what I found to be the general argument among historians. The best starting point is Nancy Cott's chapter on "Religion" in *The Bonds of Womanhood*, pp. 126–59; see her list of charitable societies, pp. 135–36; see also Nancy Woloch's summary in "Piety and Purity" in *Women and the American Experience*, pp. 120–23, and her bibliography, pp. 148–49. Nancy Hewitt summarizes the "widely accepted scenario" locating the source of later activism in domesticity and revivalism in her "Introduction" to *Women's Activism and Social Change*, pp. 19–20; see also Julie Roy Jeffrey's summary in *Frontier Women*, pp. 4–7; and Carl Degler, "The World Is Only a Large Home," in *At Odds*, pp. 298–303. Ann Douglas, in *The Feminization of American Culture*, pp. 12, 80–117, speaks to the alliance between Victorian women and ministers and the resultant "sentimentalization of theological and secular culture"; Mary Ryan studies the revival cycle of 1813–1838 for the women in Utica, New York, in *Cradle of the Middle Class*. Also useful are Barbara Welter, "The Feminization of American Religion: 1800–1860," in *Dimity Convictions*, pp. 83–102; Ryan, "A Woman's Awakening," pp. 602–23; and Ryan, "The Power of Women's Networks," pp. 66–83. Revivals and women's

piety come into many discussions of separate men's and women's "spheres" in the nineteenth century.

17 Values of Christianity: Nancy Woloch, p. 125. "Disinterested benevolence": Elsbree, pp. 146–52; see also Mercy Whitney J., Oct. 24, 1819; Jeremiah Evarts to Rev. Hiram Bingham & others, Jan. 5, 1822, ABCFM-HEA.

18 Political component: this is Andrew's argument. For further discussion of the missions as an attempt to "preserve orthodoxy at home as well as spread Christianity abroad" (p. 19), see pp. 13–24. Unitarians and Trinitarians: Andrew, p. 14.

19 Basic Christian truths: Daws, *Shoal of Time*, p. 62. Remind Christians of unity: see "Dr. Hopkin's Semi-centennial Discourse," in Anderson, *Memorial Volume*, pp. 20–24, for the mission's reliance on "essential elements of the Christian religion," not on a sectarian agenda. Members of the Board, p. 87; see Andrew, p. 79, for the "genius" of the crusade in combatting religious divisions at home. City on a hill: Bradley, *The American Frontier in Hawaii.* p. 106; also MW to Miss S. G. Bidwell, July 6, 1852, MLC.

20 Missions to American Indians: Elsbree, pp. 7, 17–18; see also "Historical Catalogue of the Missions" in Anderson, *Memorial Volume*, pp. 268–69. Relatively unsuccessful: Elsbree blames "the land hunger of the white settlers, the susceptibility of the natives to the diseases and vices of the white man, and . . . the inability of the Protestant missionaries to adapt their method of appeal to the needs and the understanding of the natives" (pp. 22–23); for an introduction to missionary efforts among the Indians, see Robert Berkhofer, *Salvation and the Savage;* Sybil Bingham read *The Life of David Brainerd:* see SB-PJ, June 2, 1813.

21 Origin of ABCFM and first missions: the "haystack" story about Mills and his friends appears in the standard histories; see especially Elsbree, pp. 99, 110–14; "Enlisting the Public" and "The System at Work: The Sandwich Island Mission," in Andrew, pp. 66–96, 97–110. $30,000: Andrew, p. 22.

22 "Collecting mission": SR to Lucia Ruggles [Holman], Nov. 14, 1817, RP. Reform movements: for discussion of missionary women as similar to other reformers, see Grimshaw, "Conflicts in Roles," pp. 491, 515n.

23 Missions to Burma: Elsbree (thinking of dates of arrival, not departure) says the missions to Bombay and Ceylon were the only ones before 1820 (p. 114); see also Andrew, p. 97; Anderson, *Memorial Volume*, pp. 227–29, 268.

24 "Obookiah": see standard histories; Edwin Dwight, *Memoirs of Obookiah;* and *A Narrative of Five Youths.*

25 George Kaumualii: Catherine Stauder, "George, Prince of Hawaii," *HJH* 6 (1972): 28–44. "Neglected": Stauder, p. 33; Anne H. Spoehr, "George, Prince Tamoree: Heir Apparent of Kauai and Niihau," *HJH* 15 (1981): 31–49; quoted p. 38.

26 50,000 copies: Andrew, p. 102. Preparations for the Sandwich Islands Mission: see Andrew, pp. 106–16.

27 Bingham in charge of preparations: Andrew, p. 106 and footnote; see also HB to Samuel Worcester, April 28, 1819, ABCFM 6, vol. 2, no. 122; Rev. Elisha Yale to Samuel Worcester, July 19, 1819, referring to Bingham as "well qualified to superintend any part of the business of the mission," ABCFM 6, vol. 2, no. 124. Thurston's resentment: "He thinks Mr. Bingham is too much disposed to take precedence of him, & has injured him": unsigned memorandum from conversation between [Jeremiah Evarts] and Rev. William Ellis, April 25, 1825, ABCFM 8.5, no. 26; when the company left for Hawaii, Andrew notes, the authority was "technically shared" by Thurston (p. 166).

28 $3,200: Andrew, p. 116. $10,000: Andrew, p. 116. $5,000: William Salisbury to TH, June 28, 1819, RP. "Little patrimony": SB to Jeremiah Evarts, Oct. 23, 1819, MLC. Articles donated: Albertine Loomis, *Grapes of Canaan: Hawaii 1820* (a historical novel based on careful research), p. 20.

29 Unmarried women: Barbara Welter discusses the increasing numbers of single women missionaries after the Civil War in "She Hath Done What She Could," in *Women in American Religion*, pp. 116–25; see also Grimshaw, "Paths of Duty," pp. 88–94, for the ABCFM's "cool response" to single women; and Jane Hunter, *The Gospel of Gentility*, for a study of the many unmarried women missionaries to China in the late nineteenth century.

30 Anderson essay on wives: Rev. Rufus Anderson, "Introductory Essay on the Marriage of Missionaries," in Rev. William Ellis, *Memoir of Mrs. Mary Ellis*, pp. vii–xv.

31 Worcester to "Females": "Instructions" printed in Heman Humphrey, *The Promised Land*, pp. xii–xiii, BP, Box 2.

32 Christianity and female character: see Grimshaw, "Conflicts in Roles," p. 495, for the notion that "the *true* gospel of Christ upheld a high status for women"; see also Welter, "She Hath Done," p. 117, for the notion of Christianity as a "liberator" of women; Cott, pp. 130–31, for the "omnipresent theme" of women's "special obligations" to Christianity.

33 Cult of true womanhood: Barbara Welter, "The Cult of True Womanhood, 1820–1860," pp. 151–74; virtues quoted, p. 151; "Introduction" and "Domesticity" in Cott, pp. 63–100; Grimshaw, "New England Missionary Wives, Hawaiian Women, and 'The Cult of True Woman-

hood,'" pp. 71–100; Woloch, pp. 148–49, gives an annotated bibliography for the doctrine of "women's sphere," explaining that historians disagree on its effect as loss or gain; Degler argues that "we ought not to conclude too hastily that the separation of the spheres was nothing more than a rationale for the subordination or diminishing of women": see "Wives and Husbands," p. 27, and pp. 26–51 generally. Carol George, editor of *"Remember the Ladies,"* argues that the cult was "ironically juxtaposed against the emergent women's rights movement" (p. 68, and see pp. 67–122 generally); see also Kathryn Kish Sklar's biography, *Catharine Beecher.* For sources of the changes in women's roles, generally attributed to an increasingly commercial economy, see Cott, pp. 19–62; Mary Ryan, "Changing Roles, New Risks: Women in Commercial America," in *Womanhood in America,* pp. 83–136.

34 Shipment of frame house: Bingham, *Residence,* pp. 61–62. "Wives endure": Anderson, *Memorial Volume,* p. 272.

35 "Sarah S.": HB to Jeremiah Evarts, Aug. 31, 1819, ABCFM 6, vol. 2, no. 2. "Mrs. Clapp": AT to Samuel Worcester, Sept. 7, 1819, ABCFM 6, vol. 2, no. 117.

36 "Most delicate mission": Rev. William Goodell, *Forty Years in the Turkish Empire,* pp. 54–58. Lucy Thurston's courtship: Thurston, pp. 2–7, 248–49. "Wives of merchants": Thurston, p. 247.

37 "Rather reserved," "good education": MW to "My Dear, Dear Bros. & Sisters," Feb. 4, 1820, MLC.

38 Bingham courtship: Hiram Bingham, Jr., quotes his father in an unidentified newspaper article: Scrapbook, BP, Box 14.

39 "Best swimmer": Daniel Chamberlain J., Dec. 31, 1819.

40 Religious content of journals: since these women belonged to either Congregational or Presbyterian churches, their meditations reflect orthodox Calvinism (not the newer, more liberal ideas of Universalist or Unitarian churches); Barbara Epstein in *The Politics of Domesticity* provides a good summary of conversion narratives and conventional theology, tracing the differences between men's and women's religious experiences as the century went on. Women tended (as here) to stress original sin, estrangement from God, and the need to replace a rebellious heart with one submissive to God. But the "antagonism" Epstein finds between women and reluctant male converts does not apply to missionary couples: see pp. 49, 58, and 45–66 generally; see also Sandra Wagner, "Mission and Motivation," pp. 62–70.

41 "Ah me . . . into thy hands": SB-PJ (subsequent references in this section are to this journal unless noted). "Thy will not mine": March 16, 1813. "All his pleasure": Jan. 1, 1815.

42 "Eighth . . . Thanksgiving": Sybil Bingham J., Dec. 7, 1819. "Low": Aug. 25, 1815.

43 "What a sermon": Nov. 1, 1811. "Earth . . . offered": "Sabbath 7th" [Jan.], 1816.

44 "Walk with God": Sept. 14, 1813.

45 "Blood of Christ": "Sabbath 7th" [Jan.], 1816. "*Devoutly*": Dec. 27, 1818. "Open a door . . . heathen": Sept. 14, 1819.

46 Earlier proposal of marriage: Dec. 27, 1818; Alfred Bingham names Levi Parsons in "Sybil's Bones," p. 13; Sybil's daughter Lydia Coan refers to a proposal from "one under appointment to a foreign field" in her memoir, *A Brief Sketch of the Missionary Life of Mrs. Sybil Moseley Bingham,* HMCS.

47 Samuel Ruggles's "Mary": SR to LR[H], March 1819, RP. Samuel's childhood: SR to Samuel Wooster [Worcester], June 7, 1817, MLC. "Worth of their souls": SR to "Dear Brothers," March 1818, RP. "Amiable disposition": Isaac Ruggles to LR[H], March 7, 1815, RP. *Keiki: Missionary Album,* p. 168.

48 Thomas Holman: Andrew, pp. 112–13 and footnote; see also SR to LR[H], March 1819, RP. Letters of July 2, 1817, and Feb. 6, 1819: RP. By June 30: Isaac Ruggles to LR[H], 1819, RP.

49 "Useful accomplishments": Isaac Ruggles to LR[H], March 28, 1814, RP. "To deny themselves": Isaac Ruggles to LR[H], June 30, 1819, RP. "To the trial": Holman, p. 25. "Our grand object": Holman, p. 36. "Necessaries also": Holman, p. 33. "Suffering enough": Holman, p. 38.

50 Elisha Loomis courtship: EL to Samuel Worcester, Sept. 16, 1819, ABCFM 6, vol. 2, no. 129.

51 "Friendly visit . . . renewed": MW to Josiah Brewer, draft, Aug. 30, 1819, MLC. "Uncommon" . . . could not speak for her: Rev. Heman Humphrey to Rev. E. Smith, Sept. 8, 1819, MLC. "Caught a Partridge": copied by Hattie [Mrs. Samuel] Whitney from *The Family Tree Book,* Pogue Family Misc., MLC.

52 "Union and cordiality": MW to Josiah Brewer, Feb. 4, 1819, MLC. "Duties . . . incumbent on me": MW to "My Dear Parents," Oct. 12, 1819, MLC. "Vale of tears": MW to Edward Partridge, Sept. 25, 1819, MLC. "Stewardship": MW to Mrs. Laura Partridge, draft, n.d. [Sept. 1819], MLC. "Undeserving the name": MW to Edward Partridge, draft, Jan. 7, 1819, MLC.

53 "Light of the gospel": MW to Josiah Brewer, draft, Aug. 30, 1819, MLC. "Lord send me," "great undertaking": MW to Wms. and Laura Partridge, draft, Sept. 27, 1819, MLC. "The hope & prospect . . . I may go": MW to "My Dear Parents," Oct. 12, 1819, MLC.

54 "Garments . . . scores": Thurston, p. 7. Sixty for Sybil: SB to Mrs. Bates,

Oct. 8, 1820, BP, Box 3. Ordination service: Andrew, p. 117. For the complete texts of the speeches discussed in the following section, see Humphrey, *The Promised Land;* both "The Charge" and "Instructions" are printed here, BP, Box 2.

55 "Through the gospel": Anderson, *Memorial Volume,* p. 277. "*Gospel preceded civilization*": Anderson, *Memorial Volume,* p. 384; see also comment on p. 100, citing R. H. Dana, that the Hawaiians had "no civilization of their own"; Howe argues (p. 113) that by the 1830s, for British missionaries, "experience had blurred the theological niceties as to whether civilisation was or was not a necessary prerequisite."

56 Leave-taking ceremonies: Goodell, p. 61; Bingham, *Residence,* pp. 63–64; Elisha Loomis J., Oct. 23, 1819.

57 Sale of *Thaddeus:* Bradley, p. 64. To Boki, TJ, Feb. 1, 1821.

58 Jerusha Chamberlain "calm": Daniel Chamberlain J., Nov. 21, 1819. "Endured the voyage": March 29, 1819.

59 References to husbands: Maria Loomis J., Feb. 21, 1819; Holman, p. 39; Thurston, p. 25.

60 "Pleasant and useful": Mercy Whitney J.

61 Roster: Humphrey, p. xvi. "Approbation": SB to Jeremiah Evarts, Oct. 23, 1819, MLC. Inequities of childhood: Thurston, p. 245. "Daughters . . . disproportionate": J., Dec. 3, 1833. $50 for girls: Anderson, *Memorial Volume,* p. 279. For women's legal status at this time, see Cott, pp. 5–7, 21.

62 "Servile lot": Thurston, p. 289. "Proud post of wife": SB to Mr. & Mrs. James Hunnewell, Aug. 22, 1846, BP, Box 3.

63 "Salvation above gender": Epstein, p. 23, is speaking for the previous century here, but the point still holds. "Glory of God": MP[W] to Edward Partridge, Sept. 25, 1819, MLC.

64 Notion of family: see reference to the cult of true womanhood. Cott refers (p. 199) to the "cultural halo" about the home and family; see Faragher, pp. 144, 158, and 144–78 generally, for the homestead as the "dominating social motif of the nineteenth-century West" and its dependence on the family unit. The mission's sense of "family" contrasts with what Faragher found for the wagon-trains: "at their best these little communities simply stumbled along" (p. 28).

65 "Composure": Maria Loomis J., Jan. 8, 1819; Samuel Ruggles J., Jan. 8, 1819; see also "calm": Sybil Bingham J., Jan. 8, 1819. "Safely through": Sybil Bingham J. Whitney overboard: Mercy Whitney J., March 27, 1820; TJ, March 27, 1820; MW to Mr. James Hunnewell, Feb. 23, 1863, MLC.

66 "Misspent": Mercy Whitney J., Dec. 11, 1819. Sermon Dec. 19: Nancy Ruggles J. "Coldness": Maria Loomis J. [Williams version].

67 "Division of time": TJ, Nov. 19, 1819. "Regularity . . . meals": MW to "My Dear, Dear Bros. & Sisters," Feb. 4, 1820, MLC. Mercy's schedule: J., Jan. 17, 1820. Sybil's schedule: J., Jan. 25, 1820. "Euclid": J., March 22, 1820. "Recitation hour": J., Nov. 20, 1820. See also schedules of Nancy Ruggles, J., Dec. 28, 1819; Maria Loomis J., Jan. 1, 1820.

68 Regularity of events: Nancy Ruggles J., Dec. 28, 1819; Daniel Chamberlain J., Feb. 5, 1820. "Concert of prayer": Elsbree, p. 136. Ebenezer: TJ, Jan. 30, 1820. "Qualities of character": TJ, Feb. 7, 1820. Communion: TJ, Feb. 27, 1819.

69 References to family: Nancy Ruggles J.; Mercy Whitney J.

70 Trouble with Holmans: DC to Samuel Worcester, Nov. 14, 1820, MLC-ts, vol. 1; "Holman Affair Report," the letter sent by HB and AT to the Board in Feb. 1821, typescript in HMCS (Bingham once threw himself on his couch in tears, pp. 13–14); see also Francis Halford's sympathetic account of Holman in *Nine Doctors and God.*

71 "Cheerfully": Nancy Ruggles J., Oct. 23, 1819; Mercy Whitney J., Oct. 23, 1819. "Happiest part": Mercy Whitney J. "Great work": Maria Loomis J., Oct. 23, 1819. "Enthusiasm": Persons, p. 91; Sybil Bingham wrote to Jeremiah Evarts that it was "not enthusiasm" that prompted her donation of $800 to the ABCFM: Oct. 23, 1819, MLC.

72 "Inconsistent walk and conversation": MLC. "Stumbling block": MW to "Bro. & Sis. [Dow]," Oct. 23, 1819, MLC.

Chapter 2: Pagan Shores

1 For references to landfall throughout this section, see Sybil Bingham, Maria Loomis, Samuel Ruggles, Mercy Whitney J., March 30, 1820; Bingham, *Residence,* p. 69.

2 "Sugar Cane and Tarrow," "*little glad*": Holman, p. 17. "All animation": Thurston, p. 25.

3 Chance: Sybil Bingham wrote, "*Chance* has no dominion in God!" to Misses Atwater and Mosely, Nov. 24, 1816, BP, Box 2; see also Hiram Bingham's reasons for storms in *Residence,* p. 64. "Sparrow falls": Sybil Bingham J. "Marvellous": ML to "a friend in this village," June 18, 1820, letter published in *Utica Sentinel,* April 13, 1821, MLC; also Maria Loomis J., March 30, 1819. "Waiting for his law": Mercy Whitney J., March 30, 1819.

4 Tumultuous year: for the factual details throughout this chapter, I am indebted to the histories listed at the beginning of the Notes. See especially "1819," in Kuykendall, pp. 61–70. *Kuhina-nui,* Kuykendall, p. 63. Kalanimoku as prime minister, Kuykendall, p. 53; Samuel Ka-

makau, "Abolition of the tabus under Liholiho," in *Ruling Chiefs,* pp. 219–28; Daws, "The King is Dead," in *Shoal of Time,* pp. 53–60. Kamehameha's legacy: Kuykendall, p. 32; Daws, *Shoal of Time,* p. 56.

5 Hawaiian civilization and *kapus:* Kamakau, "Hawaii Before Foreign Innovations," in *Ruling Chiefs,* pp. 229–45; David Malo, *Hawaiian Antiquities:* pp. 52–62 (castes), pp. 68–71 (*kauwa*), pp. 27–29 (eating *kapus*), and generally; "Ancient Hawaii," in Kuykendall, pp. 7–11 ("psychically dangerous," p. 8). *Kapus* and rank: Samuel Kamakau, "The Degrees of Chiefs," in *Ka Po'e Kahiko,* pp. 4–5, 10. The best introduction to this vast subject is David Kittelson, *The Hawaiians: An Annotated Bibliography;* a good short introduction is E. S. Craighill Handy, *Cultural Revolution in Hawaii;* W. D. Alexander, *A Brief History of the Hawaiian People,* is intended as an introductory textbook; see also E. S. Craighill Handy, K. Emory, et al., *Ancient Hawaiian Civilization; Aspects of Hawaiian Life and Environment,* a collection of lectures given at the Kamehameha Schools in 1962–1963; and some often-cited modern studies: Irvin Goldman, *Ancient Polynesian Society,* and Marshall Sahlins, *Islands of History.* Both Goldman and Handy omit the *kahunas* as a class.

6 Depopulation: Kuykendall, p. 336; Robert Schmitt, in *Historical Statistics of Hawaii,* uses the missionaries' census to suggest a population of 135,145 in 1823: see "Table 1.1: Population Estimates 1778 to 1832," p. 7; by 1850, Hawaiians numbered 82,035: see "Table 8: Population by Race 1778–1850" in Schmitt's *Demographic Statistics of Hawaii,* p. 43; David Stannard, *Before the Horror,* puts the precontact population at 800,000 to 1 million, much higher than conventional estimates, p. 79. This would make the depopulation by 1820 even more devastating. Stannard's book includes "Comments" by demographers Eleanor Nordyke and Robert Schmitt, born of whom disagree (pp. 105–21).

7 System of *kapus* toppled: Kuykendall, pp. 65–70 and footnotes. Keopuolani's part: Kamakau, *Ruling Chiefs,* p. 224; Maria Loomis J., April 6, 1820. Howe remarks (pp. 163–67) how quickly the system was toppled and with how little regret, arguing that there was "no basic change in society" for the commoners, who now had fewer demands from the priesthood but more from the *alii.* Kaahumanu ate shark meat: Daws, *Shoal of Time,* p. 56.

8 "Whimsical": Daws, *Shoal of Time,* p. 55. "Cook our tarrow": Daniel Chamberlain J., July 8, 1820.

9 Baptism: Alexander, p. 168; Kuykendall, p. 67. Jump off a cliff: Daws, *Shoal of Time,* p. 54.

10 Opinions of Hopu and Honolii: MW to "My Dear, Dear Bros. & Sisters," Feb. 4, 1820, MLC. Waiting on tables: Daniel Chamberlain J.,

Feb. 5, 1820. "Use of poisons": Thurston, p. 24. "Could not bring up their infants": Miron Winslow, *A Sketch of Missions,* p. 303.

11 "Uncivilized": Mercy Whitney J., Dec. 31, 1819. "Eat separately": Thurston, p. 18. "Oppressive shackles": Samuel Ruggles J., April 6, 1820; Maria Loomis J., Feb. 25, 1820.

12 "Martyrs in the cause": Samuel Ruggles J., Nov. 8, 1819. "Faithful . . . end": Maria Loomis J., Jan. 23, 1820. "Cross . . . erected": Mercy Whitney J. "Trust was in God": Thurston, p. 18.

13 Gifts of welcome: Mercy Whitney J., March 31, 1820. "Threshold of a nation": Thurston, p. 30. "Let the tears flow": Sybil Bingham J., March 31, 1820. "Christianized?": Bingham, *Residence,* p. 81.

14 "Children of nature": Thurston, p. 30. "Never told me": Nancy Ruggles J., April 1, 1820. Marshall Sahlins argues that the *alii* saw their relationship to commoners in the same terms—"culture" versus "nature," or "civilization" contrasted with "barbarism": see *Historical Metaphors,* pp. 30–31.

15 "Naked": Sybil Bingham J., March 31, 1820. Impressions of clothing: TJ, April 1, 1820; Thurston, p. 30; see also Mercy Whitney J., April 1, 1820; Holman, p. 18.

16 Size of Hawaiians: Nancy Ruggles J., April 1, 1820; Thurston, p. 31; Mercy Whitney J., April 6, 1820; Maria Loomis J., April 1, 1820; Bingham, *Residence,* p. 82.

17 "Present . . . potatoes": TJ, April 1, 1819. "Clasp": Thurston, p. 31. Children in laps: TJ, April 1, 1820. Wish to reside: Bingham, *Residence,* p. 82.

18 Royal visitors left on April 1: following Bingham, *Residence,* pp. 82–84.

19 "Hasty pudding": Holman, p. 19. "Muslin": Mercy Whitney J., April 4, 1820. Making poi: Maria Loomis J., April 2, April 7, 1820. "Decency of the table": Nancy Ruggles J.

20 Eating habits: Mercy Whitney J., April 4, 1820. "Even decency": Nancy Ruggles J., April 1, 1820. "Disgusted": Holman, pp. 19–20. "Satanic": Daniel Chamberlain J., April 15, 1820. "Gloomy reign": Sybil Bingham J., April 3, 1820. Smoking: Holman, p. 21. "The brutes": Mercy Whitney J., April 4, 1820. "Thick as bees": Maria Loomis J., April 2, 1820; Mercy Whitney J., April 5, 1820. "Savage tongues": Sybil Bingham J., April 3, 1820. "Far from them": Holman, p. 20.

21 "No account of time": Holman, p. 19. "Disregard of time": Sybil Bingham J., April 11, 1820. "Waiters": Mercy Whitney J., April 4, 1820. "Hogs": Holman, p. 19. "Little force": Mercy Whitney J., April 6, 1820. "Deep slumbers": Thurston, p. 35.

22 Ethnocentrism: my assessment of this problem (here and throughout) stops short of Grimshaw's description of missionary attitudes as "in-

tense ethnocentricity amounting in late twentieth-century evaluations to racism" (*Paths of Duty*, p. 194); see also "Conflicts in Roles," pp. 513–15. My evaluation follows Barbara Welter's conclusion in "She Hath Done" (p. 124) that "missionaries were far more sensitive to the societies in which they worked than is generally believed." Though ethnocentricity is undeniable, the degree of conflict in missionary attitudes, the alternation between recoil and sympathy, distinguishes these women from other Euro-Americans of their class in the nineteenth century. For comparison, see "Women, Race, Religion, and Class on the Frontier," in Myres, *Westering Women*, for a discussion of longstanding stereotypes of Catholics, Hispanics, and Indians. Though Myres finds contradictions and ambivalences, and some change in attitude after the annexation of Texas, only a "few" women were "openly sympathetic to the plight of Mexicans after the American occupation" (pp. 77–78, and see pp. 17–79 generally). Jeffrey stresses the "fear" of Indians (not a factor in the Hawaiian experience), noting that only when Indians conformed to American expectations were they praised. "Only rarely," she concludes (pp. 54–55), "could white women reach across the barriers of race and culture to establish sympathetic contact with Indian women" (see pp. 46–55 generally). My point is not to deny or excuse prejudicial attitudes toward Hawaiians (and also Catholics and Mormons), but to put them in context. Missionary insistence on "equality of souls," a potential antidote to divisive prejudice, is reflected in the attitude of missionary women. Unlike Western settlers, they came with sympathy and "compassion for souls" on their minds and were trying to engage with Hawaiians, not simply to live in their territory.

23 "Desire for . . . salvation": Maria Loomis J. "Appearance tolerable": NR to Rev. Shubard Bartlett, March 31, 1820, MLC.

24 Hawaiian generosity and gifts: Mercy Whitney J., April 8, 1820; Samuel Ruggles J., April 5, 1820. "Drooping . . . exercise": Maria Loomis J., March 19, 1820. "*Miti kanaka*": Maria Loomis J., April 5, 1820. "Best hut in the village": Mercy Whitney J., April 8, 1820. "Appear friendly": Sybil Bingham J., April 11, 1820. "Natives hurting him": Daniel Chamberlain J., July 1, 1820.

25 "Most interesting Sabbath": Nancy Ruggles J., April 2, 1820.

26 Women a novelty: one white woman did arrive before the missionary wives, the wife (or mistress) of Captain de Freycinet on the *Uranie* in 1819, though as a stowaway dressed in men's clothes; see T. Blake Clark, "Honolulu's Streets." Offers of trade: Maria Loomis J., April 5, 1820. Liholiho's "palace": Maria Loomis J., April 7, 1820.

27 "Shades of Eden": Thurston, p. 31. "Grow larger": Holman, p. 19. Sewing for Kalakua: Thurston, p. 34; Mercy Whitney J., April 3, 1820.

28 Women ashore: Maria Loomis J., April 7, 1820; Holman, pp. 21–23; Nancy Ruggles J., April 7, 1820. Long necks: Kamakau, *Ruling Chiefs*, p. 247.

29 Permission to land: Mercy Whitney J., April 3, 1820. "All his pleasure": Sybil Bingham J., April 4, 1820; Mercy Whitney also remarks that "Zion's king" can turn men's hearts "as he pleases" in J., April 4, 1820.

30 "King's visit on *Thaddeus:* Bingham, *Residence,* p. 89. "Decorum": Maria Loomis J., April 6, 1820. "Scale . . . poising": Thurston, p. 35. "Arm will protect": Nancy Ruggles J., April 7, 1820.

31 Liholiho's disclaimers, "nor any other man": Thurston, p. 36.

32 Verdict on the foreigners: Kuykendall, pp. 84–85. Buying European ships: Bradley, pp. 56, 61–64; p. 63 cites John C. Jones, the American consul. Foreigners assist Kamehameha: Kuykendall, p. 27.

33 Campbell and foreigners: Bradley, pp. 34–40; Campbell quoted, p. 40; Davis quoted, p. 38.

34 "Wicked white men": Samuel Ruggles J. Jean Rives's advice: Kamakau, *Ruling Chiefs,* pp. 246–47. John Young's advice: Bradley refutes the claim that Young supported the missionaries, p. 126 and footnotes; see also Bingham, *Residence,* p. 88; Kuykendall, pp. 41–43. John Young quoted: Bingham, *Residence,* p. 303.

35 Negotiations for landing: see Bingham, *Residence,* pp. 88–90. "Misunderstandings," Bingham, *Residence,* p. 88. "White men prefer Oahu," "hovel," "tabu," Bingham, *Residence,* p. 89; see also TJ, April 8, 9, 10, 1820. "Insist upon our stay": SB-PJ, April 8, 1820.

36 King's decision and women's reactions: Mercy Whitney J., April 11, 1820; Nancy Ruggles J., April 10, 1820; Thurston, p. 37; Holman, p. 26; Sybil Bingham J., April 11, 1820.

37 Contrast Kailua with Honolulu: Daniel Chamberlain J., April 8, 1820; Nancy Ruggles J., April 10, 1820; see also Mercy Whitney J., April 11, 1820.

38 First night in Kailua: Thurston, p. 37; Holman, pp. 26–27.

39 "Beauty of the landscape": Maria Loomis J., April 14, 1820. Arrival at Honolulu: Bingham: *Residence,* p. 92. Marin: Smith, p. 48; Bradley, p. 38; see also Ross Gast and Agnes Conrad, *Don Francisco de Paula Marin* (containing a biography by Ross Gast and Marin's journal and letters, edited by Agnes Conrad).

40 "Description of maps: Clark, pp. 6–7. No water until 1850s: see "II: The Site" in A. Lockwood Frost and Rossie M. Frost, AIA, "A Study and Report on the Old Mission Houses," 1968, HMCS (hereafter "Frost Report"); see also two pamphlets by George F. Nellist, "An Early History of Honolulu's Water System" (1951) and "The Discovery and Development of Artesian Water" (1953), both published by the Board

of Water Supply of the City and County of Honolulu, Hawaiian Historical Society Library.

41 View from Punchbowl Hill: Bingham, *Residence*, p. 93.

42 "Luxuriance . . . vegetation": TJ, April 14, 1820. "Gospel of Christ": Mercy Whitney J., April 6, 1820. "Interesting . . . saved": Bingham, *Residence*, p. 94.

43 "Intemperance": Bingham, *Residence*, p. 94. "No means unfriendly": TJ, April 17, 1820. Women's disembarking: Mercy Whitney J., April 20, 1820; Sybil Bingham J., June 20, 1820; Nancy Ruggles J., April 19, 1820.

44 "Obstinate" Captain Blanchard: SR to LH, April 23, 1820, RP. Temporary quarters: TJ, April 19, 1820; Nancy Ruggles J., April 19, 1820. Furniture: Bingham, *Residence*, p. 96.

45 Probationary year: Grimshaw, *Paths of Duty*, pp. 24–49, singles out the first company as "Intrepid Pilgrims." "Much harmony": Sybil Bingham J., July 8, 1820.

46 "Increase of labor": SB to Mrs. Bates, Oct. 8, 1820, BP, Box 3. Duties at cookstove: Maria Loomis J., May 23, 1820; Daniel Chamberlain J., June 19, 1820; SB to Mrs. Bates, Oct. 8, 1820, BP, Box 3. 33 meals: Sybil Bingham J., June 28, 1820. 39 meals: June 30, 1820. "Mice and fleas": Mercy Whitney J., July 8, 1820.

47 Laundry: Nancy Ruggles's journal refers to the "friendly assistance of the brethren," June 20, 1820; Maria Loomis refers to help from two native boys: J., May 23, 1820; Thurston, p. 45; Bingham, *Residence*, p. 108; Sybil Bingham J., June 20, 1820.

48 Sewing: NR to LH, May 10, 1820, RP; Maria Loomis J., May 10, 1820. Ruffled shirts: SB to Mrs. Bates, Oct. 8, 1820, BP, Box 3.

49 "In my life," "smoother path": Sybil Bingham J. "Mercy of GOD . . . is great": SB to Mrs. Bates, Oct. 8, 1820, BP, Box 3.

50 Loomis childbirth: Sybil Bingham J., July 16, 1820; SB to LT, June 30, 1820, BP, Box 2. Praise for Samuel: Maria Loomis J., Aug. 1, 1820. Elisha's happiness: Elisha Loomis J.

51 "Sleek goat": Sybil Bingham J., July 3, 1820. Anthony Allen's gifts: Sybil Bingham J., June 20, 1820. Tea set: TJ, May 5, 1820. Apples: Mercy Whitney J., April 19, 1820. "Fond" of poi: Daniel Chamberlain J., June 19, 1820. "Without our care": Mercy Whitney J., May 31, 1820.

52 Detractors were quiet: Sybil Bingham J., June 20, 1820. "Kind" white people: April 23, 1820. RP. Tea on May 5: TJ. Contributions to "orphan" fund: Mercy Whitney J., May 16, 1820; Maria Loomis J., May 12, 1820.

53 Visit to Anthony Allen: Sybil Bingham J., Mercy Whitney J., June 24, 1820; Maria Loomis J., June 23, 1820.

54 "Nothing to what we expected": Maria Loomis J., April 19, 1820. "Jealousy": June 21, 1820. "(Talk) Owhyhee": Sybil Bingham J., June 25, 1820. "Fill their souls": Sybil Bingham J.
55 Moment of skittishness: Sybil Bingham J., June 24, 1820.
56 "Conducted themselves with propriety": TJ, May 3, 1820. Lucy's pursuit by priest: Thurston, pp. 49–51.
57 Ate dogs: Maria Loomis J., April 23, 1820. "Indolence" and other complaints: Maria Loomis J., June 21, 1820. Seventy companions: Thurston, p. 43. "Incessant noise" and "poor ignorant creatures": Mercy Whitney J., April 30, 1820. "Smooth handle": Thurston, p. 45.
58 Liliha's visit: Mercy Whitney J., Sybil Bingham J., July 7, 1820.
59 Trouble with Holmans: Asa Thurston's letter of April 27 is quoted in TJ, May 3, 1820. Private conference between Lucy and Lucia: Thurston, pp. 39–40. Unless otherwise noted, quotations and information in this section come from the "Holman Affair Report," a letter from Hiram Bingham and Asa Thurston to Samuel Worcester at the ABCFM, Feb. 15, 1821. The report runs to 137 typewritten pages, including reminiscences and letters from the voyage and first year. HMCS typescript of original at Houghton Library, Harvard.
60 "Comfort their hearts": Mercy Whitney J., July 2, 1820. Sybil's consolation: SB to Lucy Thurston, June 30, 1820, BP, Box 2.
61 Holman's defense: TH to Prudential Committee, ABCFM, Nov. 21, 1820, MLC-ts, vol. 1. "Scarcity of water": Holman, p. 34.
62 Lucia's complaints . . . "heathenish": Holman, pp. 31–32.
63 "Visit of an angel": Thurston, p. 47.
64 "Money . . . uppermost": DC to Samuel Worcester, Nov. 14, 1820, MLC-ts, vol. 1.
65 Holman's difficult personality: Andrew, pp. 112–13.
66 News from Kauai: SR to TH, June 30, 1820, RP. Arrival: Samuel Whitney J., Samuel Ruggles J., May 3, 1820. "Heart very glad": Samuel Ruggles J., May 10, 1820: TJ, June 28, 1820. King's promises: Samuel Whitney J., May 16, 1820.
67 "*Aloha America*": Samuel Ruggles J., May 4, 1820.
68 Women offered: Samuel Ruggles J., May 8, 1820 (quoted); see also Samuel Whitney J., May 27, 1820. Reading skills: Samuel Ruggles J., June 2, June 17, 1820. Sleepless night: Samuel Whitney J., June 3, 1820. "Purposed to deceive": Samuel Ruggles J., July 25, 1820.
69 Women's arrival in Kauai: Mercy Whitney J., July 21, July 25, 1820; Nancy Ruggles J., July 25–26, 1820; NR to LH, Aug. 19, 1820, RP. "Never want for anything": SR to Jeremiah Evarts, Aug. 2, 1820, MLC-ts, vol. 1.
70 Empathy and letters to mothers: Nancy Ruggles J., July 26, 1820; Mercy Whitney J., July 26, 1820.

71 Letter from Kapule: Maria Loomis J., Aug. 23, 1820.
72 Letters from Kaumualii: Bingham, *Residence*, p. 113; TJ, Aug. 23, 1820. See also my earlier comments on ethnocentrism: such empathy combined with revulsion makes for conflict in missionary attitudes, distinguishing them from most nineteenth-century observers.
73 "Moral darkness": Nancy Ruggles J., July 26, 1820. "Cheering rays": Mercy Whitney J., July 29, 1820.
74 "Earthly things . . . passed away": NR to LH, Aug. 19, 1820, RP.

Chapter 3: This Ransomed Land

1 Character traits: "Holman Affair Report," pp. 21–22, HMCS.
2 "Vital piety": SB to "Dear Sister Lucy [Whiting]," Jan. 1824, BP, Box 3; MW's essay for a Maternal Association meeting, MLC.
3 Gospel and civilization inextricable: upon landing, Bingham wrote that there was "no time to be lost" in introducing "everything in the way of civilization, as well as religion"; see *Residence*, p. 96. Missionaries bear resemblances here to western pioneer women, who had a similar "civilizing mission" on the frontier—though among missionaries this function was not limited to women: see "Am Beginning to Feel Quite Civilized," in Jeffrey, pp. 79–106; Grimshaw argues in "New England Missionary Wives" that "the women of the mission took as their special portion . . . the 'transformation' of Hawaiian girls and women to concepts of American femininity" (p. 73), but this exclusive goal was not immediately apparent to the pioneers, who at first had less rigidly defined ambitions. By the second decade, however, (if not earlier), the women were concentrating on helping Hawaiian females.
4 "Refusal to keep wooden gods": Kamakau, *Ruling Chiefs*, pp. 270–71. Shower bath: Forbes Research Notes, vol. 1, p. 1, citing Elisha Loomis J., July 4, 1826, HMCS; Elisha Loomis J., March 16, 1821.
5 "Promote their civilization": MW to Mrs. Mary Clark, July 15, 1830, MLC. "Arts of civilization": Samuel Whitney J., Sept. 20, 1821.
6 "Adorning my profession": Mercy Whitney J., Aug. 11, 1823.
7 "Little sanctuary": Nancy Ruggles J., July 30, 1820. Reading printed sermons: Samuel Whitney to Samuel Worcester, July 1820, MLC-ts, vol. 1; one sermon read was "The Church Safe." "Not approve of haste": TJ, Dec. 31, 1820.
8 Boki lingered: Bingham, *Residence*, p. 107. "*On Heathen Ground*": Sybil Bingham J., July 13, 1820. Hannah Holmes's meetings, Opukahaia, "worship . . . in truth": TJ, Oct. 8, 1820.
9 William Kanui's excommunication: Sybil Bingham J., July 14, July 23, 1820; Maria Loomis J., July 25, 1820. I am indebted generally to Susan Bell, "Owhyhee's Prodigal," *HJH* 10 (1976): 25–32; see also obituary

in *The Friend* (Honolulu), Feb. 5, 1864. The school at Cornwall was closed in 1827: see Anderson, *Memorial Volume*, pp. 329–32.

10 George Kaumualii, "hindering the holy work": Sybil Bingham J., July 2, 1820. Wrote to Hiram Bingham: TJ, Nov. 12, 1820. Drove schooner onto reef: Maria Loomis J., April 9, 1822. Whitneys' estimate, "dissipated wretch": Samuel Whitney J., April 8, 1824. Kaumualii's will and insurrection: Samuel Whitney J., July 6, Oct. 6, 1824.

11 "Had he behaved . . . iniquity": Mercy Whitney J., Aug. 31, 1821. "Poor outcast": Samuel Whitney J., July 6, 1824.

12 Hopu and Honolii: Bingham, *Residence*, pp. 165–66; see also "Memoirs of Thomas Hopoo," *HJH* 2 (1968): 42–54; vol. 1 (1967): 41–51, and Susan Bell, "The Boys from Cornwall," in *Unforgettable True Stories of the Kingdom of Hawaii*, pp. 11–22. New church: Bingham, *Residence*, p. 133; see also Ethel M. Damon, *The Stone Church at Kawaiahao*, for general information on this church and successive ones. "These earthly courts": Lucy Thurston, "Journal cont.," Sept. 16, 1821, MLC.

13 "Dominion . . . Isles of the Sea," victory the Lord's: SB to Mrs. Bates, Oct. 8, 1820, BP, Box 3.

14 Shared schoolteaching: SW to Samuel Worcester, July 20, 1820, MLC-ts, vol. 1. As public forum: women, for example, were not allowed to speak in church or at General Meetings – see Grimshaw, "Paths of Duty," pp. 358–61. For a short history of mission schools, see Kuykendall, pp. 100–113, and W. D. Westervelt, "The First Twenty Years of Education in the Hawaiian Islands," Hawaiian Historical Society, Nineteenth Annual Report, 1911, pp. 16–26.

15 "Regular school": Samuel Whitney J., Sept. 6, 1820. Attendance: SW and SR to Samuel Worcester, Oct. 14, 1820, MLC-ts, vol. 1.

16 Liholiho's reading: TJ, July 14, 1820; Thurston, p. 42. Threats of whipping: LT to Deacon Abner Goodale, Oct. 16, 1820, MLC. "His pious heart," SW to Samuel Worcester, July 20, 1820, MLC-ts vol. 1. Elisha Loomis in Kawaihae ["Toehigh"]: Elisha Loomis J., Sept. 14, 1820.

17 First reading lessons: TJ, July 14, Aug. 1, 1820. "Vowel changes": Kamakau, *Ruling Chiefs*, p. 270.

18 "Pleasantest school . . . America": Sybil Bingham J., Feb. 2, 1821. "Satisfied": SB to Sophia, draft, n.d., cont. July 29, 1821, BP, Box 3. "Among the heathen": SB to Sister M[argaret], Sept. 10, [1821], [pp. 3–4 of draft that begins as letter to Mrs. Johns], BP, Box 3. "So much for me": Sybil Bingham J., July 22, 1820; Bingham, *Residence*, p. 106. "Happiest of my life": Lucy Thurston, "Journal cont.," July 18, 1821, MLC.

19 "Tenacious memories": Thurston, p. 90. "Alphabet the first day": SW

and SR to Samuel Worcester, Oct. 14, 1820, MLC-ts, vol. 1. Quick memories: TJ, Nov. 5, 1820, Sept. 12, 1820; see also Elisha Loomis J., March 19, 1821.

20 "Immediate attention": Daniel Chamberlain J., June 24, 1820."Adopting" a heathen child: Sybil Bingham J., Dec. 31, 1822; see also "Minutes of a General Meeting," May 16, 1825, p. 7, HMCS.

21 Sybil and William Beals: SB to Sister M[argaret], Sept. 10, 1821 (pp. 3–4 of draft that begins as letter to Mrs. Johns), BP, Box 3.

22 First quarterly examination: TJ, Sept. 12–14, 1820.

23 Later examinations (*hoike*): Kamakau, *Ruling Chiefs*, pp. 271, 270; for a dramatic description of *hoikes*, see Daws, *Shoal of Time*, p. 90, and Kuykendall, p. 108, both quoting the journal of Reuben Tinker, July 19, 1831 (HMCS).

24 Hunting wild bullock: Samuel Whitney J., Nov. 1, 1821; he sawed boards Dec. 10, 1821. Thurston's "toil": LT to Levi Chamberlain, July 19, 1825, MLC. Cleaning spring: Daniel Chamberlain J., June 19, 1820.

25 Sybil's "assistance": SB to LT, June 30, 1820, BP, Box 2.

26 Domestic labors get in the way of missionary work: an obvious but major theme. See Grimshaw, *Paths of Duty*, p. 102 for confirmation that wives in subsequent companies also found that their missionary "careers" were "marginal and unheroic." See also chapter entitled "Prudent Helpmeets," pp. 100–127. Grimshaw concludes in "Paths of Duty," p. 636, that the "sex-specific nature and role of women was used deliberately to restrain mission wives from moving the boundaries of female participation in a direction which conflicted with male dominance," citing domestic duties and attitudes toward the "place of females" as impediments. That these restrictions were internalized did not make them less cruel.

27 "Labors have smothered it": Sybil Bingham J., July 22, 1820. "Render trifling": Sybil Bingham J., Feb. 25, 1823. For background on the "heavy" physical burdens of nineteenth-century domestic life, see Degler, pp. 52–55.

28 Contradictions in nineteenth-century notions of womanhood: see Welter, "The Cult of True Womanhood," for the tension between the qualities of the true woman and those needed for reform or missionary work, westward migration, utopian communities, industrialism, and the Civil War; the cult carried the "seeds of its own destruction," and as women began to challenge it, created "guilt and confusion" (p. 174). Grimshaw, "Conflicts in Roles," p. 513, makes the same point.

29 New houses: SB to Mrs. Bates, Oct. 8, 1820, BP, Box 3; TJ, Sept. 16, 1820 (the Chamberlains moved earlier, on Sept. 14). "Valleys in the rear": Maria Loomis J., June 19, 1820.

30 Houses in Kauai: Samuel Whitney J., Aug. 10, Sept. 1, 1820; SW to "Dear Sisters," Nov. 6, 1820, MLC. Fifty men for labor: Samuel Whitney J., Sept. 1, 1820. "Cool and pleasant spot": SW and SR to Samuel Worcester, Oct. 14, 1820, MLC-ts, vol. 1.

31 "My resting place": SB to "My dear Sisters Anna, Lucy, Sophia & Abby," Aug. 17, 1820, BP, Box 3. "Within its pleasant walls": SB to Mrs. Bates, Oct. 8, 1820, BP, Box 3.

32 Furniture: Maria Loomis J., Oct. 20, 1820; Bingham, *Residence*, pp. 116–17, quoting a letter of Sybil's.

33 Honolii's house: "A Chronological List of Dates Showing History of the Frame House, Chamberlain House, & Miscellaneous Related Buildings," in Frost Report. Enclosed acres: TJ, Dec. 2, 1820. First garden: TJ, Jan. 8, 1821. "Flourishing": TJ, March 22, 1821. Native plants: TJ, Jan. 8, 1821. Shade from hala: TJ, July 17, 1821.

34 "Ten thousand worlds": Mercy Whitney J., Aug. 2, 1820. "Uncertain riches": Mercy Whitney J., March 29, 1820. "Building up his spiritual temple": Mercy Whitney J., March 26, 1821.

35 "Higher objects": Jeremiah Evarts to Rev. Hiram Bingham & others, Jan. 5, 1822, ABCFM-HEA. "Riches . . . dangerous": Mercy Whitney J., June 16, 1827. "Blended": SB to HB, Sept. 3, 1843, BP, Box 3.

36 Common stock system: Sybil Bingham J., Oct. 21, 1822. "Settled principles": SB to Sophia, draft, n.d., cont. July 29, 1821, BP, Box 3.

37 Goat's milk: Mercy Whitney J., April 7, 1820. "Our necessary wants": SB, "have found that" [fragment], n.d. [Sept. 1821], BP, Box 3.

38 "Temporal comfort": SB-PJ, Sept. 15, 1820. Rocking chair: Sybil Bingham J., June 22, 1820.

39 Cradle-swing: Maria Loomis J., Jan. 25, 1821. Chinese table: Thurston, p. 39. Rocker: Thurston, p. 54. Timber for cradle: Mercy Whitney J., Aug. 28, 1820. Bureau: Mercy Whitney J., May 10, 1831. Cupboard: LT to Levi Chamberlain, July 25, 1829, MLC.

40 Bonnets: Thurston, p. 112. Unfashionable dresses: Laura Fish Judd, *Honolulu*, p. 5. Clothing recommendations: DC to J. Evarts, Oct. 6, 1820, MLC-ts, vol. 1.

41 "This ransomed land": SB, "have found that" [fragment], n.d. [Sept. 1821], BP, Box 3.

42 "Hour of anguish": SB-PJ, Sept. 14, Oct. 22, 1820. "Sublunary world": SB to "My dear Sisters Anna, Lucy, Sophia & Abby," Aug. 17, 1820, BP, Box 3. "*He will do right*": SB to Mrs. Bates, Oct. 8, 1820, BP, Box 3.

43 Imagination: SB-PJ, Oct. 22, 1820. Sybil's fear was not unusual, though only two of the mission wives died in childbirth: Grimshaw, *Paths of Duty*, p. 97. For background on nineteenth-century childbirth prac-

tices (and the increasing reliance on male doctors rather than midwives), see Degler, pp. 55–66.

44 "A tender subject . . . exercised": SB to LT, Oct. 31, 1820, BP, Box 3.

45 Birth of Sophia: TJ, Nov. 9, 1820; Elisha Loomis J., Nov. 14, 1820; DC to J. Evarts, Nov. 10, 1820, MLC-ts, vol. 1.

46 Births: Samuel Whitney J., Oct. 20, Dec. 22, 1820; Thurston, p. 61; AT to Deacon Abner Goodale, Oct. 8, 1821, MLC; see also *Missionary Album.* Of the 76 women missionaries, 70 bore children; "Thirty-eight fertile women who lived in the islands until at least forty-four years of age or older bore a total of two hundred and fifty babies": (Grimshaw, *Paths of Duty,* p. 89). For further discussion of gynecological problems, see pp. 89–99.

47 "Most lovely objects": Maria Loomis J., Oct. 20, 1820. "Darling child": SB to Mrs. Bates, April 1821, BP, Box 3. "Most remarkable children": SB to "Beloved Sisters Betsey, Laura & Fanny [Bingham]," Dec. 22, 1821, BP, Box 3. Maria Whitney's infancy: Mercy Whitney J., April 28, 1821.

48 "Missionary work" by children: Thurston, pp. 275–76. "Caressing . . . children," gifts to Sophia: TJ, Nov. 15, 1820. Babies in arms: Maria Loomis J., Feb. 6, 1821. "Rude attention": SB to Mrs. Bates, April 1821, BP, Box 3.

49 Names of babies: *Missionary Album;* Mercy Whitney J., April 24, April 28, 1821; later, "Tapoole" was spelled "Kapule"; "Tamoree" became "Kamualii."

50 "More than my divine Master will approve": Maria Loomis J., Sept. 6, 1820. "Unspeakable goodness": TJ, Nov. 9, 1820. "Not ours": LT to Deacon Abner Goodale & family, March 20, 1823, MLC. "Loaned of our Father": SB to "Beloved Sisters Betsey, Laura & Fanny [Bingham]," Dec. 22, 1821, BP, Box 3.

51 "Master's praise": SB to Sophia, draft, n.d., cont. July 29, 1821, BP, Box 3.

52 Training children: the nineteenth-century "cult of true womanhood" was also a "cult of motherhood": see Ryan, *Womanhood,* pp. 180 and 164–91 generally; Cott, p. 46, explains that "more than ever before in New England history, the care of children appeared to be mothers' sole work and the work of mothers alone." Eighteenth-century notions that the mother was responsible for the physical care alone (the father providing moral, intellectual, and religious guidance) gave way to an increased role for the mother. Lockean ideas also contributed to emphasis on the "formative importance of early childhood": see Ryan, *Womanhood,* pp. 84, 86, and 84–94 generally. Degler speaks (pp. 72, 66–85) of the "century of the child"; Epstein (pp. 76–77) of new

attitudes toward motherhood as a woman's most important responsibility, and of the "almost sacred nature of the mother-child relationship." The emphasis was on metaphoric as well as literal motherhood. "In short," says Ryan in *Womanhood*, p. 145, "ante-bellum culture placed woman on a pedestal labeled 'mother of civilization.'"

53 "Little lambs," "how to do wisely myself," "upbraid not": SB to "Beloved Sisters Betsey, Laura, & Fanny [Bingham]," Dec. 27, 1822, BP, Box 3. "Missionary work": Lucy Thurston, "Journal cont.," Nov. 9, 1821, MLC. "Our faithfulness": Mercy Whitney J., April 28, 1821.

54 "A child dressed . . . huts": Thurston, p. 63.

55 "Heart . . . deformity": Daniel Chamberlain, "Journal Kept on Board the Brig Pearle," March 31, 1823; this notion of innate depravity, though common to Calvinistic faiths of the nineteenth century, goes against a trend toward notions of childhood innocence: Epstein, pp. 81–85; also Cott, p. 87; Degler, pp. 66–69.

56 "Immortals": SB to Sister M[argaret], Sept. 10, [1821], [pp. 3–4 of draft that begins as a letter to Mrs. Johns], BP, Box 3. "Up and doing": Mercy Whitney J., July 9, 1820. "Instructing . . . youth": J., July 22, 1821.

57 "Varieties of labor": SB to Sister M[argaret], Sept. 10, [1821], [pp. 3–4 of draft that begins as a letter to Mrs. Johns], BP, Box 3. "Necessary to be performed": Sybil Bingham J., Dec. 15, 1821.

58 Schoolteaching arrangements: Maria Loomis J., Jan. 15, 1821.

59 Sybil's health: SB to "Dear & Affectionate Friend," May 18, 1821, BP, Box 3. "Place . . . near my arms": Sybil Bingham J., Jan. 27, 1821. "My appropriate work": J., Feb. 13, 1821. "Than to change frequently": Mercy Whitney J., Aug. 13, 1821.

60 Fathers' help: Thurston, p. 62. "Cumberer": this was the Goodrich family; see *Paths of Duty*, p. 136. "These children": Sybil Bingham J., April 13, 1822. Men helped, argues Grimshaw, out of "kindness," not "duty."

61 Frustration . . . gender: Myres makes this point (p. 100): "women who went west as missionary wives viewed themselves . . . as missionaries first and as wives second"; Faragher comments (p. 244n): "feminine ideology, while a factor, was not as important as the social facts of pioneer wifery." My point is that for missionary women, religious convictions took precedence over "feminine ideology."

62 Mission life as atavistic: see summaries of eighteenth-century life in books on women's history: Hewitt's "Introduction" to *Women's Activism;* Cott's summary of preindustrial patterns (p. 59); Ryan's description in *Womanhood*, pp. 30–31, of the "self-sufficient agrarian household where male and female labor commingled in the single productive enterprise that insured survival." An interesting comparison

can be made between mission life and various utopian, communal experiments: see Ryan's accounts of the Shakers and the Oneida community in *Womanhood,* pp. 174–79.

63 Lack of male-female antagonism: this subject has received much attention. The purpose of Epstein's book, *Politics of Domesticity,* is to trace "women's consciousness of difference from, and antagonism to men" as seen in religious activities (p. 1); but many sources of conflict, such as male resistance to religion and a sense that male and female roles "repudiated the other's values" (p. 62), do not seem to me to occur in mission life. Carroll Smith-Rosenberg in "Beauty, the Beast, and the Militant Woman: A Case Study in Sex Roles and Social Stress in Jacksonian America," finds "antimale resentment and anger" in the rhetoric of members of the New York Moral Reform Society (*Disorderly Conduct,* p. 126), but, again, this was a wholly female group, whereas men and women were united as reformers in Hawaii. Ryan, however, in "The Power of Women's Networks," found that members of the Utica, N.Y., Moral Reform Society were "enthusiastic exponents" of the stereotype of the "true woman" and did not enter reform work out of discontent with their own "sphere" or resentment against men (p. 67). This description seems to me closer to the experience of missionary wives. Nancy Woloch, pp. 120–25, summarizes the relationship between Protestant ministers and middle-class women parishioners in a way that describes missionary couples: they were both "outsiders" in a society that strove for wealth and "allies who strove for morality in a competitive world."

64 "Female hands and minds . . . *his work*": SB to "Beloved Sisters [Lucy and Sophia Moseley]," Dec. 27, 1822, BP, Box 3.

65 "*Native* help": Lucy Thurston, "Journal cont.," June 15, 1821, MLC. "Thus far been trained": Mercy Whitney J., Aug. 13, 1821; see also Grimshaw on servants, *Paths of Duty* pp. 104–5, 111–13.

66 Sybil ill, rainstorm: Sybil Bingham J., Feb. 17, 1821. "Consumption": Thurston, p. 62. Healthy babies: Mercy Whitney J., April 28, 1821; SB to Mrs. Bates, April 1821, BP, Box 3. Fleas: Samuel Whitney J., Dec. 10, 1820. Levi's teething and Maria's dysentery: see respective J.

67 "Orphan": Maria Loomis J., May 7, 1821. Situation in mid-June: Lucy Thurston, "Journal cont.," June 15, 1821, MLC.

68 Sybil "quite ill": Maria Loomis J., June 22, 1821; see also TJ, June 21, 1821. Baby dead: TJ, June 29, 1821. For July events, see TJ.

69 Kauai in 1822 . . . "all his benefits": Sybil Bingham J., March 23, 1822.

70 Frame house: "Chronological List of Dates" summarizes journal entries, Frost Report, HMCS; Sybil Bingham J., Oct. 3, 1822. Rain: Maria Loomis J., Nov. 23, 1821.

71 "Mercy of God": Sybil Bingham J., Feb. 27, 1821. "As thy day": Maria Loomis J., June 18, 1821. "Joy in the morning": NR to Rev. Shubard Bartlett, March 31, 1820, cont. July 3, 1820, MLC. "More than I can bear": SB to [her sister] Lucy, [n.d.] 1821, BP, Box 3.

72 "Long table": SB, "feelings of my present state" [fragment], n.d. [1823], BP, Box 3; see also J., Oct. 3, 1822.

73 Maria Loomis's "strength unequal": J., Nov. 9, 1822. Dividing the "long table": Sybil Bingham, journal fragment, [Nov.] 6, 8, 9, [1822], BP, Box 2. "Own little family": SB to "Beloved Sisters," Dec. 27, 1822, BP, Box 3; Maria Loomis J., Nov. 9, 1822.

74 Poem: "Long Table of the Mission," HMCS offprint. "Self-denial": Bingham, *Residence*, p. 109. Not "perfectly happy": ML to Mrs. Bishop, Dec. 29, 1823; see Forbes Research Notes, vol. 4, p. 763–64, HMCS.

75 Sewing: Maria Loomis J., June 18, 1821: Sept. 1, 1822. "Plain gong": Sybil Bingham J., Oct. 5, 1822.

76 Not expect much: Maria Loomis J., April 15, 1822. "Copy it off": Maria Loomis J., March 11, 1823. "Neglect my pen": Mercy Whitney J., March 10, 1821. "How . . . filled": SB to Mrs. Bates, April 1821, BP, Box 3. "No *willing neglect*": SB to "Beloved Sisters Betsey, Laura, & Fanny [Bingham]," Dec. 22, 1821, BP, Box 3.

77 "Well enough alone": Maria Loomis J., Aug. 8, 1822. Constitution "injured": J., Aug. 22, 1822.

78 "Sad . . . frightful mountains": Maria Loomis J., Oct. 3, 1822. "Without getting *Aloha*": MW to Mrs. Mary Clark, Oct. 1830, MLC.

79 Spiritual intensity, "sweet sabbaths": Mercy Whitney J., March 30, 1821. "Quite the reverse": Mercy Whitney J., Aug. 6, 1821. This loss of "high religious fervour" was typical: Grimshaw, "Paths of Duty," p. 276; Myres also confirms (p. 103) that many missionary women "came to question the vitality of their faith."

80 "These lower shores," "do I well . . . concerned?": SB to "Dear Sister Lucy [Whiting]," Jan. 1824, BP, Box 3; see also Sybil Bingham J., Feb. 16, 1823. "In their ignorance and wretchedness": Mercy Whitney J., Aug. 6, 1821

81 Cup of tea: SB to "Beloved Sisters Betsey, Laura, & Fanny [Bingham]," Dec. 27, 1822, BP, Box 3. "Fountain": Sybil Bingham J., June 16, 1827.

Chapter 4: The Good Fight

1 Likelike's death: SB to "Dear Sister Margaret," March 2, 1821, BP, Box 3; Maria Loomis J., March 4, 1821.

2 "Stranger": Sybil Bingham J., Oct. 6, 1822.

3 Descendants: see, for example, "Unveiling Ceremonies in Memory of

the Pioneer Missionary Rev. Hiram Bingham," *The Friend,* May 1905; eulogies for Lucy and Asa Thurston, in Thurston, pp. 185–95; 297–307; Walter F. Frear, "A Century of Achievement," in *The Centennial Book,* pp. 5–15; and his "*Anti-Missionary Criticism with Reference to Hawaii,*" originally read before the Honolulu Social Science Association, Jan. 7, 1935, pp. 3–33.

4 "Continue in . . . sin": Maria Loomis J. "Darling lusts": Elisha Loomis J., Feb. 16, 1821. Grimshaw, "Paths of Duty," pp. 315–30, concludes that the women rejected the Hawaiians as "strange heathens" and the other foreigners as "heathen strangers"; see also "Devoted Missionaries" in *Paths of Duty,* pp. 154–78.

5 Sybil "happy" with Hiram: SB to Sophia, draft, n.d., cont. July 29, 1821, BP, Box 3.

6 "Domestic solicitude": SB to "My Dear Sister Nancy [Ruggles]," Dec. 16, 1827, BP, Box 3.

7 Harmonious relationships: "sincerely loved you": ML to NR, Feb. 17, [1822], MLC; "good sisters": Maria Loomis J., Dec. 13, 1821; "worthy of imitation": Mercy Whitney J., Oct. 28, 1823. The language of "love" was typical among nineteenth-century women: for a positive assessment, see Carroll Smith-Rosenberg, "The Female World of Love and Ritual: Relations Between Women in Nineteenth-Century America," in *Disorderly Conduct,* pp. 33–76. Affection among mission "family" members extended to "brothers" as well as "sisters"; see Daniel Chamberlain's praise of Sybil Bingham in J., Nov. 21, Dec. 1, 1820.

8 "This side Heaven": SR to "Sisters," Nov. 6, 1820, MLC. "Twin Samuels": MW to "Dear Sister Dow," Dec. 20, 1832, MLC.

9 "Different teachers": SB to Sophia, draft, n.d., cont. July 29, 1821, BP, Box 3.

10 "Quiet residence": TJ, Dec. 31, 1820. "None . . . slept much": Maria Loomis J., Jan. 16, 1820. Thessalonians: TJ, Jan. 21, 1821. Suffering of Samuel R.: Samuel Whitney J., Jan. 21, 1821. "New England with tears": Samuel Whitney J., June 4, 1821.

11 Prolix letter: this is the "Holman Affair Report," HMCS. Feb. 16, 1821, assembly: Maria Loomis J., Feb. 16, 1821; Sybil Bingham J., Feb. 16, 1821.

12 "Cannot say . . . sorry": Maria Loomis J., Oct. 2, 1821; see also Mercy Whitney J., Dec. 31, 1822.

13 "*This wicked heart*": SB-PJ, Jan. 26, 1821. "Sinner saved by grace": SB-PJ, July 5, 1821. "Coming . . . day of GOD": SB to Sophia, draft, n.d., cont. July 29, 1821, BP, Box 3.

14 Christ's injunction . . . rare: see NR's untypical comment on the "mission's enemies" to Mr. and Mrs. Bartlett: "O may our hearts reply, 'Fa-

ther forgive them for they know not what they do,'" Feb. 21, 1828, MLC.

15 "No more good times": Kamakau, *Ruling Chiefs,* p. 251. Advisors of Liholiho skeptical: Bingham, *Residence,* p. 110. "Cut his soul out": reported in TJ, April 4, 1821. "Clique": Thurston, p. 58.

16 "Links . . . fatherland": Thurston, p. 46. Soap: Sybil Bingham J., Aug. 21, 1821 [fragment begins Jan. 25, 1821]. Gifts recorded in journal: TJ, Nov. 2, 1820. Captains circulate list: Maria Loomis J., April 20, 1821.

17 "Bad example . . . white": Daniel Chamberlain J. "Runaway sailors": Maria Loomis J., Sept. 1, 1822. "Sodom": Sybil Bingham J., Dec. 17, 1821.

18 Rum: Kamakau, *Ruling Chiefs* p. 193; *Awa:* Samuel Kamakau, *The Works of the People of Old,* pp. 41–44. "Bathed in it": Kamakau, *Ruling Chiefs,* p. 250.

19 Liholiho and rum: for a favorable estimate of Liholiho, see Kuykendall, p. 71. Debts of king: Kamakau, *Ruling Chiefs,* p. 251. Ships bought: Kamakau, *Ruling Chiefs,* p. 251; Kuykendall, p. 91.

20 Sandalwood trade: Kuykendall, pp. 90–92, and appendix D, pp. 434–36; Bradley, pp. 66–70.

21 King's drinking habits: SB to "Uncle," draft, Sept. 17, 1821, BP, Box 3. Entry into Honolulu . . . "nerveless hand": TJ, Feb. 4, 1821. Kalanimoku refuses breakfast: Sybil Bingham J., Feb. 8, 1821; TJ, Feb. 7, 1821. Sober days: Smith, p. 71. Drink with Capt. Turner: TJ, Sept. 30, 1821.

22 Efforts at reform: TJ, April 15, 1821. "So sunk . . . vice": SB to "Uncle," draft, Sept. 17, 1821, BP, Box 3. Liholiho's illness: Sybil Bingham J., March 1, 1822; Bingham, *Residence,* p. 159. "Picking up straws": Maria Loomis J., March 3, 1822. "Five more years": Kamakau, *Ruling Chiefs,* p. 255; Bingham, *Residence,* p. 179.

23 "Access . . . call for thee": SB to "Uncle," draft, Sept. 17, 1821, BP, Box 3. Excuses from *alii:* Bingham, *Residence,* pp. 56–57.

24 Resistance from *haoles:* Sybil Bingham J., Dec. 16, 1821; Mercy Whitney J., Feb. 2, 1822. Cellar guns: Maria Loomis J., June 29, 1821. Capt. Davis and Hannah Holmes: Maria Loomis J., Sept. 13, 1821; Head in king's lap: Maria Loomis J., March 24, 1822. "Shall not soon forget": Mercy Whitney J., June 10, 1823 (she is remembering 1822). "Threatening to set fire": Elisha Loomis J., Sept. 20, 1821.

25 Treatment of Holmans criticized: TJ, Oct. 1, Oct. 10, 1821.

26 "Temporary wives": Elisha Loomis J., Aug. 27, 1821. Whaling begins: Kuykendall, p. 93. Whitney welcomes Capt. Masters: J., June 17, 1821.

27 Captain "E"'s hypocrisy: Thurston, p. 67 [this occurred in 1825, not 1822, as Thurston states; Lucy refers to a daughter of "five summers," who would be Sophia Bingham).

28 "Shout like victory": SB to [HB's] "Honored & Beloved Parents," [n.d.] 16, 1822, BP, Box 3.
29 Objections to visit to Tahiti: TJ, July 28, 1821.
30 Difficulty in reaching Kauai: Sybil Bingham J.; see also Mercy Whitney J., Aug. 28, 1822. "Fullest evidence": March 5, 1822.
31 Word of Jesus: TJ, July 28, 1821. Amputation: TJ, Sept. 26, 1820. Rumors about ammunition: Maria Loomis J., May 18, 1821; in July 1820, a directive expelled all foreigners not "belonging" to a chief, except for missionaries: Bingham, *Residence,* pp. 112–13.
32 Earlier frame buildings: Charles Peterson, "Pioneer Prefabs in Honolulu," *HJH* 5 (1971): 24–38. Permission from Liholiho to build: Sybil Bingham J., Feb. 6, 1821; Maria Loomis J., Feb. 5, 1821; TJ, Feb. 5, 1821; Thurston, pp. 57–58; Bingham, *Residence,* pp. 126–27. There are conflicting accounts of receiving permission to build. TJ and the Maria Loomis J. say that the king consented on Feb. 5 after Hiram Bingham made the argument about the women's health. Sybil puts the date at Feb. 5 as well, but sidesteps the identity of the pleader by using the passive voice: "on being told the women must suffer." Bingham's book speaks of an initial refusal, encouragement by Kalanimoku to ask again, and subsequent consent. The king did forbid the actual erecting of the house until he returned from an intended visit to Maui. But Kalanimoku in the meantime, on April 20, allowed them to start building. Lucy Thurston puts her request a few days earlier than the formal announcement on April 20. Her memory decades later may be conflating the dates of February and April, or her secretive excursion may have been redundant.
33 Women secured a "footing": Thurston, p. 69.
34 "All dwelt . . . in peace": Kamakau, *Ruling Chiefs,* p. 247.
35 Sports: Malo, pp. 214–34.
36 Practicing the hula: Sybil Bingham J., Feb. 15, 1821. "Peculiar situation": TJ, Jan. 14–15, 1821. Sermon and general account: Elisha & Maria Loomis J., Jan. 14–15, 1821.
37 *Akua* and idolatry: TJ, Dec. 20, 1820.
38 Maria Loomis watched hula: J., Jan. 30, 1821. "Surrounded by the heathen": Maria Loomis J., Feb. 22, 1821.
39 "Folly": Sybil Bingham J., Feb. 15, 1821. "Transitory trifles": TJ, Feb. 22, 1821. "Lasciviousness": Bingham, *Residence,* pp. 123–25. The insistence on "purity" for New England's "true woman" provides an obvious contrast to Hawaiian norms: once again, the efforts in Hawaii at moral reform were not the special province of women (as on the mainland) but were shared by both sexes.
40 Other foreigners and hula: see Dorothy Barrere, Mary Pukui, and Marion Kelly, *Hula: Historical Perspectives* (hereafter *Hula*). I am in-

debted to this book generally for nonmissionary accounts of the hula: Chamisso quoted, p. 23; Vancouver, p. 21; Menzies, p. 19.

41 Hula training: Mary Pukui, "The Hula, Hawaii's Own Dance," in *Hula*, pp. 70–73. Subjects for hula: Kamakau, *Ruling Chiefs*, p. 240.

42 "Never beat up for the taboos": TJ, Dec. 20, 1820. Keeping the "*laka*": TJ, Dec. 20, 1820; Feb. 20, 1821.

43 Hula as act of worship: see *Hula*, p. 2—this was the opinion of Nathaniel Emerson, *Unwritten Literature of Hawaii* (Charles E. Tuttle Co., 1982 [1909]). "Lying vanity": TJ, Dec. 20, 1820. "All in play": Maria Loomis J., Feb. 20–22, 1821. "Stumps" and questions: TJ, Feb. 22, 1821. "*We will dance*": TJ, March 10, 1821.

44 Likelike's death: TJ, March 4, 1821.

45 "Afraid to stay . . . house": Maria Loomis J., Jan. 10, 1822. Expressions of "regard": Maria Loomis J., March 5, 1821. Alum: TJ, March 5, 1821.

46 Laughter: TJ, March 5, 1821; Mercy Whitney J., Nov. 20, 1823. Hawaiian grieving: see Mary Kawena Pukui, E. W. Haertig, and Catherine Lee, *Nana I Ke Kumu* (*Look to the Source*), vol. 1:132–48, for an excellent explanation of Hawaiian practices (hereafter *Nana*, vol. 1).

47 Funeral sermon: TJ, March 10–11, 1821; Maria Loomis J., March 11, 1821.

48 Son of Man cometh: this is a common reflection—see Maria Loomis J., June 29, July 1, 1821. "Future state of rewards": Mercy Whitney J., Aug. 29, 1821. "Funeral of George Kaumualii's child: Mercy Whitney J. "Very bad": Samuel Whitney J., June 15, 1821.

49 "First *we know*": Maria Loomis J., Jan. 11, 1822. "Manner of civilized people": Maria Loomis J. "Usually . . . at night": Mercy Whitney J., Dec. 8, 1823. Thomas Hopu's father: Thurston, pp. 78–79.

50 "Unwillingness to return": Mercy Whitney J., Feb. 13, 1822. Numbers diminished: Sybil Bingham J., Dec. 14, 1821; Maria Loomis J., Sept. 14, March 3, 1821. "Sorry by and by": Sybil Bingham J., March 3, 1821. "Lost children": Sybil Bingham J., Dec. 29, 1821.

51 "Decoyed": Maria Loomis J., Sept. 1, 1822. "Aversion to labor": Sybil Bingham J., March 3, 1821. "Impatience of restraint": Maria Loomis J., March 3, 1821. "Disgraceful . . . younger part of them": Maria Loomis J., Feb. 27, 1821. "Work . . . disgraceful": Elisha Loomis J., Feb. 19, 1821. Isaac Lewis and mending clothes: Elisha Loomis J., Aug. 12, 1821. Hawaiian division of labor between sexes: mission women never reconsidered their own division of labor, confirmation of how thoroughly they had internalized the prescription of "domesticity" for "true" womanhood, and of the distance they put between themselves and the Hawaiians. Though Mr. Harwood was "prevailed upon" to help during the crisis of the long table, this was pioneer flexibility, not "going native."

52 Disciplining Charlotte: Elisha Loomis J., May 9, 1821. Flogging: Maria Loomis J. and Elisha Loomis J., Feb. 5, 1821. Little Talks: Maria Loomis J., Feb. 6–7, 1822; Mercy Whitney J., Aug. 20, 1823.

53 "My dear William": SB to William Beals, Aug. 29, 1822, MLC. "Am your child": Sybil Bingham J., Oct. 9, 1822. "Little boy Eli": Mercy Whitney J., Aug. 13, 1821. "Sarah": Maria Loomis J., March 3, 1821. Charlotte Holmes: Elisha Loomis J., May 9, 1821.

54 Children "brought up in their own ways": Elisha Loomis J., May 9, 1821. For similar comments, see SB to the Maternal Association in Hartford, Oct. 26, 1836, BP, Box 2: "The truth is they [parents] have never learned how to govern. There is lamentable deficiency in family government"; and MW, commenting on her young *alii* pupil, "Moses," as "ruined, I fear, by excessive indulgence": to NR, June 30, 1837, MLC. Pupils usually not children: Kamakau, *Ruling Chiefs,* p. 102; Kuykendall, pp. 107–8. Not "tamed": Judd, p. 55. For background on nineteenth-century childrearing practices, see "Inducting Children Into the Social Order," in Degler, pp. 86–110.

55 *Luhi, hanai: Nana,* vol. 1:49–50.

56 Giving away children: Mercy Whitney J., Nov. 25, 1821; Laura Judd (p. 46) thought this a "most unnatural state policy"; Sheldon Dibble, *History,* p. 141, thought the practice showed "how confused, indistinct, and inadequate the views of the heathen are on moral subjects." "*Hiapo: Nana,* vol. 1:51–53. Prostitution: Mary Kawena Pukui, E. W. Haertig, and Catherine Lee, *Nana I Ke Kumu* (*Look to the Source*), vol. 2: p. 92 (hereafter *Nana,* vol. 2).

57 Request for Thurston child: Thurston, pp. 88–89.

58 Sexual explicitness, Maria getting hold of language: Mercy Whitney J., May 22, 1823. "Lewd & vulgar": Mercy Whitney J., June 16, 1827; see also Sybil Bingham J., May 9, 1822.

59 Hawaiian sexuality: *Nana,* vol. 2:92; Malo, pp. 214–17. High *mana* of foreigners: *Nana,* vol. 2:91–92.

60 Infanticide: missionary references abound—see Mercy Whitney J., Oct. 24, 1828; Samuel Whitney J., April 30, 1824; SB to Members of the Maternal Association, March 16, 1837, BP, Box 3; SB to Mrs. Stewart, Jan. 1, 1830, BP, Box 3; Judd, p. 29; William Ellis, *A Narrative of a Tour Through Hawaii [in 1823],* pp. 243–48. For a brief account by an anthropologist, see Goldman, pp. 564–65; for accounts by Hawaiians, see Kamakau, *Ruling Chiefs,* pp. 233–34 and the explanation of Mary Pukui in *Nana,* vol. 1:116–17, 120–21. Infants to sharks: Sybil Bingham J., Feb. 12, 1821. Modern apologists for Hawaiian culture include Haunani-Kay Trask, "Scholars Revise History to Depict True Hawaiian Past: Western Interpretation Biased, Flawed," in *Year of the Hawaiian 1887–1987,* pp. 8–9, and David Stannard, who

argues (pp. 63–64) that "there is not a *single* piece of credible evidence that infanticide existed on a significant scale as a cultural practice in pre-*haole* Hawai'i."

61 Head-shaving: Maria and Elisha Loomis J., Nov. 27, 1820. Thefts: Maria Loomis J., March 23, 1822.

62 Praying to death: Dibble, pp. 76–78; for his censorious account of Hawaiian "ignorance" and missionary efforts to correct it, see pp. 131–49. "Days in trifling": TJ, April 12, 1821. Sunday in Waikiki: Sybil Bingham J., Aug. 9, 1822. "Adoption of our costume": Bingham, *Residence,* p. 137.

63 Kamamalu and sewing button: SB to "Dearly beloved friends," [n.d.], 1821, BP, Box 3.

64 "Servant to all": Sybil Bingham J., March 14, 1822; Bingham, *Residence,* p. 170.

65 Kaahumanu's reputation as haughty: Maria Loomis J., Jan. 10, 1822; SB to "Misses Bingham," Dec. 22, 1821, BP, Box 3; Bingham, *Residence,* p. 164. Handsome: Kamakau, *Ruling Chiefs,* p. 311 and pp. 311–13 generally; see also Jane Silverman, *Kaahumanu, Molder of Change,* pp. 78, 83, and 73–84 generally. Kaahumanu's marriage to Kaumualii, pp. 75–78; Charles Stewart remarks on the "shade of melancholy" about Kaumualii, the "royal captive" in Honolulu, in *Journal of a Residence in the Sandwich Islands,* p. 291.

66 Kaahumanu's illness: Sybil Bingham J., Dec. 22, 1821; Bingham, *Residence,* pp. 149–51.

67 Kaahumanu's tours to destroy idols: Silverman, *Kaahumanu,* pp. 79–80; Bingham, *Residence,* p. 162.

68 Thirty garments: Mercy Whitney J., Dec. 31, 1822. "Favorite clothing": Maria Loomis J., April 2, 1822. "Bonnets": Sybil Bingham J., Oct. 4, 1822; Kaahumanu's handkerchief as "rod of correction": Lydia Bingham Coan, *A Brief Sketch,* pp. 20–21.

69 Christian's "privilege": Sybil Bingham J., March 9, 1823. "Laboring directly": SB to "Dearly beloved friends," [n.d.], 1821, BP, Box 3. "Hope it is for them": Sybil Bingham J., Feb. 16, 1823.

70 "Direct efforts for their good": Sybil Bingham J., Feb. 16, 1823.

71 Plates in Maria's Bible: Maria Loomis J., Feb. 17, 1821. "Inactivity" and walks with Asa: Lucy Thurston, "Journal cont.," Aug. 9, 1822, MLC. "Keeps pretty near": Maria Loomis J., Feb. 3, 1823.

72 "Hardly worth mentioning": SB to "Dearly beloved friends," [n.d.], 1821, BP, Box 3. Feather bed: Maria Loomis J., April 4, 1821. "Little notes": Sybil Bingham J., Aug. 10, 1822.

73 "Very great patience": Maria Loomis J., June 15, 1821. "Entertain our royal guests": Sybil Bingham J., Jan. 1, 1822. "Confess themselves ignorant": Mercy Whitney J., March 8, 1823.

74 Typical, hectic days, "observe and imitate," "am *still*," "multitudes of souls": Sybil Bingham J., Feb. 11–15, 1823.

75 "Slaves of ignorance and sin": SB to "Misses Bingham," Dec. 22, 1821, BP, Box 3.

76 Printing: Bingham, *Residence*, p. 160; for a good summary, see the pamphlet by A. Grove Day and A. Loomis, *Ka Pa'i Palapala, Early Printing in Hawaii.* Description of contents: Daws, *Shoal of Time*, pp. 8–9. 500 copies: Elisha Loomis J., Feb. 26, 1822. "40 missionaries": Elisha Loomis J., Jan. 30, 1822.

77 Sybil's twenty-five scholars: J. Five Hundred: Bingham, *Residence*, p. 160. Chanting: *Nana*, vol. 2:58. Statistics on *Pi-a-pa:* Kuykendall, pp. 106–7.

78 Ellis visit, "smile upon the mission": Sybil Bingham J., Oct. 3, 1822; Bingham, *Residence*, p. 161. Preaching in Hawaiian: Bingham gives Aug. 4 as the date in *Residence*, p. 163; Elisha Loomis J. gives Aug. 6; Maria Loomis J. gives Sept. 1, 1822.

79 "Shaking of dry bones": Lucy Thurston, "Journal cont.," Aug. 9, 1822, MLC. "Day . . . reality": Sybil Bingham J., Aug. 9, 1822. "New era": Maria Loomis J., Sept. 1, 1822.

80 Cox's dream: Bingham, *Residence*, p. 163. New support for learning: see Sybil Bingham J., Aug. 9, 1822; Maria Loomis J., Sept. 1, 1822; Bingham, *Residence*, pp. 162–65. Kaahumanu's reading: there is some confusion about who taught her. Hiram's account refers to himself (though Sybil was with him); the implied day is Saturday. Sybil's journal of Aug. 9, 1822, refers to herself as the teacher, giving the day as Tuesday: Bingham, *Residence*, pp. 164–65; Silverman, *Kaahumanu*, p. 82.

81 William Beals, "so trifling": Sybil Bingham J., Aug. 9, 1822. Kaahumanu's letter from Kauai: Bingham, *Residence*, p. 172.

82 "Mite of labor . . . praise him": Sybil Bingham, J., Aug. 9, 1822.

83 "Quickening powers": SB to Mrs. Bates, March 11, 1823, BP, Box 3; for a similar description see Sybil Bingham J., Feb. 15, 1823.

Chapter 5: Children of Light

1 Mission house: see "Chronological List of Dates" and "Evolution of Frame House," in Frost Report, HMCS. The Forbes Research Notes contain excerpts from missionary journals and diaries: see "Frame House," vol. 4:556–687, HMCS. Dust: Judd, p. 26; Sereno Edwards Bishop, *Reminiscences of Old Hawaii*, pp. 34–36, remembered that "there were scarcely any trees in the town" and that "mission dooryards were almost devoid of vegetation" in the 1830s. 1835 schoolhouse: *Judd Fragments* II, p. 92, HMCS.

2 Occupants of frame house: see "Frame House Occupants," in Forbes

Research Notes, vol. 5:790, HMCS. Sybil's bedroom: J., Oct. 6, 1822.

3 "Should be recalled": J., Oct. 6, 1822. Death of Parsons at "hour unlooked for": SB to [her sister] Lucy, Sept. 14, 1826, BP, Box 2. "Redeemer leave me not": SB-PJ, Dec. 31, 1822. "Termination": SB to "Beloved Sisters," Jan. 28, 1823, BP, Box 3. Burial: SB to Mrs. Bates, March 11, 1823, BP, Box 3.

4 "Condescension": SB to Mrs. Bates, March 11, 1823, BP, Box 3. Dying gaze: SB to "My dear sister," Nov. 23, 1826, BP, Box 3. "Glories," "Saviour's precious love": SB to "Beloved Sisters," Jan. 28, 1823, BP, Box 3.

5 "Maternal love wept": SB to Mrs. Bates, March 11, 1823, BP, Box 3. Parallel phrases: SB to "Beloved Sisters," Jan. 28, 1823, BP, Box 3; see also SB to "My dear Miss Battelle," Feb. 24, 1823, BP, Box 3. Grimshaw, "Paths of Duty," p. 479, counts thirty-six mission children who died (usually under the age of two); see also *Paths of Duty*, p. 140.

6 Amanda Loomis's illness: Maria Loomis J., Feb. 29, 1823.

7 Samuel Whitney's "death-like countenance": Mercy Whitney J., July 4, 1823. "Border . . . grave": MW to "Sr. Chamberlain," Sept. 20, 1830, MLC. Samuel's eyes: Mercy Whitney J., July 22, 1822. Extracting teeth: Mercy Whitney J., July 4, 1823.

8 Whitneys' situation in Waimea: Mercy Whitney J., Aug. 11, Aug. 14, 1823. "Gloom over my mind": MW to NR, Jan. 19, 1824, MLC. "Cares & labors": MW to ML, Jan. 14, 1824, MLC. Mercy's loneliness was not unusual: "nearly half of the ordained ministers and their wives lived alone at stations," though most were located with one or two other couples; see Grimshaw, "Paths of Duty," p. 197.

9 "Preyed . . . upon her health": Maria Loomis J., Feb. 14, 1823. "Addition to our labor": Maria Loomis J., March 29, 1823.

10 Chamberlains leave: HB, AT, & EL to Jeremiah Evarts, March 20, 1823, MLC-ts, vol. 1. "Not continue long": Mercy Whitney J., July 22, 1822. Melons: Daniel Chamberlain J., June 19, 1820. Cornfields: TJ, Jan. 8, 1821. "No scope . . . agriculture": Daniel Tyerman & George Bennet, MLC-ts, vol. 1. "Lands . . . shifting": DC to J. Evarts, Nov. 11, 1822, MLC-ts, vol. 1. Jerusha had "no desire": Mercy Whitney J., July 22, 1822. "Moral death" for children, "Go home": LT to Deacon Abner Goodale & family, March 20, 1823, MLC. "Separating them from natives!": LT to Cousin William Goodell, Oct. 24, 1834, ABCFM-Hawaii. "Like parents": Mercy Whitney J., July 22, 1822. Refuse payment: J. Evarts to "Rev. Mssrs. Bingham, Thurston & their fellow laborers at the Sand. Islands," Oct. 11, 1823, ABCFM-HEA. Jerusha Chamberlain died in 1879: see *Missionary Album* and reference in *The Friend*, Nov. 1913.

11 Honolulu in 1823: Stewart, pp. 93–94. Palace, Stewart, p. 100.

Kaahumanu's house (another was built in 1824), Stewart, p. 311. William Ellis in his *Journal* put Honolulu's 1823 population at six to seven thousand (pp. 27–28); by 1825, James Macrae thought 6,000 an "underrated" figure: *With Lord Byron at the Sandwich Islands,* p. 21. Seventeen grogshops: Bradley, p. 88. "Fine appearance": Maria Loomis J., April 2, 1823; Elisha Loomis J., March 29, 1823.

12 Arrival of second company, chiefs' dress: Stewart, pp. 97, 110, 102. Four hundred garments from China: Stewart, p. 136.

13 Clothing: Judd, pp. 4–5. Weddings: Judd, p. 14. "Much amusement": Judd, p. 5.

14 Estimated by exterior: Judd, p. 20.

15 "Taciturn" Kaahumanu and material for dresses: Judd, p. 33.

16 Fourth annual celebration: see Stewart, pp. 115–20; Bingham, *Residence,* pp. 183–86; SIJ, April 24, May 10, 1823. "Last day": Bingham dates the parade to May 8, SIJ to May 10.

17 Reinforcements, no children sent: Lucy Thurston, "Journal cont.," Nov. 20, 1822, MLC. "Lost all the energy": Maria Loomis J., April 25, 1823. Domestic arrangements and hired help: Maria Loomis J., April 28, 1823. "Identity of new missionaries: Bingham, *Residence,* pp. 186–89; *Missionary Album.* Betsey Stockton: Smith, p. 99; Bell, "Black Heritage," in *Unforgettable True Stories,* pp. 49–58.

18 Brethren's meetings: Maria Loomis J., May 23, 1823. "Like Martha": Maria Loomis J., April 15, 1822 (Williams version).

19 Men's tours: Bingham, *Residence,* p. 190; William Ellis wrote up the trip in his book *A narrative of a tour through Hawaii.*

20 Situation of women left behind, eleven children: SB to Mrs. Howell, Dec. 1823, BP, Box 3. Dust storm, Sybil's health poor, long table, "tired out" from labors: ML to NR, Aug. 11, 1823, MLC. "Part to perform": SB to Mr. and Mrs. Chamberlain, July 7, 1824, BP, Box 2.

21 Men preaching in Hawaiian: see Maria Loomis J., Feb. 3, 1821; Mercy Whitney J., March 16, 1823. Language study: ML to NR, Aug. 11, 1823, MLC; SB to "Dear Sister Lucy," Jan. 1824, BP, Box 3; SB to Mrs. Bates, April 9, 1823, BP, Box 3; see also Maria Loomis J., June 3, Sept. 15, 1823.

22 Men "debating": Maria Loomis J., Sept. 11, 1823. Discuss "hardships," women's labor: SIJ, Sept. 12, 1823. "Distress" of E. Bishop: Maria Loomis J., Sept. 30, 1823. New stations: Maria Loomis J., Oct. 11, 1823 (she identifies the Elys' station as Kaarakekua, Jan. 16, 1824). "Alone again": Maria Loomis J., Jan. 16, 1824.

23 Horsemen: Maria Loomis J., Jan. 5, 1824. "Should I be taken down": Maria Loomis J., Feb. 5, 1824. J. Evarts Bingham: Maria Loomis J., May 1, 1824.

24 "Bustling cares . . . less secular": SB to "Dear Sister Lucy [Whiting]," Jan. 1824, BP, Box 3.

25 "Quite refreshed": Mercy Whitney J., June 15, 1825. Cried at palm groves: Maria Loomis J., May 30, 1825.

26 "As if on land": Maria Loomis J., May 30, 1823. Eating not "fastidious": Thurston, p. 74. "The interview . . . servants about them": Mercy Whitney J., April 21, 1821. "Most despicable heathen": Mercy Whitney J., Aug. 8, 1823. "All else trifles": SB to "Dearly beloved friends," [n.d.], 1821, BP, Box 3.

27 "Cannot . . . hire a nurse": Maria Loomis J., Feb. 5, 1824. "Trained to habits of industry," "shake it off": Mercy Whitney J., July 3, 1825. "Could I let it go": SB to NR, Jan. 1, 1825, MLC. "Northern constitution": Thurston, p. 112.

28 Letters: references abound—see, for example, Sybil Bingham J., Oct. 18, 1822; SB to [daughter] Lucy, Nov. 25, 1835, BP, Box 3; SB to Mrs. Collins, [n.d.], 1829, BP, Box 2. Sybil Bingham J., Oct. 8, 1822.

29 Letters and journals in print: Mercy Whitney J., July 22, 1822 (also Dec. 31, 1822); Maria Loomis J., Dec. 15, 1821; SB to Lucy [Whiting], Oct. 9, 1832, BP, Box 3. "Unfits my mind for writing": Maria Loomis J., May 1, 1824.

30 "Zealous . . . surrounded": Maria Loomis J., April 29, 1824. Prepared for death: Mercy Whitney J.

31 Mission expanding: Bingham, *Residence*, p. 211. "Fellow laborers . . . strangers": Mercy Whitney J., June 1, 1826. "Arrived this spring": NR to Rev. and Mrs. Ebenezer Brown, June 5, 1833, MLC.

32 Voyages: MW to Mrs. Baldwin, July 5, 1831, MLC; Mercy Whitney J., July 16, 1828, April 16, 1838, June 3, 1851; Sybil Bingham J., March 16, 1822; Thurston, pp. 74–76; quotation p. 293; see also NR to Rev. and Mrs. Ebenezer Brown, June 5, 1833, MLC.

33 "Suitable qualifications . . . little community": SB to "Dear Sister Lucy [Whiting]," Jan. 1824, BP, Box 3. Resentment of Bingham: Char Miller, *Fathers and Sons*, pp. 48–50. Problems of rapport: see also unsigned memorandum of conversation between [Evarts] and Rev. William Ellis, April 25, 1825: ABCFM, vol. 8.5, no. 26. Differences played down: see, for example, Sereno Bishop's comment (pp. 56–57) that differences of opinion "never grew to bitterness" and that a "spirit of harmony" prevailed.

34 Keopuolani's baptism and death: see accounts by Bingham, *Residence*, pp. 193–95, 182; Kamakau, *Ruling Chiefs*, pp. 261–63; Stewart, pp. 211–25; Marjorie Sinclair, *Nahi'ena'ena: Sacred Daughter of Hawaii*, pp. 43–50; I am indebted to this book for accounts of Nahienaena throughout the next chapters.

35 "Died a Christian": Mercy Whitney J., Sept. 27, 1823. "Propriety . . . baptism": Maria Loomis J., Sept. 21, 1823. "First . . . convert": Kamakau, *Ruling Chiefs*, p. 262.

36 "Mother and friend," Liholiho's remarks: Maria Loomis J., Sept. 21, 1823.

37 "Invigorated courage": Bingham, *Residence*, p. 197. Kalanimoku's baptism "good or not," "duty": SIJ, Sept. 27, 1823. Requests came "repeatedly": SIJ, March 22, 1824. Kaahumanu's note, response quoted: SIJ, April 3, 1824. Though refusing to baptize interested adults, the missionaries readily baptized their own children. This goes back to Puritan covenant theory, which asserted that "children of regenerate Christians were born within the covenant. The rite of infant baptism . . . was called a 'seal' or pledge of participation in the covenant," and it was assumed that these infants would as adults "experience regeneration as a matter of course" (Persons, *American Minds*, p. 7). See Lucy Thurston's thought upon the birth of her daughter Persis: "God's covenant is with believers & their seed. This supports my mind, & encourages me to commit my precious babe to his faithful and almighty care" (Journal fragment, Nov. 20, 1822, MLC; see also LT to Deacon Abner Goodale & family, March 20, 1823, MLC). Despite their refusal to baptize quickly, the missionaries were still trying to dispense the "essential" truths of Christianity: see William Ellis's defense that in the early years he "never noticed anything contrary to the doctines generally held by the Evangelical portion of Christendom," and that the teaching stressed "the consequences of sin, the necessity of regeneration to salvation, and the love and power of God in providing the means for securing both" ("Appendix A," pp. 34–35, in Frear, *Anti-Missionary Criticism*).

38 Liholiho's lessons: SIJ, Aug. 27, 1822. "No attention to it": Kamakau, *Ruling Chiefs*, p. 255. Liquor bottle upside-down: Bingham, *Residence*, p. 180.

39 Liholiho's visit to London: there is an account of this in every history; see especially Kamakau, *Ruling Chiefs*, pp. 255–57; Bingham, *Residence*, pp. 202–4. "Special relationship" with England: see Kuykendall, pp. 41–42; Rhoda Hackler, "Alliance or Cession? Mission Letter from Kamehameha I to King George III of England Casts Light on 1794 Agreement," *HJH* 20 (1986): 1–12.

40 Government after Liholiho's departure: Kamakau, *Ruling Chiefs*, p. 258; Kuykendall, pp. 430–34, p. 78 (Kauikeouli's age).

41 New laws, "notices": Kuykendall, pp. 120–21. "Not drinking so much": Kamakau, *Ruling Chiefs*, p. 381. Crier proclaimed: see Kuykendall, p. 117 (and footnotes). Kalanimoku's "stirring address": SIJ, April 18,

1824. Laws proclaimed in Lahaina . . . "*palapala*": Kuykendall, p. 118; Smith, p. 111.

42 April 1824, quarterly examinations: Bingham, *Residence*, p. 214; SIJ, April 19, 1824.

43 Kaahumanu defies Pele: Bingham, *Residence*, p. 227. Church in Kaawaloa: Bingham, *Residence*, p. 211. Kaahumanu's house: SIJ, April 20, 1824. Other houses: Bingham, *Residence*, p. 226; SIJ, July 6, 1824.

44 New laws about marriage: see Robert Schmitt and Rose Strombel, "Marriage and Divorce in Hawaii Before 1870," *Hawaiian Historical Review* 2, no. 2 (Jan. 1966). Public ceremonies of *alii:* Jane Silverman, "To Marry Again," *HJH* 17 (1983): 65 and generally; Judith Gething, "Christianity and Coverture," *HJH* 11 (1977): 188–220.

45 "Too wicked yet": SIJ, April 15, 1824. Singing school: SIJ, May 20, 1824. New church of 1824: SIJ, July 17, 1824.

46 Boki charges one dollar: Daws, *Shoal of Time*, p. 76, Maria Loomis J., Oct. 1, 1823.

47 Council of chiefs in 1824: Sinclair, pp. 57–59; Elisha Loomis J., June 28, 1824 (Hiram Bingham was in Kauai that summer). "Probably true": Sinclair, p. 59. Two young adolescents: Nahienaena was probably born in 1815, Kauikeaouli in 1814 or 1813 (Sinclair, p. 23). Children separated in Honolulu and Lahaina: Sinclair, p. 55. Baby: Sinclair, p. 155.

48 Depopulation: MW to NR, April 5, 1825, MLC. "Some say . . . *palapala*": Sinclair, p. 57. Death of "Governor Cox": SIJ, March 22, 1824. Empty casket: Kamakau, *Ruling Chiefs*, p. 254.

49 Death of William Beals: SIJ, Feb. 16, 1824. Sexual activity: see Grimshaw, "Paths of Duty," pp. 172–74, citing Levi Chamberlain J., Feb. 16, 1824, and Clarissa Richards J., Feb. 19, 1824. "Royal favor": SB to "Bro. & Sister" [Whiting], March 8, 1824, BP, Box 2. "Loved . . . dear child": undated fragment [summer of 1824], BP, Box 3.

50 Death of Kaumualii: SB to Mrs. Collins, Aug. 16, 1824, BP, Box 3. Accusation against Stewart, "kill the *haoles*": SIJ, May 29, 1824; Stewart, p. 294.

51 "Die with affection": Bingham, *Residence*, p. 224. "Drunkenness . . . kept up": MW to Mrs. Bishop, Aug. 2, 1824, MLC. Situation in Kauai throughout this section: SB to Mrs. Collins, draft, Aug. 16, 1824, BP, Box 3. Meditating on death: MW to LT, Aug. 5, 1824, MLC.

52 Rebellion in Kauai: Bingham, *Residence*, pp. 234–45 generally; Stewart, pp. 312–21 generally; Kamakau's account (*Ruling Chiefs*, pp. 265–69) does not name George Kaumualii as a leader.

53 Women's ordeal and quotations: see SB to Mrs. Collins, draft, Aug. 16, 1824, BP, Box 3.

54 George Kaumualii's capture: Samuel Whitney J., Oct. 6, 1824. "Iron cable": Bingham, *Residence*, p. 245.

55 New teachings: Bingham, *Residence,* p. 243. Richards uneasy: Bingham, *Residence,* p. 238. "Live": Bingham, *Residence,* p. 239. "Preservation by God": Bingham, *Residence,* p. 245.

56 A hundred Hawaiians request baptism: Bingham, *Residence,* p. 268. Schools: Kamakau, *Ruling Chiefs,* p. 270. "Goodly number": Mercy Whitney J., May 26, 1825. "I love the *palapala*": Bingham, *Residence,* pp. 256–58. Read upside-down: Judd, p. 17.

57 Kapiolani and Pele: the story is told in many histories; quotations here are from Bingham, *Residence,* pp. 255–56.

58 Kaahumanu's changes: Mercy Whitney J., March 1, 1825 (Silverman, *Kaahumanu,* p. 78, credits Mercy with being the first of the missionaries to recognize Kaahumanu's political power in 1821); SIJ, Feb. 8, 1825; Silverman, *Kaahumanu,* p. 102. "Christian character": SIJ, Feb. 11, 1825. Trips: Silverman, *Kaahumanu,* p. 87. "New" Kaahumanu: Bingham, *Residence,* p. 271.

59 Return of Liholiho's body: Stewart, quoting Richards, pp. 338–39. "Touching scene . . . minute-guns": Stewart, pp. 340–41; see also Bingham, *Residence,* pp. 262–63.

60 Funeral: Stewart, pp. 348–49.

61 Requests for baptism in May: SIJ, May 31, 1825. Changed Kaahumanu: Mercy Whitney J., Nov. 16, 1825.

62 Attendance at 3,000: Bingham, *Residence,* p. 271. Church membership: Bingham, *Residence,* p. 277, says there was "one organized church" on all the islands at this point; see also Damon, *Stone Church,* pp. 21–22 and "Appendix," pp. 141–42, which explains that in 1830 the Hawaiian churches became "separate organizations, subject to review . . . by the original mission church. The original mission church ceased to exist after 1860." Kapiolani a little while later: there is some confusion here, since Kamakau, *Ruling Chiefs,* p. 382, says Kapiolani was "baptized" in October 1825. But he may be making a distinction between baptism and church membership. "Tears of gratitude": Mercy Whitney J., Dec. 5, 1825.

Chapter 6: The Tie That Binds

1 "Medicine brought me": SB to "Beloved Brothers & Sisters," Dec. 30, 1825, BP, Box 2; relapsed in October: Mercy Whitney J., Nov. 16, 1825; "broken constitution": Bingham, *Residence,* p. 274; see also SB to "My Dear Sister Nancy [Ruggles]," Dec. 16, 1827, BP, Box 3.

2 Evarts's death, "bitter chastisement": SB to Sophia [Cushing], June 12, 1825, BP, Box 2; SB to "My Dear Hon'd Friend" [Mrs. Fowler], Sept. 9, 1825, BP, Box 2; SB to LT, July 17, 1826, BP, Box 2. "Prostrate": SB to Maria, July 1825, BP, Box 2.

3 Comfortable health: SB to "Beloved Brothers & Sisters," Dec. 30, 1825, BP, Box 2."Effect on my constitution": Sybil Bingham J., [May 7], 1827. Letter never finished: SB to NR, May 30, 1826, MLC.

4 "Debility": Bingham, *Residence,* p. 273; Mercy Whitney J., July 3, 1825, Oct. 13, 1825; SW to Hannah Smith, Nov. 16, 1826, MLC. "Injured" constitution: Maria Loomis J., Aug. 22, 1822. "Pulmonary complaint": Thurston, pp. 229–30. Miscarriage ["abortion"]: SR to Levi Chamberlain, Sept. 2, 1833, MLC. "Once blooming health": MW to "Sister Maria," Nov. 1, 1836, ML. See also Lucy Thurston's advice to the younger wives pp. 136–37, to "*take care of your health.*"; see also Grimshaw's account of gynecological complaints in *Paths of Duty,* pp. 314–48.

5 "Into the grave": Mercy Whitney J., Dec. 7, 1826. "Rest stations": SB to Mrs. Bates, Oct. 1, 1830, BP, Box 2. Land at Punahou: SB to [daughter] Sophia, Dec. 14, 1831, MLC; Judd, p. 74; Coan, *Brief Sketch,* p. 23.

6 Loomis departure: ML to "My Dear Husband," Oct. 23, 1827, MLC; obituary in *The Friend,* April 1910.

7 Deaths: Elizabeth Bishop in Thurston, pp. 92–93. Fanny Ruggles: see MW to ML, May 30, 1827, MLC. *The Missionary's Daughter: A memoir of Lucy Goodale Thurston of the Sandwich Islands,* by A. P. Cummings, was published by the American Tract Society in 1842, as the author explains, to serve the cause of "youthful piety" and of missions. Eleven wives died prematurely, though only two in childbirth: see Grimshaw, "Paths of Duty," pp. 318, 343, and *Paths of Duty,* p. 97.

8 "Too high a coloring": MW to Mrs. C. A. Ely, Nov. 13, 1832, MLC.

9 Society Islands: MW to Mrs. Ely, Nov. 24, 1832, MLC. "Error of . . . opinion": MW to Mrs. Ely, April 30, 1836, MLC. Thurston, p. 90. See also SB to Mrs. Howell, Nov. 14, 1832, BP, Box 2; LT to Cousin William Goodell, Oct. 24, 1834, ABCFM-Hawaii.

10 Sending children home: see "Minutes of the General Meeting of 1826: Report of Sending Children to Their Native Land," Sept. 1826, HMCS (hereafter Minutes, 1826). "*Let her go*": Mercy Whitney J., page inserted opposite Nov. 11, 1826. "*From us*": *Extracts from Letters of Mrs. S. M. Bingham, Relative to Sending Her Children from the Sandwich Islands to America,* p. 11 (hereafter *Extracts*), HMCS; see also Grimshaw, *Paths of Duty,* pp. 133–37; and Char Miller, "Domesticity Abroad: Work and Family in the Sandwich Islands Mission 1820–1840," in *Missions and Missionaries in the Pacific,* pp. 77–86.

11 Board did not approve: Jeremiah Evarts to "the Missionaries at the Sandwich Islands," Oct. 27, 1827, ABCFM-HEA; the Board relaxed its position by the 1830s: see MW to Mrs. Ely, March 25, 1835, MLC;

Anderson, *Memorial Volume*, pp. 278–80; see also report of the twenty-first annual meeting of the ABCFM in *Missionary Herald*, vol. 26, no. 11, Nov. 1830.

12 "Brands from the burning": Mercy Whitney J., March 17, 1829. Prison: Thurston, p. 127.

13 Maria's lot: Mercy Whitney J., Sept. 17, 1823. "At a loss" with boys: Mercy Whitney J., March 17, 1829. Sophia as lonely: HB "Extracts from a letter to Mr. Evarts" [typescript], Oct. 15, 1828, MLC; the complete letter exists in MLC-ts, vol. 2.

14 Sophia Bingham's screams: Sybil Bingham J., April 3, 1827, BP, Box 2. "Impious language": SB to "Beloved Brothers & Sisters," Dec. 30, 1825, BP, Box 2. Safety: HB, "Extracts from a letter to Mr. Evarts" [typescript], Oct. 15, 1828, MLC, and MLC-ts, vol. 2.

15 Father's labors: SB to Mrs. Howell, Nov. 14, 1832, BP, Box 2.

16 "What parents in America?" "suitable partners": Minutes, 1826.

17 "Have our children with us": Mercy Whitney J., June 16, 1827. "Hazardous either way": *Extracts*, p. 16.

18 "Except by example": MW to "Sister Thurston," Jan. 27, 1828, MLC. Motto: Thurston, p. 120. Usefulness "impeded": Mercy Whitney J., June 16, 1827. "Struggle": *Extracts*, p. 19. Decision mutual: I find no evidence that mothers had to be convinced by fathers or acquiesced in a decision made by them. Hiram Bingham insisted that mothers and fathers "are jointly bound to provide for their children" (*Residence*, p. 332); Degler explains that there was a "muting" of patriarchy's impact in the nineteenth century and that "mother and father were often seen as equally interested and involved in the upbringing of their children" (pp. 74–75).

19 "Duty to leave": MW to NR, Feb. 7, 1834, MLC.

20 "Beyond everything else": *Extracts*, p. 14. "Little children sin": MW to Henry Whitney, Aug. 26, 1834, MLC; see also Nancy Ruggles's question to daughter Sarah in letter to Rev. Ebenezer Brown, June 5, 1830, MLC. Practical advantage: the argument of MW to Mrs. Ely, April 30, 1836, MLC.

21 "Their souls too": SW to Henry Whitney, Aug. 10, 1836, MLC. Boarding schools: Kuykendall, pp. 111–13.

22 "Any sacrifice": *Extracts*, p. 9.

23 Maria Whitney's departure: Mercy Whitney J., Aug. 4, Nov. 10–11, 1826.

24 Statistics on children sent home: Bingham, *Residence*, pp. 331–33; Thurston, p. 148. Bingham cites "18 other" children besides his two, but his list makes a total of 19; Lucy Thurston counts 18, but excludes her child (Asa went home at twelve) while Bingham includes "1

Thurston." Besides those from the first company, the Bishops sent two, the Richardses six, and the Levi Chamberlains two (all from the second company), and the Armstrongs (of the fifth) sent one.

25 "Leave table": *Extracts*, p. 2. "In vain": *Extracts*, p. 4. "*Still leaks*": *Extracts*, p. 8. "Turn quietly . . . pillow": *Extracts*, p. 10. Sound of their wails: SW to Henry Whitney, Aug. 10, 1836, MLC. "Entwined themselves": MW to NR, Nov. 4, 1831, MLC. Emily's last night: MW to [daughter] Maria, Feb. 8, 1834, MLC.

26 "Conceals . . . the future": MW to Maria P. Chamberlain, Dec. 10, 1831, MLC. "Anxious heart": *Extracts*, p. 7. Helpless solicitude: MW to Samuel & Henry Whitney, Nov. 28, 1831, MLC.

27 Elisabeth's birthday: SB–PJ, March 8, 1839. Describing house and daguerreotype: MW to "My dear son Samuel," Oct. 10, 1848, MLC. Sophia's portrait: see Laura Judd, March 22, 1831, *Judd Fragments IV*, HMCS.

28 "Let the earth roll": SB to NR, Aug. 29, 1827, MLC; Mercy Whitney J., Aug. 19, 1859. "Higher objects": Jeremiah Evarts to Rev. Hiram Bingham & others, Jan. 5, 1822, ABCFM-HEA.

29 "Wandering about": MW to Mrs. Hoadly, May 20, 1830, MLC; see also Mercy Whitney J., April 10, 1828, and March 17, 1829. "Must have suffered": MW to Henry Whitney, Oct. 18, 1841, MLC. Binghams' not wanting to wrench themselves: SB to "My dear Esther," Nov. 23, 1837, BP, Box 3.

30 "Alive to God": Mercy Whitney J., Dec. 12, 1819. "*Kaawale*": MW to NR, Feb. 7, 1834. MLC.

31 Rapport with Nancy Ruggles: MW to "Sister Dow," Dec. 20, 1832, MLC. No condolences: MW to "Sister Maria," Nov. 30, 1842, MLC; Mercy Whitney J., March 7, 1856.

32 Waimea in the 1830s: MW to "Cousin Ely," March 27, 1837, MLC. Children planted trees: MW to [son] Samuel, Dec. 25, 1838, MLC; MW to Henry, Aug. 20, 1840, MLC; MW to [sons] Samuel & Henry, Oct. 2, 1833, MLC; MW to [son] Samuel, Oct. 10, 1848, MLC. Reprimands: see, for example, MW to [son] Henry, Aug. 27, 1838, MLC. Samuel's disappearance: MW to Mrs. Ely, April 25, 1844; to Mrs. Walker, Jan. 28, 1845; to "Dearly beloved *tho erring* Son," June 28, 1845, all MLC; see also Mercy's complaint in 1870 that she has given Samuel up as a correspondent, not having heard from him for eight years: MW to Hattie Whitney [Mrs. Samuel], March 15, 1870, MLC. Visit to mainland: see MW to "My dear children Sam'l & Hattie," July 22, 1862, and to "Dear Bro. & Sister Ruggles," April 29, 1864, MLC; these letters confirm that she saw both children during her visit.

33 Strained relationship with Maria: MW to Samuel, Oct. 10, 1848; Mercy

Whitney J., Sept. 6, 1848, March 29, 1849 (the journal was sent to Emily at this time). "Not fully reconciled": Levi Chamberlain J., vol. 25, May 38, 1848. Mr. Pogue: Mercy Whitney J., May 28, 1851. Childrearing advice: Mercy Whitney J., May 28, 1851.

34 "*Sad* I sometimes feel," "frank & confiding": Mercy Whitney J., Sept. 6, 1848. Rowell children: Mercy Whitney J., Oct. 13, 1848. Widowhood: MW to John Partridge, July 13, 1846, MLC; MW to Maria Chamberlain, Jan. 3, 1846, MLC.

35 "Healthier climate": MW to Eliza Goodrich, Jan. 3, 1846, MLC. "Simple diet": MW to "Sr. Pamela," Sept. 11, 1837, MLC. God's creation: Mercy Whitney J., Nov. 14, 1840. "Sea bath": J., Nov. 8, 1856.

36 Feeble health: references are numerous – see, for example, "ophthalmy": J., Feb. 7, 1830, Nov. 27, 1838, MLC; seton: J., Nov. 7, 1829, Jan. 20, 1831, Aug. 14, 1841; "old complaint": Oct. 18, 1841, Dec. 9, 1848. Henry's birth: MW to "Dear Mother & Sisters," Oct. 22, 1835, MLC. "Wonder that I am still alive": J., Sept. 23, 1848.

37 Teaching: MW to Samuel, Dec. 25, 1838, MLC; J., Aug. 11, 1834. "Labors *directly*": MW to "Sister Maria," Dec. 1, 1841, MLC.

38 Deborah Kapule: Mercy Whitney J., Nov. 14, 1839. Maria's name: MW to Maria, Oct. 30, 1837, MLC.

39 "Children": J., Nov. 4, 1851. Dress improved: J., Dec. 9, 1836. Happy marriages rare: J., Nov. 2, 1854. Sloth: J., May 2, 1854. Hawaiian help: J., Dec. 24, 1841. Habits of childrearing: J., Dec. 9, 1836. "Degraded": J., Aug. 6, 1842. "Above the beasts": MW to [son] Henry, Nov. 12, 1844, MLC.

40 People "oppressed": MW to "Sister Maria," Oct. 7, 1834, MLC.

41 "Attachment to the *old missionaries*": Mercy Whitney J., July 11, 1848. Dress of *kapa:* MW to Mrs. Ely, Nov. 22, 1833, MLC; Henry's return: J., Nov. 12, 1849. Guards: MW to Mrs. C. A. Ely, July 14, 1837, MLC. Recuperating in 1835: MW to [sons] Samuel & Henry, Dec. 17, 1835, MLC. *Lomi-lomi:* J., Nov. 14, 1854.

42 "Play day": J., Dec. 12, Dec. 19, 1850; Jan. 1857.

43 "*Circumspect*": MW to Miss S. G. Bidwell, July 6, 1852, MLC. "Lukewarmness": MW to Cousin Sarah Bidwell, May 15, 1831, MLC. Diet: MW to "Sister Maria," July 31, 1837, MLC. "Blank in Creation": MW to "Sister Dow," Aug. 14, 1867, MLC.

44 What Pioneers endured: J., Sept. 23, 1854. Improvements in material life: MW to "Sister Dow," July 25, 1862, MLC. Mail and steamer: J., Aug. 23, 1851, Dec. 9, 1854, March 7, 1856.

45 Salary: J., Jan. 9, 1856. Used native vessels: J., Jan. 9, 1856. Auction: Ethel M. Damon, *Koamalu: A Story of Pioneers on Kauai*, vol. 1:297. "Heavenly inheritance": MW to Mr. O. Partridge, Nov. 10, 1832, MLC.

46 "Sorrows have an end": J., July 4, 1827. "Rejoicing in thy love": J., Oct. 23, 1848.
47 "Lonely pilgrim": J., Sept. 23, 1854 *Pupule:* conversation, Lela Goodell.
48 Absence of friends: MW to Mrs. C. A. Ely, Sept. 12, 1834, MLC. Lucy took her five children home in 1840. Two remained for schooling, one died upon arrival, and two returned with her to Honolulu. See p. 355 *n38*. Difference . . . girls: Thurston, p. 123. "Make better provision": Thurston, p. 101. Good health: Thurston, p. 230. Binghams' stress on "pollution" of Honolulu: *Extracts*, p. 13.
49 "Dungeon": Thurston, p. 77.
50 Designed house: Thurston, pp. 78, 84–85. Jews in Gentile culture: p. 127. Not speak the language: Thurston, pp. 84–85.
51 Persis rebels: Thurston, pp. 120–21. Daughters teach Hawaiians: Thurston, pp. 130, 147–48. "Not removed": Thurston, p. 130. Twenty-year limit: Thurston, pp. 118, 139.
52 Bell for classes: Thurston, p. 123. Lucy's schoolteaching: Thurston, p. 122. Friday Female Meeting: Thurston, p. 98. Number of members: Thurston, p. 103. Letters about butter: LT to Levi Chamberlain, Sept. 9, Dec. 6, Dec. 23, 1830; Levi Chamberlain to Mr. and Mrs. Thurston, Oct. 27, 1830, MLC. Private work: Thurston, p. 103.
53 Example of Samuel Whitney: LT to Dea. David & Millicent Goodale, July 7, 1845, MLC. "Erred": Mercy Whitney J., June 3, 1857. Advice to Hiram: SB to [son] Hiram Bingham, Feb. 28, 1845, BP, Box 3.
54 Impurity of speech: Thurston, p. 90. "Awakened into life": paraphrased from Thurston, pp. 87, 113. "Deepest pity": Thurston, p. 113. "Not take care of ours": Thurston, p. 122.
55 "Standard": Thurston, p. 90. Public examples: Thurston, p. 147. Kapiolani as *haole* chiefess: Kamakau, *Ruling Chiefs*, p. 383. "Native converts to Christianity . . . *origin*": Thurston, p. 114.
56 "Severe struggle": Thurston, p. 121. Remove children from services: Thurston, pp. 120–21. Peeling potatoes: Thurston, p. 112.
57 "Commanding": Thurston, p. 307; daughter Lucy's death: Thurston, p. 150.
58 Childbirth on ship: Thurston, p. 106. Paralysis: Thurston, pp. 141–42. Quinine: Thurston, p. 160.
59 Operation for breast cancer: Thurston, pp. 170–75. "Like a river": Thurston, p. 172. "Let them come": Thurston, p. 152.
60 Asa's last illness: see LT to [daughter] Persis Taylor, March 28, 1868, MLC (this account did not get into Lucy's book). Public reading in 1870: Thurston, p. 198. Hawaiian language in the schools: see Judd, p. 62; Laura Judd to SB, Sept. 2, 1844, BP, Box 3; Bradley, 133–34n; Kuykendall, pp. 360–61. "Speedy extinction": Kuykendall, p. 337.

61 "Spasms of pain": Thurston, p. 296. Burial: Thurston, p. 296; "on top of Mr. Thurston": copy of will in MLC.

Chapter 7: Pilgrim Path

1 Ruggleses' return: SR to Levi Chamberlain, Sept. 2, 1833, MLC. "Makes me feel": SB to NR, Sept. 13, 1833, MLC. "Happy": SR to Levi Chamberlain, Feb. 19, 1834; see also Nov. 22, 1836, MLC.

2 "Tumultuous" Honolulu: SB to [sisters] Anna & Lucy, draft, Nov. 25, 1833, BP, Box 3. "Both human and divine": SB to Mrs. Sigourney, Dec. 17, 1833, BP, Box 3.

3 For accounts of violence against mission, see Bingham, *Residence*, pp. 274–76 (Lahaina and *Daniel* in 1825), pp. 283–89 (*Dolphin* and attack against Bingham); pp. 313–19 (*John Palmer* at Lahaina in 1827). For general accounts of violence throughout this section, see also Bradley, pp. 176–82; Daws, "Foreigners and French Priests," in *Shoal of Time*, pp. 75–81; Jane Litten, "Whaler Versus Missionary at Lahaina," *Hawaiian Historical Review* 1 (1963): 219–34. "Enemy is busy": SB to "My Dear Hon'd Friend, [Mrs. Fowler]," Sept. 9, 1825, BP, Box 2. Attack on Hiram Bingham: SB to "My Dear Mr. & Mrs. Osgood," March 1, 1826, BP, Box 3. Hid in the cellar, "final victory": SB to Mrs. Johns, Nov. 5, 1827, BP, Box 3.

4 "Swallow us up," "no little awe": SB to [sister] Lucy, Dec. 2, 1827, BP, Box 2. "Mad Jack" Percival: Bingham, *Residence*, p. 288.

5 "Real hatred to the gospel": Sybil Bingham J., April 4, 1827, BP, Box 2. Circular of 1826: Bingham, *Residence*, p. 300. Charges against Richards: Daws, *Shoal of Time*, pp. 80–81. Lord Byron: Kuykendall, pp. 119–20. Thomas ap Catesby Jones and *Peacock:* Bingham, *Residence*, pp. 301–303; Kuykendall, pp. 434–35 (sandalwood debts); Bradley, pp. 106–9, 181–82 (treaty). Jones rounded up deserters, helped settle sandalwood debts, and negotiated a treaty of friendship. *Vincennes:* Bradley, p. 195.

6 Relationship of church and state: Bingham, *Residence*, pp. 279–82. Kaahumanu enforces *kapu:* Silverman, *Kaahumanu*, pp. 104, 106.

7 Arrival in Honolulu: SB to [sister] Lucy, Dec. 2, 1827, BP, Box 2.

8 Catholics: Daws, *Shoal of Time*, p. 80; Silverman, *Kaahumanu*, pp. 130–32; Kamakau, *Ruling Chiefs*, pp. 324–33; Kuykendall, pp. 137–47; see SB to Mrs. Stewart, Jan. 1, 1830, BP, Box 3, for an account of Kaahumanu's comments on the priests. Boki supported the cause of the priests, mainly to embarrass the government and Kaahumanu; the two priests expelled in 1831 had by the late 1830s returned to stay. Hawaiian Catholics were harassed and punished throughout the 1830s.

9 Six to seven hundred members: SB to Rev. Aretas Kent [cousin], Aug. 12, 1833, BP, Box 3. Statistics for 1837: Daws, *Shoal of Time,* p. 98. Kauai: Bingham, *Residence,* p. 337. Married 1,222: Bingham, *Residence,* p. 328. Kauikeaouli: Bingham, *Residence,* p. 346.

10 Female Prayer Meeting: see SB to Mrs. Foot [formerly Miss Battelle], Oct. 20, 1830, BP, Box 3; SB to Misses Jane & Sally Howell, March 17, 1830, BP, Box 3.

11 Book for children: SB to Mrs. Stewart, Jan. 1, 1830 (the letter continues for several days), BP, Box 3; Bingham, *Residence,* pp. 367–69.

12 Tea party: SB to "My Dear Sister Nancy [Ruggles]", Dec. 16, 1827, BP, Box 3. "Very much engaged": SB to Misses Jane & Sally Howell, BP, Box 3.

13 "To have failed in anything": Sybil Bingham J., June 30, 1827, BP, Box 2. Rest cure, 1830: Bingham, *Residence,* p. 376; SB to Mrs. Bates, Oct. 1, 1830, BP, Box 2; SB to Miss Whitney, Oct. 6, 1830, BP, Box 2 (about "daily borders"); SB to Sophia Shepard, Oct. 15, 1830, BP, Box 3; SB to J. Evarts, Sept. 17, 1830, ABCFM-Hawaii.

14 Visits and friendship with Kaahumanu: Sybil Bingham J., June 9, June 29, 1827, BP, Box 2. Rocking chair; see Silverman, p. 127, p. 129 (photograph). Visit with Lydia Namahana: Sybil Bingham J., April 8, 1827, BP, Box 2 (I have standardized the spelling of *aroha*). Nancy Ruggles felt close to Kapiolani (see letter to Rev. Shubard Bartlett, June 27, 1833, MLC), but Grimshaw explains that such close friendships between missionaries and Hawaiians were rare, and in any case extended only to *alii,* not commoners: see "Paths of Duty," p. 222, and *Paths of Duty,* pp. 57–62.

15 Kaahumanu's death, present at deathbed: MW to [daughter] Maria, March 5, 1832, MLC (the letter continues at later dates). "Entered into rest": SB to [sister] Lucy, draft, Oct. 9, 1832, BP, Box 3; SB, n.d., draft, BP, Box 3 (similar to letter to Mrs. Sigourney, Dec. 17, 1833, in Coan, *Brief Sketch,* p. 21.). "Dying saint": MW to "the ladies who were the contributors of the box of articles," Oct. 23, 1833, MLC; see also general accounts by Judd, pp. 38–39; Bingham, *Residence,* pp. 432–33 (last visit), p. 435 (funeral); Kamakau, *Ruling Chiefs,* pp. 308–9; Silverman, *Kaahumanu,* pp. 144–46.

16 "Died a *Christian*": Kuykendall, p. 133, quoting Henry A. Pierce to James Hunnewell, June 11, 1832. "Bosom of our family" and "she truly loved us": SB to [sister] Lucy, draft, Oct. 9, 1832, BP, Box 3.

17 The thirties: see SB to Mrs. Johns, March 20, 1833, BP, Box 3, for a description of the times; see also Judd, p. 41; Kamakau, *Ruling Chiefs,* pp. 334–38; Kuykendall, pp. 133–52 ("The Troubled Thirties"); Daws, *Shoal of Time,* pp. 91–94 ("Bird Feathers"). "Fabrick . . . would fall":

SB to [sister] Lucy, draft, Oct. 9, 1832, BP, Box 3. *Hulumanu:* the term means "bird of foul feathers": Sinclair, p. 96. Kinau in despair: Judd, p. 41.

18 Kauikeaouli as ruler: Kuykendall, pp. 135–36; Daws, *Shoal of Time,* p. 94, says that Kauikeaouli "virtually abandoned the direction of affairs of state" after 1835; Kamakau, *Ruling Chiefs,* pp. 419, 428 (constitution). Hawaiians licensed to preach: Kuykendall, p. 339. General Meeting disbanded: Anderson, *Memorial Volume,* pp. 253–56; Rufus Anderson, "Appendix VI: Actions of the Board," in *Hawaiian Islands,* p. 429.

19 Depopulation, 1840: Daws, *Shoal of Time,* p. 168. By 1850 the Hawaiian population was 82,000: Schmitt, *Demographic Statistics,* p. 43. Epidemics: Daws, *Shoal of Time,* p. 141; Kamakau, *Ruling Chiefs,* pp. 416–18. "*Okuu* phenomenon": John Dominis Holt, *Monarchy in Hawaii,* pp. 12, 14.

20 Nahienaena and Kauikeaouli: I am indebted generally in this section to Marjorie Sinclair's biography (cited earlier). Gossip about incest: Sinclair, pp. 58–59 ("probably true"), pp. 105–6 (denied later). Behavior: MW to NR, Oct. 30, 1834, MLC (Mercy felt that Nahienaena ought to be made a public example). Suicide attempt: Sinclair, pp. 141–42. Sleeping together as marriage: Sinclair, p. 142. Baby's father: Sinclair, p. 155.

21 Funeral: Kamakau, *Ruling Chiefs,* pp. 340–42; Bingham, *Residence,* pp. 498–99. Kauikeaouli's changed behavior: Judd, p. 49; Kamakau, *Ruling Chiefs,* p. 341; Sinclair, pp. 160–62.

22 Moral lesson: MW to [daughter] Maria, Jan. 9, 1837, MLC. Last words: Judd, p. 48.

23 Female Associations: see Cott, pp. 149–51, for introduction; in Hawaii, the Maternal Association meetings began in 1834; the first Female Prayer Meeting (for Hawaiians) was in 1825.

24 Purpose of journal: Sybil Bingham J., April 2, 1827, BP, Box 3. "System": J., June 11, 1827. "Irregularity": SB to Mrs. [Eliza] Hubbell, Dec. 19, 1829, BP, Box 3. "Bustling, unquiet state": SB to Mrs. Howell, Feb. 8, 1839, BP, Box 3.

25 Cupboard: Sybil Bingham J., June 13, 1827, BP, Box 3; Judd, p. 25. Changes in mission house: see Frost Report and "Frame House," Forbes Research Notes, vol. 4, pp. 558–687. SB to "My dear Esther," Nov. 23, 1837, BP, Box 3 (refers to two bedrooms and a cookroom); SB to ML & EL: Sept. 1, 1829, BP, Box 3. "Pretty garden of plants": SB to "Sister Spaulding," April 1837, BP, Box 3.

26 Hawaiian help: Sybil Bingham J., June 11, 1827, BP, Box 3. "Do as well as they know how": SB to Mrs. Howell, April 1837, BP, Box 3. Stopped

doing laundry: SB to Mrs. Bates, Sept. 18, 1837, BP, Box 3; Sybil's restraint in criticism is atypical: Grimshaw finds that missionary women had "scarcely a word of praise" for Hawaiian help ("Paths of Duty," p. 405).

27 Precious "*time*": SB to Mrs. Bates, Sept. 18, 1837, BP, Box 3. Teaching: SB to Mrs. [Eliza] Hubbell, Dec. 19, 1829, BP, Box 3. "Maternal care overwhelms": Sybil Bingham J., June 16, 1827, BP, Box 3. "Misconception" that children are favored: SB to Mrs. Collins, Dec. 3, 1832, BP, Box 3. "More times than I have lines," "step abroad": SB to Mrs. Johns, Oct. 23, 1839, BP, Box 3.

28 Be alone: see J., June 9, 1827. "To dispose of first": SB to Mrs. Goodrich, March 6, 1836, BP, Box 2. "The poor people": SB to Mrs. [Eliza] Hubbell, Dec. 19, 1829, BP, Box 3.

29 "Miscellany": SB to Mrs. Sigourney, Dec. 17, 1833, BP, Box 3. "Hewers of wood": SB to "My dear Esther," Nov. 23, 1837, BP, Box 3. "Things of the body": J., May 21, 1827, BP, Box 3. "Go as it happens": SB to Mrs. [Eliza] Hubbell, Dec. 19, 1829, BP, Box 3. "Health must suffer": J., April 2, 1827, BP, Box 2. Regret . . . "what a missionary wife": SB to "Beloved Brothers & Sisters," Dec. 30, 1825, BP, Box 2.

30 "Multitudes . . . more cares": Sybil Bingham J., April 2, 1827, BP, Box 3. "Lime as anything": SB to Misses Jane & Sally Howell, March 17, 1830, BP, Box 3. "Heartily as to the Lord": SB to J. Evarts, Sept. 17, 1830, ABCFM-Hawaii. "Cheerful in it": SB to [sisters] Anna & Lucy, Nov. 25, 1833, BP, Box 3. "Thy strength be": SB to Mrs. Bates, Nov. 27, 1839, BP, Box 3.

31 "Dust . . . said or thought": Sybil Bingham J., May 19, 1827, BP, Box 3; see also April 2–3, 1827. "*Readiness to wander*": SB-PJ, Oct. 12, 1829. "Mark the years": SB-PJ, Sept. 14, 1834.

32 "Chase away . . . darkness": SB to Mrs. Bates, Sept. 18, 1837, BP, Box 3. "Happy happy": SB to [childhood friend] Eunice, Oct. 18, 1830, BP, Box 2. "Join with angels above": SB to [ ], draft, April 13, 1833, BP, Box 3.

33 Kamakau's lament: *Ruling Chiefs*, p. 242; see generally pp. 229–45. *Marai:* Elisha Loomis J., Sept. 4, 1823.

34 Correspondences between Hawaiian and Christian practices: this I take to be Sahlins's point in *Historical Metaphors:* "at the least, all structural transformation involves reproduction if not also the other way around" (p. 68).

35 "Ruinous to the people": Bingham, *Residence*, p. 174. Sermon of Rev. Abraham Akaka: "Statehood Service at Kawaiahao Church, March 13, 1959," in *A Hawaiian Reader*, ed. A. Grove Day and Carl Stroven, pp. 323–28.

36 "Unmitigatedly bad after all": from *Why and What Am I: The Confessions of an Inquirer* (1857), quoted by Frear, *Anti-Missionary Criticism,* p. 12.

37 Sybil's deteriorating health: many letters speak of this, among them SB to "My dear Esther," Nov. 23, 1837, BP, Box 3; SB to Mrs. Howell, April 1837, BP, Box 3; SB to Mrs. Bates, Oct. 28, 1836, BP, Box 3; SB to Clarissa Richards, March 3, 1837, BP, Box 3. "Invalid through the year": SB to Mrs. Bates, Sept. 18, 1837, BP, Box 3. "Strange subject": SB to Mrs. J. Evarts, Oct. 11, 1839, BP, Box 3. "Watch": SB to Mrs. Johns, Oct. 23, 1839, BP, Box 3.

38 Five Thurston children: Thurston, p. 149; see also p. 165. For verification that all five children went, see Maria Chamberlain J., Aug. 1, 1840, and Persis Thurston J., July 30, 1840.

39 Thirty-first anniversary: Mercy Whitney J.

40 Statistics: Bingham, *Residence,* p. 576. Missionary values in "retreat": my argument follows Daws, *Shoal of Time,* pp. 104–5; Twain quoted, p. 105; see also pp. 161, 163; and Gavan Daws, "The Decline of Puritanism at Honolulu in the Nineteenth Century," *HJH* 1 (1967): 31–42.

41 "Accustomed from infancy": MW to Mrs. Hoadly, Oct. 23, 1833, MLC.

42 "Great work of doing good to souls": SB-PJ, Sept. 14, 1834. "Good . . . I do not": SB to [her sister] Lucy, Sept. 14, 1826, BP, Box 2. "Imposition": *The Winter's Tale* (New York: New American Library, 1963), I.ii.73–74.

43 Life in the 1850s: Grimshaw, "New England Missionary Wives," p. 95. "Magnitude and grandeur": SB to Mrs. Howell, Feb. 2, 1839, BP, Box 3.

44 "Contrast of present-things": SB to Mrs. Bates, Sept. 18, 1837, BP, Box 3; see also SB to [daughter] Sophia, Oct. 31, 1837, BP, Box 3. "Great work . . . accomplished": SB to Mrs. Foot, Dec. 6, 1837, BP, Box 3. "Not the work of a day": SB to Mrs. Bates, Sept. 18, 1837, BP, Box 3; see also Richard Greer's description of "Honolulu in 1838," *HJH* 11 (1977): 3–38, and Bradley, pp. 254–55.

45 "Work there is finished," "glory is departed": SB to Mrs. J. Evarts, Oct. 11, 1839, BP, Box 3. "Great Awakening": Daws, *Shoal of Time,* p. 102; see also chart in Dibble, p. 307; chart in Bingham, *Residence,* p. 577. Criticism of Bingham: Miller, *Fathers and Sons,* pp. 46–55; Andrew, pp. 165–67. Mission experiment not a failure: Grimshaw concludes that although the missionary women knew that "cultural change . . . did not occur simply as a result of formal instruction," and that "every contact" and "every act which Hawaiians observed might prove the catalyst for change," the women's "final defeat" was to realize that "the effects on Hawaiian women were unsatisfactory." (See "Paths of Duty," pp. 518–19; "Devoted Missionaries," in *Paths of Duty,* pp. 154–

78; also "New England Missionary Wives.") My account of "success" may seem to contrast with Grimshaw's emphasis on the women's sense of failure. But there are two categories of effort—the attempt at setting a domestic example and the attempt at religious conversion, which is the "experiment" Sybil refers to. Both Grimshaw (p. 195) and Jeffrey in her study of pioneer women in the West (including missionaries) make a distinction between the way these women evaluated their work (often negatively) and the long-range assessment of historians. They had "expected [as did missionary women] to resist the disintegrating forces of frontier life and hoped to realize and even extend their own social role" (p. 24). Like the women in Hawaii, they often felt defeated. But Jeffrey argues (pp. 101–6) that they did play an important role in developing the West and in setting a standard for civilization.

46 "Before they sailed": MW to "Dear Sister Lyons," Nov. 21, 1840, MLC; Mercy Whitney J., Aug. 15, 1840; Stephen Reynolds in Smith, p. 237. Binghams expected to return: Bradley, p. 387 and footnotes, also pp. 387–89 generally; Bingham, *Residence*, p. 578.

47 Mercy's parting reflections: J., Aug. 15, 1840.

48 "Indescribable": SB to Mrs. Bliss, March 22, 1841, BP, Box 3. Visit to New England: I am indebted in this section to Alfred M. Bingham, "Sybil's Bones: A Chronicle of the Three Hiram Binghams," *HJH* 9 (1975): 3–36, especially for details about Sybil's burial and Samuel Williston.

49 Memoir of Kaahumanu: SB to Mrs. Upbearn, April 1, 1843, BP, Box 3. "Pilgrim & sojourner": SB to Mrs. Armstrong, Oct. 27, 1842, BP, Box 3. "Scattered flock": SB to Elisabeth Bingham, Dec. 17, 1843, BP, Box 3. Three anniversaries: SB to HB, Oct. 11, 1843, BP, Box 3. "Some loneliness": SB to [daughter] Sophia, June 1844, BP, Box 3.

50 "Embarrassments": SB to Mrs. Bates, Jan. 1, 1846, BP, Box 3. Postage: SB to [son] Hiram, Sept. 25, 1843, BP, Box 3; SB to HB, Oct. 11, 1843, BP, Box 3.

51 Cough: SB to HB, Nov. 24, 1845, BP, Box 3; to [daughter] Sophia, Dec. 20, 1846, MLC.

52 Replacement by Rev. Armstrong: SB to Levi Chamberlain, July 17, 1843, BP, Box 3. Land at Punahou: SB to Levi Chamberlain, July 17, 1843; SB to Laura Judd, Dec. 28, 1843, BP, Box 3; Hiram Bingham wrote to the members of the Sandwich Island Mission, Feb. 26, 1842, approving of the founding of a school "but with the right to the land as I did hold it, to be carefully held in my name." However, when the Binghams requested dismission, Hiram wrote to Rufus Anderson "that I consider my connexion with houses and lands at the Sandwich Islands, and with the church & people once under my care there as

quietly and entirely closed": Oct. 23, 1846, ABCFM-HEA. Both letters are found in Ethel M. Damon, "From Manoa to Punahou," Forty-ninth Annual Report of the Hawaiian Historical Society, 1940, pp. 5–11.

53 Hiram's book: Bingham, "Sybil's Bones," p. 11; HB to SB, June 13, 1847, BP, Box 1. Bequest of $800: SB to Mrs. Wood, Nov. 20, 1847; SB to HB, March 31, 1847, BP, Box 3.

54 Doctrine of *God's . . . providence:* SB to "Brothers," June 9, 1846, BP, Box 3; SB to Levi Chamberlain, July 17, 1843, BP, Box 3. "Reverse": SB to NR, Jan. 15, 1825, MLC. "Labyrinthe": SB to Clarissa Richards, Feb. 2, 1846. "Mistaken duty": SB to Mrs. Hill, Feb. 21, 1846. Not "rashly": SB to Mr. & Mrs. Hunnewell, Aug. 22, 1846, BP, Box 3.

55 Cold, hungry, "no abiding place": SB to [daughter] Sophia, Dec. 20, 1846, MLC.

56 Help from Williston: Bingham, "Sybil's Bones," pp. 13, 16–17. "Book is finished": HB to SB, June 13, 1847, BP, Box 1.

57 Coughing blood: SB to HB, March 25, 1847, BP, Box 3. "Trembling and afraid": SB to [sister] Sophia, Dec. 26, 1847, in Bingham, "Sybil's Bones," p. 17. This is not Sybil's last letter: see SB to [daughter] Sophia, Jan. 2, 1848, BP, Box 3 (Sophia's copy). "Be in her rocking chair" and last words: HB to Sophia and William Moseley, March 2, 1848, BP, Box 1 (Hiram wrote several similar letters telling of Sybil's death); see also Bingham, "Sybil's Bones," p. 17. "Bands [bonds]": as written by HB (letter above) and by one of the Bingham children, BP, Box 2. Sybil's swollen feet: HB to Daniel and Lucy Whiting, March 2, 1848, BP, Box 1.

58 Reapplication for missionary work: Bradley, p. 388n; Miller, *Fathers and Sons,* p. 55; Bingham, "Sybil's Bones," pp. 11–12 (dismission), pp. 19–20 (final appeal).

Bibliography

Hawaiian and Missionary Materials

I list here the sources mentioned in the Notes. Manuscript materials are described in the Acknowledgments and at the beginning of the Notes.

Akaka, Abraham. "Statehood Service at Kawaiahao Church, March 13, 1959." In *A Hawaiian Reader,* edited by A. Grove Day and Carl Stroven. Honolulu: Mutual Publishing Co., 1984.

Alexander, William D. *A Brief History of the Hawaiian People.* New York: American Book Company, 1891.

Anderson, Rufus. *Hawaiian Islands: Their Progress and Condition Under Missionary Labors.* Boston: Gould and Lincoln, 1864.

Anderson, Rufus. "Introductory Essay on the Marriage of Missionaries." In William Ellis, *Memoir of Mrs. Mary Mercy Ellis.* Boston: Crocker & Brewster, 1836.

Anderson, Rufus. *Memorial Volume of the First Fifty Years of the American Board of Commissioners for Foreign Missions.* Boston: ABCFM, 1863.

Andrew, John. *Rebuilding the Christian Commonwealth.* Louisville: University Press of Kentucky, 1976.

Aspects of Hawaiian Life and Environment. Honolulu: Kamehameha Schools Press, 1971.

Barrere, Dorothy, Mary Pukui, and Marion Kelly. *Hula: Historical Perspectives.* Honolulu: Bernice P. Bishop Museum, 1980.

Bell, Susan. "Owhyhee's Prodigal." *Hawaiian Journal of History* 10 (1976): 25–32.

Bell, Susan. *Unforgettable True Stories of the Kingdom of Hawaii.* Honolulu: Press Pacifica, 1986.

Benedetto, Robert. *The Hawaiian Journals of the New England Missionaries, 1813–1894: A Guide to the Holdings of the Hawaiian Mission Children's Society Library.* Honolulu: Hawaiian Mission Children's Society, 1982.

Bingham, Alfred M. "Sybil's Bones: A Chronicle of the Three Hiram Binghams." *Hawaiian Journal of History* 9 (1975): 3–36.

Bingham, Hiram. *A Residence of Twenty-one Years in the Sandwich Islands.* Rutland, Vt.: C. H. Tuttle, 1981 [1847].

Bingham, Hiram. *Selected Writings of Hiram Bingham, 1814–1869: Missionary to the Hawaiian Islands To Raise the Lord's Banner.* Edited by Char Miller. Studies in American Religion, vol. 31. New York: Edwin Mellon Press, 1987.

Bingham, Sybil. *Extracts from Letters of Mrs. S. M. Bingham, Relative to Sending Her Children from the Sandwich Islands to America.* New York: Privately printed, 1882.

Bishop, Sereno Edwards. *Reminiscences of Old Hawaii.* Honolulu: Hawaiian Gazette, 1910.

Bradley, Harold. *The American Frontier in Hawaii.* Palo Alto, Calif.: Stanford University Press, 1942.

Clark, T. Blake. "Honolulu's Streets." Papers of the Hawaiian Historical Society, no. 20, 1939.

Coan, Lydia Bingham. *A Brief Sketch of the Missionary Life of Mrs. Sybil Moseley Bingham.* N.p.: Privately printed, 1885.

Coan, Titus. *Life in Hawaii: An Autobiographical Sketch.* New York: Anson D. F. Randolph, 1882.

Cummings, A. P. *The Missionary's Daughter: A Memoir of Lucy Goodale Thurston of the Sandwich Islands.* N.p.: American Tract Society, 1842. Hawaiian Mission Children's Society Library.

Damon, Ethel M. "From Manoa to Punahou." Hawaiian Historical Society, 49th Annual Report. 1940.

Damon, Ethel M. *Koamalu: A Story of Pioneers on Kauai,* vol. 1. Honolulu: privately printed, 1931.

Damon, Ethel M. *The Stone Church at Kawaiahao.* Honolulu: Star-Bulletin Press, 1945.

Daws, Gavan. "The Decline of Puritanism at Honolulu in the Nineteenth Century." *Hawaiian Journal of History* 1 (1967): 31–42.

Daws, Gavan. *Shoal of Time: A History of the Hawaiian Islands.* Honolulu: University of Hawaii Press, 1974 [1968].

Day, A. Grove, and Albertine Loomis. *Ka Pa'i Palapala: Early Printing in Hawaii.* Honolulu: Printing Industries of Hawaii, 1973.

Dibble, Sheldon. *History and General View of the Sandwich Islands Mission.* New York: Taylor and Dodd, 1839.

Dwight, Edwin. *Memoirs of Obookiah.* Honolulu: Women's Board of Missions for the Pacific Islands, 1968 [1818].

Edwards, Jonathan. *The Life of David Brainerd.* New Haven: Yale University Press, 1985.

Ellis, William. *The American Mission in the Sandwich Islands: A Vindication and an Appeal.* Honolulu: reprinted from the London edition by H. M. Whitney, 1866.

Ellis, William. *A Narrative of a Tour through Hawaii, or Owhyhee.* Honolulu: Hawaiian Gazette Co., 1917 [reprint of 1827 London edition].

Elsbree, Oliver. *The Rise of the Missionary Spirit in America.* Williamsport, Pa.: Williamsport Printing and Binding Co., 1928.

Frear, Walter. "A Century of Achievement." In *The Centennial Book.* Honolulu: Central Committee of the Hawaiian Mission Centennial, 1920.

Frear, Walter. *Anti-Missionary Criticism with Reference to Hawaii.* Honolulu: Advertiser Publishing Co., 1935.

Friend, The (Honolulu). Newspaper. Established 1843.

Frost, A. Lockwood, and Rossie M. Frost. "A Study and Report on the Old Mission Houses." Typescript. 1968. Hawaiian Mission Children's Society Library.

Forbes Research Notes. 12 vols. Typescript. Hawaiian Mission Children's Society Library.

Gast, Ross, and Agnes Conrad. *Don Francisco de Paula Marin.* Honolulu: University Press of Hawaii, 1973.

Gething, Judith. "Christianity and Coverture: Impact on the Legal Status of Women in Hawaii, 1820–1920." *Hawaiian Journal of History* 11 (1977): 188–220.

Goldman, Irving. *Ancient Polynesian Society.* Chicago: University of Chicago Press, 1970.

Goodell, Rev. William. *Forty Years in the Turkish Empire.* Boston: n.p., 1891.

Greer, Richard. "Honolulu in 1838." *Hawaiian Journal of History* 11 (1977): 3–37.

Grimshaw, Patricia. "'Christian Woman, Pious Wife, Faithful Mother, Devoted Missionary': Conflicts in Roles of American Missionary Women in Nineteenth-Century Hawaii." *Feminist Studies* 9 (1983): 490–521.

Grimshaw, Patricia. "New England Missionary Wives, Hawaiian Women, and 'The Cult of True Womanhood.'" *Hawaiian Journal of History* 19 (1985): 71–100.

Grimshaw, Patricia. "Paths of Duty: American Missionary Wives in Early Nineteenth-Century Hawaii." Dissertation, University of Melbourne, 1986, HMCS.

Grimshaw, Patricia. *Paths of Duty: American Missionary Wives in Nineteenth-Century Hawaii.* Honolulu: University of Hawaii Press, 1989.

Gulick, Rev. Orramel H., and Anne Gulick. *The Pilgrims of Hawaii.* New York: Fleming H. Revell, 1918.

Hackler, Rhoda. "Alliance or Cession? Missing Letter from Kamehameha I to King George III of England Casts Light on 1794 Agreement." *Hawaiian Journal of History* 20 (1986): 1–12.

Halford, Francis. *Nine Doctors and God.* Honolulu: University of Hawaii Press, 1954.

Handy, E. S. Craighill. *Cultural Revolution in Hawaii.* New York: American Council, Institute of Pacific Relations, 1931.

Handy, E. S. Craighill, Kenneth Emory, et al. *Ancient Hawaiian Civilization.* Rev. ed. Rutland, Vt.: Charles H. Tuttle, 1965.

Hawaiian Historical Society. Annual Reports. Honolulu. 1892–1965.

Hawaiian Historical Society. Papers. Honolulu. 1892–1940.

Holman, Lucia Ruggles. *Journal of Lucia Ruggles Holman.* Reprint. Brookfield, Conn.: Congregational Church of Brookfield, 1979.

Holt, John Dominis. *Monarchy in Hawaii.* Honolulu: Topgallant Publishing Co., 1971.

Hopoo, Thomas. "Memoirs of Thomas Hopoo." *Hawiian Journal of History* 2 (1968): 42–54.

Howe, K. R. *Where the Waves Fall.* Honolulu: University of Hawaii Press, 1984.

Humphrey, Heman. *The Promised Land: A Sermon Delivered at Goshen, Connecticut, at the Ordination of Messrs. Hiram Bingham and Asa Thurston.* Boston: Samuel T. Armstrong, 1819. Hawaiian Mission Children's Society Library.

Ii, John Papa. *Fragments of Hawaiian History.* Translated by Mary Pukui. Honolulu: Bishop Museum Press, 1959.

Judd, Laura Fish. *Honolulu.* Honolulu: Honolulu Star-Bulletin, 1963 [1861].

Judd Fragments II. Honolulu: Paradise of the Pacific Press [privately printed], 1911. Hawaiian Mission Children's Society.

Kamakau, Samuel. *Ka Po'e Kahiko: The People of Old.* Translated by Mary Pukui. Honolulu: Bishop Museum, 1964.

Kamakau, Samuel. *Ruling Chiefs of Hawaii.* Honolulu: Kamehameha Schools Press, 1961.

Kamakau, Samuel. *The Works of the People of Old: Na Hana A Ka Po'e Kahiko.* Translated by Mary Pukui. Honolulu: Bishop Museum, 1976.

Kittelson, David. *The Hawaiians: An Annotated Bibliography.* Honolulu: University of Hawaii Press, 1985.

Kuykendall, Ralph S. *The Hawaiian Kingdom, 1788–1854: Foundation and Transformation.* Honolulu: University of Hawaii Press, 1938.

Litten, Jane. "Whaler Versus Missionary at Lahaina." *Hawaiian Historical Review* 1 (1963): 219–34.

Loomis, Albertine. *Grapes of Canaan: Hawaii 1820.* Honolulu: Hawaiian Mission Children's Society, 1966 [1951].

Macrae, James. *With Lord Byron at the Sandwich Islands in 1825.* Hilo: Petroglyph Press, 1972.

Malo, David. *Hawaiian Antiquities (Moolelo Hawaii).* Translated by Nathaniel Emerson. Honolulu: Bishop Museum Press, 1951 [1898].

Miller, Char. *Fathers and Sons: The Bingham Family and the American Mission.* Philadelphia: Temple University Press, 1982.

Miller, Char, ed. *Missions and Missionaries in the Pacific.* New York: Edwin Mellon Press, 1985.

Missionary Album. Honolulu: Hawaiian Mission Children's Society, 1969.

Missionary Herald (Boston). Periodical. 1821–1840. Hawaiian Mission Children's Society Library and University of Michigan Library.

A Narrative of Five Youths from the Sandwich Islands. New York: n.p., 1818.

Nellist, George F. "The Discovery and Development of Artesian Water." The Board of Water Supply of the City and County of Honolulu, 1953. Hawaiian Historical Society Library.

Nellist, George F. "An Early History of Honolulu's Water System." The Board of Water Supply of the City and County of Honolulu, 1951. Hawaiian Historical Society Library.

Peterson, Charles. "Pioneer Prefabs in Honolulu." *Hawaiian Journal of History* 5 (1971): 24–38.

Pukui, Mary Kawena, E. W. Haertig, and Catherine Lee. *Nana I Ke Kumu (Look to the Source).* 2 vols. Honolulu: Queen Lili'uokalani Children's Center, 1972.

Richards, William. *Memoir of Keopuolani.* Boston: Crocker & Brewster, 1825.

Sahlins, Marshall. *Historical Metaphors and Mythical Realities.* ASAO Special Publications no. 1. Ann Arbor: University of Michigan Press, 1981.

Sahlins, Marshall. *Islands of History.* Chicago: University of Chicago Press, 1985.

Schmitt, Robert. *Demographic Statistics of Hawaii.* Honolulu: University of Hawaii Press, 1968.

Schmitt, Robert. *Historical Statistics of Hawaii.* Honolulu: University of Hawaii Press, 1977.

Schmitt, Robert. "Religious Statistics of Hawaii." *Hawaiian Journal of History* 7 (1973): 41–45.

Schmitt, Robert, and Rose Strombel. "Marriage and Divorce in Hawaii Before 1870." *Hawaiian Historical Review* 2 (1966): 241–45.

Silverman, Jane. *Kaahumanu: Molder of Change.* Honolulu: Friends of the Judiciary History Center of Hawaii, 1987.

Silverman, Jane. "To Marry Again." *Hawaiian Journal of History* 17 (1983): 64–74.

Sinclair, Marjorie. *Nahi'ena'ena: Sacred Daughter of Hawaii.* Honolulu: University Press of Hawaii, 1976.

Smith, Bradford. *Yankees in Paradise: The New England Impact on Hawaii.* New York: J. B. Lippincott, 1956.

Spoehr, Anne H. "George, Prince Tamoree: Heir Apparent of Kauai and Niihau." *Hawaiian Journal of History* 15 (1981): 31–49.

Stannard, David. *Before the Horror: The Population of Hawaii on the Eve of Western Contact.* Honolulu: Social Science Research Institute, University of Hawaii, 1989.

Stauder, Catherine. "George, Prince of Hawaii." *Hawaiian Journal of History* 6 (1972): 28–44.

Stewart, Charles S. *Journal of a Residence in the Sandwich Islands.* Reprint. Honolulu: University of Hawaii Press, 1970.

Thurston, Lucy G. *Life and Times of Mrs. Lucy G. Thurston.* Ann Arbor, Mich.: S. C. Andrews, 1882.

Trask, Haunani-Kay. "Scholars Revise History to Depict True Hawaiian Past: Western Interpretation Biased, Flawed." *Year of the Hawaiian* 1887–1987. Honolulu: Honolulu Star-Bulletin/C. F. Boone, 1987.

Wagner, Sandra. "Mission and Motivation: The Theology of the Early American Mission in Hawaii." *Hawaiian Journal of History* 19 (1985): 62–70.

Wagner, Sandra. "Sojurners Among Strangers: The First Two Companies of Missionaries to the Sandwich Islands." Dissertation, University of Hawaii, 1986. Hawaiian Mission Children's Society Library.

Westervelt, W. D. "The First Twenty Years of Education in the Hawaiian Islands." Hawaiian Historical Society, Nineteenth Annual Report, 1911, pp. 16–26.

Whitney, S. *The Whitney Family of Connecticut and Its Affiliations.* Vol. 1. New York: privately printed, 1878.

Winslow, Miron. *A Sketch of Missions.* Andover: Flagg and Gould, 1819.

Zwiep, Mary. "Sending the Children Home: a dilemma for early missionaries." *Hawaiian Journal of History* 24 (1990): 39–68.

Related Sources

Ahlstrom, Sydney. *Religious History of the American People.* New Haven: Yale University Press, 1972.

Berkhofer, Robert. *Salvation and the Savage.* Lexington: University of Kentucky Press, 1965.

Cott, Nancy. *The Bonds of Womanhood: "Women's Sphere" in New England, 1780–1835.* New Haven: Yale University Press, 1977.

Degler, Carl. *At Odds: Women and the Family in America from the Revolution to the Present.* New York: Oxford University Press, 1980.

Douglas, Ann. *The Feminization of American Culture.* New York: Knopf, 1977.

Epstein, Barbara. *The Politics of Domesticity: Women, Evangelism, and Temperance in Nineteenth-Century New England.* Middletown: Wesleyan University Press, 1981.

Faragher, John. *Women and Men on the Overland Trail.* New Haven: Yale University Press, 1979.

George, Carol, ed. *"Remember the Ladies": New Perspectives on Women in American History.* Syracuse: Syracuse University Press, 1975.

Hewitt, Nancy. *Women's Activism and Social Change: Rochester, New York, 1822–1872.* Ithaca: Cornell University Press, 1984.

Hunter, Jane. *The Gospel of Gentility: American Missionary Women in Turn of the Century China.* New Haven: Yale University Press, 1984.

Jeffrey, Julie Roy. *Frontier Women: The Trans-Mississippi West 1840–1880.* New York: Hill and Wang, 1979.

Myres, Sandra L. *Westering Women and the Frontier Experience 1800–1915.* Albuquerque: University of New Mexico Press, 1982.

Persons, Stow. *American Minds: A History of Ideas.* New York: Holt, Rinehart, and Winston, 1958.

Ryan, Mary. *Cradle of the Middle Class: The Family in Oneida County, New York, 1790–1865.* Cambridge: Cambridge University Press, 1981.

Ryan, Mary. "The Power of Women's Networks: A Case Study of Female Moral Reform in Antebellum America." *Feminist Studies* 5 (1979): 66–83.

Ryan, Mary. *Womanhood in America.* New York: New Viewpoints, 1975.

Ryan, Mary. "A Woman's Awakening: Evangelical Religion and the Families of Utica, New York, 1800–1840." *American Quarterly* 30 (1978): 602–23.

Sklar, Kathryn Kish. *Catharine Beecher: A Study in American Domesticity.* New Haven: Yale, 1973.

Smith-Rosenberg, Carroll. *Disorderly Conduct: Visions of Gender in Victorian America.* New York: Knopf, 1985.

Stansell, Christine. *City of Women: Sex and Class in New York, 1789–1860.* New York: Knopf, 1986.

Welter, Barbara. "The Cult of True Womanhood." *American Quarterly* 18 (1966): 151–74. Reprinted in *Dimity Convictions: The American Woman in the Nineteenth Century,* pp. 21–41. Athens: Ohio: University Press, 1976.

Welter, Barbara. "The Feminization of American Religion: 1800–1860." In *Dimity Convictions: The American Woman in the Nineteenth Century,* pp. 83–102. Athens: Ohio University Press, 1976.

Welter, Barbara. "She Hath Done What She Could." In *Women in American Religion,* edited by Janet James, pp. 111–25. Philadelphia: University of Pennsylvania Press, 1980.

Woloch, Nancy. *Women and the American Experience.* New York: Knopf, 1984.

Index